Praise for Donna and Heather's Gluten-Free Cookbooks

"Your cookbooks have restored my confidence. I considered myself a good baker, but did I ever struggle with gluten-free baking. I had failure after failure, so I quit baking. Then my mom gave me *125 Best Gluten-Free Recipes* for Christmas, and I have had more success with your recipes than any other! Thanks so much for what you do!"

— *K. Bauer, Texas*

"I absolutely *love* your cookbooks *The Best Gluten-Free Family Cookbook* and *125 Best Gluten-Free Recipes*. Thank you so much for the recipes, as well as the 'basics,' as there is so much to learn. I highly recommend these cookbooks when chatting with 'newbies' in the health food store or bookstore."

— *Sharon Erickson, Nanaimo, British Columbia*

"Look no further than Washburn and Butts' books at www.bestbreadrecipes.com. They started out as bakers with expertise in bread machines and got hooked on gluten-free."

— *Ellen Bayens,* **The Celiac Scene**

"I purchased my first bread machine about five weeks ago. I have baked three breads so far: the Maritime Brown Bread, the Orange Chocolate Chip Loaf and the Sandwich Bread. They were all good, but I fell in love with the Sandwich Bread. It is outstanding, and it does not crumble. Until I had my bread machine, I ate purchased breads with slices the size of my palm. I am so delighted to again eat normal-size slices."

— *Monique Dubois, Saint-Lambert, Quebec*

"I love and completely agree with your approach of emphasizing whole grains and nutritious ingredients. You've *proved* that a large percentage of starch in a GF flour blend is not necessary. Your recipes taste delicious, and I believe the hearty flavor of the whole grains actually makes them tastier than the counterpart made with a traditional rice/starch GF flour mix. My favorite bread recipe is the Ancient Grains Bread. I make this regularly, and my kids (non-celiacs, age 6 and 8) actually prefer it to wheat bread. The Honey Walnut Bread is wonderful too."

— *C. Coffey, GIG Support Group, Rochester, New York*

"I want to thank you for the *Complete Gluten-Free Cookbook*. My wife has many food restrictions, and your book has helped so much. Brilliant, and the recipes work so well. Almost all the bread we eat is made from your cookbook, and it is so good. Gluten-free breads generally leave much to be desired, but yours are excellent. I eat them even though I can eat regular bread. Thanks!"

— *Jim Elphinstone, Lac La Biche, Alberta*

"I bought your book *250 Gluten-Free Favorites*. I chose the Pesto Pork and made it tonight. *It was fantastic!* I could not believe how easy it was to prepare or how *great* it tasted. It was healthy, not too heavy for me but not too light for my son. Your book has changed my whole outlook on cooking GF. I had become bored with cooking since I had to keep everything so basic, but now I have so many ways to add flavor and keep cholesterol under control."

— *Teresa Nullmeier, Houston, Texas*

"The Lemon Coconut Bars from *The Best Gluten-Free Family Cookbook* are a little piece of heaven. They cooked beautifully, the recipe was easy to follow and everything is divine! Pastry is my favorite treat and after discovering severe gluten intolerance last spring, I've been experimenting and searching out great recipes. I knew pastry would be back in my life someday, and here it is! Thank you, thank you, thank you!"

— *Julie Duggan, London, Ontario*

"Donna and Heather's cookbooks are a great addition to the Specialty Food Shop! I do not hesitate to recommend them to customers looking for quality gluten-free cookbooks that offer appetizing and nutritious recipes."

— *Cristina Cicco, RD, Hospital for Sick Children, Toronto, Ontario*

"I spoke to Donna about making muffins and how I hate to bake/cook! Donna made me feel brave, so I purchased *250 Gluten-Free Favorites* because it had the most muffin recipes. I made up the muffin mix, and I've made two types of muffins from it. So much more yummy then the other ones I had made before. Plus, I made the Cheese Sauce and the Beef and Quinoa Soup. Thank you so much for making me feel comfortable with GF cooking."

— *Jennifer Ebbs, Burlington, Ontario*

"You have outdone yourselves! Your new book looks incredible. I am just thrilled that you are using the healthy flours and grains that I've been harping on about for years and minimizing the empty starches. Wonderful! Last night I paged through every recipe. I have 37 flagged as ones to try first!"

— *Anne Wraggett, Victoria, British Columbia*

"Your cookbooks have been amazing and inspiring! Everything I have tried is delicious, and my family appreciates it too. I was diagnosed with celiac disease last year, and I was very disappointed until my daughter purchased your books for us. After receiving them, I began to read and learn, and I went shopping for the various types of new flours, etc. Since I've tried baking your bread recipes, I will never buy a frozen gluten-free bread again! Your recipes (not just the bread) are wonderful. I feel it is a healthier way of life, and for this reason, I *only* cook and bake gluten-free for the whole family. My health has since improved dramatically."

— *A. Simonetta, Richmond Hill, Ontario*

the Gluten-Free Baking book

Donna Washburn & Heather Butt

Robert
ROSE

For complete cataloguing information, see page 320.

Disclaimer
The recipes in this book have been carefully tested by our kitchen and our tasters. To the best of our knowledge, they are safe and nutritious for ordinary use and users. For those people with food or other allergies, or who have special food requirements or health issues, please read the suggested contents of each recipe carefully and determine whether or not they may create a problem for you. All recipes are used at the risk of the consumer.

We cannot be responsible for any hazards, loss or damage that may occur as a result of any recipe use.

For those with special needs, allergies, requirements or health problems, in the event of any doubt, please contact your medical adviser prior to the use of any recipe.

Design and Production: Daniella Zanchetta/PageWave Graphics Inc.
Editor: Sue Sumeraj
Recipe editor: Jennifer MacKenzie
Proofreader: Sheila Wawanash
Indexer: Gillian Watts
Photographer: Colin Erricson
Associate Photographer: Matt Johannsson
Food Stylist: Kathryn Robertson
Prop Stylist: Charlene Erricson

Cover image: Carrot Cake (variation, page 209)

We acknowledge the financial support of the Government of Canada through the Book Publishing Industry Development Program (BPIDP) for our publishing activities.

Published by Robert Rose Inc.
120 Eglinton Avenue East, Suite 800, Toronto, Ontario, Canada M4P 1E2
Tel: (416) 322-6552 Fax: (416) 322-6936
www.robertrose.ca

NOV 0 1 2011

Printed and bound in Canada

1 2 3 4 5 6 7 8 9 SP 19 18 17 16 15 14 13 12 11

We dedicate this book to those who live with gluten intolerance
and to their families. We developed these recipes with you
in mind. We hope we help make baking gluten-free
a more enjoyable experience.

Contents

Acknowledgments

THIS BOOK HAS had the support and assistance of many people from its inception to the final reality. We want to thank those who helped us along the way.

Our thanks to the following people and companies for supplying products for recipe development: Doug Yuen of Dainty Foods for an assortment of rice, brown rice flour and rice bran; George Birinyi Jr. of Grain Process Enterprises Ltd., for potato and tapioca starches, sorghum flour, amaranth flour, whole bean flour, chickpea flour, pea flour and quinoa grain and flour; Howard Selig of Valley Flaxflour Ltd. for flax flour and flaxseed, both brown and golden; Margaret Hudson of Burnbrae Farms Ltd. for Naturegg Simply Whites and Break Free liquid eggs; Egg Farmers of Ontario for whole-shell eggs; Michel Dion of Lallamand Inc. for Eagle Instaferm® yeast; Beth Armour and Tracy Perry of Cream Hill Estates Ltd. for oat flour and rolled oats; the Seaton Smith family of Gluten-Free Oats® Company for old-fashioned rolled oats; Avena Foods Inc. for Only Oats™ oat bran, flour and flakes; Best Cooking Pulses for yellow pea flour and chickpea flour; Northern Quinoa Corp. for quinoa flour; and Workinesh Spice Blends Inc. for teff flour.

Thank you to Jarden Consumer Solutions for the Sunbeam stand mixer and to Hamilton Beach Brands for the food processor.

A huge thank you to the members of our focus group, who faithfully and tirelessly tasted and tested gluten-free recipes and products from the beginning to the end of recipe development. Your comments, suggestions and critical analysis were invaluable and helped make this a better book. A very special thanks to Craig Butt for the nutritional analysis charts and to Orma McDougall and the members of the Brockville chapter of the Canadian Celiac Association.

We want to express our appreciation to photographer Colin Erricson, associate photographer Matt Johannsson, food stylist Kathryn Robertson and prop stylist Charlene Erricson. Thank you for making the photographs of our gluten-free recipes look delicious. Once again, we enjoyed baking for the photo shoot.

Bob Dees, our publisher; Marian Jarkovich, Director, Sales and Marketing; Martine Quibell, Manager, Publicity; and Nina McCreath, International Sales and Marketing at Robert Rose Inc. deserve special thanks for their ongoing support.

To Daniella Zanchetta of PageWave Graphics, thank you for working through this cookbook's design, layout and production. Thank you to Sue Sumeraj and Jennifer MacKenzie, our editors; Sheila Wawanash, our proofreader; and Gillian Watts, our indexer.

A very special thank you to Magda Fahmy-Turnbull, RD, for her work on the nutritional analysis. She has been an invaluable resource throughout this project.

Thank you to our families: Heather's husband, our sons, our daughters-in-law and our grandchildren. You help bring balance to our lives when we become too focused on our work.

And finally, to you who must follow a gluten-free diet, we sincerely hope these recipes help make your life easier and more enjoyable. We developed them with you in mind.

— *Donna and Heather*

Introduction

THE DAY WE handed in the manuscript for *125 Best Gluten-Free Bread Machine Recipes*, we were excited to receive a phone call from our publisher inviting us to get back into the test kitchen to develop another 250 gluten-free recipes for this book.

The Gluten-Free Baking Book emphasizes baking for one or two. We chose this theme because you told us how expensive you find the gluten-free ingredients. In addition, many of you now live alone or have an empty nest and would like to have just enough dessert for yourself or the two of you. You don't want to eat the same thing three nights in a row just to finish it up. A number of you have downsized and don't have a large freezer anymore, so you like the idea of baking just 6 nutritious, delicious muffins or dinner rolls at a time. You also like the ease and convenience of our various baking mixes.

So for this book, we've downsized our cakes from 13 by 9 inches (33 by 23 cm) to 9 by 5 inches (23 by 12.5 cm), our cupcake recipes now make 6 cupcakes instead of 12, our desserts are for just 2 to 3 servings, our cookie recipes make 1 1/2 dozen, and individual tarts replace whole 10-inch (25 cm) pies.

We searched our cupboards and storage areas and were surprised by how many custard cups and small casserole dishes and baking dishes we found. The time is right to invest in small pans, as there are so many modern finishes and shapes available. It is fun just to wonder through the baking section of stores. Be sure to check out the information about these baking pans on page 27.

When we spoke at the GIG Educational Conference in Minneapolis, Minnesota, about how to make desserts more nutritious, you reinforced that this was the direction you wanted to take your baking, so we have continued to increase the fiber and calcium and decrease the fat, sugar and sodium. All of our recipes use ingredients free of trans fats. We use a lot of local produce in season.

One of the best perks of working on a gluten-free cookbook is that we get to meet and talk with you. Over the past year, we have met many new celiacs and renewed old friendships as we've travelled from Minneapolis, Minnesota, to Kansas City, Missouri, to Minocqua, Wisconsin, to Hamilton, Ontario. You challenge us with your requests, inspire us with your commitment and bolster us with your enthusiasm.

We always bake and deliver the food to Toronto for the photographer; that way, when you look at the pictures, you know exactly what you can expect from our recipes.

Keep in touch with us. We appreciate your emails and letters, as they give us valuable feedback. We know you must find time in your busy lives to write. Your questions and comments are important to us.

Donna J. Washburn, P.H.Ec.,
and Heather L. Butt, P.H.Ec.
Quality Professional Services
1655 County Road 2
Mallorytown, Ontario K0E 1R0

Email: bread@ripnet.com
Website: www.bestbreadrecipes.com

Understanding Whole Grains

"A whole grain is the entire seed, including the naturally occurring nutrients of an edible plant. The size, shape and color of the seed, also referred to as the 'kernel,' vary with the species. A grain is considered a whole grain when it contains all three seed parts: bran, germ and endosperm."

— The Whole Grains Council
(www.wholegrainscouncil.org)

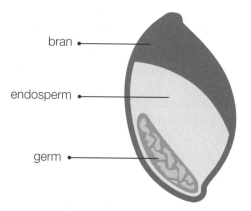

What Is Meant by "Whole Grain"?

As the quote above explains, a whole grain consists of three parts: the bran, the germ and the endosperm. The **bran**, or outer coating, is made up of several layers. It is rich in insoluble fiber and contains antioxidants and B vitamins. Just beneath the bran layers is a small structure called the **germ**. The germ is rich in healthy oils, B vitamins, minerals including magnesium and iron, and some protein. The **endosperm** is the largest portion of the grain. It contains starch, protein, soluble fiber and small amounts of vitamins and minerals.

Whole grains contain all three parts, whereas refined grains (white rice, defatted soy, degerminated cornmeal) have the bran and germ removed, leaving only the endosperm. Refined grains are not as nutritious as whole grains. Some refined grains may be enriched (some of the nutrients that were removed are added back), but few GF grains, flours or products such as cereals and pasta are enriched. It is very important to read labels every time when purchasing products made commercially with GF flours.

Whole grains can be eaten whole, cracked, ground or milled into flour. They can be the basis of commercial pastas, cereals and baked products. A whole grain that has been processed (cracked, crushed, ground, milled, rolled, extruded and/or cooked) still contains approximately the same nutrients found in the original grain seed.

Flour is the ground form of a grain. It can be milled from the whole grain or may be a refined and processed grain.

Many gluten-free flours are made from whole grains.

These include:
- amaranth
- buckwheat
- corn, including whole cornmeal
- millet
- Montina™ (Indian rice grass)
- GF oats, including oatmeal
- quinoa
- rice, both brown and colored
- wild rice
- sorghum
- teff

(Approved and endorsed by the Whole Grains Council, May 2004, www.wholegrainscouncil.org)

Amaranth

Amaranth seeds (also known as whole-grain amaranth) are off-white, golden, tan or light brown in color and are about the size of poppy seeds. The flavor ranges from mild, slightly sweet and nutty, to a more robust, peppery whole-grain taste. Stews and soups can be thickened by adding a small amount of amaranth seeds. Use amaranth seeds raw in crackers, granola, breading, crusts, toppings for casseroles and sweets with molasses or honey. The seeds can be cooked with other whole grains, or added to stir-fries, soups or stews. You can also enjoy them as a breakfast cereal. Be careful not to overcook them, as they become very gummy.

Amaranth flour is very fine and has a light cream color and a pleasant, nutty taste. Because of its high moisture content, use it in combination with other flours. It produces baked goods that are moist and dense, but added starch helps to lighten the texture. The grain of the bread is more open, the texture not as silky and the crumb color slightly darker than wheat flour breads. Amaranth flour tends to form a crust on the outside of a product during baking, sealing the outside before the product is completely cooked on the inside, so use the smallest amount of liquid you can and allow for slightly longer baking times than you might otherwise. Products baked with amaranth flour tend to brown quickly and may need to be tented with foil during the last third of the baking time. Check to make sure the internal temperature of the baked product reaches 200°F (100°C), as it may look baked on the outside before the center is done. We enjoy amaranth flour in yeast breads, muffins, cookies, pancakes, flatbreads and donuts. Amaranth flour is one of our favorites for thickening gravy, soups and stews, as it results in a dull finish and holds well.

Further Information

- www.nuworldamaranth.com
- www.lesliebeck.com

Buckwheat

Buckwheat groats are the hulled, white to cream-colored, triangular-shaped kernels of the buckwheat (saracen corn) plant. Soft in texture and bitter in flavor, they are available whole or cracked into coarse, medium or fine grinds.

> Some people have difficulty digesting buckwheat.

Finely cracked groats (grits) may be labeled "cream of buckwheat." They cook quickly and are served like rice, or are combined with rice to dilute their intense flavor. In Russia, buckwheat groats are served as a hot porridge for breakfast. They are also used to thicken gravy and sauces or added to casseroles, stews, salads and side dishes.

Kasha is roasted or toasted buckwheat groats. The groats darken to brown, the bitter flavor disappears and the nutty, earthy flavor becomes stronger. Kasha is used in dishes ranging from pilafs to meat mixtures.

Buckwheat flakes (oatmeal-style buckwheat) are rolled flakes made from buckwheat groats treated with hot steam. These small, brittle flakes look like small rolled oats, but have a slightly sweeter flavor and a slightly browner color. Those who can't tolerate oatmeal can substitute buckwheat flakes.

Buckwheat flour is very fine, with a unique, strong, musty, slightly sour, slightly nutty flavor. For light buckwheat flour, the hull is removed before the groats are ground. Dark buckwheat flour is made of unhulled groats; it is grayish, with tiny black specks of hull, and has a strong, earthy taste. Buckwheat flour tends to make baked goods heavier and give them a distinctive, stronger taste. It is usually blended with other flours. Buckwheat flour is used in pancake mixes, waffles, Russian blinis, Japanese soba noodles

> Bees use the nectar in buckwheat flowers to make a dark, strong-flavored honey. Buckwheat is sometimes planted just for the honey.

(which contain wheat), crêpes, muffins, dumplings, unleavened chapati and pastries. It can be used as a meat extender in a sausage meat mixture or combined with other GF flours to make breads and quick breads.

Further Information

- www.whfoods.com
- www.recipetips.com
- www.innvista.com

Corn

Cornmeal is milled from corn. It has larger granules than regular flour and can be yellow, white, red or blue. Although these varieties are slightly different in texture and flavor, one can be substituted for the other. The coarser the grind, the more granular the texture of the finished product and the more intense the corn flavor. Cornmeal can be used to make cornbread, spoon bread, polenta or muffins, or can be cooked and served as a hot cereal. It can also be used as a coating for fried foods or as a meat extender. Cornmeal is sometimes used to dust a greased pan, which helps keep the product from sticking to the pan and gives the crust extra crunch and a hint of flavor.

Degerminated cornmeal is ground between massive steel rollers. The fiber and corn germ are separated out, leaving a less nutritious and less flavorful grain. When you're looking for whole-grain cornmeal, avoid products that are labeled "degerminated."

Corn flour is more finely ground than cornmeal. Baked goods made using corn flour have a lighter texture than those made with cornmeal. Cornbread made with corn flour is richer and less crumbly.

Further Information

- www.momsretro.com/recipe_tips-corn.html

> Corn flour and cornstarch are not interchangeable in recipes.

Millet

Millet grain is not a true grain but is closely related to corn and sorghum. It is yellow or white, small and round, with a mild, delicate, corn-like flavor and a texture much like that of brown rice. Millet takes on the flavor of whatever it is cooked with. It can be used in pilafs or casseroles, as a stuffing for vegetables or meat, or in Asian dishes that call for rice, quinoa or buckwheat. We like to add dry millet grain to yeast breads, biscuits and muffins, for a crunchy texture.

Millet grits are coarsely ground millet grain; **millet meal** is more finely ground and has a slightly sweet flavor, similar to that of corn.

Millet flour is made from finely ground millet grain. It can be substituted for rice flour in small amounts in most recipes and adds a lovely cream color to baked goods. Millet flour is used in flatbreads or is mixed with other GF flours for baking. It produces light, dry, delicate breads with a thin, buttery, smooth crust. A small amount can be substituted for other GF flours, but results may vary.

Further Information

- www.chetday.com/millet.html

Montina™

Montina is the registered trade name for flour milled from the seed of a native North American grass called Indian rice grass (which is not related to rice, despite its name). In 2001, the Amazing Grains Grower Cooperative of Montana was formed to grow and market Montina. It is now available in almost every state in the U.S., but is not available in Canada.

Forms of Montina

- **Montina Pure Baking Flour Supplement** is 100% Indian rice grass and is used in combination with other

GF flours. It is a light brown-gray color and has a nutty but slightly sweet flavor. Substitute Montina Pure Baking Flour Supplement for 15% to 20% of any other GF flour in a recipe.

- **Montina All-Purpose Flour Blend** is a combination of white rice flour, tapioca flour and Montina Pure. Montina All-Purpose Flour Blend can be used cup for cup (mL for mL) to replace any GF flour or wheat flour. It doesn't need to be mixed with another GF flour, but xanthan gum or guar gum must be added. It can be used to make muffins, breads and pancakes and to thicken gravies, soups and stews.

Further Information

- www.amazinggrains.com

Oats

Oat groats, the whole-grain form of oats, are the oat kernel with the hull removed. They look like brown rice: long and thin, with a smooth, shiny surface. Groats have a sweet, nutty taste with a slight hint of pecan flavor. Combine them with other grains, such as rice, cook and serve instead of potatoes or plain rice or in a pilaf.

Rolled oats (oat flakes or oatmeal) result when groats are steamed and then rolled to flatten. Some rolled oats are also roasted to provide more flavor. These large, separate flakes are also called old-fashioned, thick-cut or porridge oats; they take longer to cook than quick-cooking oats (which are cut into smaller pieces to reduce the cooking time), but they also retain more flavor and nutrition. This is what most people think of as "oatmeal." Rolled oats can be eaten as a hot breakfast cereal, added to muesli, breads and scones, used to thicken soups and stews or added as a filler or extender to meatloaf and casseroles. Popular uses in North America are in cookies and granolas.

Oat flour is made from finely ground groats, which contain much of the bran. Depending on how it is ground, the flour can be almost as nutritious as the whole grain itself (it is heat during grinding that causes nutrient loss). The high oil content provides a sweet, nutty flavor. Oat flour makes baked items moist and more crumbly, but the products stay fresh longer than items baked with wheat flour. Use it in quick breads, yeast breads, cookies and cakes or to thicken soups, stews, sauces and gravies.

> To make your own oat flour, process rolled oats in a blender or food processor until finely ground.

Oat bran is the outer layer of the oat groat, the part of the grain that contains soluble fiber, which is known to lower cholesterol. Light tan in color, it provides a distinctive texture and a rich, nutty flavor. When used in baked goods such as muffins, pancakes, scones, breads and cookies, it increases their fiber content. It can also be added to breakfast cereals or eaten alone as a hot cereal. Breads may be dusted with oat bran before they are baked, to create a flavorful topping. Oat bran can also be used as a meat extender, as a thickener for gravies, sauces and stews, or as a coating (alone or mixed with a dry rub) for meat or fish.

> The North American celiac organizations have each taken an individual position on the use of oats in the gluten-free diet, but all agree on the need to consult your doctor before adding oats to your diet. Look for oats labeled "pure," "uncontaminated" or "gluten-free."

Further Information

- www.creamhillestates.com
- www.glutenfreeoats.com
- www.onlyoats.ca
- www.bobsredmill.com
- www.innvista.com

Quinoa

Quinoa seeds are small and flat, with a pointed oval shape. The color can range from cream or pale yellow to pink, orange, purple and black. Quinoa seeds have a delicate, almost bland flavor. Cooked quinoa has a fluffy consistency and is excellent as a hot cereal, in casseroles, soups and stews or in stir-fries. Serve as the base for salad or tabbouleh. Quinoa can replace rice as a side dish or be cooked in combination with rice as a pilaf. For information on cooking quinoa, see the Techniques Glossary, page 310. As quinoa cooks, the outer germ around each grain twists outward, forming a small white spiraled tail that is attached to the kernel. The grain itself is soft and delicate, while the tail is crunchy; this creates an interesting texture combination and a pleasant crunch.

Quinoa flakes are whole quinoa kernels rolled flat into flakes of $\frac{1}{8}$ to $\frac{1}{4}$ inch (0.25 to 0.5 cm) in diameter. Add quinoa flakes to cookie recipes or use them to replace GF oatmeal or buckwheat flakes in toppings for fruit crisps.

Quinoa flour is finely ground and tan-colored, with a strong, slightly nutty flavor. Because of its strong flavor, use it in small amounts. Baked products made with quinoa flour have a tender, moist crumb and keep well. We enjoy quinoa flour in pancakes, bread, muffins and crackers.

Further Information

- www.quinoa.com
- www.quinoa.net

Rice Flours

Brown rice flour is milled from the whole grain. It has a grainy texture and provides more fiber and nutrients than white rice flour. It is only a shade darker than white rice flour and has a mild, nutty flavor. Brown rice flour results in a product with a grainy texture and a fine, dry crumb. Use it in recipes calling for rice flour.

Rice bran and **rice polish** are the two outer parts of the rice kernel, removed during milling for white rice flour. Rice bran is the outermost layer. When bran and polish are added in small amounts to recipes, the fiber content is increased. They are interchangeable in recipes.

Sweet rice flour (glutinous rice flour, mochiko flour, sticky rice flour, mochi flour, sushi rice flour) is made from short-grain rice. It contains more starch than brown or white rice flour. There are two grades: one is beige, grainy and sandy-textured; the other is white, starchy, sticky and less expensive. The latter works better in recipes. It is often used to bread foods before frying or to thicken Asian dishes. We use it to dust baking pans or our fingers for easier handling of sticky dough.

Wild rice flour is gray-brown to black and has a nutty flavor and an interesting texture. It can be added to pancakes, muffins, scones and cookies or used to thicken casseroles, sauces, gravies and stews. Try it in fish, chicken and tempura batters.

Further Information

- www.bobsredmill.com
- www.wildfoods.ca

Sorghum

Sorghum grains (also known as milo) are white ovals smaller than peppercorns, with a hearty, chewy texture and a slightly sweet, nutty, earthy taste. They can be extruded, steam-flaked, popped, or puffed and micronized. Sorghum grains are used to make porridges, tortillas and rice substitute. They can be used in place of barley in soups. They are also sold popped, just like popcorn.

> Sorghum should not be used as a sprouting grain, as the young shoots are very poisonous.

Sorghum flour ranges in color from a gray-tan to eggshell white, and the grinds vary from coarse (stone-ground) to very fine. Because its flavor is neutral, it absorbs other flavors well. The most wheat-like of all GF flours, it is the best general-purpose flour, giving baked items a warm, creamy color. Sorghum flour adds protein to home-baked goods such as scones, cakes, cookies, breads, muffins, pizza dough, waffles, cereals, energy bars, salty snack foods, pastas and chapati (an unleavened Indian flatbread).

> The protein and starch in sorghum endosperm are more slowly digested than those in other grains, making it beneficial for people with diabetes. Some sorghum varieties are so rich in antioxidants, which protect against cell damage, that they are comparable to blueberries (known for their high antioxidant levels).

Other sorghum products include: puffed sorghum (used in snacks, granola, cereals, granola bars, baked products and dry snack cakes, and added to soups as a GF substitute for couscous, bulgur and pearled barley); cracked sorghum (used in legume and/ or vegetable mixtures); sorghum syrup, a molasses-like sweetener that is not as popular today as it once was; sorghum grits, which are similar in texture to cream of wheat porridge; and sorghum beer.

> Rather than using a standard mix of flours in our recipes, we like to vary the proportions of flours and starches so that each recipe has a unique flavor and texture. We love the results we get when we use a mixture of sorghum flour and bean flour with strong flavors such as pumpkin, chocolate, molasses, dates and rhubarb.

Further Information

- www.csaceliacs.org
- www.innvista.com
- www.recipetips.com
- www.sorghumgrowers.com

Teff

Teff grain is the smallest grain in the world, tinier than a poppy seed and only twice the size of the period at the end of this sentence. The seeds can be white, ivory or brown. Brown teff has a subtle hazelnut, almost chocolate-like flavor; white teff has a chestnut-like flavor; ivory teff has a mild, slightly molasses-like sweetness and nutty taste. The darker varieties are earthier-tasting. The grain can be sprouted to use in salads and sandwiches. Raw teff grain can substitute for some of the seeds, nuts or other small grains in recipes. Due to its small size, use only $1/2$ cup (125 mL) of teff to replace 1 cup (250 mL) of sesame seeds. Teff grain is a good thickener for soups, stews and gravies.

> Due to a low glycemic index, teff is digested slowly, which makes it beneficial for diabetics and athletes.

Use teff grain in stir-fry dishes and casseroles and to make grain burgers. Cook it to make breakfast porridge, a polenta-like side dish, stuffing or pilaf. It can be cooked alone or in combination with other grains and vegetables. It combines well with brown rice, millet, kasha (toasted buckwheat groats) and cornmeal. Cooked teff can be seasoned with cinnamon, ginger, garlic, cardamom, chiles, basil or cilantro. Ethiopians use teff as the main ingredient in their staple bread, injera.

Teff flour milled from brown teff has a sweet, nutty flavor, while flour from white teff is milder. Teff flour has excellent baking qualities. Use it in breads, quick breads, pancakes, waffles, pie crusts, gingerbread, crackers and cookies. Teff flour is also a good thickener for soups, sauces, stews, gravies and puddings.

> Like rice, teff cooks quickly. Cook it just long enough to open the grain. For extra flavor, toast the grains first.

Further Information

- www.hort.purdue.edu/newcrop/ cropfactsheets/teff.html
- www.innvista.com
- www.recipetips.com
- www.teffco.com

> A hundred and fifty teff seeds weigh as much as one kernel of wheat; seven grains will fit onto the head of a pin.

How Much Should I Eat?

The U.S. Department of Agriculture's MyPyramid (www.mypyramid.gov), revised in 2005, recommends that adults eat a total of 6 ounce (175 g) equivalents of grains a day (based on a 2,000-calorie diet). At least 3 ounces (90 g) of this should include whole-grain cereals, breads, crackers, rice or pasta. One ounce (30 g) equals 1 slice of bread, 1 cup (250 mL) of breakfast cereal or ½ cup (125 mL) of cooked rice, cereal or pasta, all of which can be considered one ounce (30 g) equivalent.

Canada's Food Guide (www.hc-sc.gc.ca), revised in 2007, recommends that children and adults eat 3 to 8 servings from the grain products group each day. The recommended number of servings depends on age and sex. For example, females between 19 and 50 should eat 6 to 7 servings; males in the same age range should eat 8 servings. Of

these servings, health experts suggest that at least half should be whole-grain products, especially those low in fat, sugar and salt. One serving is 1 slice of bread, 1 ounce (30 g) of cold cereal, ¾ cup (175 mL) of hot cereal or ½ cup (125 mL) of pasta or rice.

Suggestions for Including Whole Grains in a GF Diet

- Eat a variety of whole grains, such as teff, brown rice, quinoa, wild rice and pure, uncontaminated oats.
- Bake whole-grain breads using a combination of whole grains.
- Choose whole-grain flours to bake muffins, breads and desserts.
- Add whole grains such as millet grain and amaranth seeds to whole-grain flours when preparing baked goods.
- Use whole grains to prepare your own granola or snacks.
- Prepare pilafs, stir-fries, salads and stuffings with wild rice, brown rice, quinoa and oat groats, or a combination of these.
- Buy GF cereals made from whole grains. The first ingredient listed should be a whole grain such as oats, amaranth, brown rice, wild rice or quinoa.
- Select GF pasta made from whole grains, including quinoa or wild rice. Some GF pastas are enriched with nutrients lost during processing.
- Look for a label that states "100% whole grain," not just "whole grain" — the latter may contain only a small proportion of whole grains.
- Get in the habit of reading the Nutrition Facts table, as well as ingredient lists, to become familiar with the amounts of nutrients in specific products.

Other Gluten-Free Baking Ingredients

Fats

Fats are either saturated or unsaturated.

Saturated fats are solid at room temperature. They come mainly from animal sources and include butter, cheese, whole milk, cream, ice cream, egg yolks, lard, suet, drippings and fatty meats. Some plant fats, such as coconut oil, palm oil and other tropical oils, are also high in saturated fat; these are semisolid at room temperature.

> Cholesterol is made in our bodies, but we also get it from meat, poultry, seafood, eggs, dairy, lard and butter.

Unsaturated fats come mainly from vegetable sources and are liquid at room temperature. There are two types: monounsaturated and polyunsaturated.

- **Monounsaturated fats** are found in fruit, seed and nut oils, including avocado, olive, sesame seed, peanut and canola oils. They can start to solidify in the refrigerator, but become liquid again at room temperature.

- **Polyunsaturated fats** are found in vegetable, seed and nut oils, including corn, sunflower, safflower, soybean, cottonseed and sesame seed oils. Omega-3 and omega-6 fatty acids are also polyunsaturated fats. Natural sources of omega-3 fats include seafood and certain plants (see box, following). Omega-6 fats are found in vegetable oils.

> - Fish, including salmon, mackerel, albacore tuna, sardines, rainbow trout, herring and anchovies, are particularly good sources of omega-3 fatty acids.
> - Plant sources of omega-3s include flaxseed, flax oil and walnut oil. Small amounts are found in canola and soybean oil and some soft, non-hydrogenated margarine.
> - Many foods, including some eggs, milk, bread and soy beverages, are now enriched with omega-3 fats.

Trans fats are produced during hydrogenation, which is the process that adds hydrogen to liquid oils, changing them into solid fats such as shortening or margarine. In the process, any health benefits the oils may have had are destroyed, and trans fats behave like saturated fats in the body. Soft margarine sold in tubs has some hydrogen added to the oil and is "partially hydrogenated"; solid or stick margarine has more added and is a fully hydrogenated product. In addition, many fast foods and processed foods have a high trans fat content.

For health reasons, the majority of your fat intake should be from monounsaturated oils and soft, non-hydrogenated margarines. Wherever you can in cooking and baking, use vegetable oils or soft margarine instead of butter, lard, shortening or hard margarine.

> "Smoke point" is the temperature at which a heated oil or fat begins to smoke.

Flaxseed

Whole flaxseed (also known as linseed) refers to the unbroken seed. The seeds are small, flat and tear-shaped. They range in color from dark reddish-brown to golden and have a nutty flavor and a crisp, yet chewy texture.

Cracked flaxseed is not sold in stores but can be prepared at home: use a coffee grinder to crack the outer coating of the seed slightly, resulting in pieces of different sizes and textures. Cracked flaxseed is easier to digest than whole flaxseed. For extra crunch, add slightly cracked flaxseed to yeast breads and quick breads or sprinkle it on salads and hot or cold cereals. Add just before serving, as it becomes sticky.

> Use a coffee grinder or food processor to crack or grind whole flaxseed to the consistency you want for your recipe. For optimum freshness, grind it as you need it. Refrigerate any extra.

Ground flaxseed is sold as flax flour, milled flaxseed or sprouted flax flour. All forms of ground flaxseed are interchangeable in recipes. You can prepare your own by grinding whole flaxseed to a gold to medium brown powder with slightly darker flecks. Replace up to $1/3$ cup (75 mL) of vegetable oil in recipes with 1 cup (250 mL) of ground flaxseed. You can add up to 1 tbsp (15 mL) ground flaxseed to the batter for cookies, cakes or pancakes without decreasing the other flours or starches. If you add more, the amount of liquid and other flours may have to be adjusted.

> Ground Salba can be substituted for ground flaxseed. Grind Salba seeds even finer than flaxseed, or the product might be slightly gritty.

Further Information

- www.flaxcouncil.ca
- www.flaxflour.com
- www.saskflax.com

Leaveners

Leaveners in cakes, quick breads and yeast breads produce carbon dioxide, which, when heated, expands the cell wall structure, resulting in a light, even texture.

- **Baking powder** is used in cakes, biscuits and muffins. However, some baking powders contain wheat starch, which will be specified on the label. Gluten-free baking powder is available in some areas and can be substituted in equal amounts. If it's not available in your area, here's a recipe you can use to make your own: In a small bowl, sift together 2 tsp (10 mL) cream of tartar, 2 tsp (10 mL) cornstarch or arrowroot starch and 1 tsp (5 mL) baking soda. Make only small amounts at a time and store in an airtight container.

- **Yeast** converts the carbohydrates in flour and sugar to produce the carbon dioxide gas that causes dough to rise. The recipes in this cookbook were developed using bread machine or instant yeast. We always recommend using the type of yeast called for in the recipe.

  The expiry date on the package indicates that it should be opened before that date and used within a 2-month period. Yeast should be kept in an airtight container in the freezer. There's no need to defrost before measuring; use yeast directly from the container in the freezer. Do not transfer the yeast from one container to another, as exposing it to air can shorten its life.

If you suspect that the yeast has become less active, perform this test for freshness: Dissolve 1 tsp (5 mL) granulated sugar in $1/2$ cup (125 mL) lukewarm water. Add 2 tsp (10 mL) yeast and stir gently. In 10 minutes, the mixture should have a strong yeasty smell and be foamy. If it doesn't, the yeast is too old — time to buy fresh yeast!

Legume Flours

Legumes (also called pulses) include peas, beans, lentils and peanuts. Besides using dried legumes in our recipes, we also use their flours.

> Legume flours combine well with other GF flours.

- **Fava bean flour** is made from earthy-flavored fava beans.
- **Chickpea flour** (garbanzo bean flour, gram, besan, chana dal) has a mild, nut-like taste, with a hint of lemon. It adds a rich, sweet flavor to baked foods. It is used in East Indian cuisine and to thicken soups and gravies.
- **Garfava flour** (sold as garbanzo-fava bean flour in Canada) is a blend of garbanzo bean (chickpea) flour and fava bean flour. It has a nutty taste.
- **Whole bean flour** is made from Romano beans (also called cranberry beans or speckled sugar beans). The dried beans are cooked (heat-treated, micronized) to help reduce flatulence, then stone-ground to a uniform, fine, dark, strong-tasting flour. When one

> All legume flours are a shade of yellow and have a very fine texture. They complement recipes made with molasses, brown sugar, chocolate, pumpkin, applesauce and rhubarb.

of our recipes calls for whole bean flour, use this one; however, if it's not available, any bean or pea flour can be substituted.

- **White (navy) bean flour** is made from small, white round or oval beans. The white flour has a mild flavor and a powdery texture. Use it to thicken sauces, gravies and soups.
- **Pinto bean flour** has a slightly pink tinge, although the pinto beans it is made from have a spotty beige and brown color.
- **Pea flours** are produced from dried field peas with the bran (hull) removed. Green pea flour has a sweeter flavor than yellow pea flour. Pea flours keep baked products softer longer and improve dough made in a bread machine. They can be used as a natural colorant in baked goods, homemade noodles and other foods. Pea flours complement recipes made with banana, peanut butter and strong spices such as cloves.

> All types of bean flours (except soy flour) can be used interchangeably with pea flours in our recipes.

- **Pea fiber**, ground from yellow pea hulls, is a fine-textured, light-yellow-colored, bland-tasting powder. It increases the volume of doughs and can replace fat in a recipe because of its ability to bind with water. It is a source of insoluble dietary fiber and increases the fiber content of products made with it. Use it in breads, cakes, cookies, tortillas, pasta, soups and fiber drinks.
- **Soy flour** (soya flour), made from soybeans, is powdery fine, with a pungent, nutty, slightly bitter flavor that is enhanced by the flavors of accompanying flours. Soy flour is available in full-fat (natural), low-fat

and defatted versions. The higher the fat content, the deeper the color. Full-fat soy flour contains the natural oils found in the soybean; defatted soy flour has had the oils removed during processing.

> Soy is one of the top 10 allergens in Canada and one of the top 8 in the U.S.

Soy flour has a strong odor when wet that disappears with baking. It adds rich color, fine texture, a pleasant nutty flavor, tenderness and moistness to baked goods. Products containing soy flour bake faster and tend to brown quickly, so the baking time may need to be shortened or the oven temperature lowered. Tenting baked goods with foil partway through the baking time also helps.

Soy flour can also be used to thicken sauces and gravies, to add a nutty flavor and extra protein to pancake batter and to enrich pasta and breakfast cereals. Added to fried foods such as donuts, soy flour reduces the amount of fat absorbed by the dough.

> Studies have shown that 15% of celiacs cannot tolerate soybeans or soy products.

Further Information

- www.farmbuilt.com
- www.foodprocessing.com
- www.thumboilseed.com/soy-flour.htm
- www.soyfoods.org
- www.bestcookingpulses.com

Nut Flours and Meals

Nut flours and meals are made from very finely ground nuts such as almonds, hazelnuts and pecans. They are not as smooth or as fine as grain flours. Nut flours can be purchased, or you can grind them yourself (see the Techniques Glossary, page 309). Grind the nuts when you're ready to prepare the recipe. We like to toast them first, for a nuttier flavor (see page 309). Toasting also dries nut flour, helping to prevent clumping.

- **Almond flour**, or **meal**, is made from blanched almonds and is creamy white. Sugar or flour is sometimes added during grinding to absorb the oil from the almonds and prevent clumping, so check purchased almond flour to be sure it is gluten-free. Combine almond flour with rice flour or amaranth flour when a white, delicate-flavored product is desired.

- **Hazelnut flour** is a creamy color with dark brown to black flecks. It has a full, rich flavor that is sweet and nutty. We enjoy it in pastry and anything with orange or chocolate.

- **Pecan meal** is a warm brown, similar in color to ground flaxseed. It complements recipes made with maple, pumpkin and dried fruits such as apricots and dates.

> Nut meals and flours are interchangeable in recipes.

Further Information

- www.bluediamond.com
- www.diamondnuts.com

Starches

Starches, which are complex carbohydrates, have two purposes in gluten-free cooking: to lighten baked products and to thicken liquids for sauces or gravies.

Baking with Starches

- **Arrowroot** (arrowroot starch, arrowroot powder, arrowroot starch flour) is a fine, white, tasteless starchy powder with a mild aroma. Arrowroot is more expensive and may be more difficult to find than other starches. When mixed with GF flours to make breads, cookies and pastries, arrowroot helps the baked goods bind better and lightens the finished product.

- **Cornstarch** (corn flour, maize, *crème de maïs*) is a fine, silky, white, tasteless starchy powder. When mixed with GF flours to make breads, cookies and pastries, cornstarch helps the baked goods bind better and lightens the finished product.

- **Potato flour** is made from the whole potato, including the skin. Because it has been cooked, it absorbs large amounts of water. Potato flour is much denser and heavier than potato starch and has a definite potato flavor. Potato flour is not used like other flours in baking as it would absorb too much liquid and make the product gummy, but small amounts can be used in breads, puddings and cakes to hold the product together. We rarely use potato flour, but we frequently use potato starch.

- **Potato starch** (potato starch flour) is made from only the starch of potatoes, and is therefore less expensive than

Potato starch is often confused with potato flour, but one cannot be substituted for the other.

potato flour. It is a very fine, silky, white powder with a bland taste. It lumps easily and must be sifted frequently. When combined with other GF flours, it adds moistness to baked goods and gives them a light and airy texture. It also causes breads to rise higher.

A permitted ingredient for Passover (unlike cornstarch and other grain-based foods), potato starch is often found with kosher products in supermarkets

- **Tapioca starch** (tapioca flour, tapioca starch flour, cassava flour, yucca starch, manioc, manihot or *almidón de la yuca*) is powdery fine, white and mildly sweet. Tapioca starch lightens baked goods and gives them a slightly sweet, chewy texture.

Thickening with Starches

All starches can be used to thicken soups, gravies, sauces, stews and meat dishes.

- **Arrowroot** thickens liquids almost immediately at a lower temperature than either cornstarch or wheat flour, which means it's less likely to burn, but it loses its thickening ability if it's boiled even a little bit too long, so always add it at the end of the cooking process. Due to its greater thickening ability, use only half as much arrowroot as wheat flour. Its consistency does not hold as long after cooking. Use arrowroot as a thickener for acidic liquids such as Chinese dishes, stir-fries, clear glazes for fruit pies and clear fruit sauces. It should not be used to thicken dairy-based sauces, as it turns them slimy.

Sauces thickened with arrowroot can be frozen and defrosted.

- **Cornstarch** doesn't thicken well when mixed with acidic liquids such as lemon juice. Use cornstarch to thicken cream fillings, custards and puddings and in clear glazes for fruit pies and clear fruit sauces. To avoid lumps, cornstarch must be dissolved in an equal amount of cold water before it is added to hot liquids. (Mixing it with a granular solid, such as granulated sugar, also disperses it into a liquid.) Cornstarch has twice the thickening power of wheat flour. It helps prevent eggs from curdling in custards and causes heat to be transmitted more evenly throughout. Sauces made with cornstarch turn spongy when frozen.

- **Potato flour** mixes well in cold water, cooks quickly without lumps and turns transparent after heating. Potato flour is always used in very small quantities. It thickens quickly when heated with water, and at a lower temperature than cornstarch, so it can be added to sauces at the last minute.

- **Potato starch** should be mixed with twice the amount of cold water before it is added to hot liquids, for the best thickening results. Liquids thickened with potato starch should never be boiled, or the thickening ability will be lost. Sauce thickened using potato starch becomes watery again when cooled.

- **Tapioca starch** gives a transparent high gloss to fruits and makes a perfectly smooth filling. It's the perfect product to use with high-acid fruits. In addition to sauces, it is used to thicken glazes, puddings, custards and juicy fruit pie fillings.

> If you plan to freeze a dish, use tapioca starch, as it remains stable when frozen.

Further Information
- www.glutenfreemall.com
- www.recipetips.com
- www.foodsubs.com
- www.jodelibakery.netfirms.com

Sugars

Most sugar is made from either sugarcane or sugar beets and varies in color, flavor, sweetness and crystal size (coarse, medium, fine, extra-fine, superfine). It can be either refined or raw.

> In this book, recipes labeled "white sugar–free" contain no white (granulated) sugar as an added ingredient but may contain another type of sugar, including brown sugar, honey, molasses, corn syrup or maple syrup. And some of the ingredients we call for, such as dried cranberries, may contain white sugar added during processing. There is much discussion about the type of sugar we use today. Nutritionally, the important point is not the kind of sugar but the quantity we consume. Excess sugar is the problem.

White (Granulated) Sugar

White (granulated) sugar is highly refined and is sold in various crystal sizes:

- **Coarse sanding sugar** has large crystals that sparkle when light is reflected through them. It is used to decorate cookies and other desserts.

- The most common size is sold as **white sugar** or **granulated sugar**; it's what we often simply call sugar. The finer grades are made by sieving white sugar.

- **Fruit sugar** is slightly finer than regular white sugar. It is used in gelatin, pudding and powdered drink mixes.

> White sugar (granulated sugar) is dried to prevent clumping.

- **Superfine sugar** (also known as bar sugar, berry sugar in B.C. and castor sugar in Britain) is finer than granulated sugar but not as fine as confectioner's sugar. The tiny crystals dissolve instantly and completely. It is used to make caramel, fine-textured cakes, drinks and meringues.
- **Confectioner's sugar** (also called icing sugar, powdered sugar and fondant) is simply white sugar that has been ground to a fine powder, then sifted. It usually contains 3% cornstarch as an anticaking agent, to prevent clumping. It is used in icings, confections and whipped cream. Canadian icing sugar may contain wheat starch, so check the label. Always sift confectioner's sugar just before using.

Brown Sugar

Brown sugar (brilliant yellow, golden yellow, light yellow, yellow, dark brown) is from late stages of refining. The crystals are brown and fine and contain moisture and varying amounts of molasses. The darker the color, the higher the molasses content, the stronger the flavor and the higher the moisture. Light brown sugar is used for baking and to make butterscotch, condiments and glazes. Dark brown sugar is used to make gingerbread, mincemeat and baked beans.

Raw Sugars

Raw sugars are the products of the first stage of the sugarcane refining process. There are slight differences among them.

- **Demerara sugar** has large crystals that are light to golden brown in color. It is very moist and adds a crunchy texture when sprinkled on hot and cold cereals, cakes, cookies, fruit and desserts. It is also used as a sweetener for tea or coffee.

Brown sugar should be stored in an airtight container so it doesn't lose moisture and become hard. If it does harden, put a slice of bread, a piece of apple or a damp paper towel in the container to provide moisture until the sugar softens.

If you need to use hardened brown sugar immediately, heat the required amount in a 250°F (120°C) oven for a few minutes, or microwave it on Low (10%) for 1 to 2 minutes per cup (250 mL).

- **Muscovado sugar** (Barbados sugar) is coarser and moister than regular brown sugar. It ranges in color from light to very dark brown, and has a strong molasses flavor.
- **Turbinado sugar** (plantation sugar) is a specialty raw brown sugar that has been steam-cleaned. It has a mild caramel flavor and is golden in color. It is used to sweeten tea and other beverages.

Liquid Sugars

- **Molasses** is a by-product of the sugarcane and sugar beet refining process. In the United States, molasses is sold in three varieties: light, dark and blackstrap. In Canada, the varieties are called fancy molasses, cooking molasses and blackstrap molasses. Light (fancy) molasses is, as you would expect, the lightest in both color and flavor; it is used in baked goods and main dishes. Cooking (dark) molasses is a combination of light and blackstrap; it is used in dishes where a more pronounced molasses flavor is desired. Blackstrap molasses is very dark and bitter, but it contains minerals, vitamins and trace elements lost in the refining of the other grades; it is used in baked goods.

- **Treacle**, most commonly used in the U.K., is a syrup made during the refining of sugarcane. There are two kinds: light treacle (also called golden syrup) and dark treacle. Dark treacle is similar to molasses, while light treacle has a lighter flavor.

- **Corn syrup** is made from cornstarch. It keeps foods moist and prevents them from spoiling quickly. It is common for corn syrup to be flavored with vanilla extract. You will find corn syrup in numerous commercial products and in home-baked items such as frosting and fudge.

- **High-fructose corn syrup (HCFS)** is manufactured from cornstarch. It has a higher sugar content than white (granulated) sugar and is an ingredient in most processed foods, including soft drinks, cereals, ketchup, crackers and many more. It is used to improve taste and keep foods and beverages fresher longer.

- **Maple syrup** is made by boiling the sap of the sugar maple tree to concentrate the flavor. Forty gallons (150 L) of sap yield 1 gallon (4 L) of maple syrup. If made properly, it never freezes because of its low moisture and high sugar content. It can be stored in the refrigerator for up to 2 months or in the freezer for up to 1 year. If it crystallizes, heat it gently by standing the container in a bowl of warm water until the crystals dissolve, or microwave it on High for 90 seconds per cup (250 mL).

- **Honey** is a natural sugar made by bees. The flavor depends on the variety of flower it is made from; common flavors include clover, orange blossom and lavender. The color indicates the strength of flavor and ranges from near white to deep golden yellow to deep brown or black. The texture ranges from thin to heavy. Honey has a natural emulsifying quality, so it is a good addition to oil-and-vinegar salad dressings.

> Honey can trigger allergic reactions in some individuals. Children under 12 months of age should not eat honey because of a rare but serious risk of botulism.

Store honey in a cool location, away from direct sunlight, in a tightly covered container. It will last indefinitely. If cloudiness develops and hard crystals form over time, simply warm the honey gently by placing the jar in a pan of hot water and stirring the honey. If honey is overheated, the sugars will caramelize and the flavor and color may change.

Before measuring honey, coat the measuring cup with vegetable spray — the honey will flow more easily and rapidly.

Xanthan Gum

Xanthan gum is a natural carbohydrate produced from the fermentation of glucose. It helps prevent baked goods from crumbling, gives them greater volume, improves their texture and extends their shelf life. It also helps prevent pastry fillings from "weeping," so your crust won't get soggy. Do not omit xanthan gum from a recipe.

Xanthan gum can be purchased at health food stores, online or where you purchase other gluten-free ingredients. Before working with xanthan gum, be sure to wipe counters and containers with a dry cloth; when it comes in contact with water, it becomes slippery, slimy and almost impossible to wipe up.

> Guar gum is gluten-free, but it may act as a laxative in some people. It can be substituted for xanthan gum in equal proportions.

Storing Other Gluten-Free Baking Ingredients

Ingredient	Room temperature*	Refrigerator	Freezer	Additional information
Baking powder and baking soda	6 months			
Flaxseed, whole	1 year			
Flaxseed, cracked or ground		6 months	1 year	For optimum freshness, grind only as needed.
Hemp seeds, hulled		Once open, use within 1 year		Purchase hemp seeds and hemp seed flour only from stores that sell refrigerated products.
Legumes, canned	5 years			
Legumes, dried	1 year			
Legumes, cooked		Lentils and split peas: 4 days Beans: 5 days	6 months	
Legume flours		6 months	1 year	
Nut flours and meals**		3 months	1 year	Store away from foods with strong odors, such as fish and onions.
Nuts, unshelled**	6 months		1 year	
Salba seeds		6 months		Prepare ground Salba and Salba gel as needed.
Seeds (pumpkin, poppy, sesame and sunflower)**		6 months	1 year	
Soybeans, dried	1 year			
Soy flour, full-fat		6 months	1 year	
Soy flour, defatted	1 year			
Starches	Indefinitely			
Xanthan gum and guar gum	6 months		Indefinitely	
Yeast (instant and bread machine)	2 months		12 months	Open before expiry date.

  * All gluten-free baking ingredients should be stored in airtight containers in a cool, dry, dark place.
 ** Because of their high oil content, seeds, nuts and nut flours tend to become rancid quickly. Purchase in small quantities and taste before using.

Nutrient Content of Gluten-Free Flours and Starches

Gluten-free flour (per 1 cup/250 mL)	Protein (g)	Fat (g)	Carbohydrates (g)	Fiber (g)	Calcium (mg)	Iron (mg)
Whole-grain flours						
Amaranth flour	17	8	80	18	51	9
Brown rice flour	11	4	124	7	17	3
Oat flour	21	9	78	12	50	7
Quinoa flour	13	8	84	6	61	9
Sorghum flour	12	4	88	8	35	6
Teff flour	16	4	88	16	201	7
Other flours and starches						
Almond flour	24	56	24	12	750	5
Cornstarch	0	0	117	1	3	1
Flax flour	24	45	38	36	332	8
Garfava flour	35	6	72	12	104	8
Soy flour (low-fat)	47	6	38	18	241	9

Sources: USDA, Case Nutrition Consulting Inc., Bob's Red Mill, Nu-World Amaranth, Northern Quinoa Corp., Twin Valley Mills and Nutrition Data.

Protein helps us maintain and repair body tissues. Complete proteins (meat, fish, poultry, milk and milk products and eggs) provide all the amino acids necessary for a healthy body; incomplete proteins (grains, legumes, vegetables) lack some of the essential amino acids. However, the body has the ability to use amino acids from a variety of sources to form complete proteins. Here are some suggested combinations: beans and rice, cereals and milk, nuts and grains; whole-grain breads and legumes. All grains are not created equal: some contain more and higher levels of essential amino acids than others. It is therefore important to bake with a variety of nutritious grains.

Fat provides the essential fatty acids that the body cannot produce. It protects the organs and muscles with padding and insulation. Although fats are necessary for a healthy diet, they have two and a half times as many calories per gram as protein and carbohydrates, so the amount of fat consumed should be controlled.

Carbohydrates are the primary source of energy for the body. They provide fuel as the body breaks down complex carbohydrates into simple sugars.

Fiber is found only in plants and plays a significant role in keeping us healthy. Insoluble fiber aids in digestion, while soluble fiber can lower cholesterol. Sources of insoluble fiber include rice bran, brown rice, almond meal and legumes. Sources of soluble fiber include flaxseed and pears. Oat bran, whole-grain oats and soybeans contain both types. When increasing fiber in the diet, do so gradually.

Calcium helps the body build strong bones and teeth. It is also required for blood clotting and nerve and muscle function.

Iron is necessary for the formation of hemoglobin in red blood cells. It also helps the immune system function.

All About Baking Pans

Choosing Baking Pans

Baking pans are now available in a wide variety of materials: nonstick, aluminum, stainless steel, ceramic and silicone. There are different qualities within each type. For evenly risen and uniformly browned baked goods, purchase the best quality you can afford. We recommend using heavy, well-insulated pans. A heavy pan ensures a uniform thickness and even browning. A lighter, inexpensive pan might cause the product to rise higher in the middle than at the edges.

A shiny, light-colored metal pan reflects heat away from the baked product so it doesn't brown too much before it is done baking. Darker pans absorb more heat and can leave edges crisp and over-browned. When using dark pans, check for doneness 5 minutes before the low end of the recommended baking time. For example, if a recipe says to bake for 35 to 45 minutes, check for doneness after 30 minutes.

Glass baking dishes and metal baking pans with a dark nonstick finish conduct and retain heat, causing foods to bake more quickly. Therefore, if using these containers, reduce the oven temperature by 25°F (10°C). For example, if a recipe says to bake at 350°F (180°C), bake at 325°F (160°C) instead. When we baked cheesecakes using a dark, nonstick, glass-bottomed springform pan, we were much happier with the results we got baking them at the lower temperature.

Silicone pans seem to bake in the same length of time as metal pans. They have the added bonus that they don't need to be greased and are convenient to store. When using larger silicone pans, and filling them with heavy or wet batters, we place the filled pan on a baking sheet to help transfer it to the oven. We then carefully slide the pan off the baking sheet onto the oven rack. When removing the pan from the oven at the end of baking, slide the pan onto the baking sheet for easy transfer to the cooling rack.

For the best results, it is important to use the size of pan called for in the recipe. When checking the pan size, measure from the top inside edge to the opposite top inside edge. If you don't have the exact size, choose a slightly larger pan over a smaller one. You'll have to adjust the baking time as well. That is why knowing the tests for doneness is so important.

Pan Sizes

Baking pans are available in many sizes and shapes, so it is important to know how much they can hold. To determine volume capacity, fill the pan to the top with water, then measure the water in a measuring cup. Remember, the batter should fill the pan only two-thirds to three-quarters full.

The following chart lists some of the common pans we used for the recipes in this book.

Pan Type	Pan Size	Approximate Volume of Pan
Loaf pan	9 by 5 inches (23 by 12.5 cm) 8 by 4 inches (20 by 10 cm)	8 cups (2 L) 6 cups (1.5 L)
Mini loaf pan	5¾ by 3¼ inches (14 by 8 cm) 5¼ by 2½ inches (13 by 6 cm)	2 cups (500 mL) 1 cup (250 mL)
Muffin cups	2½ inches (6 cm)	¼ cup (60 mL)
Mini springform pan	4½ inches (11 cm)	3 cups (750 mL)
Square baking pan	8 by 8 by 1½ inches (20 by 20 by 4 cm)	6 cups (1.5 L)
Round baking pan	8 by 1¼ inches (20 by 3 cm)	5 cups (1.25 L)
Jelly roll pan	15 by 10 inches (40 by 25 cm)	n/a
Ramekin	3½ by 1¾ inches (9 by 4.5 cm)	¾ cup (175 mL)
Round casserole dish	2½ quarts (2.5 L) 5 inches (12.5 cm) 6 inches (15 cm)	10 cups (2.5 L) 3 cups (750 mL) 5 cups (1.25 L)
Oval baking dish	10 ounces (300 mL)	1¼ cups (300 mL)
Pizza pan	8 inches (20 cm)	n/a
Fluted tart shell	4¼ by ½ inches (11 by 1 cm)	n/a
Mini Bundt or kugelhopf pan (mini tube pan)	4 by 1¾ inches (10 by 4.5 cm)	1 cup (250 mL)

Preparing Pans for Baking

In our recipes, the equipment list above the ingredient list will tell you whether, and how, the baking pan needs to be prepared. For some recipes, the pan needs no preparation; for others, it is either greased or both greased and lined with parchment or waxed paper.

Greasing Pans

We no longer use butter to grease pans, as it burns. Today, "greasing" commonly means spraying the pan with nonstick vegetable oil. Be sure the spray is gluten-free.

Greasing and Lining Pans

Greasing the pan before lining it with parchment paper helps secure the parchment to the base. To line a pan, trace the outline of the bottom of the pan on parchment paper, then cut it out with paper scissors. Place the paper in the pan with the clean side up (the side used for tracing down).

Using an Instant-Read Thermometer

WHEN WE BAKE gluten-free, it is important to use a thermometer to test foods for doneness, as it is more difficult to tell when they are baked: the outside of the bread or cake may look browned enough when the inside is still raw. The indicators you may be used to looking for when baking with wheat may not be reliable, as gluten-free foods often have a different appearance. A thermometer is the only accurate way to be sure the food is done.

Purchasing

The best thermometer for this purpose is a bimetallic stemmed thermometer often called an instant-read or chef's thermometer. It has a round or oval head at the top, a long metal stem and a pointed end that senses the temperature. There are both digital and dial versions available. Check the temperature range to be sure it covers the temperatures you need. Instant-read thermometers are widely available in department stores, some grocery stores, specialty shops, hardware stores and big-box stores, and can also be purchased online.

Use

To test baked goods for doneness, insert the thermometer into the center of the product. (Some of the newer thermometers only need to be inserted to a depth of 3/4 inch/2 cm, so check the manufacturer's instructions.) With thin or small products, it may be necessary to insert the stem horizontally. Gluten-free baked goods, whether breads, cakes or muffins, are baked at 200°F (100°C).

Do not leave the thermometer in the product during baking, as the plastic cover will melt, ruining the thermometer. Clean the probe thoroughly after each use and store the thermometer in the plastic sleeve that came with it. Some of the more expensive ones (but not all) are dishwasher-safe. Read the manufacturer's instructions

How to Calibrate Your Dial Thermometer

It is important to make sure your dial thermometer is reading temperatures accurately, so you'll want to test it periodically. There are two ways of doing this, and either will work, though we prefer the boiling-water method.

- Bring a pot of water to a boil. Insert the thermometer probe into the boiling water, making sure it doesn't touch the pot. It should read 212°F or 100°C. (Be careful not to burn yourself on the steam; we hold the thermometer with needle-nose pliers.)

- Fill a container with crushed ice and cold water (mostly ice; just use water to fill the gaps). Insert the thermometer probe into the center of the ice water, making sure it doesn't touch the container. It should read 32°F or 0°C. Only use this method if your thermometer is designed for this low temperature.

If the temperature reading is not exact, hold the calibration nut (found right under the round head) with a wrench and rotate the head until it reads the correct number of degrees.

Speaking Our Language: Are We All on the Same Page?

- "GF" means "gluten-free," such as GF sour cream, GF mayonnaise, etc., when both gluten-free and gluten-containing products are available. We recommend that you read package labels every time you purchase a GF product. Manufacturers frequently change the ingredients.

Keeping the following points in mind as you prepare our recipes will help you get the same great results we did:

- We selected specific GF flour combinations for individual recipes based on the desired texture and flavor of the final product. Unless mentioned as a variation, we have not tested other GF flours in the recipes. Substituting other flours may adversely affect the results.

- GF recipes can be temperamental. Even an extra tablespoon (15 mL) of water in a baked product can cause the recipe to fail. Use a graduated, clear, liquid measuring cup for all liquids. Place it on a flat surface and read it at eye level.

- Select either metric or imperial measures and stick to that for the whole recipe; do not mix.

- Select the correct dry measures (e.g., $\frac{1}{2}$ cup and $\frac{1}{4}$ cup when the recipe calls for $\frac{3}{4}$ cup, or 125 mL and 50 mL for 175 mL). For accuracy and perfect products, use the "spoon lightly, heap and level once" method

of measuring. For small amounts, use measuring spoons, not kitchen cutlery. (Long-handled, narrow measuring spoons made especially to fit spice jars are accurate and fun to use.)

- We used large eggs, liquid honey, light (fancy) molasses, bread machine or instant yeast, unsweetened fruit juice (not fruit drinks) and salted butter. Expect different results if you make substitutions.

- We tested with 2%, 1% or nonfat milk and yogurt, and fat-free or 5% sour cream.

- Unless otherwise stated in the recipe, eggs and dairy products are used cold from the refrigerator.

- All foods that require washing are washed before preparation. Foods such as bananas are peeled, but fresh peaches and apples are not (unless specified).

- If the preparation method (chopped, melted, diced, sliced) is listed before the food, it means that you prepare the food before measuring. If it is listed after the food, measure first, then prepare. Examples are "melted butter" vs. "butter, melted"; "ground flaxseed" vs. "flaxseed, ground"; and "cooked brown rice" vs. "brown rice, cooked."

- If in doubt about a food term, a piece of equipment or a specific recipe technique, refer to the glossaries, located on pages 299 to 310.

A Page from Deanna's Diary

MOVING AWAY FROM home can seem scary enough, but when you have to eat gluten-free it can feel even more overwhelming. I am in my second year of university and have been surviving just fine. Preparing for the first year was definitely the hardest, between choosing a school and figuring out what I would eat when I moved out.

The program I wanted to take was offered at multiple schools, so I did my research to find out which school offered the best options for eating gluten-free. Many schools have a number of gluten-free selections in their cafeterias, but I wanted to attend a school with apartment-style residences, where you have three or four roommates who share a kitchen, a living room and two or three bathrooms. This type of residence would work perfectly for me, because I could cook any food I want and not be restricted to what the cafeteria had on offer.

When you apply for school and residence, they ask if you have any health concerns or other reasons for needing a certain type of residence. I asked my doctor to write a note saying I am a celiac and require a gluten-free diet, and it would be best for me to have an apartment-style residence with a kitchen. My request was granted, and when I moved in I explained everything to my roommates and we never had any problems.

The next step was learning to make all of my favorite foods so that I could cook them whenever I wanted. It was tough at first, but it definitely helped to know that I could simply go to the cafeteria if I wanted. My advice is, when you're first learning to cook, focus on what you love to eat so that it will be more fun. Then learn the hard stuff later.

I was surprised by how many of my new friends also had celiac disease. We started getting together and making all of our favorite dishes, and it was great to sample everything they grew up eating.

For my second year, I got a house with the same roommates, so there was no need to explain everything all over again. We even make meals together that all of us can eat, such as stir-fries, chicken and omelets, or I just use my own noodles when we make spaghetti.

Moving away from home is definitely tough, and there can be many struggles, but food should never have to be one of them!

— *Deanna Jennet, Trent University, Ontario*

Deanna and her mother, Sue, have been celiac friends of ours since before we began developing gluten-free recipes in 2001. Deanna, now a university student, shares her point of view in each of our gluten-free cookbooks to help other young celiacs.

No-Knead Yeast Breads

■■■

Tips for No-Knead Bread Baking

- Select a heavy-duty mixer with a paddle attachment (flat beater) for the best mixing.

- Gradually add the dry ingredients to the liquids as the machine is mixing, then stop the machine and use a rubber spatula to scrape the bottom and sides of the bowl.

- The consistency of GF bread dough is more like thick cake batter than the traditional dough ball. You don't need to spend 10 minutes kneading the dough (hence the term "no-knead").

- All 9- by 5-inch (23 by 12.5 cm) loaf pans are not the same size. A celiac found that our breads came out only 2 inches (5 cm) high when baked in her pans. After verifying that she had followed the recipes exactly, measured accurately and used the same ingredients, she sent a picture that gave us the clue that her 9- by 5-inch pan was larger than ours. We have two different types: one with straight sides and the other slightly sloped. The height of your bread can vary with the size and shape of your pan.

- Fill the lightly greased pan only two-thirds full (if you have extra dough, bake it in a mini loaf pan or muffin tin), then set it, uncovered, in a warm, draft-free place until the dough has risen to the top of the pan (or almost to the top, as directed in the recipe). This usually takes 60 to 75 minutes, but may be shorter or longer. Rising time may vary due to:
  - the temperature of the liquids and other ingredients used in the recipe;
  - the temperature of the room, whether there are drafts from heating or air conditioning units, altitude and the level of humidity;
  - what your loaf pan is made of (see page 27).

- Be patient: the loaf does most of its rising in the last 15 minutes of the rising time. Do not let it over-rise, or it could collapse during baking.

- During baking, if the loaf gets as dark as desired before it is fully baked, tent it with foil for the remainder of the baking time (see the Techniques Glossary, page 310).

- Before removing the loaf from the oven, use an instant-read thermometer to take the internal temperature. It should read 200°F (100°C). If it doesn't, continue baking until it does, even if the loaf looks baked. (See Using an Instant-Read Thermometer, page 29.)

- After removing the loaf from the oven, immediately remove it from the pan and place it on a cooling rack. This will prevent a soggy loaf.

- Once the loaf has cooled, slice it with an electric knife or bread knife with a serrated blade.

- Store bread wrapped airtight at room temperature for 1 to 2 days. Bread stored in the refrigerator dries and stales quickly. For longer storage, place one or two slices in individual plastic bags, then place those bags in a larger sealable freezer bag. Freeze for up to 3 weeks. Remove a slice or two at a time.

White Bread

This is sure to become your favorite nutritious white sandwich bread. It won't crumble in your packed lunch.

■■■■■■■■■■■■■■■

Tips

Be sure not to substitute or omit any ingredients and to measure accurately.

To ensure success, see page 34 for tips on baking no-knead breads.

Nutritional value per serving	
Calories	121
Fat, total	4 g
Fat, saturated	1 g
Cholesterol	25 mg
Sodium	243 mg
Carbohydrate	18 g
Fiber	2 g
Protein	3 g
Calcium	18 mg
Iron	2 mg

■ **9- by 5-inch (23 by 12.5 cm) loaf pan, lightly greased**

1 cup	brown rice flour	250 mL
1/2 cup	amaranth flour	125 mL
1/3 cup	almond flour	75 mL
1/3 cup	quinoa flour	75 mL
1/4 cup	potato starch	60 mL
2 tbsp	tapioca starch	30 mL
1 tbsp	xanthan gum	15 mL
1 tbsp	bread machine or instant yeast	15 mL
1 1/2 tsp	salt	7 mL
2	large eggs	2
1 cup	water	250 mL
2 tbsp	vegetable oil	30 mL
2 tbsp	liquid honey	30 mL
1 tsp	cider vinegar	5 mL

1. In a large bowl or plastic bag, combine brown rice flour, amaranth flour, almond flour, quinoa flour, potato starch, tapioca starch, xanthan gum, yeast and salt. Mix well and set aside.

2. In a separate bowl, using a heavy-duty electric mixer with paddle attachment, combine eggs, water, oil, honey and vinegar until well blended. With the mixer on its lowest speed, slowly add the dry ingredients until combined. Stop the machine and scrape the bottom and sides of the bowl with a rubber spatula. With the mixer on medium speed, beat for 1 minute or until smooth.

3. Spoon dough into prepared pan. Let rise, uncovered, in a warm, draft-free place for 60 to 75 minutes or until dough has risen to the top of the pan. Meanwhile, preheat oven to 350°F (180°C).

4. Bake for 35 to 40 minutes or until internal temperature of loaf registers 200°F (100°C) on an instant-read thermometer. Remove from the pan immediately and let cool completely on a rack.

Variation

Raisin Bread: Add 1/2 cup (125 mL) raisins and 1 tsp (5 mL) ground cinnamon with the dry ingredients.

Brown Sandwich Bread

For those who want a rich, golden, wholesome, nutritious sandwich bread to carry for lunch, this is your loaf.

■■■■■■■■■■■■■■■

Tips

The batter fills the pan only two-thirds full before it rises, but bakes to fill the pan.

Be sure to tent with foil partway through the baking time, as this is a very dark-colored loaf.

To ensure success, see page 34 for tips on baking no-knead breads.

Nutritional value per serving

Calories	116
Fat, total	4 g
Fat, saturated	1 g
Cholesterol	25 mg
Sodium	247 mg
Carbohydrate	18 g
Fiber	2 g
Protein	4 g
Calcium	17 mg
Iron	2 mg

■ **9- by 5-inch (23 by 12.5 cm) loaf pan, lightly greased**

1 cup	sorghum flour	250 mL
½ cup	pea flour	125 mL
⅓ cup	tapioca starch	75 mL
⅓ cup	rice bran	75 mL
2 tbsp	packed brown sugar	30 mL
1 tbsp	xanthan gum	15 mL
2 tsp	bread machine or instant yeast	10 mL
1½ tsp	salt	7 mL
2	large eggs	2
1	large egg white	1
1¼ cups	water	300 mL
3 tbsp	vegetable oil	45 mL
2 tbsp	light (fancy) molasses	30 mL
1 tsp	cider vinegar	5 mL

1. In a large bowl or plastic bag, combine sorghum flour, pea flour, tapioca starch, rice bran, brown sugar, xanthan gum, yeast and salt. Mix well and set aside.

2. In a separate bowl, using a heavy-duty electric mixer with paddle attachment, combine eggs, egg white, water, oil, molasses and vinegar until well blended. With the mixer on its lowest speed, slowly add the dry ingredients until combined. Stop the machine and scrape the bottom and sides of the bowl with a rubber spatula. With the mixer on medium speed, beat for 1 minute or until smooth.

3. Spoon dough into prepared pan. Let rise, uncovered, in a warm, draft-free place for 60 to 75 minutes or until dough has risen to the top of the pan. Meanwhile, preheat oven to 350°F (180°C), with rack set in bottom third of oven.

4. Bake for 25 minutes. Tent with foil and bake for 10 to 15 minutes or until internal temperature of loaf registers 200°F (100°C) on an instant-read thermometer. Remove from the pan immediately and let cool completely on a rack.

Variations

Substitute any kind of bean flour for the pea flour.

Substitute GF oat bran for the rice bran.

Herbed Brown Bread

The fragrant aroma of this zesty herb bread makes waiting for it to bake extremely difficult. Serve it with any course — soup, salad or entrée.

▪▪▪▪▪▪▪▪▪▪▪▪▪▪▪

Tips

This is an excellent loaf to use for making croutons and bread crumbs. See the Techniques Glossary, page 307, for information about bread crumbs. Turn them into a stuffing for beef, pork or poultry.

To ensure success, see page 34 for tips on baking no-knead breads.

Nutritional value per serving	
Calories	130
Fat, total	6 g
Fat, saturated	1 g
Cholesterol	25 mg
Sodium	207 mg
Carbohydrate	17 g
Fiber	2 g
Protein	3 g
Calcium	18 mg
Iron	1 mg

▪ 9- by 5-inch (23 by 12.5 cm) loaf pan, lightly greased

1 1/4 cups	sorghum flour	300 mL
2/3 cup	whole bean flour	150 mL
1/3 cup	tapioca starch	75 mL
1/4 cup	granulated sugar	60 mL
1 tbsp	xanthan gum	15 mL
1 tbsp	bread machine or instant yeast	15 mL
1 1/4 tsp	salt	6 mL
1/3 cup	snipped fresh parsley	75 mL
1/4 cup	snipped fresh marjoram	60 mL
1/4 cup	snipped fresh thyme	60 mL
2	large eggs	2
1	large egg white	1
1 cup	water	250 mL
1/3 cup	vegetable oil	75 mL
1 tsp	cider vinegar	5 mL

1. In a large bowl or plastic bag, combine sorghum flour, whole bean flour, tapioca starch, sugar, xanthan gum, yeast, salt, parsley, marjoram and thyme. Mix well and set aside.

2. In a separate bowl, using a heavy-duty electric mixer with paddle attachment, combine eggs, egg white, water, oil and vinegar until well blended. With the mixer on its lowest speed, slowly add the dry ingredients until combined. Stop the machine and scrape the bottom and sides of the bowl with a rubber spatula. With the mixer on medium speed, beat for 1 minute or until smooth.

3. Spoon dough into prepared pan. Let rise, uncovered, in a warm, draft-free place for 60 to 75 minutes or until dough has risen almost to the top of the pan. Meanwhile, preheat oven to 350°F (180°C).

4. Bake for 35 to 45 minutes or until internal temperature of loaf registers 200°F (100°C) on an instant-read thermometer. Remove from the pan immediately and let cool completely on a rack.

Variation

Substitute one-third the amount of dried herbs for the fresh.

Triple-Seed Brown Bread

A sandwich bread with a rich color and added crunch — what a treat!

■■■■■■■■■■■■■■■

Tips

You can purchase buttermilk powder in bulk stores and health food stores.

Toasting the seeds gives them a nuttier flavor. For instructions, see the Techniques Glossary, page 310.

■ **9- by 5-inch (23 by 12.5 cm) loaf pan, lightly greased**

1¼ cups	sorghum flour	300 mL
½ cup	whole bean flour	125 mL
¼ cup	tapioca starch	60 mL
¼ cup	rice bran	60 mL
¼ cup	buttermilk powder	60 mL
1 tbsp	xanthan gum	15 mL
1 tbsp	bread machine or instant yeast	15 mL
1¼ tsp	salt	6 mL
¼ cup	unsalted green pumpkin seeds, toasted	60 mL
¼ cup	unsalted raw sunflower seeds, toasted	60 mL
2 tbsp	sesame seeds, toasted	30 mL
2	large eggs	2
1	large egg white	1
1 cup	water	250 mL
2 tbsp	vegetable oil	30 mL
2 tbsp	liquid honey	30 mL
1 tbsp	light (fancy) molasses	15 mL
1 tsp	cider vinegar	5 mL

1. In a large bowl or plastic bag, combine sorghum flour, whole bean flour, tapioca starch, rice bran, buttermilk powder, xanthan gum, yeast, salt, pumpkin seeds, sunflower seeds and sesame seeds. Mix well and set aside.

2. In a separate bowl, using a heavy-duty electric mixer with paddle attachment, combine eggs, egg white, water, oil, honey, molasses and vinegar until well blended. With the mixer on its lowest speed, slowly add the dry ingredients until combined. Stop the machine and scrape the bottom and sides of the bowl with a rubber spatula. With the mixer on medium speed, beat for 1 minute or until smooth.

Nutritional value per serving	
Calories	142
Fat, total	7 g
Fat, saturated	1 g
Cholesterol	26 mg
Sodium	218 mg
Carbohydrate	18 g
Fiber	2 g
Protein	5 g
Calcium	40 mg
Iron	2 mg

Tips

Slice this or any bread with an electric knife for thin, even sandwich slices.

To ensure success, see page 34 for tips on baking no-knead breads.

3. Spoon dough into prepared pan. Let rise, uncovered, in a warm, draft-free place for 60 to 75 minutes or until dough has risen almost to the top of the pan. Meanwhile, preheat oven to 350°F (180°C).

4. Bake for 20 minutes. Check to see if loaf is getting too dark and tent with foil if necessary. Bake for 15 to 25 minutes or until internal temperature of loaf registers 200°F (100°C) on an instant-read thermometer. Remove from the pan immediately and let cool completely on a rack.

Variations

For a milder bread, substitute packed brown sugar for the molasses.

Substitute brown rice flour, raw hemp powder or ground flaxseed for the rice bran.

Replace the sesame seeds with cracked flaxseed, Hemp Hearts or poppy seeds.

Egg-Free, Corn-Free, Dairy-Free, Soy-Free Brown Bread

Makes 15 slices
Serving size: 1 slice

Though shorter than some loaves, this is the perfect brown sandwich bread for those who must eliminate eggs, corn, dairy and/or soy from their diet. It carries well, for a tasty lunch.

■■■■■■■■■■■■■■■■

Tip

To ensure success, see page 34 for tips on baking no-knead breads.

Variations

For a milder bread, substitute 1 tbsp (15 mL) packed brown sugar for the molasses.

The rice bran can be replaced by an equal amount of GF oat bran or brown or white rice flour.

Nutritional value per serving

Calories	139
Fat, total	4 g
Fat, saturated	0 g
Cholesterol	0 mg
Sodium	200 mg
Carbohydrate	24 g
Fiber	3 g
Protein	3 g
Calcium	23 mg
Iron	2 mg

■ **9- by 5-inch (23 by 12.5 cm) loaf pan, lightly greased**

¼ cup	flax flour or ground flaxseed	60 mL
⅓ cup	warm water	75 mL
1¼ cups	brown rice flour	300 mL
¾ cup	sorghum flour	175 mL
⅓ cup	rice bran	75 mL
3 tbsp	tapioca starch	45 mL
1 tbsp	xanthan gum	15 mL
1 tbsp	bread machine or instant yeast	15 mL
1¼ tsp	salt	6 mL
1 cup	water	250 mL
2 tbsp	vegetable oil	30 mL
3 tbsp	liquid honey	45 mL
1 tbsp	light (fancy) molasses	15 mL
1 tsp	cider vinegar	5 mL

1. In a small bowl or measuring cup, combine flax flour and warm water; set aside for 5 minutes.

2. In a large bowl or plastic bag, combine brown rice flour, sorghum flour, rice bran, tapioca starch, xanthan gum, yeast and salt. Mix well and set aside.

3. In a separate bowl, using a heavy-duty electric mixer with paddle attachment, combine water, oil, honey, molasses, vinegar and flax flour mixture until well blended. With the mixer on its lowest speed, slowly add the dry ingredients until combined. Stop the machine and scrape the bottom and sides of the bowl with a rubber spatula. With the mixer on medium speed, beat for 1 minute or until smooth.

4. Spoon dough into prepared pan. Let rise, uncovered, in a warm, draft-free place for 75 to 90 minutes or until dough has risen almost to the top of the pan. Meanwhile, preheat oven to 350°F (180°C).

5. Bake for 25 minutes. Check to see if loaf is getting too dark and tent with foil if necessary. Bake for 10 to 20 minutes or until internal temperature of loaf registers 200°F (100°C) on an instant-read thermometer. Remove from the pan immediately and let cool completely on a rack.

Egg-Free, Corn-Free, Dairy-Free, Soy-Free Flax Bread

Makes 15 slices
Serving size: 1 slice

Don't be alarmed when this one turns out shorter than some loaves.

▪▪▪▪▪▪▪▪▪▪▪▪▪▪

Tips

For information on how to crack flaxseed, see the Techniques Glossary, page 308.

To ensure success, see page 34 for tips on baking no-knead breads.

Variation

Make a dozen dinner rolls by following the method for Egg-Free, Corn-Free, Dairy-Free, Soy-Free White Dinner Rolls (page 94).

Nutritional value per serving	
Calories	140
Fat, total	6 g
Fat, saturated	1 g
Cholesterol	0 mg
Sodium	200 mg
Carbohydrate	21 g
Fiber	3 g
Protein	3 g
Calcium	29 mg
Iron	1 mg

■ **9- by 5-inch (23 by 12.5 cm) loaf pan, lightly greased**

¼ cup	flax flour or ground flaxseed	60 mL
⅓ cup	warm water	75 mL
1¾ cups	brown rice flour	425 mL
¼ cup	almond flour	60 mL
⅓ cup	tapioca starch	75 mL
2 tbsp	granulated sugar	30 mL
2½ tsp	xanthan gum	12 mL
1 tbsp	bread machine or instant yeast	15 mL
1¼ tsp	salt	6 mL
⅓ cup	cracked flaxseed	75 mL
1⅓ cups	water	325 mL
2 tbsp	vegetable oil	30 mL
2 tsp	cider vinegar	10 mL

1. In a small bowl or measuring cup, combine flax flour and warm water; set aside for 5 minutes.

2. In a large bowl or plastic bag, combine brown rice flour, almond flour, tapioca starch, sugar, xanthan gum, yeast, salt and cracked flaxseed. Mix well and set aside.

3. In a separate bowl, using a heavy-duty electric mixer with paddle attachment, combine water, oil, vinegar and flax flour mixture until well blended. With the mixer on its lowest speed, slowly add the dry ingredients until combined. Stop the machine and scrape the bottom and sides of the bowl with a rubber spatula. With the mixer on medium speed, beat for 1 minute or until smooth.

4. Spoon dough into prepared pan. Let rise, uncovered, in a warm, draft-free place for 60 to 75 minutes or until dough has risen almost to the top of the pan. Meanwhile, preheat oven to 350°F (180°C).

5. Bake for 20 minutes. Check to see if loaf is getting too dark and tent with foil if necessary. Bake for 15 to 20 minutes or until internal temperature of loaf registers 200°F (100°C) on an instant-read thermometer. Remove from the pan immediately and let cool completely on a rack.

Country Harvest Bread

Makes 15 slices
Serving size: 1 slice

This sandwich bread with a crunch is one of our favorites.

▪▪▪▪▪▪▪▪▪▪▪▪▪▪

Tips

To prevent seeds from becoming rancid, store them in an airtight container in the refrigerator.

For information on cracking flaxseed, see the Techniques Glossary, page 308.

To ensure success, see page 34 for tips on baking no-knead breads.

Variation

Try different types of seeds, such as poppy seeds or unsalted green pumpkin seeds, but keep the total amount the same.

Nutritional value per serving

Calories	161
Fat, total	10 g
Fat, saturated	1 g
Cholesterol	25 mg
Sodium	212 mg
Carbohydrate	17 g
Fiber	3 g
Protein	5 g
Calcium	40 mg
Iron	1 mg

■ 9- by 5-inch (23 by 12.5 cm) loaf pan, lightly greased

1 cup	sorghum flour	250 mL
1/2 cup	whole bean flour	125 mL
2 tbsp	flax flour	30 mL
1/3 cup	tapioca starch	75 mL
3 tbsp	packed brown sugar	45 mL
1 tbsp	xanthan gum	15 mL
1 tbsp	bread machine or instant yeast	15 mL
1 1/4 tsp	salt	6 mL
1/2 cup	cracked flaxseed	125 mL
1/3 cup	unsalted raw sunflower seeds	75 mL
2 tbsp	sesame seeds	30 mL
2	large eggs	2
1	large egg white	1
1 cup	water	250 mL
1/4 cup	vegetable oil	60 mL
1 tsp	cider vinegar	5 mL

1. In a large bowl or plastic bag, combine sorghum flour, whole bean flour, flax flour, tapioca starch, brown sugar, xanthan gum, yeast, salt, flaxseed, sunflower seeds and sesame seeds. Mix well and set aside.

2. In a separate bowl, using a heavy-duty electric mixer with paddle attachment, combine eggs, egg white, water, oil and vinegar until well blended. With the mixer on its lowest speed, slowly add the dry ingredients until combined. Stop the machine and scrape the bottom and sides of the bowl with a rubber spatula. With the mixer on medium speed, beat for 1 minute or until smooth.

3. Spoon dough into prepared pan. Let rise, uncovered, in a warm, draft-free place for 60 to 75 minutes or until dough has risen almost to the top of the pan. Meanwhile, preheat oven to 350°F (180°C).

4. Bake for 20 minutes. Check to see if loaf is getting too dark and tent with foil if necessary. Bake for 15 to 20 minutes or until internal temperature of loaf registers 200°F (100°C) on an instant-read thermometer. Remove from the pan immediately and let cool completely on a rack.

Pumpernickel Bread

Makes 15 slices
Serving size: 1 slice

With all the hearty flavor of traditional pumpernickel, this version is great for sandwiches. Try it filled with sliced turkey, accompanied by a crisp garlic dill pickle.

■■■■■■■■■■■■■■

Tips

Sift cocoa just before measuring, as it lumps easily.

To ensure success, see page 34 for tips on baking no-knead breads.

Variations

Add 2 tbsp (30 mL) caraway, fennel or anise seeds with the dry ingredients.

Substitute an equal quantity of strong brewed room-temperature coffee for the water.

Nutritional value per serving	
Calories	123
Fat, total	4 g
Fat, saturated	0 g
Cholesterol	25 mg
Sodium	248 mg
Carbohydrate	20 g
Fiber	2 g
Protein	3 g
Calcium	21 mg
Iron	1 mg

■ **9- by 5-inch (23 by 12.5 cm) loaf pan, lightly greased**

1 cup	sorghum flour	250 mL
1/2 cup	whole bean flour	125 mL
1/3 cup	brown rice flour	75 mL
2 tbsp	quinoa flour	30 mL
1/4 cup	potato starch	60 mL
2 tbsp	tapioca starch	30 mL
2 tbsp	packed brown sugar	30 mL
1 tbsp	xanthan gum	15 mL
1 tbsp	bread machine or instant yeast	15 mL
1 1/2 tsp	salt	7 mL
1 tbsp	instant coffee granules	15 mL
1 tbsp	sifted unsweetened cocoa powder	15 mL
3/4 tsp	ground ginger	3 mL
2	large eggs	2
1	large egg white	1
1 cup	water	250 mL
3 tbsp	vegetable oil	45 mL
3 tbsp	light (fancy) molasses	45 mL
1 tsp	cider vinegar	5 mL

1. In a large bowl or plastic bag, combine sorghum flour, whole bean flour, brown rice flour, quinoa flour, potato starch, tapioca starch, brown sugar, xanthan gum, yeast, salt, coffee granules, cocoa powder and ginger. Mix well and set aside.

2. In a bowl, using a heavy-duty electric mixer with paddle attachment, combine eggs, egg white, water, oil, molasses and vinegar until well blended. With the mixer on its lowest speed, slowly add the dry ingredients until combined. Stop the machine and scrape the bottom and sides of the bowl with a rubber spatula. With the mixer on medium speed, beat for 1 minute or until smooth.

3. Spoon dough into prepared pan. Let rise, uncovered, in a warm, draft-free place for 60 to 75 minutes or until dough has risen to the top of the pan. Meanwhile, preheat oven to 350°F (180°C).

4. Bake for 35 to 45 minutes or until internal temperature of loaf registers 200°F (100°C) on an instant-read thermometer. Remove from the pan immediately and let cool completely on a rack.

Mock Swedish Limpa

The traditional Scandinavian trio of anise, caraway and fennel seeds gives this orange-scented loaf a unique flavor.

■■■■■■■■■■■■■■■■

Tips

For a smoother texture, use a food mill or a clean coffee or spice grinder to grind the seeds.

To ensure success, see page 34 for tips on baking no-knead breads.

Variation

Substitute 3 tbsp (45 mL) flaxseed or poppy seeds for the anise, caraway and fennel seeds.

Nutritional value per serving	
Calories	119
Fat, total	3 g
Fat, saturated	0 g
Cholesterol	25 mg
Sodium	208 mg
Carbohydrate	19 g
Fiber	2 g
Protein	4 g
Calcium	26 mg
Iron	2 mg

■ **9- by 5-inch (23 by 12.5 cm) loaf pan, lightly greased**

1²⁄₃ cups	sorghum flour	400 mL
¹⁄₃ cup	quinoa flour	75 mL
¹⁄₃ cup	tapioca starch	75 mL
1 tbsp	xanthan gum	15 mL
1 tbsp	bread machine or instant yeast	15 mL
1¹⁄₄ tsp	salt	6 mL
2 tsp	anise seeds	10 mL
2 tsp	caraway seeds	10 mL
2 tsp	fennel seeds	10 mL
2 tbsp	grated orange zest	30 mL
2	large eggs	2
1	large egg white	1
1 cup	water	250 mL
3 tbsp	light (fancy) molasses	45 mL
2 tbsp	vegetable oil	30 mL
1 tsp	cider vinegar	5 mL

1. In a large bowl or plastic bag, combine sorghum flour, quinoa flour, tapioca starch, xanthan gum, yeast, salt, anise seeds, caraway seeds, fennel seeds and orange zest. Mix well and set aside.

2. In a separate bowl, using a heavy-duty electric mixer with paddle attachment, combine eggs, egg white, water, molasses, oil and vinegar until well blended. With the mixer on its lowest speed, slowly add the dry ingredients until combined. Stop the machine and scrape the bottom and sides of the bowl with a rubber spatula. With the mixer on medium speed, beat for 1 minute or until smooth.

3. Spoon dough into prepared pan. Let rise, uncovered, in a warm, draft-free place for 60 to 75 minutes or until dough has risen almost to the top of the pan. Meanwhile, preheat oven to 350°F (180°C).

4. Bake for 35 to 45 minutes or until internal temperature of loaf registers 200°F (100°C) on an instant-read thermometer. Remove from the pan immediately and let cool completely on a rack.

Lemon Millet Bread

Makes 15 slices
Serving size: 1 slice

This rich, golden loaf is studded with white dots of millet. The refreshing addition of lemon makes it a real taste treat.

■■■■■■■■■■■■■■■

Tips

No need to cook the millet seeds — they soften enough during baking to provide an interesting crunch.

To ensure success, see page 34 for tips on baking no-knead breads.

Nutritional value per serving

Calories	163
Fat, total	4 g
Fat, saturated	1 g
Cholesterol	25 mg
Sodium	169 mg
Carbohydrate	27 g
Fiber	3 g
Protein	4 g
Calcium	18 mg
Iron	3 mg

■ **9- by 5-inch (23 by 12.5 cm) loaf pan, lightly greased**

1⅓ cups	brown rice flour	325 mL
1 cup	amaranth flour	250 mL
3 tbsp	tapioca starch	45 mL
1 tbsp	xanthan gum	15 mL
1 tbsp	bread machine or instant yeast	15 mL
1 tsp	salt	5 mL
½ cup	millet seeds	125 mL
2 tbsp	grated lemon zest	30 mL
2	large eggs	2
1	large egg white	1
¾ cup	water	175 mL
3 tbsp	vegetable oil	45 mL
3 tbsp	liquid honey	45 mL
2 tbsp	freshly squeezed lemon juice	30 mL

1. In a large bowl or plastic bag, combine brown rice flour, amaranth flour, tapioca starch, xanthan gum, yeast, salt, millet seeds and lemon zest. Mix well and set aside.

2. In a separate bowl, using a heavy-duty electric mixer with paddle attachment, combine eggs, egg white, water, oil, honey and lemon juice until well blended. With the mixer on its lowest speed, slowly add the dry ingredients until combined. Stop the machine and scrape the bottom and sides of the bowl with a rubber spatula. With the mixer on medium speed, beat for 1 minute or until smooth.

3. Spoon dough into prepared pan. Let rise, uncovered, in a warm, draft-free place for 60 to 75 minutes or until dough has risen almost to the top of the pan. Meanwhile, preheat oven to 350°F (180°C).

4. Bake for 20 minutes. Check to see if loaf is getting too dark and tent with foil if necessary. Bake for 15 to 25 minutes or until internal temperature of loaf registers 200°F (100°C) on an instant-read thermometer. Remove from the pan immediately and let cool completely on a rack.

Variation

Substitute orange zest and juice for the lemon.

Sun-Dried Tomato Cornbread

Serve this moist savory cornbread, flavored with salty bursts of sun-dried tomatoes, with salad for lunch.

■■■■■■■■■■■■■■■

Tips

Use dry, not oil-packed, sun-dried tomatoes in this recipe.

To ensure success, see page 34 for tips on baking no-knead breads.

Nutritional value per serving

Calories	142
Fat, total	5 g
Fat, saturated	0 g
Cholesterol	25 mg
Sodium	224 mg
Carbohydrate	21 g
Fiber	2 g
Protein	4 g
Calcium	18 mg
Iron	3 mg

■ **9- by 5-inch (23 by 12.5 cm) loaf pan, lightly greased**

1¼ cups	cornmeal	300 mL
1 cup	amaranth flour	250 mL
¼ cup	tapioca starch	60 mL
3 tbsp	granulated sugar	45 mL
1 tbsp	xanthan gum	15 mL
1 tbsp	bread machine or instant yeast	15 mL
1 tsp	salt	5 mL
2	large eggs	2
1	large egg white	1
1 cup	water	250 mL
¼ cup	vegetable oil	60 mL
1 tsp	cider vinegar	5 mL
¾ cup	snipped sun-dried tomatoes	175 mL

1. In a large bowl or plastic bag, combine cornmeal, amaranth flour, tapioca starch, sugar, xanthan gum, yeast and salt. Mix well and set aside.

2. In a separate bowl, using a heavy-duty electric mixer with paddle attachment, combine eggs, egg white, water, oil and vinegar until well blended. With the mixer on its lowest speed, slowly add the dry ingredients until combined. Stop the machine and scrape the bottom and sides of the bowl with a rubber spatula. With the mixer on medium speed, beat for 1 minute or until smooth. Stir in sun-dried tomatoes.

3. Spoon dough into prepared pan. Let rise, uncovered, in a warm, draft-free place for 60 to 75 minutes or until dough has risen almost to the top of the pan. Meanwhile, preheat oven to 350°F (180°C).

4. Bake for 20 minutes. Check to see if loaf is getting too dark and tent with foil if necessary. Bake for 25 to 30 minutes or until internal temperature of loaf registers 200°F (100°C) on an instant-read thermometer. Remove from the pan immediately and let cool completely on a rack.

Variation

Add ½ cup (125 mL) thinly sliced green onions with the sun-dried tomatoes.

Oatmeal Date Loaf

We enjoy the natural
sweetness of oatmeal
in this loaf.

▪▪▪▪▪▪▪▪▪▪▪▪▪▪

Tips

If you purchase chopped
dates instead of whole ones,
be sure to check the label
for hidden gluten.

Instead of chopping with
a knife, snip dates with
kitchen shears. Dip the
blades in hot water when
they become sticky.

Variation

For a subtle orange
flavor, add 2 tbsp
(30 mL) grated orange
zest with the dry
ingredients.

Nutritional value per serving

Calories	164
Fat, total	5 g
Fat, saturated	1 g
Cholesterol	25 mg
Sodium	247 mg
Carbohydrate	28 g
Fiber	3 g
Protein	4 g
Calcium	18 mg
Iron	1 mg

■ **9- by 5-inch (23 by 12.5 cm) loaf pan, lightly greased**

1⅓ cups	sorghum flour	325 mL
⅓ cup	GF large-flake (old-fashioned) rolled oats	75 mL
⅓ cup	GF oat flour	75 mL
¼ cup	tapioca starch	60 mL
¼ cup	packed brown sugar	60 mL
1 tbsp	xanthan gum	15 mL
2½ tsp	bread machine or instant yeast	12 mL
1½ tsp	salt	7 mL
1½ tsp	ground nutmeg	7 mL
2	large eggs	2
1	large egg white	1
1 cup	water	250 mL
¼ cup	vegetable oil	60 mL
1 tsp	cider vinegar	5 mL
1 cup	snipped pitted dates	250 mL

1. In a large bowl or plastic bag, combine sorghum flour, oats, oat flour, tapioca starch, brown sugar, xanthan gum, yeast, salt and nutmeg. Mix well and set aside.

2. In a separate bowl, using a heavy-duty electric mixer with paddle attachment, combine eggs, egg white, water, oil and vinegar until well blended. With the mixer on its lowest speed, slowly add the dry ingredients until combined. Stop the machine and scrape the bottom and sides of the bowl with a rubber spatula. With the mixer on medium speed, beat for 1 minute or until smooth. Stir in dates.

3. Spoon dough into prepared pan. Let rise, uncovered, in a warm, draft-free place for 60 to 75 minutes or until dough has risen to the top of the pan. Meanwhile, preheat oven to 350°F (180°C).

4. Bake for 25 minutes. Check to see if loaf is getting too dark and tent with foil if necessary. Bake for 15 to 20 minutes or until internal temperature of loaf registers 200°F (100°C) on an instant-read thermometer. Remove from the pan immediately and let cool completely on a rack.

Date Nut Loaf

You'll enjoy this moist, dark, sweet loaf. It's delicious spread with cream cheese.

■■■■■■■■■■■■■■■

Tips

If you purchase chopped dates instead of whole ones, be sure to check the label for hidden gluten.

For information on toasting nuts, see the Techniques Glossary, page 309.

To ensure success, see page 34 for tips on baking no-knead breads.

Variation

Replace half the dates with dried figs.

Nutritional value per serving	
Calories	179
Fat, total	7 g
Fat, saturated	1 g
Cholesterol	25 mg
Sodium	208 mg
Carbohydrate	28 g
Fiber	3 g
Protein	4 g
Calcium	27 mg
Iron	1 mg

■ **9- by 5-inch (23 by 12.5 cm) loaf pan, lightly greased**

1½ cups	sorghum flour	375 mL
¾ cup	whole bean flour	175 mL
½ cup	tapioca starch	125 mL
1 tbsp	xanthan gum	15 mL
2½ tsp	bread machine or instant yeast	12 mL
1¼ tsp	salt	6 mL
2	large eggs	2
1	large egg white	2
1¼ cups	water	300 mL
¼ cup	vegetable oil	60 mL
3 tbsp	light (fancy) molasses	45 mL
1 tsp	cider vinegar	5 mL
1 cup	snipped pitted dates	250 mL
⅓ cup	toasted chopped walnuts	75 mL

1. In a large bowl or plastic bag, combine sorghum flour, whole bean flour, tapioca starch, xanthan gum, yeast and salt. Mix well and set aside.

2. In a separate bowl, using a heavy-duty electric mixer with paddle attachment, combine eggs, egg white, water, oil, molasses and vinegar until well blended. With the mixer on its lowest speed, slowly add the dry ingredients until combined. Stop the machine and scrape the bottom and sides of the bowl with a rubber spatula. With the mixer on medium speed, beat for 1 minute or until smooth. Stir in dates and walnuts.

3. Spoon dough into prepared pan. Let rise, uncovered, in a warm, draft-free place for 60 to 75 minutes or until dough has risen to the top of the pan. Meanwhile, preheat oven to 350°F (180°C).

4. Bake for 20 minutes. Check to see if loaf is getting too dark and tent with foil if necessary. Bake for 20 to 25 minutes or until internal temperature of loaf registers 200°F (100°C) on an instant-read thermometer. Remove from the pan immediately and let cool completely on a rack.

Cranberry Raisin Bread

Makes 15 slices
Serving size: 1 slice

This recipe was inspired by a request for a GF raisin bread that is not too sweet. One of our celiac friends likes it toasted for breakfast.

■■■■■■■■■■■■■■■

Tips

Don't omit the xanthan gum, as it gives structure to the bread. The loaf is more apt to collapse without it.

To ensure success, see page 34 for tips on baking no-knead breads.

Variation

Try substituting chocolate chips for the raisins.

Nutritional value per serving	
Calories	143
Fat, total	5 g
Fat, saturated	1 g
Cholesterol	25 mg
Sodium	208 mg
Carbohydrate	22 g
Fiber	2 g
Protein	3 g
Calcium	17 mg
Iron	2 mg

■ **9- by 5-inch (23 by 12.5 cm) loaf pan, lightly greased**

1 cup	sorghum flour	250 mL
1/2 cup	amaranth flour	125 mL
1/3 cup	brown rice flour	75 mL
1/4 cup	tapioca starch	60 mL
3 tbsp	packed brown sugar	45 mL
2 1/2 tsp	xanthan gum	12 mL
1 tbsp	bread machine or instant yeast	15 mL
1 1/4 tsp	salt	6 mL
1 1/4 tsp	ground cardamom	6 mL
2	large eggs	2
1	large egg white	1
1 cup	water	250 mL
1/4 cup	vegetable oil	60 mL
1 tsp	cider vinegar	5 mL
1/3 cup	dried cranberries	75 mL
1/3 cup	raisins	75 mL

1. In a large bowl or plastic bag, combine sorghum flour, amaranth flour, brown rice flour, tapioca starch, brown sugar, xanthan gum, yeast, salt and cardamom. Mix well and set aside.

2. In a separate bowl, using a heavy-duty electric mixer with paddle attachment, combine eggs, egg white, water, oil and vinegar until well blended. With the mixer on its lowest speed, slowly add the dry ingredients until combined. Stop the machine and scrape the bottom and sides of the bowl with a rubber spatula. With the mixer on medium speed, beat for 1 minute or until smooth. Stir in cranberries and raisins.

3. Spoon dough into prepared pan. Let rise, uncovered, in a warm, draft-free place for 60 to 75 minutes or until dough has risen to the top of the pan. Meanwhile, preheat oven to 350°F (180°C).

4. Bake for 25 minutes. Check to see if loaf is getting too dark and tent with foil if necessary. Bake for 17 to 20 minutes or until internal temperature of loaf registers 200°F (100°C) on an instant-read thermometer. Remove from the pan immediately and let cool completely on a rack.

Cranberry Orange Bread

Makes 15 slices
Serving size: 1 slice

You can make this tart but sweet loaf any time of the year — no need to wait for fresh cranberries in the fall.

■■■■■■■■■■■■■■■

■ **9- by 5-inch (23 by 12.5 cm) loaf pan, lightly greased**

1⅓ cups	brown rice flour	325 mL
½ cup	amaranth flour	125 mL
⅓ cup	tapioca starch	75 mL
¼ cup	granulated sugar	60 mL
2½ tsp	xanthan gum	12 mL
1 tbsp	bread machine or instant yeast	15 mL
1½ tsp	salt	7 mL
2 tbsp	grated orange zest	30 mL
2	large eggs	2
1	large egg white	1
¾ cup	water	175 mL
¼ cup	frozen orange juice concentrate, thawed	60 mL
¼ cup	vegetable oil	60 mL
2 tsp	cider vinegar	10 mL
1 cup	dried cranberries	250 mL

1. In a large bowl or plastic bag, combine brown rice flour, amaranth flour, tapioca starch, sugar, xanthan gum, yeast, salt and orange zest. Mix well and set aside.

2. In a separate bowl, using a heavy-duty electric mixer with paddle attachment, combine eggs, egg white, water, orange juice concentrate, oil and vinegar until well blended. With the mixer on its lowest speed, slowly add the dry ingredients until combined. Stop the machine and scrape the bottom and sides of the bowl with a rubber spatula. With the mixer on medium speed, beat for 1 minute or until smooth. Stir in cranberries.

3. Spoon dough into prepared pan. Let rise, uncovered, in a warm, draft-free place for 60 to 75 minutes or until dough has risen to the top of the pan. Meanwhile, preheat oven to 350°F (180°C).

Nutritional value per serving	
Calories	161
Fat, total	5 g
Fat, saturated	1 g
Cholesterol	25 mg
Sodium	249 mg
Carbohydrate	27 g
Fiber	2 g
Protein	3 g
Calcium	14 mg
Iron	1 mg

Tips

Orange zest is the bright orange portion of an orange peel. The easiest way to grate it is with a rasp grater — a very sharp, thin tool.

There's no need to thaw the orange juice concentrate before measuring it; simply scoop it into a dry measure directly from your freezer. That way, you only need to thaw the amount needed.

To ensure success, see page 34 for tips on baking no-knead breads.

4. Bake for 20 minutes. Tent with foil and bake for 25 to 30 minutes or until internal temperature of loaf registers 200°F (100°C) on an instant-read thermometer. Remove from the pan immediately and let cool completely on a rack.

Variations

Substitute 1 cup (250 mL) freshly squeezed orange juice for the water and orange juice concentrate.

Substitute dried blueberries for the cranberries.

Dried Apple Nut Bread

White dots of dried apple make this bread interesting and enjoyable.

■■■■■■■■■■■■■■■

Tips

Use either dried apple rings or dried apple slices.

See the Techniques Glossary, page 309, for information on toasting nuts.

To ensure success, see page 34 for tips on baking no-knead breads.

Variation

Substitute dried apricots for the apples and walnuts for the pecans.

Nutritional value per serving	
Calories	198
Fat, total	8 g
Fat, saturated	1 g
Cholesterol	25 mg
Sodium	278 mg
Carbohydrate	31 g
Fiber	4 g
Protein	4 g
Calcium	25 mg
Iron	2 mg

■ **9- by 5-inch (23 by 12.5 cm) loaf pan, lightly greased**

1¼ cups	sorghum flour	300 mL
¼ cup	GF oat flour	60 mL
¼ cup	teff flour	60 mL
⅓ cup	tapioca starch	75 mL
¼ cup	packed brown sugar	60 mL
1 tbsp	xanthan gum	15 mL
1 tbsp	bread machine or instant yeast	15 mL
1¼ tsp	salt	6 mL
2 tsp	ground cinnamon	10 mL
2	large eggs	2
1	large egg white	1
1 cup	water	250 mL
¼ cup	vegetable oil	60 mL
1 tsp	cider vinegar	5 mL
¾ cup	chopped dried apples	175 mL
½ cup	toasted chopped pecans	125 mL

1. In a large bowl or plastic bag, combine sorghum flour, oat flour, teff flour, tapioca starch, brown sugar, xanthan gum, yeast, salt and cinnamon. Mix well and set aside.

2. In a separate bowl, using a heavy-duty electric mixer with paddle attachment, combine eggs, egg white, water, oil and vinegar until well blended. With the mixer on its lowest speed, slowly add the dry ingredients until combined. Stop the machine and scrape the bottom and sides of the bowl with a rubber spatula. With the mixer on medium speed, beat for 1 minute or until smooth. Stir in apples and pecans.

3. Spoon dough into prepared pan. Let rise, uncovered, in a warm, draft-free place for 60 to 75 minutes or until dough has risen to the top of the pan. Meanwhile, preheat oven to 350°F (180°C).

4. Bake for 20 minutes. Check to see if loaf is getting too dark and tent with foil if necessary. Bake for 15 to 25 minutes or until internal temperature of loaf registers 200°F (100°C) on an instant-read thermometer. Remove from the pan immediately and let cool completely on a rack.

Apricot Pecan Loaf

A slice of this nutritious, warm, dark teff loaf with contrasting chunks of golden apricots is a delicious take-to-work coffee break accompaniment.

■■■■■■■■■■■■■■■

Tips

Instead of chopping dried apricots with a knife, snip them with kitchen shears. Dip the blades in hot water when they become sticky.

To ensure success, see page 34 for tips on baking no-knead breads.

Variation

Replace half the apricots with dried figs, chopped into large pieces.

Nutritional value per serving	
Calories	165
Fat, total	7 g
Fat, saturated	1 g
Cholesterol	25 mg
Sodium	207 mg
Carbohydrate	23 g
Fiber	3 g
Protein	4 g
Calcium	27 mg
Iron	2 mg

■ **9- by 5-inch (23 by 12.5 cm) loaf pan, lightly greased**

1 cup	sorghum flour	250 mL
2/3 cup	teff flour	150 mL
1/3 cup	amaranth flour	75 mL
1/3 cup	tapioca starch	75 mL
1 tbsp	xanthan gum	15 mL
1 tbsp	bread machine or instant yeast	15 mL
1 1/4 tsp	salt	6 mL
2	large eggs	2
1	large egg white	1
1 cup	water	250 mL
3 tbsp	vegetable oil	45 mL
3 tbsp	liquid honey	45 mL
1 tsp	cider vinegar	5 mL
1/2 cup	snipped dried apricots	125 mL
1/2 cup	toasted chopped pecans	125 mL

1. In a large bowl or plastic bag, combine sorghum flour, teff flour, amaranth flour, tapioca starch, xanthan gum, yeast and salt. Mix well and set aside.

2. In a separate bowl, using a heavy-duty electric mixer with paddle attachment, combine eggs, egg white, water, oil, honey and vinegar until well blended. With the mixer on its lowest speed, slowly add the dry ingredients until combined. Stop the machine and scrape the bottom and sides of the bowl with a rubber spatula. With the mixer on medium speed, beat for 1 minute or until smooth. Stir in apricots and pecans

3. Spoon dough into prepared pan. Let rise, uncovered, in a warm, draft-free place for 60 to 75 minutes or until dough has risen to the top of the pan. Meanwhile, preheat oven to 350°F (180°C).

4. Bake for 20 minutes. Check to see if loaf is getting too dark and tent with foil if necessary. Bake for 22 to 25 minutes or until internal temperature of loaf registers 200°F (100°C) on an instant-read thermometer. Remove from the pan immediately and let cool completely on a rack.

Chocolate Hazelnut Dessert Bread

Makes 15 slices
Serving size: 1 slice

Plan to eat this one warm from the oven, as that's when the chocolate flavor is the strongest.

■■■■■■■■■■■■■■■

Tips

See the Techniques Glossary, page 308, for information on toasting hazelnuts. For this recipe, there's no need to remove the skin after toasting them.

You can "stir in" with the mixer on its lowest speed.

Variation

For a stronger hazelnut flavor, add 1 tbsp (15 mL) hazelnut liqueur (such as Frangelico) with the liquids.

Nutritional value per serving	
Calories	181
Fat, total	9 g
Fat, saturated	2 g
Cholesterol	26 mg
Sodium	179 mg
Carbohydrate	24 g
Fiber	3 g
Protein	5 g
Calcium	44 mg
Iron	2 mg

■ **9- by 5-inch (23 by 12.5 cm) loaf pan, lightly greased**

1⅓ cups	sorghum flour	325 mL
⅔ cup	whole bean flour	150 mL
¼ cup	tapioca starch	60 mL
¼ cup	granulated sugar	60 mL
1 tbsp	xanthan gum	15 mL
2½ tsp	bread machine or instant yeast	12 mL
1 tsp	salt	5 mL
¼ cup	unsweetened cocoa powder, sifted	60 mL
2	large eggs	2
1	large egg white	1
1⅓ cups	milk, warmed to room temperature	325 mL
¼ cup	vegetable oil	60 mL
1 tsp	cider vinegar	5 mL
⅔ cup	semisweet or dark chocolate chips	150 mL
⅓ cup	toasted coarsely chopped hazelnuts	75 mL

1. In a large bowl or plastic bag, combine sorghum flour, whole bean flour, tapioca starch, sugar, xanthan gum, yeast, salt and cocoa. Mix well and set aside.

2. In a separate bowl, using a heavy-duty electric mixer with paddle attachment, combine eggs, egg white, milk, oil and vinegar until well blended. With the mixer on its lowest speed, slowly add the dry ingredients until combined. Stop the machine and scrape the bottom and sides of the bowl with a rubber spatula. With the mixer on medium speed, beat for 1 minute or until smooth. Stir in chocolate chips and hazelnuts.

3. Spoon dough into prepared pan. Let rise, uncovered, in a warm, draft-free place for 60 to 75 minutes or until dough has risen to the top of the pan. Meanwhile, preheat oven to 350°F (180°C).

4. Bake for 20 minutes. Check to see if loaf is getting too dark and tent with foil if necessary. Bake for 15 to 25 minutes or until internal temperature of loaf registers 200°F (100°C) on an instant-read thermometer. Remove from the pan immediately and let cool completely on a rack.

Fruited Barm Brack

Barm brack, meaning "yeast bread" in Gaelic (although it is not always made with yeast), is an Irish bread with raisins or currants and candied fruit peel. Try our fruited version, made with tea, apricots, currants and cranberries. Perfect with an entrée or dessert!

■■■■■■■■■■■■■■■■■

Tips

Powdered ice tea mixes are too sweet and too strongly flavored with lemon to be substituted for the tea in this recipe.

We allow our tea to steep longer than normal to make it extra strong for this recipe.

To ensure success, see page 34 for tips on baking no-knead breads.

Nutritional value per serving	
Calories	145
Fat, total	3 g
Fat, saturated	0 g
Cholesterol	21 mg
Sodium	210 mg
Carbohydrate	27 g
Fiber	3 g
Protein	4 g
Calcium	28 mg
Iron	2 mg

■ **Three 5³/₄- by 3¹/₄-inch (14 by 8 cm) loaf pans, lightly greased**

1¹/₃ cups	sorghum flour	325 mL
¹/₂ cup	amaranth flour	125 mL
¹/₂ cup	teff flour	125 mL
¹/₂ cup	tapioca starch	125 mL
¹/₄ cup	packed brown sugar	60 mL
1 tbsp	xanthan gum	15 mL
1 tbsp	bread machine or instant yeast	15 mL
1¹/₂ tsp	salt	7 mL
1¹/₂ tsp	ground cinnamon	7 mL
¹/₂ tsp	ground nutmeg	2 mL
2	large eggs	2
2	large egg whites	2
1¹/₃ cups	strong brewed black tea, at room temperature	325 mL
2 tbsp	vegetable oil	30 mL
1 tsp	cider vinegar	5 mL
¹/₂ cup	snipped dried apricots	125 mL
¹/₂ cup	dried currants	125 mL
¹/₂ cup	dried cranberries	125 mL

1. In a large bowl or plastic bag, combine sorghum flour, amaranth flour, teff flour, tapioca starch, brown sugar, xanthan gum, yeast, salt, cinnamon and nutmeg. Mix well and set aside.

2. In a separate bowl, using a heavy-duty electric mixer with paddle attachment, combine eggs, egg whites, tea, oil and vinegar until well blended. With the mixer on its lowest speed, slowly add the dry ingredients until combined. Stop the machine and scrape the bottom and sides of the bowl with a rubber spatula. With the mixer on medium speed, beat for 1 minute or until smooth. Stir in apricots, currants and cranberries.

3. Spoon dough into prepared pans, dividing evenly. Let rise, uncovered, in a warm, draft-free place for 60 to 75 minutes or until dough has risen to the top of the pan. Meanwhile, preheat oven to 350°F (180°C).

4. Bake for 33 to 38 minutes or until internal temperature of loaf registers 200°F (100°C) on an instant-read thermometer. Remove from the pan immediately and let cool completely on a rack.

Mini Chop Suey Loaves

This old standby is chock full of mixed candied fruit. Keep one loaf for yourself and share the others.

■■■■■■■■■■■■■

Tips

For a lighter, less sweet loaf, rinse the fruit under cold water and dry well before adding it to the dough.

To ensure success, see page 34 for tips on baking no-knead breads.

Variation

Kulich: Substitute raisins for some of the candied fruit.

Nutritional value per serving	
Calories	178
Fat, total	4 g
Fat, saturated	0 g
Cholesterol	21 mg
Sodium	211 mg
Carbohydrate	32 g
Fiber	2 g
Protein	4 g
Calcium	23 mg
Iron	13 mg

■ **Three 5³⁄₄- by 3¹⁄₄-inch (14 by 8 cm) loaf pans, lightly greased**

1¹⁄₂ cups	amaranth flour	375 mL
1¹⁄₄ cups	brown rice flour	300 mL
¹⁄₂ cup	potato starch	125 mL
1 tbsp	xanthan gum	15 mL
1³⁄₄ tsp	bread machine or instant yeast	8 mL
1¹⁄₂ tsp	salt	7 mL
2	large eggs	2
2	large egg whites	2
1¹⁄₄ cups	water	300 mL
2 tbsp	vegetable oil	30 mL
3 tbsp	liquid honey	45 mL
1 tsp	cider vinegar	5 mL
2 tsp	almond extract	10 mL
1 cup	chopped mixed candied fruit	250 mL
¹⁄₄ cup	slivered almonds	60 mL

1. In a large bowl or plastic bag, combine amaranth flour, brown rice flour, potato starch, xanthan gum, yeast and salt. Mix well and set aside.

2. In a separate bowl, using a heavy-duty electric mixer with paddle attachment, combine eggs, egg whites, water, oil, honey, vinegar and almond extract until well blended. With the mixer on its lowest speed, slowly add the dry ingredients until combined. Stop the machine and scrape the bottom and sides of the bowl with a rubber spatula. With the mixer on medium speed, beat for 1 minute or until smooth. Stir in candied fruit and almonds.

3. Spoon dough into prepared pans, dividing evenly. Let rise, uncovered, in a warm, draft-free place for 60 to 75 minutes or until dough has risen to the top of the pan. Meanwhile, preheat oven to 350°F (180°C).

4. Bake for 38 to 42 minutes or until internal temperature of loaf registers 200°F (100°C) on an instant-read thermometer. Remove from the pan immediately and let cool completely on a rack.

No-Knead Pizzas and Flatbreads

Pizza Crust

**Use this thin crust
to make Florentine
Pizza (page 63) or
Sausage and Leek
Pizza (page 64).**

■■■■■■■■■■■■■■

Tip

If you don't have an 8-inch
(20 cm) round pizza pan,
use a 12-inch (30 cm) pan.
After transferring dough to
the pan, top it with waxed
paper and roll out to an
8½-inch (21 cm) circle.
Form a ¼-inch (0.5 cm)
ridge all the way around
the edge.

- ■ **Preheat oven to 400°F (200°C), with rack set in the bottom third**
- ■ **8-inch (20 cm) round pizza pan, lightly greased**

¼ cup	sorghum flour	60 mL
¼ cup	quinoa flour	60 mL
1 tbsp	tapioca starch	15 mL
1 tsp	granulated sugar	5 mL
2 tsp	xanthan gum	10 mL
1 tbsp	bread machine or instant yeast	15 mL
¼ tsp	salt	1 mL
⅓ cup	water	75 mL
1 tbsp	extra virgin olive oil	15 mL
1 tsp	cider vinegar	5 mL

1. In a bowl or plastic bag, combine sorghum flour, quinoa flour, tapioca starch, sugar, xanthan gum, yeast and salt. Mix well and set aside.

2. In a separate bowl, using a heavy-duty electric mixer with paddle attachment, combine water, oil and vinegar until well blended. With the mixer on its lowest speed, slowly add the dry ingredients until combined. Stop the machine and scrape the bottom and sides of the bowl with a rubber spatula. With the mixer on medium speed, beat for 1 minute or until smooth.

3. Gently transfer dough to prepared pan. Using a moist rubber spatula, carefully spread to the edges.

4. Bake in preheated oven for 10 minutes or until bottom is golden and crust is partially baked.

5. Use right away to make pizza with your favorite toppings, or wrap airtight and store in the freezer for up to 1 month. Thaw in the refrigerator overnight before using.

Nutritional value per serving	
Calories	230
Fat, total	9 g
Fat, saturated	1 g
Cholesterol	0 mg
Sodium	301 mg
Carbohydrate	33 g
Fiber	7 g
Protein	7 g
Calcium	19 mg
Iron	3 mg

Thin Pizza Crust

<table>
<tr><td>

Makes 1 to 2 servings

</td></tr>
</table>

Here's a thin and crunchy crust for those who like more topping than crust.

■■■■■■■■■■■■■■■■

Tips

This recipe can easily be doubled to make 2 pizza crusts. Partially bake both, then top one to bake immediately and freeze the other for a future meal.

Warming leftover pizza for 5 to 10 minutes in the oven results in a very crisp crust.

If you don't have an 8-inch (20 cm) round pizza pan, use a 12-inch (30 cm) pan. After transferring dough to the pan, top it with waxed paper and roll out to an 8½-inch (21 cm) circle. Form a ¼-inch (0.5 cm) ridge all the way around the edge.

Nutritional value per serving	
Calories	181
Fat, total	8 g
Fat, saturated	1 g
Cholesterol	0 mg
Sodium	294 mg
Carbohydrate	26 g
Fiber	2 g
Protein	2 g
Calcium	17 mg
Iron	1 mg

■ **8-inch (20 cm) round pizza pan, lightly greased**

¼ cup	brown rice flour	60 mL
2 tbsp	potato starch	30 mL
1 tsp	granulated sugar	5 mL
½ tsp	xanthan gum	2 mL
1 tsp	bread machine or instant yeast	5 mL
¼ tsp	salt	1 mL
1 tsp	dried oregano	5 mL
¼ cup	water	60 mL
1 tbsp	vegetable oil	15 mL
1 tsp	cider vinegar	5 mL

1. In a bowl or plastic bag, combine brown rice flour, potato starch, sugar, xanthan gum, yeast, salt and oregano. Mix well and set aside.

2. In a separate bowl, using a heavy-duty electric mixer with paddle attachment, combine water, oil and vinegar until well blended. With the mixer on its lowest speed, slowly add the dry ingredients until combined. Stop the machine and scrape the bottom and sides of the bowl with a rubber spatula. With the mixer on medium speed, beat for 1 minute or until smooth.

3. Gently transfer dough to prepared pan. Using a moist rubber spatula, carefully spread to the edges.

4. Place in a cold oven and set oven temperature to 400°F (200°C). Bake for 12 to 17 minutes or until bottom is golden and crust is partially baked.

5. Use right away to make pizza with your favorite toppings, or wrap airtight and store in the freezer for up to 1 month. Thaw in the refrigerator overnight before using.

Variation

Substitute your favorite herb for the oregano — try basil, marjoram or thyme.

Classic Pizza Crust

**Makes 1 to
2 servings**

Crave pizza tonight?
Here's a quick supper
for one or two!

■■■■■■■■■■■■■■

Tips

If you bake 2 crusts at
one time, switch the oven
positions of the pans after
7 minutes.

If you only have a 9-inch
(23 cm) pizza pan, there is
enough batter to use it.

If you don't have an 8-inch
(20 cm) round pizza pan,
use a 12-inch (30 cm) pan.
After transferring dough to
the pan, top it with waxed
paper and roll out to an
8½-inch (21 cm) circle.
Form a ¼-inch (0.5 cm)
ridge all the way around
the edge.

Nutritional value per serving

Calories	219
Fat, total	8 g
Fat, saturated	1 g
Cholesterol	0 mg
Sodium	584 mg
Carbohydrate	34 g
Fiber	4 g
Protein	6 g
Calcium	33 mg
Iron	2 mg

■ **8-inch (20 cm) round pizza pan, lightly greased**

⅓ cup	whole bean flour	75 mL
⅓ cup	sorghum flour	75 mL
2 tbsp	tapioca starch	30 mL
1 tsp	granulated sugar	5 mL
½ tsp	xanthan gum	2 mL
1½ tsp	bread machine or instant yeast	7 mL
½ tsp	salt	2 mL
1 tsp	dried thyme	5 mL
½ cup	water	125 mL
1 tbsp	vegetable oil	15 mL
1 tsp	cider vinegar	5 mL

1. In a bowl or plastic bag, combine whole bean flour, sorghum flour, tapioca starch, sugar, xanthan gum, yeast, salt and thyme. Mix well and set aside.

2. In a separate bowl, using a heavy-duty electric mixer with paddle attachment, combine water, oil and vinegar until well blended. With the mixer on its lowest speed, slowly add the dry ingredients until combined. Stop the machine and scrape the bottom and sides of the bowl with a rubber spatula. With the mixer on medium speed, beat for 1 minute or until smooth.

3. Gently transfer dough to prepared pan. Using a moist rubber spatula, carefully spread to the edges.

4. Place in a cold oven and set oven temperature to 400°F (200°C). Bake for 12 to 17 minutes or until bottom is golden and crust is partially baked.

5. Use right away to make pizza with your favorite toppings, or wrap airtight and store in the freezer for up to 1 month. Thaw in the refrigerator overnight before using.

Variations

For a tender crust, substitute GF beer for the water.

Use 1 tbsp (15 mL) chopped fresh thyme in place of dried.

Herbed Pizza Crust

Makes 1 to 2 servings

Try our twist on traditional pizza crust.

■■■■■■■■■■■■■■■

Tip

If you don't have an 8-inch (20 cm) round pizza pan, use a 12-inch (30 cm) pan. After transferring dough to the pan, top it with waxed paper and roll out to an 8½-inch (21 cm) circle. Form a ¼-inch (0.5 cm) ridge all the way around the edge.

■ **Preheat oven to 425°F (220°C), with rack set in the bottom third**
■ **8-inch (20 cm) round pizza pan, greased and generously sprinkled with cornmeal**

¼ cup	amaranth flour	60 mL
¼ cup	quinoa flour	60 mL
2 tbsp	cornmeal	30 mL
1 tsp	xanthan gum	5 mL
1 tbsp	bread machine or instant yeast	15 mL
½ tsp	salt	2 mL
¼ cup	snipped fresh basil	60 mL
⅓ cup	water	75 mL
1 tbsp	extra virgin olive oil	15 mL
1 tsp	cider vinegar	5 mL

1. In a bowl or plastic bag, combine amaranth flour, quinoa flour, cornmeal, xanthan gum, yeast, salt and basil. Mix well and set aside.

2. In a separate bowl, using a heavy-duty electric mixer with paddle attachment, combine water, oil and vinegar until well blended. With the mixer on lowest speed, slowly add the dry ingredients until combined. Stop the machine and scrape the bottom and sides of the bowl with a rubber spatula. With the mixer on medium speed, beat for 1 minute or until smooth.

3. Gently transfer dough to prepared pan. With a moist rubber spatula, carefully spread to the edges.

4. Bake in preheated oven for 10 minutes or until bottom is golden and crust is partially baked.

5. Use right away to make pizza with your favorite toppings, or wrap airtight and store in the freezer for up to 1 month. Thaw in the refrigerator overnight before using.

Variations

Substitute an equal amount of chopped fresh rosemary for the basil.

Add 2 tbsp (30 mL) freshly grated Parmesan cheese with the dry ingredients.

Nutritional value per serving	
Calories	234
Fat, total	9 g
Fat, saturated	1 g
Cholesterol	0 mg
Sodium	591 mg
Carbohydrate	31 g
Fiber	7 g
Protein	7 g
Calcium	42 mg
Iron	6 mg

Herbed Pizza with Greek Topping

This vegetarian pizza topping, with an easy-to-prepare crust, is delicious served hot or at room temperature for a snack, lunch or brunch.

■ ■ ■ ■ ■ ■ ■ ■ ■ ■ ■ ■ ■ ■ ■

Tips

To make the pizza kid-friendly, top with their favorite fixings. Keep one wrapped airtight in the freezer for up to 1 month, for when they are invited to a pizza party. Reheat in a 400°F (200°C) oven for 12 to 15 minutes or until cheese is bubbly and crust is crisp.

For information on roasting garlic, see the Techniques Glossary, page 308.

For fast, easy cutting, use a pizza wheel.

Cut into bite-size appetizers or wedges for your next party.

Nutritional value per serving	
Calories	475
Fat, total	28 g
Fat, saturated	12 g
Cholesterol	63 mg
Sodium	1329 mg
Carbohydrate	37 g
Fiber	8 g
Protein	20 g
Calcium	454 mg
Iron	7 mg

■ **Preheat oven to 425°F (220°C)**

1	partially baked Herbed Pizza Crust (page 61), at room temperature	1
1	plum (Roma) tomato, thinly sliced	1
2	cloves garlic, roasted and chopped	2
1/4 cup	sliced black olives	60 mL
2 tbsp	snipped fresh basil	30 mL
1/4 tsp	freshly ground black pepper	1 mL
1/2 cup	shredded Monterey Jack cheese	125 mL
1/2 cup	crumbled feta cheese	125 mL

1. Arrange tomato slices over crust; sprinkle with garlic, olives, basil and pepper. Sprinkle with Monterey Jack and feta.

2. Bake in preheated oven for 20 to 25 minutes or until cheese is bubbly and crust is golden. Transfer to a cutting board and cut into wedges. Serve immediately. Transfer any extra wedges to a wire rack to prevent the crust from getting soggy.

Variations

Substitute mozzarella, fontina or provolone cheese for the Monterey Jack.

Substitute an equal amount of chopped fresh rosemary for the basil, both in the crust and in the topping.

Florentine Pizza

This vegetarian pizza
has generous amounts
of spinach, feta cheese
and kalamata olives.

■■■■■■■■■■■■■■

Tips

Drain the spinach well in
a colander before drying
completely with paper
towels.

Reheat leftover pizza under
the broiler to enjoy crisp
pizza.

■ **Preheat oven to 400°F (200°C)**

2 cups	fresh baby spinach, washed and trimmed	500 mL
1	partially baked Pizza Crust (page 58)	1
2	cloves garlic, minced	2
1/2 cup	freshly grated Parmesan cheese	125 mL
1 tbsp	extra virgin olive oil	15 mL
2 tsp	dried oregano	10 mL
1 cup	crumbled feta cheese	250 mL
1/2 cup	kalamata olives, sliced	125 mL

1. In a microwave-safe bowl, microwave spinach, uncovered, on High for 2 to 3 minutes or until wilted, stirring halfway through. Drain, place between layers of paper towels and pat dry. Spread over crust in a single layer to within 1/4 inch (0.5 cm) of the edges.

2. In a small bowl, combine garlic, Parmesan cheese, oil and oregano. Spread over spinach; sprinkle with feta cheese and olives.

3. Bake in preheated oven for 20 to 25 minutes or until spinach is crisp and crust is golden. Serve hot.

Variations

For a stronger, more prominent garlic flavor, add an extra 1 to 2 cloves minced garlic.

Add 1/2 cup (125 mL) snipped sun-dried tomatoes.

Substitute Swiss chard or kale for the spinach and microwave until wilted.

Nutritional value per serving	
Calories	665
Fat, total	43 g
Fat, saturated	18 g
Cholesterol	86 mg
Sodium	1942 mg
Carbohydrate	43 g
Fiber	11 g
Protein	30 g
Calcium	846 mg
Iron	7 mg

Sausage and Leek Pizza

This recipe is sure
to fill up even the
hungriest teen.

■■■■■■■■■■■■■■

Tip

For information on cleaning
leeks, see the Techniques
Glossary, page 309.

■ **Preheat oven to 400°F (200°C)**

5 oz	GF pork sausage, casings removed and meat crumbled	150 g
1	carrot, finely chopped	1
1	leek, white and light green part only, cut into 1/2-inch (1 cm) slices	1
1/3 cup	sliced mushrooms	75 mL
1 tbsp	crumbled dried rosemary	15 mL
1 tbsp	dry white wine	15 mL
1	partially baked Pizza Crust (page 58)	1
1/2 cup	shredded mozzarella cheese	125 mL

1. In a large skillet, over medium heat, brown sausage meat until no pink remains. Using a slotted spoon, remove to a plate and set aside. Drain off all but 1 tbsp (15 mL) fat from the skillet.

2. In the fat remaining in the skillet, over medium heat, cook carrot, leek, mushrooms and rosemary, stirring occasionally, for 15 minutes or until carrots are tender. Drain off fat. Return browned sausage to skillet with wine; mix gently and set aside to cool slightly.

3. Spread filling over crust to within 1/4 inch (0.5 cm) of the edges. Sprinkle with mozzarella.

4. Bake in preheated oven for 20 to 25 minutes or until cheese is bubbly and crust is golden. Serve hot.

Variations

Add 1/2 cup (125 mL) snipped sun-dried tomatoes with the mozzarella.

Try a mixture of Cheddar and mozzarella cheeses.

Substitute unsweetened apple juice for the wine.

Use lean ground pork in place of GF sausage.

Nutritional value per serving	
Calories	564
Fat, total	26 g
Fat, saturated	9 g
Cholesterol	75 mg
Sodium	579 mg
Carbohydrate	48 g
Fiber	11 g
Protein	35 g
Calcium	299 mg
Iron	6 mg

Hawaiian Pizza

Hawaiian topping is Donna's grandson's favorite.

■■■■■■■■■■■■■■■

Tips

Keep one of these pizzas wrapped airtight in the freezer for up to 1 month, for when you are invited to a pizza party. Reheat in a 400°F (200°C) oven for 12 to 15 minutes or until cheese is bubbly and crust is crisp.

For fast, easy cutting, use a pizza wheel.

Cut into bite-size appetizers or wedges for your next party.

■ **Preheat oven to 400°F (200°C)**

1	partially baked Thin Pizza Crust (page 59), at room temperature	1
½ cup	GF pizza sauce	125 mL
¾ cup	cubed GF cooked ham	175 mL
½ cup	drained pineapple tidbits	125 mL
⅓ cup	thinly sliced green bell pepper	75 mL
1 cup	shredded mozzarella cheese	250 mL

1. Spread sauce over crust to within ¼ inch (0.5 cm) of the edges. Sprinkle with ham, pineapple, green pepper and mozzarella.

2. Bake in preheated oven for 20 to 25 minutes or until cheese is bubbly and crust is golden. Transfer to a cutting board and cut into wedges. Serve immediately. Transfer any extra wedges to a wire rack to prevent the crust from getting soggy.

Variations

Substitute Asiago, fontina or provolone cheese for the mozzarella.

Substitute an equal amount of GF barbecue sauce for the GF pizza sauce and replace the ham with 1 cup (250 mL) of cooked cubed chicken.

Nutritional value per serving	
Calories	461
Fat, total	20 g
Fat, saturated	8 g
Cholesterol	54 mg
Sodium	1698 mg
Carbohydrate	41 g
Fiber	4 g
Protein	29 g
Calcium	451 mg
Iron	2 mg

Top-Your-Own Pizza

Have you ever wondered
if you have enough
leftover topping
ingredients to make
a pizza for supper?
This recipe can act as
a general guideline
for you.

▪▪▪▪▪▪▪▪▪▪▪▪▪▪▪

Tip

For the toppings, choose a
mixture of sliced mushrooms
(any variety), sliced bell
peppers, finely chopped
onions, diced tomatoes,
sliced GF pepperoni, cooked
ground beef, cooked diced
chicken, crisp GF bacon
and/or GF prosciutto.

■ **Preheat oven to 400°F (200°C)**

1	partially baked pizza crust (see recipes, pages 58–61), at room temperature	1
$\frac{1}{2}$ cup	GF pasta sauce	125 mL
1$\frac{1}{2}$ cups	toppings (see tip, at left)	375 mL
$\frac{1}{2}$ tsp	dried oregano	2 mL
1 cup	shredded mozzarella cheese	250 mL
2 tbsp	freshly grated Parmesan cheese	30 mL

1. Spread sauce over crust to within $\frac{1}{4}$ inch (0.5 cm) of the edges. Sprinkle with toppings and oregano. Sprinkle with mozzarella and Parmesan.

2. Bake in preheated oven for 20 to 25 minutes or until cheese is bubbly and crust is golden. Transfer to a cutting board and cut into wedges. Serve immediately. Transfer any extra wedges to a wire rack to prevent the crust from getting soggy.

Variation

Substitute GF pizza sauce for the pasta sauce and dried basil for the oregano.

Nutritional value per serving	
Calories	525
Fat, total	26 g
Fat, saturated	10 g
Cholesterol	35 mg
Sodium	1370 mg
Carbohydrate	44 g
Fiber	10 g
Protein	31 g
Calcium	528 mg
Iron	4 mg

Ciabatta

Makes 4 wedges
Serving size: 1 wedge

From the Italian for "old slipper," ciabatta are flat, chewy loaves that are fun to make. Poke them full of dimples before letting them rise. The flour-coated crust provides an interesting open texture. Our round version is easily cut into wedges.

■ ■ ■ ■ ■ ■ ■ ■ ■ ■ ■ ■ ■ ■ ■

Tips

When dusting with rice flour, use a flour sifter for a light, even sprinkle.

This bread freezes well. Cut into wedges and freeze individually for sandwiches.

Be sure the internal temperature reaches 200°F (100°C), as the ciabatta will look done before it really is.

Nutritional value per serving	
Calories	141
Fat, total	5 g
Fat, saturated	1 g
Cholesterol	47 mg
Sodium	309 mg
Carbohydrate	21 g
Fiber	3 g
Protein	4 g
Calcium	14 mg
Iron	1 mg

■ **6-inch (15 cm) round baking pan, lightly greased and bottom lined with parchment paper**

1/4 cup	whole bean flour	60 mL
1/4 cup	brown rice flour	60 mL
3 tbsp	tapioca starch	45 mL
1 tbsp	granulated sugar	15 mL
2 tsp	xanthan gum	10 mL
1 tbsp	bread machine or instant yeast	15 mL
1/2 tsp	salt	2 mL
1	large egg	1
1/3 cup	water	75 mL
1 tbsp	extra virgin olive oil	15 mL
1 tsp	cider vinegar	5 mL
2 to 3 tsp	sweet rice flour	10 to 15 mL

1. In a bowl or plastic bag, combine whole bean flour, brown rice flour, tapioca starch, sugar, xanthan gum, yeast and salt. Mix well and set aside.

2. In a separate bowl, using a heavy-duty electric mixer with paddle attachment, combine egg, water, oil and vinegar until well blended. With the mixer on its lowest speed, slowly add the dry ingredients until combined. Stop the machine and scrape the bottom and sides of the bowl with a rubber spatula. With the mixer on medium speed, beat for 1 minute or until smooth.

3. Gently transfer dough to prepared pan and spread evenly to the edges, leaving the top rough and uneven. Generously dust top with sweet rice flour. With well-floured fingers, make deep indents all over the dough, pressing all the way down to the pan. Let rise, uncovered, in a warm, draft-free place for 40 to 50 minutes or until almost doubled in volume. Meanwhile, preheat oven to 425°F (220°C).

4. Bake for 15 minutes. Tent with foil and bake for 5 minutes or until internal temperature of loaf registers 200°F (100°C) on an instant-read thermometer. Remove from the pan immediately and let cool on a rack. Cut into 4 wedges and serve warm.

Grilled Ham and Cheese Ciabatta Sandwich

Here's a quick lunch for two adults (or, as we learned, one teenage boy with a large appetite). Try our grilled version.

■■■■■■■■■■■■■■■

Tip

You can also use an indoor contact grill or a panini grill; in that case, there's no need to turn the sandwich, as both sides cook at once.

■ **Preheat barbecue grill to high or preheat broiler**

1	Ciabatta (page 67), left whole	1
1 tbsp	Dijon mustard	15 mL
4 oz	GF smoked ham, thinly sliced	125 g
4 oz	Swiss cheese, thinly sliced	125 g
1	large tomato, sliced	1
	Extra virgin olive oil	

1. Slice ciabatta in half horizontally. Spread Dijon mustard on the bottom half. Layer with ham, cheese and tomatoes. Cover with top half of ciabatta and brush both sides of the sandwich with a thin layer of oil.

2. Place on preheated barbecue or under preheated broiler. Cook, turning once, until ciabatta is browned and crisp and cheese is melted. Cut into 4 wedges and serve hot.

Variations

Feel free to pile on lots of thinly sliced GF cold cuts.

If you prefer a cold sandwich to a grilled one, you can add some mixed salad greens.

Nutritional value per serving	
Calories	318
Fat, total	18 g
Fat, saturated	8 g
Cholesterol	85 mg
Sodium	823 mg
Carbohydrate	24 g
Fiber	3 g
Protein	18 g
Calcium	275 mg
Iron	1 mg

Sun-Dried Tomato Ciabatta

Sun-dried tomatoes, Parmesan cheese and fresh rosemary take this Italian flatbread a step above the ordinary. It's fabulous served with soup or salad.

■■■■■■■■■■■■■■■

Tip

We like this ciabatta best served hot out of the oven.

Variation

Substitute 2 to 3 tbsp (30 to 45 mL) dried basil or oregano for the fresh rosemary and sprinkle the risen dough with 2 tbsp (30 mL) freshly grated Parmesan cheese.

Nutritional value per serving

Calories	249
Fat, total	13 g
Fat, saturated	4 g
Cholesterol	57 mg
Sodium	466 mg
Carbohydrate	25 g
Fiber	3 g
Protein	10 g
Calcium	218 mg
Iron	2 mg

■ **6-inch (15 cm) round baking pan, lightly greased and bottom lined with parchment paper**

1/4 cup	brown rice flour	60 mL
1/4 cup	whole bean flour	60 mL
3 tbsp	tapioca starch	45 mL
1 tbsp	granulated sugar	15 mL
1 1/2 tsp	xanthan gum	7 mL
1 tbsp	bread machine or instant yeast	15 mL
1/8 tsp	salt	0.5 mL
2	cloves garlic, minced	2
1/2 cup	snipped sun-dried tomatoes	125 mL
1/2 cup	freshly grated Parmesan cheese	125 mL
1/4 cup	snipped fresh rosemary	60 mL
1	large egg	1
1/3 cup	water	75 mL
2 tbsp	extra virgin olive oil	30 mL
1 tsp	cider vinegar	5 mL
2 to 3 tsp	sweet rice flour	10 to 15 mL

1. In a bowl or plastic bag, combine brown rice flour, whole bean flour, tapioca starch, sugar, xanthan gum, yeast, salt, garlic, tomatoes, Parmesan and rosemary. Mix well and set aside.

2. In a separate bowl, using a heavy-duty electric mixer with paddle attachment, combine egg, water, oil and vinegar until well blended. With the mixer on its lowest speed, slowly add the dry ingredients until combined. Stop the machine and scrape the bottom and sides of the bowl with a rubber spatula. With the mixer on medium speed, beat for 1 minute or until smooth.

3. Gently transfer dough to prepared pan and spread evenly to the edges, leaving the top rough and uneven. Generously dust top with sweet rice flour. With well-floured fingers, make deep indents all over the dough, pressing all the way down to the pan. Let rise, uncovered, in a warm, draft-free place for 40 to 50 minutes or until almost doubled in volume. Meanwhile, preheat oven to 400°F (200°C).

4. Bake for 15 minutes. Tent with foil and bake for 5 to 10 minutes or until internal temperature of loaf registers 200°F (100°C) on an instant-read thermometer. Remove from the pan immediately and let cool on a rack. Cut into 4 wedges and serve warm.

Olive Ciabatta

Black and green olives and a good-quality olive oil combine to make this strong-flavored, irresistible Italian bread. We've adapted the shape to accommodate the batter-like gluten-free dough.

■■■■■■■■■■■■■■ ■■

■ **6-inch (15 cm) round baking pan, lightly greased and bottom lined with parchment paper**

1/4 cup	hazelnut flour	60 mL
3 tbsp	whole bean flour	45 mL
2 tbsp	quinoa flour	30 mL
1 tbsp	tapioca starch	15 mL
1 tbsp	granulated sugar	15 mL
1 tsp	xanthan gum	5 mL
1 tbsp	bread machine or instant yeast	15 mL
1/2 tsp	salt	2 mL
1 tbsp	dried oregano	15 mL
1 tbsp	dried rosemary	15 mL
1	large egg	1
1/3 cup	water	75 mL
1 tbsp	extra virgin olive oil	15 mL
1 tsp	cider vinegar	5 mL
1/3 cup	sliced pitted kalamata olives	75 mL
1/4 cup	sliced pitted green olives	60 mL
1/4 cup	chopped hazelnuts	60 mL
2 to 3 tsp	sweet rice flour	10 to 15 mL

1. In a bowl or plastic bag, combine hazelnut flour, whole bean flour, quinoa flour, tapioca starch, sugar, xanthan gum, yeast, salt, oregano and rosemary. Mix well and set aside.

2. In a separate bowl, using a heavy-duty electric mixer with paddle attachment, combine egg, water, oil and vinegar until well blended. With the mixer on its lowest speed, slowly add the dry ingredients until combined. Stop the machine and scrape the bottom and sides of the bowl with a rubber spatula. With the mixer on medium speed, beat for 1 minute or until smooth. Stir in kalamata olives, green olives and hazelnuts.

Nutritional value per serving	
Calories	215
Fat, total	16 g
Fat, saturated	2 g
Cholesterol	47 mg
Sodium	479 mg
Carbohydrate	15 g
Fiber	4 g
Protein	6 g
Calcium	74 mg
Iron	3 mg

When dusting with sweet rice flour, use a flour sifter for a light, even sprinkle.

Be sure olives are well drained and pat dry with paper towels.

3. Gently transfer dough to prepared pan and spread evenly to the edges, leaving the top rough and uneven. Generously dust top with sweet rice flour. With well-floured fingers, make deep indents all over the dough, pressing all the way down to the pan. Let rise, uncovered, in a warm, draft-free place for 40 to 50 minutes or until almost doubled in volume. Meanwhile, preheat oven to 425°F (220°C).

4. Bake for 15 minutes. Tent with foil and bake for 3 to 10 minutes or until internal temperature of loaf registers 200°F (100°C) on an instant-read thermometer. Remove from the pan immediately and let cool on a rack. Cut into 4 wedges and serve warm.

Variations

To make 2 individual ciabatta, use English muffin rings on a baking sheet lined with parchment paper and fill two-thirds full. Bake for 15 minutes or until internal temperature of loaves registers 200°F (100°C) on an instant-read thermometer.

To turn this into a Mediterranean-style ciabatta, add ¼ cup (60 mL) finely chopped red onion with the kalamata olives and substitute 1 tbsp (15 mL) snipped fresh cilantro or mint for the green olives.

Substitute pecan flour for the hazelnut flour and pecans for the hazelnuts.

Blue Cheese Walnut Ciabatta

We've had many requests for ciabatta with this flavor combination. Right from the oven, this quick and easy flatbread with a tangy crunch complements soup, salad or stew.

■■■■■■■■■■■■■■■■

Tips

This dough is thicker than most gluten-free doughs. Resist the temptation to add extra liquid.

When dusting with sweet rice flour, use a flour sifter for a light, even sprinkle.

Variations

Dust with either brown rice flour or whole bean flour instead of the sweet rice flour.

Substitute GF Stilton for the blue cheese.

Nutritional value per serving

Calories	236
Fat, total	14 g
Fat, saturated	3 g
Cholesterol	55 mg
Sodium	320 mg
Carbohydrate	20 g
Fiber	3 g
Protein	9 g
Calcium	93 mg
Iron	3 mg

■ **6-inch (15 cm) round baking pan, lightly greased and bottom lined with parchment paper**

1/4 cup	whole bean flour	60 mL
3 tbsp	amaranth flour	45 mL
3 tbsp	tapioca starch	45 mL
1 tbsp	granulated sugar	15 mL
1 tsp	xanthan gum	5 mL
1 tbsp	bread machine or instant yeast	15 mL
1 tbsp	snipped fresh marjoram	15 mL
1/4 tsp	salt	1 mL
1/4 tsp	freshly ground black pepper	1 mL
1/3 cup	chopped walnuts	75 mL
1	large egg	1
1/3 cup	water	75 mL
1 tbsp	vegetable oil	15 mL
1 tsp	cider vinegar	5 mL
1/3 cup	cubed GF blue cheese (1/2-inch/1 cm cubes)	75 mL
2 to 3 tsp	sweet rice flour	10 to 15 mL

1. In a bowl or plastic bag, combine whole bean flour, amaranth flour, tapioca starch, sugar, xanthan gum, yeast, marjoram, salt, pepper and walnuts. Mix well and set aside.

2. In a separate bowl, using a heavy-duty electric mixer with paddle attachment, combine egg, water, oil and vinegar until well blended. With the mixer on its lowest speed, slowly add the dry ingredients until combined. Stop the machine and scrape the bottom and sides of the bowl with a rubber spatula. With the mixer on medium speed, beat for 1 minute or until smooth. Stir in blue cheese.

3. Gently transfer dough to prepared pan and spread evenly to the edges, leaving the top rough and uneven. Generously dust top with sweet rice flour. With well-floured fingers, make deep indents all over the dough, pressing all the way down to the pan. Let rise, uncovered, in a warm, draft-free place for 40 to 50 minutes or until almost doubled in volume. Meanwhile, preheat oven to 425°F (220°C).

4. Bake for 15 minutes. Tent with foil and bake for 3 to 10 minutes or until internal temperature of loaf registers 200°F (100°C) on an instant-read thermometer. Remove from the pan immediately and let cool on a rack. Cut into 4 wedges and serve warm.

Focaccia

Plan to serve this chewy flatbread hot from the oven along with soup or salad lunches, or cut into smaller pieces and serve as hors d'oeuvres.

■■■■■■■■■■■■■■■■

Tips

Can't decide which topping to make? Make a different one each time.

Reheat leftovers under the broiler to enjoy crisp focaccia.

Focaccia can be reheated in just a few minutes in a toaster oven set to 375°F (190°C).

Nutritional value per serving	
Calories	126
Fat, total	3 g
Fat, saturated	0 g
Cholesterol	0 mg
Sodium	293 mg
Carbohydrate	21 g
Fiber	2 g
Protein	4 g
Calcium	22 mg
Iron	3 mg

■ **8-inch (20 cm) square baking pan, lightly greased and lined with parchment paper**

1/3 cup	amaranth flour	75 mL
1/4 cup	pea flour	60 mL
3 tbsp	potato starch	45 mL
2 tbsp	tapioca starch	30 mL
1 tsp	granulated sugar	5 mL
1 tsp	xanthan gum	5 mL
1 tbsp	bread machine or instant yeast	15 mL
1/2 tsp	salt	2 mL
3/4 cup	water	175 mL
2 tsp	extra virgin olive oil	10 mL
1 tsp	cider vinegar	5 mL
	Topping mixture (pages 74–75)	

1. In a bowl or plastic bag, combine amaranth flour, pea flour, potato starch, tapioca starch, sugar, xanthan gum, yeast and salt. Mix well and set aside.

2. In a separate bowl, using a heavy-duty electric mixer with paddle attachment, combine water, oil and vinegar until well blended. With the mixer on its lowest speed, slowly add the dry ingredients until combined. Stop the machine and scrape the bottom and sides of the bowl with a rubber spatula. With the mixer on medium speed, beat for 1 minute or until smooth.

3. Gently transfer dough to prepared pan and spread evenly to the edges, leaving the top rough and uneven. Do not smooth. Let rise, uncovered, in a warm, draft-free place for 30 minutes or until almost doubled in volume. Meanwhile, preheat oven to 400°F (200°C).

4. Bake for 10 minutes or until bottom is golden. Cover with preferred topping mixture. Bake for 20 to 25 minutes or until top is golden. Remove from the pan immediately. Cut into 4 pieces and serve hot.

Variation

Substitute any type of bean flour for the pea flour.

continued...

Focaccia (continued)

Walnuts with freshly grated Parmesan cheese is a combination of flavors sure to please.

■■■■■■■■■■■■■■

Tip

Store walnuts in the refrigerator and taste for freshness before using.

Parmesan Walnut Focaccia Topping

2	cloves garlic, minced	2
2 tbsp	extra virgin olive oil	30 mL
¾ cup	finely chopped walnuts	175 mL
3 tbsp	freshly grated Parmesan cheese	45 mL

1. In a small bowl, combine garlic and oil; let stand while focaccia rises and partially bakes.

2. Drizzle over the partially baked focaccia. Sprinkle with walnuts and Parmesan.

Variation

Substitute pine nuts for the walnuts and Romano or Asiago cheese for the Parmesan.

Top focaccia with sweet onions, slowly caramelized in a small amount of olive oil until golden.

■■■■■■■■■■■■■■

Tip

No need for extra oil: if onions start to stick, add 1 tbsp (15 mL) white wine or water.

Mediterranean Focaccia Topping

2 tbsp	extra virgin olive oil	30 mL
4 cups	sliced Vidalia or other sweet onions	1 L
2 tbsp	snipped fresh thyme	30 mL
1 tbsp	balsamic vinegar	15 mL
12	kalamata olives, pitted and sliced	12
½ cup	crumbled feta cheese	125 mL

1. In a skillet, heat oil over medium-low heat. Sauté onions for 20 minutes or until tender and light golden brown. Remove from heat and stir in thyme and vinegar. Let cool slightly.

2. Spoon over the partially baked focaccia. Sprinkle with olives and feta.

Variation

Add ½ cup (125 mL) snipped sun-dried tomatoes with the olives.

A trio of cheeses sprinkled over focaccia dough creates the perfect bread to accompany gazpacho on a hot summer day.

■■■■■■■■■■■■■■■■

Tip
Use the amount of cheese stated in the recipe: too much results in a greasy focaccia.

Triple-Cheese Focaccia Topping

2	cloves garlic, minced	2
2 tbsp	extra virgin olive oil	30 mL
1 tbsp	dried basil	15 mL
⅔ cup	shredded Asiago cheese	150 mL
⅔ cup	shredded mozzarella cheese	150 mL
⅓ cup	freshly grated Parmesan cheese	75 mL
1 cup	GF salsa	250 mL

1. In a small bowl, combine garlic, oil and basil; let stand while focaccia rises and partially bakes.

2. In another small bowl, combine Asiago, mozzarella and Parmesan.

3. Drizzle garlic-oil mixture over the partially cooked focaccia. Top with salsa and cheese mixture.

Variation
Substitute your favorite lower-fat varieties for the cheeses.

Parmesan Walnut Focaccia Topping Nutritional value per serving	
Calories	234
Fat, total	23 g
Fat, saturated	3 g
Cholesterol	4 mg
Sodium	88 mg
Carbohydrate	4 g
Fiber	2 g
Protein	6 g
Calcium	91 mg
Iron	1 mg

Mediterranean Focaccia Topping Nutritional value per serving	
Calories	191
Fat, total	14 g
Fat, saturated	4 g
Cholesterol	17 mg
Sodium	397 mg
Carbohydrate	13 g
Fiber	2 g
Protein	4 g
Calcium	125 mg
Iron	1 mg

Triple Cheese Focaccia Topping Nutritional value per serving	
Calories	241
Fat, total	18 g
Fat, saturated	8 g
Cholesterol	33 mg
Sodium	484 mg
Carbohydrate	6 g
Fiber	2 g
Protein	15 g
Calcium	470 mg
Iron	1 mg

Honey Dijon Toastie

Makes 4 wedges
Serving size: 1 wedge

Honey mustard added to the dough makes this open-textured bread an ideal sandwich bread.

■■■■■■■■■■■■■■■

Tips

Measure any oil in the recipe before any sticky ingredients, such as molasses or honey. This greases the measuring spoon, allowing the sticky ingredient to slide right out.

You can use a plain Dijon mustard in place of the honey Dijon.

We like this toastie best served hot out of the oven.

If you find this too sweet, decrease the honey to 1 tbsp (15 mL).

Nutritional value per serving	
Calories	301
Fat, total	13 g
Fat, saturated	2 g
Cholesterol	47 mg
Sodium	218 mg
Carbohydrate	41 g
Fiber	5 g
Protein	7 g
Calcium	43 mg
Iron	3 mg

■ **6-inch (15 cm) round casserole dish, lightly greased and lined with parchment paper**

¾ cup	whole bean flour	175 mL
¼ cup	quinoa flour	60 mL
¼ cup	tapioca starch	60 mL
2 tsp	xanthan gum	10 mL
2 tbsp	bread machine or instant yeast	30 mL
¼ tsp	salt	1 mL
1 tbsp	dried thyme	15 mL
1	clove garlic, minced	1
1	large egg	1
¾ cup	water	175 mL
2 tbsp	extra virgin olive oil	30 mL
¼ cup	liquid honey	60 mL
2 tbsp	honey Dijon mustard	30 mL
1 tsp	cider vinegar	5 mL

1. In a bowl or plastic bag, combine whole bean flour, quinoa flour, tapioca starch, xanthan gum, yeast, salt and thyme. Mix well and set aside.

2. In a separate bowl, using a heavy-duty electric mixer with paddle attachment, combine garlic, egg, water, oil, honey, mustard and vinegar until well blended. With the mixer on its lowest speed, slowly add the dry ingredients until combined. Stop the machine and scrape the bottom and sides of the bowl with a rubber spatula. With the mixer on medium speed, beat for 1 minute or until smooth.

3. Gently transfer dough to prepared dish and spread evenly to the edges. With wet fingers, make deep indents all over the dough, pressing all the way down to the bottom. Let rise, uncovered, in a warm, draft-free place for 60 minutes or until dough has doubled in volume. Meanwhile, preheat oven to 375°F (190°C).

4. Bake for 20 minutes. Check to see if loaf is getting too dark and tent with foil if necessary. Bake for 14 to 17 minutes or until top is deep golden. Remove from the dish immediately. Cut into 4 wedges and serve hot, or transfer to a rack and let cool completely.

Barbecued Tuscan Toastie

Makes 4 wedges
Serving size: 1 wedge

Try this sandwich, and you'll understand the Tuscan attitude to food: "With love, from the heart."

■■■■■■■■■■■■■■

Tips

Choose two to three kinds of cold cuts, such as GF prosciutto, GF smoked turkey, GF salami or mild, hot or extra-hot GF capicollo.

Choose a couple of kinds of cheese, such as Swiss, Cheddar, mozzarella, American or roasted garlic–flavored.

You can also use an indoor contact grill or a panini grill; in that case, there's no need to turn the toastie, as both sides cook at once.

■ **Preheat broiler or preheat barbecue grill to high**

1	Honey Dijon Toastie (page 76), left whole	1
1 tbsp	GF mayonnaise	15 mL
2 tsp	Dijon mustard	10 mL
8 oz	thinly sliced GF cold cuts	250 g
4 oz	sliced cheese	125 g
²⁄₃ cup	mesclun	150 mL
2 tsp	extra virgin olive oil	10 mL

1. Slice toastie in half horizontally. Spread mayonnaise and mustard on the bottom half. Layer with cold cuts, cheese and mesclun. Cover with top half of toastie and press together. Brush both sides of the sandwich with oil.

2. Place under preheated broiler or on preheated barbecue. Cook, turning once, until toastie is browned and crisp and cheese is melted. Cut into 4 wedges and serve hot.

Nutritional value per serving	
Calories	525
Fat, total	24 g
Fat, saturated	6 g
Cholesterol	87 mg
Sodium	1810 mg
Carbohydrate	44 g
Fiber	6 g
Protein	34 g
Calcium	235 mg
Iron	5 mg

Savory Onion Toastie

Instead of using this open-textured bread to make a sandwich, we've put an onion topping on it.

■■■■■■■■■■■■■■■

Tip

You can also use a food processor to mix the dough. First, in a small bowl, combine the water, oil and vinegar. In the food processor, pulse the dry ingredients. With the motor running, through the feed tube, gradually add water mixture in a steady stream. Pulse until dough holds together.

■ **6-inch (15 cm) round casserole dish, lightly greased and sprinkled with cornmeal**

Onion Topping

1 tbsp	butter	15 mL
2	onions, finely chopped	2
1 tbsp	snipped fresh thyme	15 mL
1 tbsp	liquid honey	15 mL

Toastie

1/2 cup	sorghum flour	125 mL
1/2 cup	whole bean flour	125 mL
3 tbsp	tapioca starch	45 mL
1 tsp	granulated sugar	5 mL
1 tsp	xanthan gum	5 mL
1 tbsp	bread machine or instant yeast	15 mL
1/2 tsp	salt	2 mL
3/4 cup	water	175 mL
2 tbsp	vegetable oil	30 mL
1 tsp	cider vinegar	5 mL
1 to 2 tsp	sweet rice flour	5 to 10 mL
1/4 cup	freshly grated Parmesan cheese	60 mL

1. *Topping:* In a skillet, melt butter over medium-low heat. Sauté onions for 20 minutes or until tender and light golden brown. Remove from heat and stir in thyme and honey. Let cool slightly.

2. *Toastie:* In a bowl or plastic bag, combine sorghum flour, whole bean flour, tapioca starch, sugar, xanthan gum, yeast and salt. Mix well and set aside.

3. In a separate bowl, using a heavy-duty electric mixer with paddle attachment, combine water, oil and vinegar until well blended. With the mixer on its lowest speed, slowly add the dry ingredients until combined. Stop the machine and scrape the bottom and sides of the bowl with a rubber spatula. With the mixer on medium speed, beat for 1 minute or until smooth.

Nutritional value per serving	
Calories	268
Fat, total	12 g
Fat, saturated	4 g
Cholesterol	13 mg
Sodium	440 mg
Carbohydrate	34 g
Fiber	4 g
Protein	8 g
Calcium	117 mg
Iron	2 mg

Before measuring honey, coat the measuring spoon with vegetable spray; the honey will flow more easily and rapidly.

Xanthan gum helps prevent baked goods from crumbling, gives them greater volume, improves their texture and extends their shelf life.

4. Drop dough by large spoonfuls onto prepared dish. Using a moistened rubber spatula, spread evenly to the edges. Generously dust top with sweet rice flour. With well-floured fingers, make deep indents all over the dough, pressing all the way down to the bottom. Let rise, uncovered, in a warm, draft-free place for 20 minutes. Meanwhile, preheat oven to 400°F (200°C).

5. Sprinkle dough with Parmesan. Spread topping over cheese.

6. Bake for 20 to 25 minutes or until top is golden. Remove from the dish immediately. Cut into 4 wedges and serve warm.

Variation

For a more tender crust, substitute GF beer for the water.

Swedish Wraps

Use these to make the
ever-popular wrap
instead of a sandwich
for lunch.

■■■■■■■■■■■■■■

Tips

Xanthan gum helps
prevent baked goods from
crumbling, gives them
greater volume, improves
their texture and extends
their shelf life.

Roll these wraps around
your favorite sandwich
fillings.

Dipping the spatula
repeatedly into warm water
makes it easier to spread
this dough thinly and evenly.

■ Preheat oven to 400°F (200°C), with rack set in the top third
■ 15- by 10-inch (40 by 25 cm) jelly roll pan, lightly greased and lined with parchment paper

1/2 cup	sorghum flour	125 mL
1/4 cup	amaranth flour	60 mL
1/4 cup	tapioca starch	60 mL
1 tsp	granulated sugar	5 mL
2 tsp	xanthan gum	10 mL
1 tbsp	bread machine or instant yeast	15 mL
3/4 tsp	salt	3 mL
1 tsp	anise seeds	5 mL
1 tsp	caraway seeds	5 mL
1 tsp	fennel seeds	5 mL
3/4 cup	milk	175 mL
1 tsp	extra virgin olive oil	5 mL
1 tsp	cider vinegar	5 mL

1. In a bowl or plastic bag, combine sorghum flour, amaranth flour, tapioca starch, sugar, xanthan gum, yeast, salt, anise seeds, caraway seeds and fennel seeds. Mix well and set aside.

2. In a separate bowl, using a heavy-duty electric mixer with paddle attachment, combine milk, oil and vinegar until well blended. With the mixer on its lowest speed, slowly add the dry ingredients until combined. Stop the machine and scrape the bottom and sides of the bowl with a rubber spatula. With the mixer on medium speed, beat for 1 minute or until smooth.

3. Transfer dough to prepared pan. Using a moistened rubber spatula, spread evenly to the edges.

4. Bake in preheated oven for 12 to 14 minutes or until edges are brown and top begins to brown. Let cool completely on pan on a rack. Remove from pan and cut into quarters.

Variation

Try adding dried herbs to the soft dough in place of the three varieties of seeds. To make a plainer variety, omit seeds and herbs.

Nutritional value per serving	
Calories	168
Fat, total	3 g
Fat, saturated	1 g
Cholesterol	2 mg
Sodium	463 mg
Carbohydrate	31 g
Fiber	4 g
Protein	6 g
Calcium	88 mg
Iron	4 mg

Scandinavian Sesame Wafers

Makes 30 wafers
Serving size: 1 wafer

Enjoy these rich, sweet, flavorful sesame wafers with a salad, soup or just as a snack!

■■■■■■■■■■■■■■

Tips

Watch these carefully during baking — even as little as 1 minute too long can cause the bottoms to burn.

If only higher-fat soy flour is available, substitute an equal amount, but be even more vigilant about watching for burning.

Store in an airtight container at room temperature for up to 3 weeks.

■ Preheat oven to 325°F (160°C), with oven rack placed in the top position
■ Baking sheets, lined with parchment paper

⅓ cup	low-fat soy flour	75 mL
¼ cup	granulated sugar	60 mL
1 cup	sesame seeds, toasted	250 mL
1½ tsp	anise seeds	7 mL
1½ tsp	caraway seeds	7 mL
1½ tsp	fennel seeds	7 mL
¼ cup	water	60 mL
3 tbsp	vegetable oil	45 mL

1. In a bowl or plastic bag, combine soy flour, sugar, sesame seeds, anise seeds, caraway seeds and fennel seeds. Mix well and set aside.

2. In a separate bowl, combine water and oil until blended. Slowly stir in the dry ingredients until combined.

3. Drop dough by small spoonfuls at least 2 inches (5 cm) apart onto prepared baking sheets. Using a small square of parchment paper, cover each mound, then flatten with a flat-bottomed drinking glass. Remove parchment.

4. Bake, one sheet at a time, in preheated oven for 7 to 8 minutes or until lightly browned. Let cool on baking sheet for 2 to 3 minutes. Transfer to a rack and let cool completely.

Variations

Substitute untoasted poppy seeds, amaranth seeds or millet seeds for the sesame seeds.

For a mild-flavored wafer, substitute 1 tbsp (15 mL) flaxseed or poppy seeds for the anise, caraway and fennel seeds.

For a stronger sesame flavor, substitute sesame oil for the vegetable oil.

Nutritional value per serving	
Calories	55
Fat, total	1 g
Fat, saturated	0 g
Cholesterol	0 mg
Sodium	0 mg
Carbohydrate	2 g
Fiber	0 g
Protein	1 g
Calcium	5 mg
Iron	7 mg

Yeast-Free Lavosh

**Keep this thin, low-fat,
crisp Armenian flatbread
on hand to serve as
a snack with fresh
vegetables, for dipping
in salsa or with soups
or salads.**

Tips

To more easily pat out the dough, place waxed paper dusted with sweet rice flour on top. Gently pat the waxed paper to spread the dough, lifting the paper frequently to check the thickness of the dough. The thinner the dough is spread, the more authentic the cracker will be.

Store in an airtight container at room temperature for up to 1 month. If necessary, crisp the lavosh in a 300°F (150°C) oven for 5 minutes before serving.

Nutritional value per serving	
Calories	60
Fat, total	2 g
Fat, saturated	0 g
Cholesterol	0 mg
Sodium	147 mg
Carbohydrate	9 g
Fiber	1 g
Protein	1 g
Calcium	3 mg
Iron	0 mg

■ **Preheat oven to 375°F (190°C)**

⅓ cup	brown rice flour	75 mL
3 tbsp	tapioca starch	45 mL
1 tsp	granulated sugar	5 mL
1½ tsp	xanthan gum	7 mL
½ tsp	salt	2 mL
⅓ cup	water	75 mL
1 tbsp	vegetable oil	15 mL
1 tsp	cider vinegar	5 mL
1 tbsp	sesame seeds	15 mL
1 to 2 tbsp	sweet rice flour	15 to 30 mL

1. In a bowl or plastic bag, combine brown rice flour, tapioca starch, sugar, xanthan gum and salt. Mix well and set aside.

2. In a separate bowl, using a heavy-duty electric mixer with paddle attachment, combine water, oil and vinegar until well blended. With the mixer on its lowest speed, slowly add the dry ingredients until combined. Stop the machine and scrape the bottom and sides of the bowl with a rubber spatula. With the mixer on medium speed, beat for 1 minute or until smooth.

3. Sprinkle a baking sheet with half the sesame seeds. Dollop dough by large spoonfuls onto prepared sheet. Sprinkle generously with sweet rice flour. With floured fingers, gently pat out the dough to a 10-inch (25 cm) square, sprinkling with sweet rice flour if dough becomes too sticky to handle. Sprinkle with the remaining sesame seeds and press lightly into dough.

4. Bake in preheated oven for 15 minutes or until lightly browned. Turn off oven and let cool in the oven for 1 hour. Remove from oven and break into pieces.

Variations

Add dried herbs to the soft dough, then sprinkle it with freshly grated Parmesan cheese while patting it out.

Substitute millet seeds or amaranth seeds for the sesame seeds.

Sun-Dried Tomato Lavosh

Makes about 16 crackers
Serving size: ⅛th recipe

This delicious crisp is the perfect addition to a basket of fresh rolls.

■ ■ ■ ■ ■ ■ ■ ■ ■ ■ ■ ■ ■ ■

Tips

Purchase dry, not oil-packed, sun-dried tomatoes. Snip them with kitchen shears.

To more easily pat out the dough, place waxed paper dusted with sweet rice flour on top. Gently pat the waxed paper to spread the dough, lifting the paper frequently to check the thickness of the dough. The thinner the dough is spread, the more authentic the cracker will be.

Store in an airtight container at room temperature for up to 1 month. If necessary, crisp the lavosh in a 300°F (150°C) oven for 5 minutes before serving.

Nutritional value per serving	
Calories	72
Fat, total	4 g
Fat, saturated	1 g
Cholesterol	3 mg
Sodium	144 mg
Carbohydrate	8 g
Fiber	1 g
Protein	3 g
Calcium	50 mg
Iron	1 mg

■ **Preheat oven to 375°F (190°C)**
■ **Small baking sheet, lightly greased**

¼ cup	sorghum flour	60 mL
3 tbsp	whole bean flour	45 mL
2 tbsp	tapioca starch	30 mL
1 tsp	granulated sugar	5 mL
½ tsp	xanthan gum	2 mL
1½ tsp	bread machine or instant yeast	7 mL
¼ tsp	salt	1 mL
2 tbsp	snipped fresh basil	30 mL
⅓ cup	snipped sun-dried tomatoes (see tip, at left)	75 mL
⅓ cup	water	75 mL
1 tbsp	extra virgin olive oil	15 mL
1 tsp	cider vinegar	5 mL
¼ cup	freshly grated Parmesan cheese, divided	60 mL

1. In a bowl or plastic bag, combine sorghum flour, whole bean flour, tapioca starch, sugar, xanthan gum, yeast, salt, basil and tomatoes. Mix well and set aside.

2. In a separate bowl, using a heavy-duty electric mixer with paddle attachment, combine water, oil and vinegar until well blended. With the mixer on its lowest speed, slowly add the dry ingredients until combined. Stop the machine and scrape the bottom and sides of the bowl with a rubber spatula. With the mixer on medium speed, beat for 1 minute or until smooth.

3. Sprinkle prepared baking sheet with half the Parmesan. Dollop dough by large spoonfuls onto prepared sheet. Sprinkle generously with sweet rice flour. With floured fingers, gently pat out the dough to a 9-inch (23 cm) square. Sprinkle with the remaining Parmesan and press lightly into dough.

4. Bake in preheated oven for 16 to 18 minutes or until lightly browned. Turn off oven and let cool in the oven for 1 hour. Remove from oven and break into pieces.

Variation

Add 2 to 3 cloves of roasted garlic with the dry ingredients or, for a stronger flavor, use minced fresh garlic.

Moroccan Anise Crackers

Making dough doesn't get much easier or faster than this. The hands-on preparation is less than 15 minutes. Dip these crackers in hummus or a vegetable dip.

■■■■■■■■■■■■■■■

Tips

For a milder flavor, decrease the anise seeds to 2 tsp (10 mL).

Make lots of holes with the fork, as this gives an interesting finish to the top crust.

Nutritional value per serving

Calories	66
Fat, total	2 g
Fat, saturated	0 g
Cholesterol	0 mg
Sodium	156 mg
Carbohydrate	11 g
Fiber	1 g
Protein	2 g
Calcium	11 mg
Iron	1 mg

■ **Baking sheet, sprinkled with cornmeal**

3/4 cup	sorghum flour	175 mL
1/3 cup	teff flour	75 mL
2 tbsp	cornmeal	30 mL
1/4 cup	tapioca starch	60 mL
1/2 tsp	granulated sugar	2 mL
1 1/2 tsp	xanthan gum	7 mL
2 tsp	bread machine or instant yeast	10 mL
1 tsp	salt	5 mL
1 tbsp	anise seeds	15 mL
1 cup	water	250 mL
2 tbsp	vegetable oil	30 mL
1 tsp	cider vinegar	5 mL

1. In a bowl or plastic bag, combine sorghum flour, teff flour, cornmeal, tapioca starch, sugar, xanthan gum, yeast, salt and anise seeds. Mix well and set aside.

2. In a separate bowl, using a heavy-duty electric mixer with paddle attachment, combine water, oil and vinegar until well blended. With the mixer on its lowest speed, slowly add the dry ingredients until combined. Stop the machine and scrape the bottom and sides of the bowl with a rubber spatula. With the mixer on medium speed, beat for 1 minute or until smooth.

3. Immediately pour dough onto prepared baking sheet. Using a moistened rubber spatula, spread evenly into a 10-inch (25 cm) round, leaving the top rough. Let rise, uncovered, in a warm, draft-free place for 10 to 15 minutes. Meanwhile, preheat oven to 400°F (200°C).

4. Using a fork, pierce the dough all over, pressing all the way down to the baking sheet.

5. Bake in preheated oven for 15 minutes or until firm. Remove from pan and place directly on oven rack. Bake for 8 to 10 minutes or until crisp. Remove from the oven immediately and let cool completely on a rack. Break into pieces.

Variation

Substitute an equal quantity of cumin seeds for the anise seeds.

No-Knead Hearth Breads and Rolls

Crusty French Baguette

You'll be amazed by
this one — a crusty loaf
with a typical French
bread texture.

■■■■■■■■■■■■■■■

Tips

Store this bread loosely
covered in a paper bag to
maintain the crisp crust.

Use an electric or serrated
knife to thickly slice this loaf
on the diagonal.

See the Equipment
Glossary, page 299, for
information about baguette
pans.

Nutritional value per serving	
Calories	59
Fat, total	1 g
Fat, saturated	0 g
Cholesterol	0 mg
Sodium	151 mg
Carbohydrate	13 g
Fiber	1 g
Protein	1 g
Calcium	2 mg
Iron	0 mg

■ **Baguette pan or baking sheet, lightly greased, then lined with parchment paper and sprinkled with cornmeal**

1 cup	brown rice flour	250 mL
1/3 cup	potato starch	75 mL
1 tsp	granulated sugar	5 mL
2 tsp	xanthan gum	10 mL
2 tsp	bread machine or instant yeast	10 mL
3/4 tsp	salt	3 mL
1	large egg white	1
3/4 cup	water	175 mL
1 tsp	cider vinegar	5 mL

1. In a bowl or plastic bag, combine brown rice flour, potato starch, sugar, xanthan gum, yeast and salt. Mix well and set aside.

2. In a separate bowl, using a heavy-duty electric mixer with paddle attachment, combine egg white, water and vinegar until well blended. With the mixer on its lowest speed, slowly add the dry ingredients until combined. Stop the machine and scrape the bottom and sides of the bowl with a rubber spatula. With the mixer on medium speed, beat for 1 minute or until smooth.

3. Spoon dough into one side of prepared pan or onto the baking sheet in the shape of a French loaf. Using the edge of a moistened rubber spatula or a sharp knife, draw 3 or 4 diagonal lines, 1/4 inch (0.5 cm) deep, across the top of the loaf. Let rise, uncovered, in a warm, draft-free place for 60 minutes. Meanwhile, preheat oven to 425°F (220°C).

4. Bake for 20 to 23 minutes or until internal temperature of loaf registers 200°F (100°C) on an instant-read thermometer. Remove from the pan immediately and let cool completely on a rack.

Variation

Make 3 mini loaves by spooning dough into three 5¾- by 3¼-inch (14 by 8 cm) mini loaf pans. Make 2 diagonal slashes in the top of each loaf. Let rise, uncovered, in a warm, draft-free place for 60 minutes. Meanwhile, preheat oven to 400°F (200°C). Bake for 25 to 30 minutes.

Herbed Hearth Bread

Makes one 6-inch (15 cm) round loaf, 8 wedges
Serving size: 2 wedges

Instead of slicing this loaf, split it in half horizontally and fill with your favorite sandwich filling.

■■■■■■■■■■■■■■

Tips

Use an electric or serrated knife to thickly slice the loaf into wedges.

For a traditional hearth bread shape, draw a 6-inch (15 cm) circle on parchment paper lining a baking sheet. Sprinkle with cornmeal. Using a moistened spatula or large spoon, form the dough into a loaf within the circle, mounding the top.

Nutritional value per serving

Calories	235
Fat, total	9 g
Fat, saturated	1 g
Cholesterol	0 mg
Sodium	457 mg
Carbohydrate	37 g
Fiber	3 g
Protein	5 g
Calcium	40 mg
Iron	3 mg

■ **6-inch (15 cm) round baking pan, lightly greased and sprinkled with cornmeal**

¾ cup	brown rice flour	175 mL
¼ cup	amaranth flour	60 mL
¼ cup	potato starch	60 mL
1½ tsp	granulated sugar	7 mL
2 tsp	xanthan gum	10 mL
1 tbsp	bread machine or instant yeast	15 mL
¾ tsp	salt	3 mL
¼ cup	snipped fresh oregano	60 mL
¼ cup	snipped fresh parsley	60 mL
1	large egg white	1
¾ cup	water	175 mL
2 tbsp	extra virgin olive oil	30 mL
1 tsp	cider vinegar	5 mL

1. In a bowl or plastic bag, combine brown rice flour, amaranth flour, potato starch, sugar, xanthan gum, yeast, salt, oregano and parsley. Mix well and set aside.

2. In a separate bowl, using a heavy-duty electric mixer with paddle attachment, combine egg white, water, oil and vinegar until well blended. With the mixer on its lowest speed, slowly add the dry ingredients until combined. Stop the machine and scrape the bottom and sides of the bowl with a rubber spatula. With the mixer on medium speed, beat for 1 minute or until smooth.

3. Spoon dough into prepared pan, mounding the top. With a sharp knife, cut a ¼-inch (0.5 cm) deep X across the top. Let rise, uncovered, in a warm, draft-free place for 70 minutes. Meanwhile, preheat oven to 350°F (180°C).

4. Bake for 25 to 28 minutes or until internal temperature of loaf registers 200°F (100°C) on an instant-read thermometer. Remove from the pan immediately and let cool completely on a rack.

Variations

Omit the oregano and parsley for a plain Jane hearth bread.

Substitute basil, dill, marjoram or thyme for the oregano.

Crunchy Multigrain Batard

The attractive grainy slices from this loaf are the perfect accompaniment to your favorite soup or salad.

■■■■■■■■■■■■■■■

Tips

Store this bread loosely covered in a paper bag to maintain the crisp crust.

Use an electric or serrated knife to thickly slice this loaf on the diagonal.

See the Equipment Glossary, page 299, for information about baguette pans.

Nutritional value per serving

Calories	100
Fat, total	2 g
Fat, saturated	0 g
Cholesterol	0 mg
Sodium	201 mg
Carbohydrate	18 g
Fiber	2 g
Protein	3 g
Calcium	13 mg
Iron	1 mg

■ Baguette pan or baking sheet, lightly greased and lined with parchment paper

¾ cup	brown rice flour	175 mL
¼ cup	quinoa flour	60 mL
⅓ cup	potato starch	75 mL
1 tsp	granulated sugar	5 mL
2 tsp	xanthan gum	10 mL
2 tsp	bread machine or instant yeast	10 mL
1 tsp	salt	5 mL
¼ cup	millet seeds	60 mL
¼ cup	cracked flaxseed	60 mL
2 tbsp	GF large-flake (old-fashioned) rolled oats	30 mL
1	large egg white	1
¾ cup	water	175 mL
1 tsp	cider vinegar	5 mL

1. In a bowl or plastic bag, combine brown rice flour, quinoa flour, potato starch, sugar, xanthan gum, yeast, salt, millet seeds, flaxseed and oats. Mix well and set aside.

2. In a separate bowl, using a heavy-duty electric mixer with paddle attachment, combine egg white, water and vinegar until well blended. With the mixer on its lowest speed, slowly add the dry ingredients until combined. Stop the machine and scrape the bottom and sides of the bowl with a rubber spatula. With the mixer on medium speed, beat for 1 minute or until smooth.

3. Spoon dough into one side of prepared pan or onto the baking sheet in the shape of a French loaf. Using a sharp knife, draw 3 or 4 diagonal lines, ¼ inch (0.5 cm) deep, across the top of the loaf. Let rise, uncovered, in a warm, draft-free place for 70 minutes. Meanwhile, preheat oven to 425°F (220°C).

4. Bake for 18 to 22 minutes or until internal temperature of loaf registers 200°F (100°C) on an instant-read thermometer. Remove from the pan immediately and let cool completely on a rack.

Oatmeal Casserole Bread

Casserole breads are so easy to make. Cut this soft, sweet loaf into slices for a breakfast buffet when company arrives.

■■■■■■■■■■■■■■■■

Tip

This is a larger loaf than some of the others in this book. It keeps for a couple of days at room temperature and freezes well (see page 34).

Variation

Add 1 cup (250 mL) raisins or chopped dates with the dry ingredients.

Nutritional value per serving	
Calories	144
Fat, total	3 g
Fat, saturated	1 g
Cholesterol	24 mg
Sodium	236 mg
Carbohydrate	25 g
Fiber	2 g
Protein	4 g
Calcium	36 mg
Iron	1 mg

■ **10-cup (2.5 L) casserole dish, lightly greased**

¾ cup	brown rice flour	175 mL
1 cup	GF large-flake (old-fashioned) rolled oats	250 mL
½ cup	GF oat flour	125 mL
½ cup	sorghum flour	125 mL
⅓ cup	tapioca starch	75 mL
2½ tsp	xanthan gum	12 mL
1 tbsp	bread machine yeast	15 mL
1½ tsp	salt	7 mL
¼ cup	nonfat dry milk or skim milk powder	60 mL
2	large eggs	2
1¼ cups	water	300 mL
2 tbsp	vegetable oil	30 mL
⅓ cup	liquid honey	75 mL
1 tsp	cider vinegar	5 mL
2 tbsp	GF large-flake (old-fashioned) rolled oats (optional)	30 mL

1. In a bowl or plastic bag, combine brown rice flour, 1 cup (250 mL) oats, oat flour, sorghum flour, tapioca starch, xanthan gum, yeast, salt and dry milk. Mix well and set aside.

2. In a separate bowl, using a heavy-duty electric mixer with paddle attachment, combine eggs, water, oil, honey and vinegar until well blended. With the mixer on its lowest speed, slowly add the dry ingredients until combined. Stop the machine and scrape the bottom and sides of the bowl with a rubber spatula. With the mixer on medium speed, beat for 1 minute or until smooth.

3. Using a rubber spatula, pour dough into prepared dish, making sure not to fill it more than half full. Sprinkle with 2 tbsp (30 mL) oats, if desired. Let rise, uncovered, in a warm, draft-free place for 1 hour. Meanwhile, preheat oven to 350°F (180°C).

4. Bake for 25 minutes. Tent with foil and bake for 15 to 20 minutes or until deep golden brown and internal temperature of loaf registers 200°F (100°C) on an instant-read thermometer. Remove from the dish immediately. Serve warm.

Breadsticks

Serve these breadsticks as Italian restaurants do — with a dish of flavored olive oil for dipping.

■■■■■■■■■■■■■■■■

Tips

Thoroughly mix the dry ingredients before adding them to the liquids — they are powder-fine and can clump together.

Don't worry when seeds move as you spread the dough to the edges of the pan — they will still coat the breadsticks.

Nutritional value per serving	
Calories	77
Fat, total	3 g
Fat, saturated	0 g
Cholesterol	0 mg
Sodium	147 mg
Carbohydrate	12 g
Fiber	1 g
Protein	1 g
Calcium	27 mg
Iron	1 mg

■ **9-inch (23 cm) square baking pan, lightly greased**

²⁄₃ cup	brown rice flour	150 mL
2 tbsp	almond flour	30 mL
¼ cup	potato starch	60 mL
2 tbsp	tapioca starch	30 mL
1 tbsp	granulated sugar	15 mL
1¼ tsp	xanthan gum	6 mL
2 tsp	bread machine or instant yeast	10 mL
¾ tsp	salt	3 mL
¾ cup	water	175 mL
1 tbsp	vegetable oil	15 mL
1 tsp	cider vinegar	5 mL
3 tbsp	sesame seeds, divided	45 mL

1. In a bowl or plastic bag, combine brown rice flour, almond flour, potato starch, tapioca starch, sugar, xanthan gum, yeast and salt. Mix well and set aside.

2. In a separate bowl, using a heavy-duty electric mixer with paddle attachment, combine water, oil and vinegar until well blended. With the mixer on its lowest speed, slowly add the dry ingredients until combined. Stop the machine and scrape the bottom and sides of the bowl with a rubber spatula. With the mixer on medium speed, beat for 1 minute or until smooth.

3. Sprinkle 2 tbsp (30 mL) of the sesame seeds in bottom of prepared pan. Drop dough by spoonfuls over the sesame seeds. Using a moistened rubber spatula, spread dough evenly to the edges of the pan. Sprinkle with the remaining sesame seeds. Using moistened rubber spatula, press seeds into dough. Let rise, uncovered, in a warm, draft-free place for 30 minutes. Meanwhile, preheat oven to 400°F (200°C).

Tips

For uniform breadsticks, cut bread in half, then lengthwise into quarters. Finally, cut each quarter lengthwise into 3 strips.

If breadsticks become soft, crisp in a toaster oven or conventional oven at 350°F (180°C) for a few minutes.

Use any leftover breadsticks to make dry bread crumbs (see the Techniques Glossary, page 307).

4. Bake for 10 to 12 minutes or until light brown. Remove from the pan and transfer immediately to a cutting board. Reduce oven temperature to 350°F (180°C). Using a pizza wheel or a sharp knife, cut bread into 12 equal strips. Roll strips in loose sesame seeds in pan, pressing seeds into cut sides.

5. Arrange slices, with cut sides exposed, at least $1/2$ inch (1 cm) apart on a baking sheet. Bake for 20 to 25 minutes or until dry, crisp and golden brown. Remove from the pan immediately and let cool completely on a rack.

Variations

Substitute poppy seeds for the sesame seeds.

For an Italian herb flavor, add 2 to 3 tsp (10 to 15 mL) of your favorite Italian dried herb with the dry ingredients and use extra virgin olive oil instead of vegetable oil.

Mozzarella Toast

Makes 6 slices
Serving size: 1 slice

Here's a tasty bread to serve with chili the next time you invite the gang over.

■■■■■■■■■■■■■■■■■■

Tip

Be sure to preheat the broiler fully so you will quickly melt the cheese rather than bake it. Preheating will take 8 to 10 minutes for an electric broiler or 3 to 4 minutes for a gas broiler.

■ **Preheat broiler**

½	Crusty French Baguette (page 86), diagonally sliced 1 inch (2.5 cm) thick, toasted on 1 side	½
3	anchovy fillets, minced	3
1	clove garlic, minced	1
1 tbsp	snipped fresh cilantro	15 mL
¼ cup	butter, softened	60 mL
½ cup	shredded mozzarella cheese	125 mL

1. Place baguette slices, toasted side down, on a baking sheet. In a bowl, combine anchovies, garlic, cilantro and butter. Spread on baguette slices and sprinkle with cheese.

2. Toast under preheated broiler for 1 to 2 minutes or until cheese is melted.

Variation

Try a Havarti and goat cheese combination in place of the mozzarella and grill on the barbecue.

Nutritional value per serving	
Calories	151
Fat, total	9 g
Fat, saturated	6 g
Cholesterol	25 mg
Sodium	282 mg
Carbohydrate	14 g
Fiber	1 g
Protein	4 g
Calcium	75 mg
Iron	0 mg

Rich Dinner Rolls

Makes 6 rolls
Serving size: 1 roll

This is the answer to a special request for a recipe to make just a half-dozen everyday dinner rolls.

■■■■■■■■■■■■■■■■

Tips

If you only have a 12-cup muffin pan, fill the empty cups one-quarter full with water before baking.

For instructions on making your own almond flour, see under Nut flour in the Techniques Glossary, page 309.

Nutritional value per serving

Calories	232
Fat, total	11 g
Fat, saturated	1 g
Cholesterol	33 mg
Sodium	337 mg
Carbohydrate	28 g
Fiber	3 g
Protein	7 g
Calcium	94 mg
Iron	2 mg

■ **6-cup muffin pan, lightly greased**

1/2 cup	almond flour	125 mL
1/2 cup	brown rice flour	125 mL
1/4 cup	amaranth flour	60 mL
1/4 cup	potato starch	60 mL
2 tsp	xanthan gum	10 mL
1 3/4 tsp	bread machine or instant yeast	8 mL
3/4 tsp	salt	3 mL
1	large egg	1
1	large egg white	1
3/4 cup	plain yogurt	175 mL
2 tbsp	vegetable oil	30 mL
2 tbsp	liquid honey	30 mL

1. In a bowl or plastic bag, combine almond flour, brown rice flour, amaranth flour, potato starch, xanthan gum, yeast and salt. Mix well and set aside.

2. In a separate bowl, using a heavy-duty electric mixer with paddle attachment, combine egg, egg white, yogurt, oil and honey until well blended. With the mixer on its lowest speed, slowly add the dry ingredients until combined. Stop the machine and scrape the bottom and sides of the bowl with a rubber spatula. With the mixer on medium speed, beat for 1 minute or until smooth.

3. Using a 1/4-cup (60 mL) scoop, divide dough into 6 equal amounts and place in cups of prepared muffin pan. Let rise, uncovered, in a warm, draft-free place for 60 to 75 minutes or until dough has risen to the top of the cups. Meanwhile, preheat oven to 400°F (200°C).

4. Bake for 18 to 20 minutes or until internal temperature of rolls registers 200°F (100°C) on an instant-read thermometer. Remove from the pan immediately and let cool completely on a rack.

Variation

To make a dozen dinner rolls, double the ingredients, except for the xanthan gum and the yeast.

Egg-Free, Corn-Free, Dairy-Free, Soy-Free White Dinner Rolls

Makes 5 rolls
Serving size: 1 roll

These rolls are perfect for those who must eliminate eggs, corn, dairy and/or soy from their diet but enjoy a roll with dinner.

■■■■■■■■■■■■■■■■

Tip

For information about egg replacer, see the Ingredient Glossary, page 302.

Nutritional value per serving

Calories	189
Fat, total	7 g
Fat, saturated	1 g
Cholesterol	0 mg
Sodium	359 mg
Carbohydrate	30 g
Fiber	3 g
Protein	3 g
Calcium	14 mg
Iron	2 mg

■ **Baking sheet, lightly greased**

¾ cup	brown rice flour	175 mL
¼ cup	amaranth flour	60 mL
¼ cup	tapioca starch	60 mL
1 tbsp	powdered egg replacer	15 mL
1 tbsp	granulated sugar	15 mL
2½ tsp	xanthan gum	12 mL
1 tbsp	bread machine or instant yeast	15 mL
¾ tsp	salt	3 mL
¾ cup	water	175 mL
2 tbsp	vegetable oil	30 mL
1 tsp	cider vinegar	5 mL

1. In a bowl or plastic bag, combine brown rice flour, amaranth flour, tapioca starch, egg replacer, sugar, xanthan gum, yeast and salt. Mix well and set aside.

2. In a separate bowl, using a heavy-duty electric mixer with paddle attachment, combine water, oil and vinegar until well blended. With the mixer on its lowest speed, slowly add the dry ingredients until combined. Stop the machine and scrape the bottom and sides of the bowl with a rubber spatula. With the mixer on medium speed, beat for 1 minute or until smooth.

3. Using a ¼-cup (60 mL) scoop, drop 5 scoops of dough at least 2 inches (5 cm) apart onto prepared baking sheet. Let rise, uncovered, in a warm, draft-free place for 75 minutes. Meanwhile, preheat oven to 350°F (180°C).

4. Bake for 20 to 22 minutes or until internal temperature of rolls registers 200°F (100°C) on an instant-read thermometer. Remove from the pan immediately and let cool completely on a rack.

Variation

Add ¼ cup (60 mL) unsalted raw sunflower seeds or green pumpkin seeds with the dry ingredients.

French Onion Rolls

White as snow, these crispy, crusty rolls have a fantastic flavor.

Tips

Store these rolls loosely covered in a paper bag to maintain the crisp crust.

Do not add onion salt; the flavor is strong enough, and it will inhibit the action of the yeast.

Do not substitute fresh onion; there is too much water in it for this recipe.

Nutritional value per serving	
Calories	165
Fat, total	1 g
Fat, saturated	0 g
Cholesterol	0 mg
Sodium	365 mg
Carbohydrate	35 g
Fiber	3 g
Protein	5 g
Calcium	12 mg
Iron	1 mg

■ **Baking sheet, sprinkled with cornmeal**

1 cup	brown rice flour	250 mL
1/4 cup	potato starch	60 mL
1 tsp	granulated sugar	5 mL
1 1/2 tsp	xanthan gum	7 mL
2 tbsp	bread machine or instant yeast	30 mL
3/4 tsp	salt	3 mL
2 tbsp	dried minced onion	30 mL
1	large egg white	1
3/4 cup	water	175 mL
1 tsp	cider vinegar	5 mL

1. In a bowl or plastic bag, combine brown rice flour, potato starch, sugar, xanthan gum, yeast, salt and onion. Mix well and set aside.

2. In a separate bowl, using a heavy-duty electric mixer with paddle attachment, combine egg white, water and vinegar until well blended. With the mixer on its lowest speed, slowly add the dry ingredients until combined. Stop the machine and scrape the bottom and sides of the bowl with a rubber spatula. With the mixer on medium speed, beat for 1 minute or until smooth.

3. Using a 1/4-cup (60 mL) scoop, drop 5 scoops of dough at least 2 inches (5 cm) apart onto prepared baking sheet. Let rise, uncovered, in a warm, draft-free place for 70 minutes. Meanwhile, preheat oven to 350°F (180°C).

4. Bake for 20 to 22 minutes or until internal temperature of rolls registers 200°F (100°C) on an instant-read thermometer. Remove from the pan immediately and let cool completely on a rack.

Variation

For plain crusty white roll, omit the onion.

Brown Seed Dinner Rolls

Makes 6 rolls
Serving size: 1 roll

Longing for a rich, golden brown dinner roll? We've added three kinds of seeds for extra crunch.

■■■■■■■■■■■■■■■

Tips

If you don't have a scoop, use a large serving spoon and drop into muffin cups by large rounded spoonfuls.

If you only have a 12-cup muffin pan, fill the empty cups one-quarter full with water before baking.

If you don't have a muffin pan, drop 6 scoops of dough at least 2 inches (5 cm) apart onto a lightly greased baking sheet.

Nutritional value per serving

Calories	238
Fat, total	14 g
Fat, saturated	2 g
Cholesterol	31 mg
Sodium	505 mg
Carbohydrate	24 g
Fiber	4 g
Protein	8 g
Calcium	32 mg
Iron	3 mg

■ **6-cup muffin pan, lightly greased**

1/2 cup	sorghum flour	125 mL
1/3 cup	whole bean flour	75 mL
2 tbsp	potato starch	30 mL
3 tbsp	rice bran	45 mL
2 1/2 tsp	xanthan gum	12 mL
1 tbsp	bread machine or instant yeast	15 mL
1 1/4 tsp	salt	6 mL
1/4 cup	unsalted green pumpkin seeds	60 mL
1/4 cup	unsalted raw sunflower seeds	60 mL
2 tbsp	sesame seeds	30 mL
1	large egg	1
2/3 cup	water	150 mL
2 tbsp	vegetable oil	30 mL
1 tbsp	liquid honey	15 mL
1 tbsp	light (fancy) molasses	15 mL
1 tsp	cider vinegar	5 mL

1. In a bowl or plastic bag, combine sorghum flour, whole bean flour, potato starch, rice bran, xanthan gum, yeast, salt, pumpkin seeds, sunflower seeds and sesame seeds. Mix well and set aside.

2. In a separate bowl, using a heavy-duty electric mixer with paddle attachment, combine egg, water, oil, honey, molasses and vinegar until well blended. With the mixer on its lowest speed, slowly add the dry ingredients until combined. Stop the machine and scrape the bottom and sides of the bowl with a rubber spatula. With the mixer on medium speed, beat for 1 minute or until smooth.

3. Using a 1/4-cup (60 mL) scoop, divide dough into 6 equal amounts and place in cups of prepared muffin pan. Let rise, uncovered, in a warm, draft-free place for 60 to 75 minutes or until dough has risen to the top of the cups. Meanwhile, preheat oven to 350°F (180°C).

4. Bake for 18 to 20 minutes or until internal temperature of rolls registers 200°F (100°C) on an instant-read thermometer. Remove from the pan immediately and let cool completely on a rack.

Sun-Dried Tomato Cornbread (variation, page 46)

Florentine Pizza (page 63)

Mediterranean Focaccia (pages 73–74)

Crunchy Multigrain Batard (page 88)
and French Onion Rolls (page 95)

Lemon Buttermilk Scones (page 117)

Classic Banana Bread (page 133)

Cranberry Pistachio Muffins
(page 158)

Citrus Bars (page 190) and
Coconut Mango Icebox Cookies (page 180)

Oatmeal Dinner Rolls

Everyone loves these easy-to-make, golden brown dinner rolls.

■■■■■■■■■■■■■■

Tips

If you only have a 12-cup muffin pan, fill the empty cups one-quarter full with water before baking.

For a softer crust, brush the rolls with melted butter as soon as you remove them from the oven.

See the Techniques Glossary, page 310, for information on toasting seeds.

Variation

Substitute unsalted raw sunflower seeds for the pumpkin seeds, or use a combination.

Nutritional value per serving	
Calories	240
Fat, total	12 g
Fat, saturated	2 g
Cholesterol	32 mg
Sodium	320 mg
Carbohydrate	27 g
Fiber	3 g
Protein	8 g
Calcium	59 mg
Iron	4 mg

■ **6-cup muffin pan, lightly greased**

²⁄₃ cup	sorghum flour	150 mL
¼ cup	GF large-flake (old-fashioned) rolled oats	60 mL
2 tbsp	GF oat flour	30 mL
3 tbsp	tapioca starch	45 mL
1 tbsp	packed brown sugar	15 mL
2 tsp	xanthan gum	10 mL
1 tbsp	bread machine or instant yeast	15 mL
¾ tsp	salt	3 mL
1½ tsp	ground ginger	7 mL
½ cup	unsalted green pumpkin seeds, toasted	125 mL
1	large egg	1
¾ cup	milk	175 mL
2 tbsp	vegetable oil	30 mL
1 tsp	cider vinegar	5 mL

1. In a bowl or plastic bag, combine sorghum flour, oats, oat flour, tapioca starch, brown sugar, xanthan gum, yeast, salt, ginger and pumpkin seeds. Mix well and set aside.

2. In a separate bowl, using a heavy-duty electric mixer with paddle attachment, combine egg, milk, oil and vinegar until well blended. With the mixer on its lowest speed, slowly add the dry ingredients until combined. Stop the machine and scrape the bottom and sides of the bowl with a rubber spatula. With the mixer on medium speed, beat for 1 minute or until smooth.

3. Using a ¼-cup (60 mL) scoop, divide dough into 6 equal amounts and place in cups of prepared muffin pan. Let rise, uncovered, in a warm, draft-free place for 60 to 75 minutes or until dough has risen to the top of the cups. Meanwhile, preheat oven to 350°F (180°C).

4. Bake for 18 to 20 minutes or until internal temperature of rolls registers 200°F (100°C) on an instant-read thermometer. Remove from the pan immediately and let cool completely on a rack.

Grainy Mustard Mock Rye Buns

Heather takes these to the home of her son and daughter-in-law for Easter dinner, to serve with the ham.

■■■■■■■■■■■■■■■■

Tips

Do not substitute Dijonnaise for the Dijon mustard — it is too high in fat. You can, however, substitute a green peppercorn Dijon, if you like.

If you only have a 12-cup muffin pan, fill the empty cups one-quarter full with water before baking.

Nutritional value per serving	
Calories	186
Fat, total	7 g
Fat, saturated	1 g
Cholesterol	67 mg
Sodium	504 mg
Carbohydrate	26 g
Fiber	3 g
Protein	6 g
Calcium	34 mg
Iron	2 mg

■ **6-cup muffin pan, lightly greased**

$2/3$ cup	sorghum flour	150 mL
$1/2$ cup	whole bean flour	125 mL
$1/4$ cup	tapioca starch	60 mL
2 tbsp	packed brown sugar	30 mL
2 tsp	xanthan gum	10 mL
1 tbsp	bread machine or instant yeast	15 mL
$3/4$ tsp	salt	3 mL
1	large egg	1
1	large egg white	1
$2/3$ cup	water	150 mL
2 tbsp	grainy Dijon mustard	30 mL
2 tbsp	vegetable oil	30 mL
1 tsp	cider vinegar	5 mL

Grainy Dijon Mustard Glaze

1	large egg yolk	1
1 tbsp	grainy Dijon mustard	15 mL

1. In a bowl or plastic bag, combine sorghum flour, whole bean flour, tapioca starch, brown sugar, xanthan gum, yeast and salt. Mix well and set aside.

2. In a separate bowl, using a heavy-duty electric mixer with paddle attachment, combine egg, egg white, water, mustard, oil and vinegar until well blended. With the mixer on its lowest speed, slowly add the dry ingredients until combined. Stop the machine and scrape the bottom and sides of the bowl with a rubber spatula. With the mixer on medium speed, beat for 1 minute or until smooth.

3. Using a $1/4$-cup (60 mL) scoop, divide dough into 6 equal amounts and place in cups of prepared muffin pan. Let rise, uncovered, in a warm, draft-free place for 60 to 75 minutes or until dough has risen to the top of the cups. Meanwhile, preheat oven to 350°F (180°C).

4. *Glaze:* Combine egg yolk and mustard. Gently brush over risen buns.

5. Bake for 18 to 20 minutes or until internal temperature of buns registers 200°F (100°C) on an instant-read thermometer. Remove from the pan immediately and let cool completely on a rack.

Hamburger Buns

Makes
4 hamburger buns
Serving size: 1 bun

Though formed into the traditional shape for hamburger buns, these white bread rolls are also great both for sandwiches and as a dinner accompaniment.

■■■■■■■■■■■■■■■

Tips

You'll use 4 cups of the hamburger bun pan. Fill the remaining cups half full with water.

If you don't have a hamburger bun pan, try a cast-iron corncob-shaped bread pan or English muffin rings, or make free-form buns on a lightly greased baking sheet.

Nutritional value per serving	
Calories	341
Fat, total	10 g
Fat, saturated	1 g
Cholesterol	48 mg
Sodium	635 mg
Carbohydrate	57 g
Fiber	3 g
Protein	8 g
Calcium	66 mg
Iron	1 mg

■ **Hamburger bun baking pan, 4 cups lightly greased**

1 cup	brown rice flour	250 mL
1/3 cup	potato starch	75 mL
1/4 cup	tapioca starch	60 mL
2 tbsp	granulated sugar	30 mL
2 1/2 tsp	xanthan gum	12 mL
1 tbsp	bread machine or instant yeast	15 mL
1 tsp	salt	7 mL
1	large egg	1
1	large egg white	1
2/3 cup	milk	150 mL
2 tbsp	vegetable oil	30 mL
1 tsp	cider vinegar	5 mL

1. In a bowl or plastic bag, combine brown rice flour, potato starch, tapioca starch, sugar, xanthan gum, yeast and salt. Mix well and set aside.

2. In a separate bowl, using a heavy-duty electric mixer with paddle attachment, combine egg, egg white, milk, oil and vinegar until well blended. With the mixer on its lowest speed, slowly add the dry ingredients until combined. Stop the machine and scrape the bottom and sides of the bowl with a rubber spatula. With the mixer on medium speed, beat for 1 minute or until smooth.

3. Spoon dough into prepared cups of pan, dividing evenly. Flatten tops slightly. Let rise in a warm, draft-free place for 45 to 60 minutes or until dough has almost doubled in volume. Meanwhile, preheat oven to 350°F (180°C).

4. Bake for 15 to 20 minutes or until internal temperature of buns registers 200°F (100°C) on an instant-read thermometer. Remove from the pan immediately and let cool completely on a rack.

Variations

Make 2 mini sub buns by using a hot dog bun pan and 1/2 cup (125 mL) dough for each bun.

Sprinkle the tops with sesame seeds before the dough rises.

English Muffins

A popular breakfast or brunch treat! Just split with a fork and toast. Your butter and jam will ooze into the crevices.

■■■■■■■■■■■■■■■

Tip

To serve, use a fork to split each English muffin horizontally in half. Toast until golden and serve warm.

- **6 English muffin rings (optional)**
- **Baking sheet, lined with parchment and generously sprinkled with cornmeal**

1/3 cup	sorghum flour	75 mL
1/3 cup	brown rice flour	75 mL
3 tbsp	tapioca starch	45 mL
2 tsp	potato flour (not potato starch)	10 mL
2 tsp	granulated sugar	10 mL
2 tsp	xanthan gum	10 mL
2 tbsp	bread machine or instant yeast	30 mL
1/2 tsp	salt	2 mL
1	large egg	1
1	large egg yolk	1
1/2 cup	milk	125 mL
2 tbsp	vegetable oil	30 mL
1/4 to 1/3 cup	cornmeal	60 to 75 mL

1. In a bowl or plastic bag, combine sorghum flour, brown rice flour, tapioca starch, potato flour, sugar, xanthan gum, yeast and salt. Mix well and set aside.

2. In a separate bowl, using a heavy-duty electric mixer with paddle attachment, combine egg, egg yolk, milk and oil until well blended. With the mixer on its lowest speed, slowly add the dry ingredients until combined. Stop the machine and scrape the bottom and sides of the bowl with a rubber spatula. With the mixer on medium speed, beat for 1 minute or until smooth.

3. Using a 1/4-cup (60 mL) scoop, drop 6 scoops of dough at least 2 inches (5 cm) apart, in English muffin rings (if using), on prepared baking sheet. Sprinkle each with cornmeal. Top with a sheet of parchment paper. Gently pat each into a 1/2-inch (1 cm) thick circle. Remove parchment. Let rise, uncovered, in a warm, draft-free place for 30 minutes. Meanwhile, preheat oven to 400°F (200°C).

4. Bake for 13 to 15 minutes or until internal temperature of muffins registers 200°F (100°C) on an instant-read thermometer. Remove from the pan immediately and let cool completely on a rack.

Nutritional value per serving	
Calories	183
Fat, total	7 g
Fat, saturated	1 g
Cholesterol	67 mg
Sodium	218 mg
Carbohydrate	25 g
Fiber	3 g
Protein	6 g
Calcium	39 mg
Iron	2 mg

Yeast-Free Breads, Scones and Biscuits

■■■■■■■■■■■■■■■■■■■■■■■■■■■■■■■■■■■■

Irish Soda Bread

Like the traditional hearth bread, this loaf features a crusty exterior and a soft, tangy interior. It's perfect with Irish stew or baked beans.

■■■■■■■■■■■■■■■■

Tip

For instructions on making your own almond flour, see under Nut flour in the Techniques Glossary, page 309.

- ■ **Preheat oven to 375°F (190°C)**
- ■ **Two 1¼-cup (300 mL) ovenproof bowls or ramekins or one 5¾- by 3¼-inch (14 by 8 cm) mini loaf pan, lightly greased**

⅓ cup	brown rice flour	75 mL
¼ cup	almond flour	60 mL
2 tbsp	tapioca starch	30 mL
1½ tsp	granulated sugar	7 mL
1½ tsp	xanthan gum	7 mL
1½ tsp	baking soda	7 mL
2 tbsp	cold butter, cut into ½-inch (1 cm) cubes	30 mL
½ cup	plain yogurt	125 mL

1. In a bowl, combine brown rice flour, almond flour, tapioca starch, sugar, xanthan gum and baking soda. Using a pastry blender or two knives, cut in butter until mixture resembles coarse crumbs about the size of small peas. Add yogurt all at once, stirring with a fork to make a soft, slightly sticky dough.

2. Spoon dough into prepared bowls. Bake in preheated oven for 20 minutes. Check to see if loaf is getting too dark and tent with foil if necessary. Bake for 5 to 10 minutes or until internal temperature of loaf registers 200°F (100°C) on an instant-read thermometer. Let cool in bowls on a rack for 5 minutes. Remove from bowls and serve hot.

Variation

For a fruited and/or nutty version, add ½ cup (125 mL) raisins, dried currants and/or chopped walnuts to the dry ingredients.

Nutritional value per serving	
Calories	174
Fat, total	10 g
Fat, saturated	4 g
Cholesterol	17 mg
Sodium	500 mg
Carbohydrate	19 g
Fiber	2 g
Protein	4 g
Calcium	78 mg
Iron	0 mg

Yeast-Free Ciabatta

**Judy Degeling of
Newmarket, Ontario,
came up with the idea of
making our ciabatta with
baking powder instead
of yeast. It has a chewy
texture and toasts nicely,
either for sandwiches or
simply spread with jam.
She reminds folks who
cannot tolerate yeast not to
expect it to be like a yeast
bread — but it's very tasty!**

■ ■ ■ ■ ■ ■ ■ ■ ■ ■ ■ ■ ■ ■ ■

Tips

When dusting with rice flour,
use a flour sifter for a light,
even sprinkle.

This bread freezes well.
Cut into wedges and freeze
individually for sandwiches.

Be sure the internal
temperature reaches 200°F
(100°C), as the ciabatta will
look done before it really is.

Nutritional value per serving	
Calories	134
Fat, total	7 g
Fat, saturated	1 g
Cholesterol	62 mg
Sodium	427 mg
Carbohydrate	16 g
Fiber	1 g
Protein	4 g
Calcium	125 mg
Iron	1 mg

■ **Preheat oven to 425°F (220°C)**
■ **5-inch (12.5 cm) round baking pan, lightly greased
and bottom lined with parchment paper**

²/₃ cup	whole bean flour	150 mL
¹/₃ cup	brown rice flour	75 mL
2 tbsp	tapioca starch	30 mL
1 tbsp	granulated sugar	15 mL
2 tsp	xanthan gum	10 mL
1 tbsp	GF baking powder	15 mL
1 tsp	baking soda	5 mL
¹/₂ tsp	salt	2 mL
2	large eggs	2
¹/₃ cup	water	75 mL
2 tbsp	extra virgin olive oil	30 mL
1 tsp	cider vinegar	5 mL
2 to 3 tsp	sweet rice flour	10 to 15 mL

1. In a bowl or plastic bag, combine whole bean flour, brown rice flour, tapioca starch, sugar, xanthan gum, baking powder, baking soda and salt. Mix well and set aside.

2. In a separate bowl, using a heavy-duty electric mixer with paddle attachment, combine eggs, water, oil and vinegar until well blended. With the mixer on its lowest speed, slowly add the dry ingredients until combined. Stop the machine and scrape the bottom and sides of the bowl with a rubber spatula. With the mixer on medium speed, beat for 1 minute or until smooth.

3. Gently transfer dough to prepared pan and spread evenly to the edges, leaving the top rough and uneven. Generously dust top with sweet rice flour. With well-floured fingers, make deep indents all over the dough, pressing all the way down to the pan.

4. Bake in preheated oven for 26 minutes or until internal temperature of loaf registers 200°F (100°C) on an instant-read thermometer. Remove from the pan immediately and let cool on a rack. Cut into wedges and serve warm.

Variation

For a creamier-colored ciabatta, omit the whole bean flour and increase the brown rice flour to ¹/₂ cup (125 mL).

Yeast-Free Sun-Dried Tomato Ciabatta

<table>
<tr><td>Makes 4 to
6 wedges
Serving size: 1 wedge</td></tr>
</table>

If you cannot tolerate yeast but want to serve a sun-dried tomato ciabatta, you'll enjoy this one, which also features Parmesan and lots of fresh rosemary.

■■■■■■■■■■■■■■■

- ■ Preheat oven to 400°F (200°C)
- ■ 5-inch (12.5 cm) round baking pan, lightly greased and bottom lined with parchment paper

1/4 cup	brown rice flour	60 mL
1/4 cup	whole bean flour	60 mL
3 tbsp	tapioca starch	45 mL
1 tbsp	granulated sugar	15 mL
1 1/2 tsp	xanthan gum	7 mL
1 tbsp	GF baking powder	15 mL
1/8 tsp	salt	0.5 mL
2	cloves garlic, minced	2
1/2 cup	snipped sun-dried tomatoes	125 mL
1/2 cup	freshly grated Parmesan cheese	125 mL
1/4 cup	snipped fresh rosemary	60 mL
1	large egg	1
1/3 cup	water	75 mL
2 tbsp	extra virgin olive oil	30 mL
1 tsp	cider vinegar	5 mL
2 to 3 tsp	sweet rice flour	10 to 15 mL

1. In a bowl or plastic bag, combine brown rice flour, whole bean flour, tapioca starch, sugar, xanthan gum, baking powder, salt, garlic, tomatoes, Parmesan and rosemary. Mix well and set aside.

2. In a separate bowl, using a heavy-duty electric mixer with paddle attachment, combine egg, water, oil and vinegar until well blended. With the mixer on its lowest speed, slowly add the dry ingredients until combined. Stop the machine and scrape the bottom and sides of the bowl with a rubber spatula. With the mixer on medium speed, beat for 1 minute or until smooth.

Nutritional value per serving	
Calories	160
Fat, total	8 g
Fat, saturated	3 g
Cholesterol	38 mg
Sodium	311 mg
Carbohydrate	17 g
Fiber	1 g
Protein	6 g
Calcium	242 mg
Iron	1 mg

We like this ciabatta best served hot out of the oven.

Be sure the internal temperature reaches 200°F (100°C), as the ciabatta will look done before it really is.

3. Gently transfer dough to prepared pan and spread evenly to the edges, leaving the top rough and uneven. Generously dust top with sweet rice flour. With well-floured fingers, make deep indents all over the dough, pressing all the way down to the pan.

4. Bake in preheated oven for 25 to 28 minutes or until internal temperature of loaf registers 200°F (100°C) on an instant-read thermometer. Remove from the pan immediately and let cool on a rack. Cut into wedges and serve warm.

Variation

Substitute 2 to 3 tbsp (30 to 45 mL) dried basil or oregano for the fresh rosemary and sprinkle the risen dough with 2 tbsp (30 mL) freshly grated Parmesan cheese.

Yeast-Free Swedish Wraps

Makes 4 wraps
Serving size: 1 wrap

You asked us for a yeast-free sandwich wrap, and we were happy to oblige. These are perfect for lunch, filled with your favorite GF sliced cold cuts and veggies.

■■■■■■■■■■■■■■■

Tips

Xanthan gum helps prevent baked goods from crumbling, gives them greater volume, improves their texture and extends their shelf life.

Roll these wraps around your favorite sandwich fillings.

Dipping the spatula repeatedly into warm water makes it easier to spread this dough thinly and evenly.

Nutritional value per serving	
Calories	163
Fat, total	3 g
Fat, saturated	2 g
Cholesterol	2 mg
Sodium	465 mg
Carbohydrate	31 g
Fiber	3 g
Protein	5 g
Calcium	250 mg
Iron	3 mg

- Preheat oven to 400°F (200°C), with rack set in the top third
- 15- by 10-inch (40 by 25 cm) jelly roll pan, lightly greased and lined with parchment paper

½ cup	sorghum flour	125 mL
¼ cup	amaranth flour	60 mL
¼ cup	tapioca starch	60 mL
1 tsp	granulated sugar	5 mL
2 tsp	xanthan gum	10 mL
1 tbsp	GF baking powder	15 mL
¾ tsp	salt	3 mL
1 tsp	anise seeds	5 mL
1 tsp	caraway seeds	5 mL
1 tsp	fennel seeds	5 mL
¾ cup	milk	175 mL
1 tsp	extra virgin olive oil	5 mL
1 tsp	cider vinegar	5 mL

1. In a bowl or plastic bag, combine sorghum flour, amaranth flour, tapioca starch, sugar, xanthan gum, baking powder, salt, anise seeds, caraway seeds and fennel seeds. Mix well and set aside.

2. In a separate bowl, using a heavy-duty electric mixer with paddle attachment, combine milk, oil and vinegar until well blended. With the mixer on its lowest speed, slowly add the dry ingredients until combined. Stop the machine and scrape the bottom and sides of the bowl with a rubber spatula. With the mixer on medium speed, beat for 1 minute or until smooth.

3. Remove dough to prepared pan. Using a moistened rubber spatula, spread evenly to the edges.

4. Bake in preheated oven for 14 to 16 minutes or until edges and bottom are brown. Let cool completely on pan on a rack. Remove from pan and cut into quarters.

Variation

Try adding dried herbs to the soft dough in place of the three varieties of seeds. To make a plainer variety, omit seeds and herbs.

Make Your Own
Cornbread Mix (Single Portion)

**Makes 1 cup
(250 mL)
Serving size: 1/3 cup
(75 mL)**

Try making this single-portion mix before moving on to the larger batches on page 108. You can use this mix to make Mini Cornbread Loaf (page 109), Provolone and Sage Cornbread (page 110), Tomato and Spinach Cornbread (page 111), Bacon and Cheddar Cornbread (page 112) and Tarragon Cornbread Scones (page 115).

■■■■■■■■■■■■■■■

1/3 cup	cornmeal	75 mL
1/3 cup	brown rice flour	75 mL
3 tbsp	amaranth flour	45 mL
1 tbsp	tapioca starch	15 mL
1 1/2 tsp	granulated sugar	7 mL
1 tsp	xanthan gum	5 mL
1 tsp	GF baking powder	5 mL
1/2 tsp	baking soda	2 mL
1/4 tsp	salt	1 mL

1. In a bowl, combine cornmeal, brown rice flour, amaranth flour, tapioca starch, sugar, xanthan gum, baking powder, baking soda and salt.

2. Use right away or seal tightly in a plastic bag, removing as much air as possible. Store at room temperature for up to 3 days or in the freezer for up to 6 months.

Nutritional value per serving	
Calories	130
Fat, total	1 g
Fat, saturated	0 g
Cholesterol	0 mg
Sodium	409 mg
Carbohydrate	35 g
Fiber	3 g
Protein	3 g
Calcium	86 mg
Iron	2 mg

Make Your Own
Cornbread Mix (Double Portion)

**Makes 2 cups
(500 mL)
Serving size: 1/3 cup
(75 mL)**

Here's a double portion of our cornbread mix. You can use it to make Mini Cornbread Loaf (page 109), Provolone and Sage Cornbread (page 110), Tomato and Spinach Cornbread (page 111), Bacon and Cheddar Cornbread (page 112) and Tarragon Cornbread Scones (page 115).

3/4 cup	cornmeal	175 mL
2/3 cup	brown rice flour	150 mL
1/3 cup	amaranth flour	75 mL
2 tbsp	tapioca starch	30 mL
1 tbsp	granulated sugar	15 mL
2 tsp	xanthan gum	10 mL
2 tsp	GF baking powder	10 mL
1 tsp	baking soda	5 mL
1/2 tsp	salt	2 mL

1. In a bowl, combine cornmeal, brown rice flour, amaranth flour, tapioca starch, sugar, xanthan gum, baking powder, baking soda and salt.

2. Immediately divide into 2 equal portions of about 1 cup (250 mL) each. Seal tightly in plastic bags, removing as much air as possible. Store at room temperature for up to 3 days or in the freezer for up to 6 months.

Make Your Own
Cornbread Mix (8 Portions)

**Makes 8 cups (2 L)
Serving size: 1/3 cup
(75 mL)**

Here's a big batch of our cornbread mix.

3 cups	cornmeal	750 mL
2 2/3 cups	brown rice flour	650 mL
1 1/3 cups	amaranth flour	325 mL
1/2 cup	tapioca starch	125 mL
1/4 cup	granulated sugar	60 mL
3 tbsp	xanthan gum	45 mL
3 tbsp	GF baking powder	45 mL
1 tbsp	baking soda	15 mL
2 tsp	salt	10 mL

1. In a very large bowl, combine cornmeal, brown rice flour, amaranth flour, tapioca starch, sugar, xanthan gum, baking powder, baking soda and salt.

2. Immediately divide into 8 equal portions of about 1 cup (250 mL) each. Seal tightly in plastic bags, removing as much air as possible. Store at room temperature for up to 3 days or in the freezer for up to 6 months.

Mini Cornbread Loaf

No one can resist a slice of warm cornbread at any time of the day or night!

■■■■■■■■■■■■■■■■

Tips

If you don't have buttermilk on hand, add ½ tsp (2 mL) lemon juice or vinegar to ½ cup (125 mL) milk and let stand for 5 minutes.

For a softer, less gritty texture, let the batter stand for 30 minutes before baking.

- **Preheat oven to 375°F (190°C)**
- **5¾- by 3¼-inch (14 by 8 cm) mini loaf pan, lightly greased**

½ cup	buttermilk	125 mL
¼ cup	butter, melted and cooled	60 mL
1	portion Make Your Own Cornbread Mix (pages 107–108)	1

1. In a medium bowl, combine buttermilk and butter. Add cornbread mix all at once, stirring with a fork to make a soft, slightly sticky dough.

2. Spoon dough into prepared pan, leaving the top rough. Bake in preheated oven for 24 to 26 minutes or until top is golden and a tester inserted in the center comes out clean. Serve immediately.

Nutritional value per serving	
Calories	301
Fat, total	16 g
Fat, saturated	9 g
Cholesterol	39 mg
Sodium	595 mg
Carbohydrate	37 g
Fiber	3 g
Protein	5 g
Calcium	138 mg
Iron	2 mg

Provolone and Sage Cornbread

This hot and spicy treat is great for lunch.

■■■■■■■■■■■■■■■■

Tips

For the amount of provolone cheese to purchase, see the weight/volume equivalents in the Ingredient Glossary, page 305.

If you don't have buttermilk on hand, add 1/2 tsp (2 mL) lemon juice or vinegar to 1/2 cup (125 mL) milk and let stand for 5 minutes.

■ **Preheat oven to 350°F (180°C)**
■ **5³/₄- by 3¹/₄-inch (14 x 8 cm) mini loaf pan, lightly greased**

1	portion Make Your Own Cornbread Mix (pages 107–108)	1
1/3 cup	shredded provolone cheese	75 mL
1 tsp	rubbed dried sage	5 mL
1/4 tsp	coarsely ground white pepper	1 mL
1/8 tsp	cayenne pepper	0.5 mL
1	large egg	1
1/2 cup	buttermilk	125 mL

1. In a bowl or plastic bag, combine cornbread mix, cheese, sage, white pepper and cayenne. Set aside.

2. In a separate bowl, using an electric mixer, beat egg and buttermilk until combined. Add dry ingredients and stir just until combined.

3. Spoon dough into prepared pan, leaving the top rough. Bake for 23 to 26 minutes or until top is golden and a tester inserted in the center comes out clean. Serve hot.

Variations

Substitute an equal amount of dried dillweed for the sage.

Try this recipe with any tangy cheese, such as Asiago or Swiss.

Nutritional value per serving	
Calories	296
Fat, total	10 g
Fat, saturated	6 g
Cholesterol	83 mg
Sodium	709 mg
Carbohydrate	38 g
Fiber	3 g
Protein	14 g
Calcium	351 mg
Iron	3 mg

Tomato and Spinach Cornbread

Makes 4 to 6 wedges
Serving size: 1 wedge

Served hot or cold, this is the ideal treat for a summer luncheon.

■■■■■■■■■■■■■■■

Tip

Be sure to wash and dry spinach well before chopping and packing it into a measuring cup.

■ **Preheat oven to 350°F (180°C)**
■ **5-inch (12.5 cm) round baking pan, lightly greased and bottom lined with parchment paper**

1	portion Make Your Own Cornbread Mix (pages 107–108)	1
2 tbsp	snipped fresh oregano	30 mL
1	large egg	1
1/3 cup	milk	75 mL
2 tbsp	extra virgin olive oil	30 mL
2/3 cup	packed chopped spinach	150 mL
2/3 cup	coarsely chopped plum (Roma) tomatoes	150 mL

1. In a bowl or plastic bag, combine cornbread mix and oregano. Set aside.

2. In a separate bowl, using an electric mixer, beat egg, milk and olive oil until combined. Add dry ingredients and stir just until combined. Fold in spinach and tomatoes.

3. Spoon dough into prepared pan, leaving the top rough. Bake in preheated oven for 20 to 25 minutes or until top is golden and a tester inserted in the center comes out clean. Cut into wedges and serve immediately.

Variation

Substitute an equal amount of basil for the oregano.

Nutritional value per serving	
Calories	145
Fat, total	6 g
Fat, saturated	1 g
Cholesterol	32 mg
Sodium	225 mg
Carbohydrate	19 g
Fiber	2 g
Protein	3 g
Calcium	74 mg
Iron	1 mg

Bacon and Cheddar Cornbread

Enjoy the comforting goodness of cornbread, accented with the complementary flavors of bacon and Cheddar.

■ ■ ■ ■ ■ ■ ■ ■ ■ ■ ■ ■ ■ ■ ■ ■

Tip

For the amount of cheese to purchase, see the weight/volume equivalents in the Ingredient Glossary, page 302.

■ **Preheat oven to 350°F (180°C)**
■ **5-inch (12.5 cm) round baking pan, lightly greased and bottom lined with parchment paper**

1	large egg, lightly beaten	1
¾ cup	GF cream-style corn	175 mL
4	slices GF bacon, cooked crisp and crumbled	4
1	portion Make Your Own Cornbread Mix (pages 107–108)	1
⅓ cup	shredded sharp (old) Cheddar cheese	75 mL

1. In a small bowl, combine egg and corn. Set aside.

2. In a bowl, combine bacon, cornbread mix and cheese. Add corn mixture, stirring with a fork to make a thick dough.

3. Spoon dough into prepared pan, leaving the top rough. Bake in preheated oven for 23 to 25 minutes or until top is deep golden and a tester inserted in the center comes out clean. Cut into wedges and serve immediately.

Variation

Substitute ¼ cup (60 mL) chopped GF ham for the bacon.

Nutritional value per serving	
Calories	214
Fat, total	11 g
Fat, saturated	4 g
Cholesterol	45 mg
Sodium	453 mg
Carbohydrate	24 g
Fiber	2 g
Protein	6 g
Calcium	93 mg
Iron	1 mg

Broccoli and Cheddar Cornbread

Makes 12 pieces
Serving size: 1 piece

This tasty cornbread is ideal for entertaining. Cut into bite-size pieces, it can be served hot or cold as an hors d'oeuvre. It's also great for family meals.

■■■■■■■■■■■■■■■

Tip
Cut into larger pieces and serve with soup or a salad for lunch.

■ **9- by 5-inch (23 by 12.5 cm) loaf pan, lightly greased**

1/3 cup	cornmeal	75 mL
1/3 cup	brown rice flour	75 mL
2 tbsp	tapioca starch	30 mL
1 tbsp	potato starch	15 mL
1 tsp	xanthan gum	5 mL
2 tsp	GF baking powder	10 mL
1/2 tsp	baking soda	2 mL
1/4 tsp	salt	1 mL
1/3 cup	small broccoli florets	75 mL
1/4 cup	chopped onion	60 mL
1/4 cup	chopped red bell pepper	60 mL
1/3 cup	shredded sharp (old) Cheddar cheese	75 mL
2 tbsp	freshly grated Parmesan cheese	30 mL
1	large egg	1
1 tbsp	liquid honey	15 mL
1 tsp	cider vinegar	5 mL
1/3 cup	GF cream-style corn	75 mL

1. In a bowl, combine cornmeal, brown rice flour, tapioca starch, potato starch, xanthan gum, baking powder, baking soda and salt. Stir in broccoli, onion, red pepper, Cheddar and Parmesan. Set aside.

2. In a separate bowl, using an electric mixer, beat egg, honey and vinegar until combined. Stir in corn. Pour over dry ingredients and stir just until combined.

3. Spoon dough into prepared pan, leaving the top rough. Let stand for 30 minutes. Meanwhile, preheat oven to 350°F (180°C).

4. Bake for 35 to 45 minutes or until top is golden and a tester inserted in the center comes out clean. Serve hot.

Variation
Add diced GF ham or 3 slices of GF bacon, cooked crisp and crumbled, with the dry ingredients.

Nutritional value per serving

Calories	67
Fat, total	2 g
Fat, saturated	1 g
Cholesterol	18 mg
Sodium	167 mg
Carbohydrate	12 g
Fiber	1 g
Protein	3 g
Calcium	78 mg
Iron	0 mg

Blueberry Cornbread

This moist, flavorful cornbread is perfect with chili, stew or salad.

■■■■■■■■■■■■■■■■

Tips

You can use cooked fresh, thawed frozen or well-drained canned corn.

To quickly thaw blueberries, run them under cold running water. Drain well and pat dry with a paper towel.

For blue cornbread, choose blue cornmeal.

■ **Preheat oven to 350°F (180°C)**
■ **3-cup (750 mL) casserole dish, lightly greased and coated with cornmeal**

½ cup	cornmeal	125 mL
⅓ cup	amaranth flour	75 mL
2 tbsp	cornstarch	30 mL
2 tbsp	packed brown sugar	30 mL
1½ tsp	xanthan gum	7 mL
1 tbsp	GF baking powder	15 mL
½ tsp	baking soda	2 mL
¼ tsp	salt	1 mL
1	large egg	1
½ cup	buttermilk	125 mL
2 tbsp	butter, melted and cooled	30 mL
½ cup	corn kernels (see tip, at left)	125 mL
⅓ cup	frozen blueberries, thawed	75 mL

1. In a bowl, combine cornmeal, amaranth flour, cornstarch, brown sugar, xanthan gum, baking powder, baking soda and salt. Set aside.

2. In a small bowl, whisk together egg, buttermilk and butter. Stir in corn. Pour over dry ingredients and stir just until combined. Gently fold in blueberries.

3. Spoon dough into prepared casserole dish, smoothing top. Bake in preheated oven for 38 to 42 minutes or until deep golden and a tester inserted in the center comes out clean. Let cool in pan on a rack for 5 minutes. Remove from pan and serve warm.

Nutritional value per serving	
Calories	251
Fat, total	8 g
Fat, saturated	4 g
Cholesterol	63 mg
Sodium	362 mg
Carbohydrate	40 g
Fiber	3 g
Protein	6 g
Calcium	228 mg
Iron	3 mg

Tarragon Cornbread Scones

Tarragon gives a natural sweetness to these cornbread scones.

■■■■■■■■■■■■■■■

Tips

If you don't have buttermilk on hand, substitute plain yogurt or GF sour cream.

You can use cooked fresh, thawed frozen or well-drained canned corn.

Nutritional value per serving	
Calories	163
Fat, total	7 g
Fat, saturated	4 g
Cholesterol	47 mg
Sodium	332 mg
Carbohydrate	21 g
Fiber	2 g
Protein	4 g
Calcium	79 mg
Iron	1 mg

■ Preheat oven to 350°F (180°C)
■ 5-inch (12.5 cm) round baking pan, lightly greased and bottom lined with parchment paper

1	large egg	1
½ cup	buttermilk	125 mL
1	portion Make Your Own Cornbread Mix (pages 107–108)	1
2 tsp	dried tarragon	10 mL
3 tbsp	cold butter, cut into ½-inch (1 cm) cubes	45 mL
⅓ cup	corn kernels (see tip, at left)	75 mL

Traditional Method

1. In a measuring cup or small bowl, whisk together egg and buttermilk. Set aside.

2. In a bowl, combine cornbread mix and tarragon. Using a pastry blender or two knives, cut in butter until mixture resembles coarse crumbs about the size of small peas. Add egg mixture all at once, stirring with a fork to make a thick dough. Fold in corn.

Food Processor Method

1. In a measuring cup or small bowl, whisk together egg and buttermilk. Set aside.

2. In a small food processor fitted with a metal blade, combine cornbread mix and tarragon; pulse 3 or 4 times to combine. Add butter and pulse for 3 to 5 seconds or until mixture resembles coarse crumbs about the size of small peas. Add egg mixture all at once and process until dough holds together. Transfer to a bowl and fold in corn.

For Both Methods

3. Spoon dough into prepared pan, leaving the top rough. Bake in preheated oven for 30 to 35 minutes or until top is deep golden. Cut into wedges and serve immediately.

Variation

For a spicy cornbread, substitute 1 tsp (5 mL) hot pepper flakes for the tarragon.

Orange Raisin Scones

We're sure you'll love these delicious, golden-colored dessert scones.

■■■■■■■■■■■■■■■

Tip

There's no need to thaw the orange juice concentrate before measuring it; simply scoop it into a dry measure directly from your freezer. That way, you only need to thaw the amount needed.

■ **Preheat oven to 350°F (180°C)**
■ **5-inch (12.5 cm) round baking pan, lightly greased and bottom lined with parchment paper**

1	large egg yolk	1
1/4 cup	frozen orange juice concentrate, thawed	60 mL
1/3 cup	amaranth flour	75 mL
1/4 cup	almond flour	60 mL
2 tbsp	tapioca starch	30 mL
2 tbsp	granulated sugar	30 mL
1 tbsp	GF baking powder	15 mL
1 tsp	baking soda	5 mL
1 tsp	xanthan gum	5 mL
1/8 tsp	salt	0.5 mL
3 tbsp	cold butter, cut into 1/2-inch (1 cm) cubes	45 mL
1/3 cup	raisins	75 mL

1. In a measuring cup or small bowl, whisk together egg yolk and orange juice concentrate. Set aside.

2. In a bowl, combine amaranth flour, almond flour, tapioca starch, sugar, baking powder, baking soda, xanthan gum and salt. Using a pastry blender or two knives, cut in butter until mixture resembles coarse crumbs about the size of small peas. Add egg yolk mixture all at once, stirring with a fork to make a thick dough. Stir in raisins.

3. Spoon dough into prepared pan, leaving the top rough. Bake in preheated oven for 20 minutes. Tent with foil and bake for 7 to 10 minutes or until top is deep golden. Cut into wedges and serve immediately.

Variations

Omit the raisins for a plainer scone.

Substitute chocolate chips for the raisins.

Nutritional value per serving	
Calories	188
Fat, total	9 g
Fat, saturated	4 g
Cholesterol	51 mg
Sodium	267 mg
Carbohydrate	25 g
Fiber	2 g
Protein	3 g
Calcium	144 mg
Iron	2 mg

Lemon Buttermilk Scones

Makes 4 to 6 wedges
Serving size: 1 wedge

These scones with a delightful lemon tang are perfect to serve with fresh raspberries.

■■■■■■■■■■■■■■

Tips

If you don't have buttermilk on hand, substitute plain yogurt or GF sour cream.

Lemon zest is the bright yellow portion of a lemon peel. When the lemon is cold from the refrigerator, zest is easily grated with a rasp, a very sharp, thin tool.

Variation

To turn this into a dessert scone, increase the granulated sugar to ¼ cup (60 mL).

Nutritional value per serving

Calories	141
Fat, total	7 g
Fat, saturated	4 g
Cholesterol	51 mg
Sodium	276 mg
Carbohydrate	18 g
Fiber	1 g
Protein	2 g
Calcium	137 mg
Iron	2 mg

■ **Preheat oven to 350°F (180°C)**
■ **5-inch (12.5 cm) round baking pan, lightly greased and bottom lined with parchment paper**

1	large egg yolk	1
¼ cup	buttermilk	60 mL
⅓ cup	brown rice flour	75 mL
¼ cup	amaranth flour	60 mL
2 tbsp	tapioca starch	30 mL
2 tbsp	granulated sugar	30 mL
1 tbsp	GF baking powder	15 mL
1 tsp	baking soda	5 mL
1 tsp	xanthan gum	5 mL
⅛ tsp	salt	0.5 mL
2 tbsp	grated lemon zest	30 mL
3 tbsp	cold butter, cut into ½-inch (1 cm) cubes	45 mL

Traditional Method

1. In a measuring cup or small bowl, whisk together egg yolk and buttermilk. Set aside.

2. In a bowl, combine brown rice flour, amaranth flour, tapioca starch, sugar, baking powder, baking soda, xanthan gum, salt and lemon zest. Using a pastry blender or two knives, cut in butter until mixture resembles coarse crumbs about the size of small peas. Add egg yolk mixture all at once, stirring with a fork to make a thick dough.

Food Processor Method

1. In a measuring cup or small bowl, whisk together egg yolk and buttermilk. Set aside.

2. In a small food processor fitted with a metal blade, combine brown rice flour, amaranth flour, tapioca starch, sugar, baking powder, baking soda, xanthan gum, salt and lemon zest; pulse 3 or 4 times to combine. Add butter and pulse for 3 to 5 seconds or until mixture resembles coarse crumbs about the size of small peas. Add egg yolk mixture all at once and process until dough holds together.

For Both Methods

3. Spoon dough into prepared pan, leaving the top rough. Bake in preheated oven for 24 to 28 minutes or until top is deep golden. Cut into wedges and serve immediately.

Honey Walnut Scones

These rich, dark scones
are reminiscent of the
color and texture of a
date and nut loaf.

■■■■■■■■■■■■■■■■

Tips

For information on toasting
nuts, see the Techniques
Glossary, page 309.

To warm honey, microwave
it on High for 20 to
30 seconds.

Brush with lots of honey
for a sweet treat.

■ **Preheat oven to 350°F (180°C)**
■ **5-inch (12.5 cm) round baking pan, lightly greased
and bottom lined with parchment paper**

1	large egg yolk	1
1/3 cup	buttermilk	75 mL
2 tbsp	liquid honey	30 mL
1/3 cup	teff flour	75 mL
1/4 cup	whole bean flour	60 mL
2 tbsp	tapioca starch	30 mL
1 tbsp	GF baking powder	15 mL
1 tsp	baking soda	5 mL
1 tsp	xanthan gum	5 mL
1/8 tsp	salt	0.5 mL
1/3 cup	toasted coarsely chopped walnuts	75 mL
1/4 cup	cold butter, cut into 1/2-inch (1 cm) cubes	60 mL
1 to 2 tbsp	liquid honey, warmed (see tip, at left)	15 to 30 mL

1. In a measuring cup or small bowl, whisk together
   egg yolk, buttermilk and 2 tbsp (30 mL) honey.
   Set aside.

2. In a bowl, combine teff flour, whole bean flour,
   tapioca starch, baking powder, baking soda, xanthan
   gum, salt and walnuts. Using a pastry blender or two
   knives, cut in butter until mixture resembles coarse
   crumbs about the size of small peas. Add egg yolk
   mixture all at once, stirring with a fork to make a
   thick dough.

3. Spoon dough into prepared pan, leaving the top
   rough. Bake in preheated oven for 20 minutes. Tent
   with foil and bake for 7 to 10 minutes or until top
   is deep golden. Brush with warmed honey. Cut into
   wedges and serve immediately.

Variation

Add 1/2 cup (125 mL) coarsely chopped dates with
the walnuts.

Nutritional value per serving	
Calories	202
Fat, total	13 g
Fat, saturated	5 g
Cholesterol	57 mg
Sodium	280 mg
Carbohydrate	20 g
Fiber	2 g
Protein	4 g
Calcium	152 mg
Iron	1 mg

Black Olive and Goat Cheese Scones

Makes 4 to 6 wedges
Serving size: 1 wedge

The flavor of these soft, golden, slightly sweet scones contrasts with the sharpness of the ripe olives.

Tips

If you use canned olives, rinse them under cold running water and drain well.

Goat cheese (also known as chèvre, the French word for "goat") has a saltier, stronger flavor than cheeses made of cow's milk.

Nutritional value per serving	
Calories	244
Fat, total	12 g
Fat, saturated	6 g
Cholesterol	60 mg
Sodium	456 mg
Carbohydrate	31 g
Fiber	2 g
Protein	5 g
Calcium	173 mg
Iron	3 mg

- Preheat oven to 350°F (180°C)
- 5-inch (12.5 cm) round baking pan, lightly greased and bottom lined with parchment paper

1	large egg yolk	1
1/2 cup	buttermilk	125 mL
1/2 cup	amaranth flour	125 mL
1/2 cup	brown rice flour	125 mL
3 tbsp	tapioca starch	45 mL
1/4 cup	granulated sugar	60 mL
1 tbsp	GF baking powder	15 mL
1 tsp	baking soda	5 mL
1 1/2 tsp	xanthan gum	7 mL
1/4 tsp	salt	1 mL
1/4 cup	cold butter, cut into 1/2-inch (1 cm) cubes	60 mL
1/4 cup	crumbled goat cheese	60 mL
1/2 cup	sliced black olives	125 mL

1. In a measuring cup or small bowl, whisk together egg yolk and buttermilk. Set aside.

2. In a bowl, combine amaranth flour, brown rice flour, tapioca starch, sugar, baking powder, baking soda, xanthan gum and salt. Using a pastry blender or two knives, cut in butter and goat cheese until mixture resembles coarse crumbs about the size of small peas. Add egg yolk mixture all at once, stirring with a fork to make a thick dough. Fold in olives.

3. Spoon dough into prepared pan, leaving the top rough. Bake in preheated oven for 25 minutes. Tent with foil and bake for 8 to 12 minutes or until top is deep golden. Cut into wedges and serve immediately.

Variation

Substitute softened brick-style cream cheese for the goat's milk cheese.

Working with Biscuit Mix

■ If making one of the larger mix sizes, stir the mix before spooning very lightly into the dry measures when dividing into portions. Do not pack.

■ Be sure to divide the mix into equal portions before using to make up an individual recipe. Depending on how much air you incorporate into the mix and the texture of the individual gluten-free flours, the total volume of the mix can vary slightly. The important thing is to make the number of portions the recipe states.

■ Label and date packages before storing. We add the page number of the recipe to the label as a quick reference.

■ Let warm to room temperature and mix well before using.

Better Biscuits

■ When you're cutting cold butter into the dry ingredients, keep in mind that the task goes more quickly when the butter is pre-cut into $1/2$-inch (1 cm) cubes.

■ You only need to stir the liquids into the dry ingredients until they are just combined.

■ To make drop biscuits, scoop up the dough with a large serving spoon and push it off onto the baking sheet with the back of another.

■ Biscuits should all be the same size to bake in the same length of time.

■ Biscuits are done when they are golden on both top and bottom. Immediately remove them from baking sheets or the bottoms may become soggy.

■ Make only a few biscuits at a time. They are at their best served warm from the oven.

■ To reheat leftover biscuits, wrap loosely in a paper towel and microwave each biscuit on Medium (50%) power for a few seconds.

Biscuit Mix for 4 Biscuits

Makes about 1 cup (250 mL), enough for 4 biscuits
Serving size: $\frac{1}{4}$ cup (60 mL)

Crave hot, homemade, melt-in-your-mouth biscuits? Choose any one of the six variations found on pages 123 to 127 and page 130. Have this mix ready to quickly whip up a batch for breakfast, lunch or dinner. They'll disappear right before your eyes.

$\frac{1}{3}$ cup	brown rice flour	75 mL
$\frac{1}{4}$ cup	sorghum flour	60 mL
2 tbsp	tapioca starch	30 mL
2 tsp	granulated sugar	10 mL
1 tbsp	GF baking powder	15 mL
$\frac{1}{2}$ tsp	baking soda	2 mL
1 tsp	xanthan gum	5 mL
$\frac{1}{8}$ tsp	salt	0.5 mL

1. In a large bowl, combine brown rice flour, sorghum flour, tapioca starch, sugar, baking powder, baking soda, xanthan gum and salt.

2. Seal tightly in a plastic bag, removing as much air as possible. Store at room temperature for up to 3 days or in the freezer for up to 6 months.

Biscuit Mix for 12 Biscuits

Makes 3 cups (750 mL), enough for 12 biscuits
Serving size: $\frac{1}{4}$ cup (60 mL)

1 cup	brown rice flour	250 mL
1 cup	sorghum flour	250 mL
$\frac{1}{3}$ cup	tapioca starch	75 mL
2 tbsp	granulated sugar	30 mL
1 tbsp	xanthan gum	15 mL
3 tbsp	GF baking powder	45 mL
$1\frac{1}{2}$ tsp	baking soda	7 mL
$\frac{1}{2}$ tsp	salt	2 mL

1. In a large bowl, combine brown rice flour, sorghum flour, tapioca starch, sugar, xanthan gum, baking powder, baking soda and salt.

2. Immediately divide into 3 equal portions of about 1 cup (250 mL) each. Seal tightly in plastic bags, removing as much air as possible. Store at room temperature for up to 3 days or in the freezer for up to 6 months.

Nutritional value per serving	
Calories	99
Fat, total	1 g
Fat, saturated	0 g
Cholesterol	0 mg
Sodium	236 mg
Carbohydrate	23 g
Fiber	2 g
Protein	2 g
Calcium	168 mg
Iron	1 mg

Biscuit Mix for 24 Biscuits

2 cups	brown rice flour	500 mL
2 cups	sorghum flour	500 mL
2/3 cup	tapioca starch	150 mL
1/4 cup	granulated sugar	60 mL
2 tbsp	xanthan gum	30 mL
1/4 cup	GF baking powder	60 mL
1 tbsp	baking soda	15 mL
1 1/2 tsp	salt	7 mL

1. In a large bowl, combine brown rice flour, sorghum flour, tapioca starch, sugar, xanthan gum, baking powder, baking soda and salt.

2. Immediately divide into 6 equal portions of about 1 cup (250 mL) each. Seal tightly in plastic bags, removing as much air as possible. Store at room temperature for up to 3 days or in the freezer for up to 6 months.

Biscuit Mix for 48 Biscuits

4 cups	brown rice flour	1 L
4 cups	sorghum flour	1 L
1 2/3 cups	tapioca starch	400 mL
1/2 cup	granulated sugar	125 mL
1/4 cup	xanthan gum	60 mL
1/2 cup	GF baking powder	125 mL
2 tbsp	baking soda	30 mL
2 tsp	salt	10 mL

1. In a large bowl, combine brown rice flour, sorghum flour, tapioca starch, sugar, xanthan gum, baking powder, baking soda and salt.

2. Immediately divide into 12 equal portions of about 1 cup (250 mL) each. Seal tightly in plastic bags, removing as much air as possible. Store at room temperature for up to 3 days or in the freezer for up to 6 months.

Everyday Biscuits

Makes 4 biscuits
Serving size: 1 biscuit

For those who love their flavors pure and uncomplicated — a true plain biscuit!

■■■■■■■■■■■■■■■■

Tips

To drop the dough in step 3, spoon it onto a large serving spoon and push it off onto the baking sheet with the back of another.

Biscuits should all be the same size to bake in the same length of time.

This is great drop biscuit to top a stew or chili.

■ **Preheat oven to 400°F (200°C)**
■ **Baking sheet, lightly greased**

⅓ cup	milk	75 mL
½ tsp	freshly squeezed lemon juice	2 mL
1	portion Biscuit Mix (pages 121–122)	1
¼ cup	cold butter, cut into ½-inch (1 cm) cubes	60 mL

1. In a measuring cup or small bowl, combine milk and lemon juice; set aside for 5 minutes.

2. Place biscuit mix in a medium bowl. Using a pastry blender or two knives, cut in butter until mixture resembles coarse crumbs about the size of small peas. Add milk mixture all at once, stirring with a fork to make a soft, slightly sticky dough.

3. Drop dough by heaping spoonfuls 2 inches (5 cm) apart on prepared baking sheet.

4. Bake in preheated oven for 13 to 15 minutes or until golden on both top and bottom. Serve immediately.

Nutritional value per serving	
Calories	209
Fat, total	13 g
Fat, saturated	7 g
Cholesterol	32 mg
Sodium	248 mg
Carbohydrate	24 g
Fiber	2 g
Protein	3 g
Calcium	196 mg
Iron	1 mg

Cheese Biscuits

The perennial favorite of all cheese lovers, this is great drop biscuit to top a stew or chili.

■■■■■■■■■■■■■■■■

Tips

If you don't have buttermilk on hand, add 2 tbsp (30 mL) buttermilk powder to the dry ingredients and use ½ cup (125 mL) water.

You can purchase a packaged mix of grated Asiago, Parmesan and Romano cheeses to use in this recipe.

To drop the dough in step 2, spoon it onto a large serving spoon and push it off onto the baking sheet with the back of another.

■ **Preheat oven to 400°F (200°C)**
■ **Baking sheet, lightly greased**

1	portion Biscuit Mix (pages 121–122)	1
Pinch	dry mustard	Pinch
2 tbsp	shredded Asiago cheese	30 mL
2 tbsp	freshly grated Parmesan cheese	30 mL
2 tbsp	freshly grated Romano cheese	30 mL
¼ cup	cold butter, cut into ½-inch (1 cm) cubes	60 mL
½ cup	buttermilk	125 mL

1. In a medium bowl, combine biscuit mix, mustard, Asiago, Parmesan and Romano. Using a pastry blender or two knives, cut in butter until mixture resembles coarse crumbs about the size of small peas. Add buttermilk all at once, stirring with a fork to make a soft, slightly sticky dough.

2. Drop dough by heaping spoonfuls 2 inches (5 cm) apart on prepared baking sheet.

3. Bake in preheated oven for 13 to 15 minutes or until golden on both top and bottom. Serve immediately.

Variation

Add 4 slices of GF bacon, cooked crisp and crumbled, with the dry ingredients.

Nutritional value per serving	
Calories	248
Fat, total	15 g
Fat, saturated	9 g
Cholesterol	41 mg
Sodium	346 mg
Carbohydrate	25 g
Fiber	2 g
Protein	6 g
Calcium	303 mg
Iron	1 mg

Multi-Seed Biscuits

Enjoy some crunch in your biscuits? Try these!

■■■■■■■■■■■■■■

Tips

If you don't have buttermilk on hand, add 2 tbsp (30 mL) buttermilk powder to the dry ingredients and use ½ cup (125 mL) water.

To drop the dough in step 2, spoon it onto a large serving spoon and push it off onto the baking sheet with the back of another.

Biscuits should all be the same size to bake in the same length of time.

■ **Preheat oven to 400°F (200°C)**
■ **Baking sheet, lightly greased**

1	portion Biscuit Mix (pages 121–122)	1
1 tbsp	unsalted green pumpkin seeds	15 mL
1 tbsp	sesame seeds	15 mL
1 tbsp	unsalted raw sunflower seeds	15 mL
¼ cup	cold butter, cut into ½-inch (1 cm) cubes	60 mL
½ cup	buttermilk	125 mL

1. In a medium bowl, combine biscuit mix, pumpkin seeds, sesame seeds and sunflower seeds. Using a pastry blender or two knives, cut in butter until mixture resembles coarse crumbs about the size of small peas. Add buttermilk all at once, stirring with a fork to make a soft, slightly sticky dough.

2. Drop dough by heaping spoonfuls 2 inches (5 cm) apart on prepared baking sheet.

3. Bake in preheated oven for 13 to 15 minutes or until golden on both top and bottom. Serve immediately.

Variation

Substitute cracked flaxseed for the sunflower seeds and poppy seeds for the sesame seeds.

Nutritional value per serving	
Calories	249
Fat, total	16 g
Fat, saturated	8 g
Cholesterol	32 mg
Sodium	270 mg
Carbohydrate	26 g
Fiber	2 g
Protein	4 g
Calcium	231 mg
Iron	2 mg

Flaxseed Biscuits

Here's the perfect choice for those who want a high-fiber biscuit with a crunch!

■■■■■■■■■■■■■■■■

Tips

You can use either gold or brown flaxseed. For information on cracking flaxseed, see the Techniques Glossary, page 308.

To drop the dough in step 3, spoon it onto a large serving spoon and push it off onto the baking sheet with the back of another.

■ **Preheat oven to 400°F (200°C)**
■ **Baking sheet, lightly greased**

½ cup	milk	125 mL
½ tsp	freshly squeezed lemon juice	2 mL
1	portion Biscuit Mix (pages 121–122)	1
¼ cup	cracked flaxseed	60 mL
¼ cup	cold butter, cut into ½-inch (1 cm) cubes	60 mL

1. In a measuring cup or small bowl, combine milk and lemon juice; set aside for 5 minutes.

2. In a medium bowl, combine biscuit mix and flaxseed. Using a pastry blender or two knives, cut in butter until mixture resembles coarse crumbs about the size of small peas. Add milk mixture all at once, stirring with a fork to make a soft, slightly sticky dough.

3. Drop dough by heaping spoonfuls 2 inches (5 cm) apart on prepared baking sheet.

4. Bake in preheated oven for 13 to 15 minutes or until golden on both top and bottom. Serve immediately.

Variation

Substitute buttermilk for the milk and lemon juice.

Nutritional value per serving	
Calories	257
Fat, total	17 g
Fat, saturated	8 g
Cholesterol	32 mg
Sodium	255 mg
Carbohydrate	28 g
Fiber	4 g
Protein	5 g
Calcium	232 mg
Iron	1 mg

Onion Walnut Biscuits

Makes 4 biscuits
Serving size: 1 biscuit

The walnuts taste toasted in these biscuits, even though they're not!

■■■■■■■■■■■■■■■

Tip
To drop the dough in step 3, spoon it onto a large serving spoon and push it off onto the baking sheet with the back of another.

■ **Preheat oven to 400°F (200°C)**
■ **Baking sheet, lightly greased**

½ cup	milk	125 mL
½ tsp	freshly squeezed lemon juice	2 mL
1	portion Biscuit Mix (pages 121–122)	1
¼ cup	cold butter, cut into ½-inch (1 cm) cubes	60 mL
¼ cup	chopped walnuts	60 mL
1 tbsp	dried minced onion	15 mL

1. In a measuring cup or small bowl, combine milk and lemon juice; set aside for 5 minutes.

2. Place biscuit mix in a medium bowl. Using a pastry blender or two knives, cut in butter until mixture resembles coarse crumbs about the size of small peas. Stir in walnuts and onion. Add milk mixture all at once, stirring with a fork to make a soft, slightly sticky dough.

3. Drop dough by heaping spoonfuls 2 inches (5 cm) apart on prepared baking sheet.

4. Bake in preheated oven for 13 to 15 minutes or until golden on both top and bottom. Serve immediately.

Variation
Substitute 2 tbsp (30 mL) crumbled GF blue cheese for the onion.

Nutritional value per serving	
Calories	272
Fat, total	17 g
Fat, saturated	8 g
Cholesterol	32 mg
Sodium	256 mg
Carbohydrate	29 g
Fiber	3 g
Protein	5 g
Calcium	226 mg
Iron	1 mg

Buckwheat Hazelnut Drop Biscuits

What a tasty way to incorporate buckwheat into your diet — combined with hazelnut, the flavor is delightful.

■■■■■■■■■■■■■■■■

Tip

To ensure success, see page 120 for tips on making biscuits.

Nutritional value per serving

Calories	198
Fat, total	14 g
Fat, saturated	6 g
Cholesterol	25 mg
Sodium	400 mg
Carbohydrate	18 g
Fiber	2 g
Protein	3 g
Calcium	165 mg
Iron	1 mg

■ **Preheat oven to 350°F (180°C)**
■ **Baking sheet, lightly greased**

1/3 cup	buckwheat flour	75 mL
1/4 cup	hazelnut flour	60 mL
2 tbsp	tapioca starch	30 mL
2 tbsp	granulated sugar	30 mL
1 tbsp	GF baking powder	15 mL
1 tsp	baking soda	5 mL
1 1/2 tsp	xanthan gum	7 mL
1/4 tsp	salt	1 mL
3 tbsp	cold butter, cut into 1/2-inch (1 cm) cubes	45 mL
3/4 cup	GF sour cream	175 mL
1/4 cup	coarsely chopped hazelnuts	60 mL

Traditional Method

1. In a medium bowl, combine buckwheat flour, hazelnut flour, tapioca starch, sugar, baking powder, baking soda, xanthan gum and salt. Using a pastry blender or two knives, cut in butter until mixture resembles coarse crumbs about the size of small peas. Add sour cream and hazelnuts all at once, stirring with a fork to make a thick dough.

Food Processor Method

1. In a small food processor fitted with a metal blade, combine buckwheat flour, hazelnut flour, tapioca starch, sugar, baking powder, baking soda, xanthan gum and salt; pulse 3 or 4 times to combine. Add butter and pulse for 3 to 5 seconds or until mixture resembles coarse crumbs about the size of small peas. Add sour cream and hazelnuts all at once; process until dough holds together.

Tips

To drop the dough in step 2, spoon it onto a large serving spoon and push it off onto the baking sheet with the back of another.

Biscuits should all be the same size to bake in the same length of time.

For Both Methods

2. Drop dough by large spoonfuls 2 inches (5 cm) apart on prepared baking sheet.

3. Bake in preheated oven for 16 to 18 minutes or until golden on both top and bottom. Serve immediately.

Variation

Substitute plain yogurt for the GF sour cream.

Pumpkin Ginger Biscuits

We enjoy these unique biscuits, which are larger than most, for dessert, along with a fresh pear.

■■■■■■■■■■■■■■

Tips

To drop the dough in step 3, spoon it onto a large serving spoon and push it off onto the baking sheet with the back of another.

Biscuits should all be the same size to bake in the same length of time.

■ **Preheat oven to 400°F (200°C)**
■ **Baking sheet, lightly greased**

½ cup	pumpkin purée (not pie filling)	125 mL
¼ cup	milk	60 mL
1	portion Biscuit Mix (pages 121–122)	1
1 tbsp	granulated sugar	15 mL
1½ tsp	ground ginger	7 mL
¼ cup	cold butter, cut into ½-inch (1 cm) cubes	60 mL

1. In a measuring cup or small bowl, combine pumpkin purée and milk; set aside.

2. In a medium bowl, combine biscuit mix, sugar and ginger. Using a pastry blender or two knives, cut in butter until mixture resembles coarse crumbs about the size of small peas. Add pumpkin mixture all at once, stirring with a fork to make a soft, slightly sticky dough.

3. Drop dough by heaping spoonfuls 2 inches (5 cm) apart on prepared baking sheet.

4. Bake in preheated oven for 15 to 18 minutes or until golden on both top and bottom. Serve immediately.

Variations

Substitute 2 tbsp (30 mL) diced crystallized ginger for the ground ginger.

Make 6 smaller biscuits and bake for 13 to 16 minutes.

Nutritional value per serving	
Calories	232
Fat, total	13 g
Fat, saturated	7 g
Cholesterol	32 mg
Sodium	247 mg
Carbohydrate	30 g
Fiber	2 g
Protein	3 g
Calcium	199 mg
Iron	1 mg

Quick Breads and Muffins

▪▪

Baking Tips for Quick Breads and Muffins

- The batters should be the same consistency as wheat flour batters, but you can mix them more without producing tough products, full of tunnels.

- Use a portion scoop to quickly divide the batter into prepared muffin cups to ensure muffins are equal in size and bake in the same length of time.

- If you don't have a 6-cup muffin pan, use a 12-cup pan and fill the empty cups one-quarter full with water before baking. Be careful when removing the pan from the oven, as the water will be very hot.

- Bake in muffin pans of a different size. Mini muffins take 12 to 15 minutes to bake, while jumbo muffins bake in 20 to 40 minutes. Check jumbo muffins for doneness after 20 minutes, then again every 5 to 10 minutes. Keep in mind that the baking time will vary with the amount of batter in each muffin cup.

- Fill muffin pans and loaf pans no more than three-quarters full.

- Let batter-filled pans stand for 30 minutes for a more tender product. It's worth the wait. We set a timer for 20 minutes, then preheat the oven so both the oven and the batter are ready at the same time.

- If muffins stick to the lightly greased pans, let stand for a minute or two and try again. Loosen with a spatula, if necessary.

- Muffins can be reheated in the microwave, wrapped in a paper towel, for a few seconds on Medium (50%) power.

- To freeze, place individual muffins or loaf slices in small freezer bags, then place them all in a large freezer bag. Freeze for up to 1 month.

Working with Muffin Mix

- If making one of the larger mix sizes, stir the mix before spooning very lightly into the dry measures when dividing into portions. Do not pack or shake the measures.

- Be sure to divide the mix into equal portions before using to make up an individual recipe. Depending on how much air you incorporate into the mix and the texture of the individual gluten-free flours, the total volume of the mix can vary slightly. The important thing is to make the number of portions the recipe states.

- Label and date packages before storing. We add the page number of the recipe to the label as a quick reference. Store at room temperature for up to 3 days or in the freezer for up to 6 months.

- Let mix warm to room temperature and mix well before using.

Classic Banana Bread

This classic recipe almost missed inclusion in this book — how could we forget it?

■■■■■■■■■■■■■■■

Tips

You'll need about 2 very ripe medium bananas for ¾ cup (175 mL) mashed. Do not add extra.

This is a very dark loaf, and will appear baked before it is, so it is important to take the internal temperature.

Nutritional value per serving

Calories	183
Fat, total	6 g
Fat, saturated	1 g
Cholesterol	36 mg
Sodium	213 mg
Carbohydrate	30 g
Fiber	2 g
Protein	5 g
Calcium	91 mg
Iron	2 mg

■ 5¾- by 3¼-inch (14 by 8 cm) mini loaf pan, lightly greased

¾ cup	mashed bananas	175 mL
2 tbsp	milk	30 mL
½ tsp	cider vinegar	2 mL
½ cup	sorghum flour	125 mL
⅓ cup	low-fat soy flour	75 mL
2 tbsp	tapioca starch	30 mL
¼ cup	packed brown sugar	60 mL
1½ tsp	GF baking powder	7 mL
½ tsp	baking soda	2 mL
1 tsp	xanthan gum	5 mL
¼ tsp	salt	1 mL
1	large egg yolk	1
2 tbsp	vegetable oil	30 mL

1. In a large bowl, combine bananas, milk and vinegar. Let stand for 5 minutes.

2. In a bowl or plastic bag, combine sorghum flour, soy flour, tapioca starch, brown sugar, baking powder, baking soda, xanthan gum and salt. Mix well and set aside.

3. Add egg yolk and oil to banana mixture and, using an electric mixer, beat until combined. Add dry ingredients and mix just until combined.

4. Spoon batter into prepared pan. Let stand for 30 minutes. Meanwhile, preheat oven to 350°F (180°C).

5. Bake for 20 minutes. Check to see if loaf is getting too dark and tent with foil if necessary. Bake for 15 to 20 minutes or until internal temperature of loaf registers 200°F (100°C) on an instant-read thermometer. Let cool in pan on a rack for 5 minutes. Remove from pan and let cool completely on rack.

Variation

Stir in ⅓ cup (75 mL) chopped walnuts or pecans at the end of step 3.

Date Cashew Loaf

This dark loaf will satisfy your need for something slightly sweet and crunchy. We love cashews!

Tips

Instead of chopping with a knife, snip dates with kitchen shears. Dip the blades in hot water when they become sticky.

This is a very dark loaf, and will appear baked before it is, so it is important to take the internal temperature.

Nutritional value per serving

Calories	261
Fat, total	11 g
Fat, saturated	2 g
Cholesterol	35 mg
Sodium	212 mg
Carbohydrate	38 g
Fiber	4 g
Protein	5 g
Calcium	95 mg
Iron	2 mg

■ 5³/₄- by 3¹/₄-inch (14 by 8 cm) mini loaf pan, lightly greased

²/₃ cup	coarsely snipped dates	150 mL
¹/₂ cup	boiling water	125 mL
¹/₂ cup	teff flour	125 mL
¹/₄ cup	brown rice flour	60 mL
2 tbsp	tapioca starch	30 mL
2 tbsp	packed brown sugar	30 mL
1¹/₂ tsp	GF baking powder	7 mL
¹/₂ tsp	baking soda	2 mL
1 tsp	xanthan gum	5 mL
¹/₄ tsp	salt	1 mL
1	large egg yolk	1
2 tbsp	vegetable oil	30 mL
¹/₂ cup	cashews	125 mL

1. In a large bowl, combine dates and boiling water. Let stand for 5 minutes.

2. In a bowl or plastic bag, combine teff flour, brown rice flour, tapioca starch, brown sugar, baking powder, baking soda, xanthan gum and salt. Mix well and set aside.

3. Add egg yolk and oil to date mixture and, using an electric mixer, beat until combined. Add dry ingredients and mix just until combined. Stir in cashews.

4. Spoon batter into prepared pan. Let stand for 30 minutes. Meanwhile, preheat oven to 350°F (180°C).

5. Bake for 25 minutes. Check to see if loaf is getting too dark and tent with foil if necessary. Bake for 11 to 15 minutes or until internal temperature of loaf registers 200°F (100°C) on an instant-read thermometer. Let cool in pan on a rack for 5 minutes. Remove from pan and let cool completely on rack.

Variation

Substitute macadamia nuts for the cashews.

Oatmeal Muffin Mix for 6 Muffins

Makes 1½ cups (375 mL), enough for 6 muffins
Serving size: ¼ cup (60 mL)

Two of our earlier cookbooks included muffin mix recipes. Since then, we have often been asked for an oatmeal muffin mix. Here you go — we know you will enjoy it. Be sure to check with your physician before introducing GF oats into your diet.

■■■■■■■■■■■■■■■■

Tips
See page 132 for tips on working with muffin mix.

Try this single-batch recipe before moving on to the larger batches on pages 136 to 138.

Nutritional value per serving	
Calories	111
Fat, total	1 g
Fat, saturated	0 g
Cholesterol	0 mg
Sodium	206 mg
Carbohydrate	23 g
Fiber	3 g
Protein	3 g
Calcium	84 mg
Iron	2 mg

⅔ cup	sorghum flour	150 mL
¼ cup	GF oat flour	60 mL
¼ cup	GF large-flake (old-fashioned) rolled oats	60 mL
1 tbsp	GF oat bran	15 mL
2 tbsp	tapioca starch	30 mL
2 tsp	GF baking powder	10 mL
½ tsp	baking soda	2 mL
1 tsp	xanthan gum	5 mL
¼ tsp	salt	1 mL

1. In a bowl or plastic bag, combine sorghum flour, oat flour, oats, oat bran, tapioca starch, baking powder, baking soda, xanthan gum and salt. Mix well.

2. Seal tightly in a plastic bag, removing as much air as possible. Store at room temperature for up to 3 days or in the freezer for up to 6 months.

Oatmeal Muffin Mix
for 12 Muffins

This double batch of our oatmeal muffin mix is twice as nice! Be sure to check with your physician before introducing GF oats into your diet.

■■■■■■■■■■■■■■■

Tips

See page 132 for tips on working with muffin mix.

If you don't have a 2-tsp (10 mL) measuring spoon, the most accurate way to measure 4 tsp (20 mL) is to use a 1-tbsp (15 mL) measuring spoon plus a 1-tsp (5 mL) measuring spoon.

Stir the mix before spooning very lightly into the dry measures. Do not pack.

Nutritional value per serving	
Calories	108
Fat, total	1 g
Fat, saturated	0 g
Cholesterol	0 mg
Sodium	205 mg
Carbohydrate	22 g
Fiber	2 g
Protein	3 g
Calcium	84 mg
Iron	2 mg

1⅓ cups	sorghum flour	325 mL
½ cup	GF oat flour	125 mL
½ cup	GF large-flake (old-fashioned) rolled oats	125 mL
2 tbsp	GF oat bran	30 mL
¼ cup	tapioca starch	60 mL
4 tsp	GF baking powder	20 mL
1 tsp	baking soda	5 mL
2 tsp	xanthan gum	10 mL
½ tsp	salt	2 mL

1. In a large bowl or plastic bag, combine sorghum flour, oat flour, oats, oat bran, tapioca starch, baking powder, baking soda, xanthan gum and salt. Mix well.

2. Immediately divide into 2 equal portions of about 1½ cups (375 mL) each. Seal tightly in plastic bags, removing as much air as possible. Store at room temperature for up to 3 days or in the freezer for up to 6 months.

Oatmeal Muffin Mix for 24 Muffins

Makes 6 cups (1.5 L), enough for 24 muffins
Serving size: $1/4$ cup (60 mL)

We like to make up larger amounts of muffin mix so we always have it on hand when we want to bake fresh muffins for breakfast. Be sure to check with your physician before introducing GF oats into your diet.

■■■■■■■■■■■■■■■

Tips

See page 132 for tips on working with muffin mix.

Stir the mix before spooning very lightly into the dry measures. Do not pack.

$2^2/3$ cups	sorghum flour	650 mL
1 cup	GF oat flour	250 mL
1 cup	GF large-flake (old-fashioned) rolled oats	250 mL
$1/2$ cup	GF oat bran	125 mL
$1/2$ cup	tapioca starch	125 mL
3 tbsp	GF baking powder	45 mL
2 tsp	baking soda	10 mL
4 tsp	xanthan gum	20 mL
1 tsp	salt	5 mL

1. In a large bowl or plastic bag, combine sorghum flour, oat flour, oats, oat bran, tapioca starch, baking powder, baking soda, xanthan gum and salt. Mix well.

2. Immediately divide into 4 equal portions of about $1^1/2$ cups (375 mL) each. Seal tightly in plastic bags, removing as much air as possible. Store at room temperature for up to 3 days or in the freezer for up to 6 months.

Nutritional value per serving	
Calories	114
Fat, total	1 g
Fat, saturated	0 g
Cholesterol	0 mg
Sodium	205 mg
Carbohydrate	23 g
Fiber	3 g
Protein	3 g
Calcium	94 mg
Iron	2 mg

Oatmeal Muffin Mix for 36 Muffins

Makes 9 cups (2.25 L), enough for 36 muffins
Serving size: ¼ cup (60 mL)

You asked us for a large mix to make up for a family reunion. Here is one you can make all at once or use in small amounts. Be sure to check with your physician before introducing GF oats into your diet.

■■■■■■■■■■■■■■■

Tips

See page 132 for tips on working with muffin mix.

Stir the mix before spooning very lightly into the dry measures. Do not pack.

4 cups	sorghum flour	1 L
1½ cups	GF oat flour	375 mL
1½ cups	GF large-flake (old-fashioned) rolled oats	375 mL
¾ cup	GF oat bran	175 mL
¾ cup	tapioca starch	175 mL
¼ cup	GF baking powder	60 mL
1 tbsp	baking soda	15 mL
2 tbsp	xanthan gum	30 mL
1½ tsp	salt	7 mL

1. In a large bowl or plastic bag, combine sorghum flour, oat flour, oats, oat bran, tapioca starch, baking powder, baking soda, xanthan gum and salt. Mix well.

2. Immediately divide into 6 equal portions of about 1½ cups (375 mL) each. Seal tightly in plastic bags, removing as much air as possible. Store at room temperature for up to 3 days or in the freezer for up to 6 months.

Nutritional value per serving	
Calories	113
Fat, total	1 g
Fat, saturated	0 g
Cholesterol	0 mg
Sodium	205 mg
Carbohydrate	23 g
Fiber	3 g
Protein	3 g
Calcium	85 mg
Iron	2 mg

Triple Oat Muffins

Don't want your sweet oatmeal muffin cluttered with other flavors or textures? You'll love this one!

■■■■■■■■■■■■■■■

Tips

See the baking tips on page 132 before trying this recipe.

To make a dozen muffins, double all ingredients.

If you prefer a sweeter muffin, increase the brown sugar to $1/3$ cup (75 mL).

■ **6-cup muffin pan, lightly greased**

$1/4$ cup	packed brown sugar	60 mL
1	large egg	1
$1/2$ cup	milk	125 mL
3 tbsp	vegetable oil	45 mL
1 tsp	freshly squeezed lemon juice	5 mL
1	portion Oatmeal Muffin Mix (pages 135–138)	1

1. In a bowl, using an electric mixer, beat brown sugar, egg, milk, oil and lemon juice until combined. Add muffin mix and mix just until combined.

2. Spoon batter into prepared muffin cups, dividing evenly. Let stand for 30 minutes. Meanwhile, preheat oven to 350°F (180°C).

3. Bake for 18 to 20 minutes or until firm to the touch. Remove from the pan immediately and let cool completely on a rack.

Variation

Add $1/2$ tsp (2 mL) of any sweet spice, such as ground ginger, cinnamon, nutmeg or allspice, and $1/2$ cup (125 mL) raisins, dried currants, coarsely chopped nuts or unsweetened shredded coconut with the muffin mix.

Nutritional value per serving	
Calories	226
Fat, total	9 g
Fat, saturated	1 g
Cholesterol	32 mg
Sodium	229 mg
Carbohydrate	33 g
Fiber	3 g
Protein	5 g
Calcium	121 mg
Iron	2 mg

Banana Oatmeal Muffins

**Speckled as bananas
should be, these
muffins are wonderful
for breakfast, a snack
or dessert.**

▪▪▪▪▪▪▪▪▪▪▪▪▪▪▪

Tips

See the baking tips on page 132 before trying this recipe.

If you prefer a sweeter muffin, increase the sugar to ¼ cup (60 mL).

Freeze individually in small freezer bags for carried lunches for the whole family.

▪ **6-cup muffin pan, lightly greased**

3 tbsp	granulated sugar	45 mL
1	large egg	1
1¼ cups	mashed bananas	300 mL
3 tbsp	vegetable oil	45 mL
1 tsp	cider vinegar	5 mL
1	portion Oatmeal Muffin Mix (pages 135–138)	1
2 tsp	ground nutmeg	10 mL

1. In a bowl, using an electric mixer, beat sugar, egg, bananas, oil and vinegar until combined. Add muffin mix and nutmeg; mix just until combined.

2. Spoon batter into prepared muffin cups, dividing evenly. Let stand for 30 minutes. Meanwhile, preheat oven to 350°F (180°C).

3. Bake for 22 to 25 minutes or until firm to the touch. Remove from the pan immediately and let cool completely on a rack.

Variation

Add ½ cup (125 mL) coarsely chopped nuts or raisins with the muffin mix.

Nutritional value per serving	
Calories	190
Fat, total	7 g
Fat, saturated	1 g
Cholesterol	3 mg
Sodium	162 mg
Carbohydrate	30 g
Fiber	3 g
Protein	4 g
Calcium	69 mg
Iron	2 mg

Blueberry Oat Muffins

Even your doctor would recommend that you enjoy these nutritious muffins!

■■■■■■■■■■■■■■■

Tips

See the baking tips on page 132 before trying this recipe.

We defrosted small frozen blueberries in a single layer on a microwave-safe plate in the microwave for 45 seconds on High. For large blueberries, double the microwave time and check for partially thawed (berries are not warm to the touch and still hold their shape).

If you prefer a sweeter muffin, increase the brown sugar to 1/4 cup (60 mL).

Nutritional value per serving	
Calories	229
Fat, total	9 g
Fat, saturated	1 g
Cholesterol	31 mg
Sodium	218 mg
Carbohydrate	34 g
Fiber	4 g
Protein	4 g
Calcium	99 mg
Iron	2 mg

■ **6-cup muffin pan, lightly greased**

3 tbsp	packed brown sugar	45 mL
2 tsp	grated orange zest	10 mL
1	large egg	1
1/2 cup	freshly squeezed orange juice	125 mL
3 tbsp	vegetable oil	45 mL
1 tsp	cider vinegar	5 mL
1	portion Oatmeal Muffin Mix (pages 135–138)	1
1/2 tsp	ground mace	2 mL
3/4 cup	fresh or partially thawed frozen blueberries	175 mL

1. In a bowl, using an electric mixer, beat brown sugar, orange zest, egg, orange juice, oil and vinegar until combined. Add muffin mix and mace; mix just until combined. Stir in blueberries.

2. Spoon batter into prepared muffin cups, dividing evenly. Let stand for 30 minutes. Meanwhile, preheat oven to 350°F (180°C).

3. Bake for 20 to 23 minutes or until firm to the touch. Remove from the pan immediately and let cool completely on a rack.

Variations

Substitute cranberries for the blueberries.

For a stronger flavor, substitute ground cardamom for the mace.

Oatmeal Date Muffins

Makes 6 muffins
Serving size: 1 muffin

Donna's all-time favorite
muffins, these stay moist
for days!

■■■■■■■■■■■■■■

Tips

See the baking tips on
page 132 before trying this
recipe.

Instead of chopping with
a knife, snip dates with
kitchen shears. Dip the
blades in hot water when
they become sticky.

If you prefer a sweeter
muffin, increase the brown
sugar to ¼ cup (60 mL).

■ **6-cup muffin pan, lightly greased**

⅔ cup	coarsely snipped dates	150 mL
⅓ cup	boiling water	75 mL
3 tbsp	packed brown sugar	45 mL
1 tbsp	grated orange zest	15 mL
1	large egg	1
¼ cup	freshly squeezed orange juice	60 mL
3 tbsp	vegetable oil	45 mL
1	portion Oatmeal Muffin Mix (pages 135–138)	1

1. In a small bowl, combine dates and boiling water. Let cool to room temperature.

2. In a bowl, using an electric mixer, beat brown sugar, orange zest, egg, orange juice and oil until combined. Stir in date mixture. Add muffin mix and mix just until combined.

3. Spoon batter into prepared muffin cups, dividing evenly. Let stand for 30 minutes. Meanwhile, preheat oven to 350°F (180°C).

4. Bake for 20 to 23 minutes or until firm to the touch. Remove from the pan immediately and let cool completely on a rack.

Variation

Substitute dried figs for the dates.

Nutritional value per serving	
Calories	268
Fat, total	9 g
Fat, saturated	1 g
Cholesterol	31 mg
Sodium	218 mg
Carbohydrate	45 g
Fiber	5 g
Protein	5 g
Calcium	103 mg
Iron	2 mg

Chocolate Banana Oatmeal Muffins

Makes 6 muffins
Serving size: 1 muffin

These muffins are so delightfully rich, they make a wonderful dessert.

■■■■■■■■■■■■■■■■

Tips

See the baking tips on page 132 before trying this recipe.

Be sure to take the time to sift the cocoa powder, as it lumps easily. Sift right before measuring.

If you prefer a sweeter muffin, increase the sugar to ¼ cup (60 mL).

■ **6-cup muffin pan, lightly greased**

1	portion Oatmeal Muffin Mix (pages 135–138)	1
2 tbsp	sifted unsweetened cocoa powder	30 mL
3 tbsp	granulated sugar	45 mL
1	large egg	1
1 cup	mashed bananas	250 mL
3 tbsp	vegetable oil	45 mL
1 tsp	cider vinegar	5 mL

1. In a bowl, combine muffin mix and cocoa. Mix well and set aside.

2. In a separate bowl, using an electric mixer, beat sugar, egg, bananas, oil and vinegar until combined. Add dry ingredients and mix just until combined.

3. Spoon batter into prepared muffin cups, dividing evenly. Let stand for 30 minutes. Meanwhile, preheat oven to 350°F (180°C).

4. Bake for 20 to 23 minutes or until firm to the touch. Remove from the pan immediately and let cool completely on a rack.

Variation

For a stronger chocolate flavor, stir in ½ cup (125 mL) semisweet chocolate chips with the dry ingredients.

Nutritional value per serving	
Calories	245
Fat, total	9 g
Fat, saturated	1 g
Cholesterol	31 mg
Sodium	216 mg
Carbohydrate	39 g
Fiber	5 g
Protein	5 g
Calcium	93 mg
Iron	2 mg

Oatmeal Chocolate Chip Muffins

You'll notice how the sour cream softens the texture of these muffins.

■■■■■■■■■■■■■■■

Tips

See the baking tips on page 132 before trying this recipe.

You can use any size of chocolate chip, from minis to chunks.

If you prefer a sweeter muffin, increase the honey to ¼ cup (60 mL).

■ **6-cup muffin pan, lightly greased**

1	large egg	1
⅔ cup	GF sour cream	150 mL
3 tbsp	vegetable oil	45 mL
3 tbsp	liquid honey	45 mL
1	portion Oatmeal Muffin Mix (pages 135–138)	1
½ cup	semisweet chocolate chips	125 mL

1. In a bowl, using an electric mixer, beat egg, sour cream, oil and honey until combined. Add muffin mix and chocolate chips; mix just until combined.

2. Spoon batter into prepared muffin cups, dividing evenly. Let stand for 30 minutes. Meanwhile, preheat oven to 350°F (180°C).

3. Bake for 20 to 23 minutes or until firm to the touch. Remove from the pan immediately and let cool completely on a rack.

Variation

Substitute plain yogurt for the GF sour cream.

Nutritional value per serving	
Calories	321
Fat, total	17 g
Fat, saturated	6 g
Cholesterol	41 mg
Sodium	228 mg
Carbohydrate	41 g
Fiber	4 g
Protein	6 g
Calcium	120 mg
Iron	2 mg

Carrot Oatmeal Muffins

These golden muffins are speckled with moist orange strands of carrot.

■■■■■■■■■■■■■■

Tips

See the baking tips on page 132 before trying this recipe.

Don't grate the carrots too far ahead, as they can darken. You can, however, grate extra and freeze in a freezer bag for up to 1 month.

If you prefer a sweeter muffin, increase the honey to 3 tbsp (45 mL).

■ **6-cup muffin pan, lightly greased**

2 tsp	grated orange zest	10 mL
1	large egg	1
1/2 cup	freshly squeezed orange juice	125 mL
3 tbsp	vegetable oil	45 mL
2 tbsp	liquid honey	30 mL
1 tbsp	light (fancy) molasses	15 mL
1	portion Oatmeal Muffin Mix (pages 135–138)	1
2/3 cup	shredded carrots	150 mL

1. In a bowl, using an electric mixer, beat orange zest, egg, orange juice, oil, honey and molasses until combined. Add muffin mix and carrots; mix just until combined.

2. Spoon batter into prepared muffin cups, dividing evenly. Let stand for 30 minutes. Meanwhile, preheat oven to 350°F (180°C).

3. Bake for 20 to 23 minutes or until firm to the touch. Remove from the pan immediately and let cool completely on a rack.

Variation

Add 1/2 cup (125 mL) raisins or coarsely chopped pecans with the muffin mix.

Nutritional value per serving	
Calories	228
Fat, total	9 g
Fat, saturated	1 g
Cholesterol	31 mg
Sodium	221 mg
Carbohydrate	34 g
Fiber	4 g
Protein	5 g
Calcium	102 mg
Iron	2 mg

Cornmeal Muffin Mix
for 6 Muffins

Makes 1¼ cups (300 mL), enough for 6 muffins
Serving size: 3 tbsp (45 mL)

Try this recipe first, to be sure the sweetness and flavor is what you want. Then make the larger batch below to have on hand when you are in a hurry.

■■■■■■■■■■■■■■■■

Tip
See page 132 for tips on working with muffin mix.

½ cup	teff flour	125 mL
½ cup	cornmeal	125 mL
2 tbsp	cornstarch	30 mL
2 tsp	GF baking powder	10 mL
½ tsp	baking soda	2 mL
1 tsp	xanthan gum	5 mL
¼ tsp	salt	1 mL

1. In a bowl or plastic bag, combine teff flour, cornmeal, cornstarch, baking powder, baking soda, xanthan gum and salt. Mix well.

2. Seal tightly in a plastic bag, removing as much air as possible. Store at room temperature for up to 3 days or in the freezer for up to 6 months.

Nutritional value per serving			
Calories	93	Carbohydrate	20 g
Fat, total	1 g	Fiber	2 g
Fat, saturated	0 g	Protein	2 g
Cholesterol	0 mg	Calcium	94 mg
Sodium	207 mg	Iron	1 mg

Cornmeal Muffin Mix
for 24 Muffins

Makes 5 cups (1.25 L), enough for 24 muffins
Serving size: 3 tbsp (45 mL)

We like to make up larger amounts of muffin mix so we always have it on hand when we want to bake fresh muffins.

■■■■■■■■■■■■■■■■

2 cups	teff flour	500 mL
2 cups	cornmeal	500 mL
½ cup	cornstarch	125 mL
3 tbsp	GF baking powder	45 mL
2 tsp	baking soda	10 mL
1 tbsp	xanthan gum	15 mL
1 tsp	salt	5 mL

1. In a large bowl or plastic bag, combine teff flour, cornmeal, cornstarch, baking powder, baking soda, xanthan gum and salt. Mix well.

2. Immediately divide into 4 equal portions of about 1¼ cups (300 mL) each. Seal tightly in plastic bags, removing as much air as possible. Store at room temperature for up to 3 days or in the freezer for up to 6 months.

Cornmeal Muffins

Serve these rich, dark muffins warm right out of the oven with chili or soup for a cold winter's lunch or light supper.

■■■■■■■■■■■■■■■

Tips

See the baking tips on page 132 before trying this recipe.

To make a dozen muffins, double all ingredients.

■ **6-cup muffin pan, lightly greased**

½ cup	milk	125 mL
1 tsp	freshly squeezed lemon juice	5 mL
3 tbsp	granulated sugar	45 mL
1	large egg	1
3 tbsp	vegetable oil	45 mL
1	portion Cornmeal Muffin Mix (page 146)	1

1. In a small bowl or measuring cup, combine milk and lemon juice; let stand for 5 minutes.

2. In a bowl, using an electric mixer, beat milk mixture, sugar, egg and oil until combined. Add muffin mix and mix just until combined.

3. Spoon batter into prepared muffin cups, dividing evenly. Let stand for 30 minutes. Meanwhile, preheat oven to 350°F (180°C).

4. Bake for 18 to 20 minutes or until firm to the touch. Remove from the pan immediately and let cool completely on a rack.

Variation

Stir ¼ cup (60 mL) chopped red bell pepper into the batter at the end of step 2.

Nutritional value per serving	
Calories	197
Fat, total	8 g
Fat, saturated	1 g
Cholesterol	32 mg
Sodium	226 mg
Carbohydrate	27 g
Fiber	2 g
Protein	4 g
Calcium	122 mg
Iron	1 mg

Cranberry Cornmeal Muffins

These cornmeal muffins contain a delightful surprise: a tangy burst of flavor when you bite into a cranberry.

Tips

See the baking tips on page 132 before trying this recipe.

Measure any oil in the recipe before any sticky ingredients, such as molasses or honey. This greases the measuring spoon, allowing the sticky ingredient to slide right out.

If using thawed frozen cranberries, make sure to drain them well before adding them to the batter.

To make a dozen muffins, double all ingredients.

■ **6-cup muffin pan, lightly greased**

1	large egg	1
1 tbsp	grated orange zest	15 mL
1/2 cup	freshly squeezed orange juice	125 mL
3 tbsp	vegetable oil	45 mL
1/4 cup	liquid honey	60 mL
1	portion Cornmeal Muffin Mix (page 146)	1
3/4 cup	fresh or thawed frozen cranberries	175 mL

1. In a bowl, using an electric mixer, beat egg, orange zest, orange juice, oil and honey until combined. Add muffin mix and mix just until combined. Stir in cranberries.

2. Spoon batter into prepared muffin cups, dividing evenly. Let stand for 30 minutes. Meanwhile, preheat oven to 350°F (180°C).

3. Bake for 18 to 20 minutes or until firm to the touch. Remove from the pan immediately and let cool completely on a rack.

Nutritional value per serving	
Calories	223
Fat, total	8 g
Fat, saturated	1 g
Cholesterol	31mg
Sodium	217 mg
Carbohydrate	36 g
Fiber	3 g
Protein	4 g
Calcium	103 mg
Iron	1 mg

Asiago, Sage and Cornmeal Muffins

Hot, spicy and cheesy, these muffins are wonderful as part of a carried lunch.

■■■■■■■■■■■■■■■

Tips

See the baking tips on page 132 before trying this recipe.

To make a dozen muffins, double all ingredients.

For Asiago cheese weight/ volume equivalents, see the Ingredient Glossary, page 301.

If you don't have buttermilk on hand, substitute ²⁄₃ cup (150 mL) water and add ¼ cup (60 mL) buttermilk powder to the dry ingredients.

Nutritional value per serving	
Calories	211
Fat, total	11 g
Fat, saturated	3 g
Cholesterol	7 mg
Sodium	268 mg
Carbohydrate	22 g
Fiber	3 g
Protein	7 g
Calcium	221 mg
Iron	1 mg

■ **6-cup muffin pan, lightly greased**

1	portion Cornmeal Muffin Mix (page 146)	1
½ cup	shredded Asiago cheese	125 mL
2 tsp	dried rubbed sage	10 mL
½ tsp	coarsely ground black pepper	2 mL
Pinch	cayenne pepper	Pinch
1	large egg	1
²⁄₃ cup	buttermilk	150 mL
3 tbsp	vegetable oil	45 mL

1. In a bowl or plastic bag, combine muffin mix, cheese, sage, black pepper and cayenne. Mix well and set aside.

2. In a separate bowl, using an electric mixer, beat egg, buttermilk and oil until combined. Add dry ingredients and mix just until combined.

3. Spoon batter into prepared muffin cups, dividing evenly. Let stand for 30 minutes. Meanwhile, preheat oven to 350°F (180°C).

4. Bake for 18 to 20 minutes or until firm to the touch. Remove from the pan immediately and let cool completely on a rack.

Variation

Substitute any tangy cheese, such as provolone or Swiss, for the Asiago.

Corn and Ham Muffins

Specks of yellow, green and pink add interest to these muffins. Enjoy one for lunch!

■■■■■■■■■■■■■■■

Tips

See the baking tips on page 132 before trying this recipe.

To make a dozen muffins, double all ingredients.

If you prefer, you can use cooked fresh or thawed frozen corn kernels.

■ **6-cup muffin pan, lightly greased**

1	large egg	1
½ cup	milk	125 mL
3 tbsp	vegetable oil	45 mL
3 tbsp	liquid honey	45 mL
1	portion Cornmeal Muffin Mix (page 146)	1
3 oz	GF ham, diced	90 g
⅓ cup	well-drained canned corn kernels	75 mL
¼ cup	snipped fresh parsley	60 mL
1 tbsp	dried tarragon	15 mL

1. In a bowl, using an electric mixer, beat egg, milk, oil and honey until combined. Add muffin mix and mix just until combined. Stir in ham, corn, parsley and tarragon.

2. Spoon batter into prepared muffin cups, dividing evenly. Let stand for 30 minutes. Meanwhile, preheat oven to 350°F (180°C).

3. Bake for 18 to 20 minutes or until firm to the touch. Remove from the pan immediately and let cool completely on a rack.

Variation

Substitute 2 to 3 slices of GF bacon, cooked crisp and crumbled, for the ham.

Nutritional value per serving	
Calories	234
Fat, total	9 g
Fat, saturated	1 g
Cholesterol	39 mg
Sodium	386 mg
Carbohydrate	32 g
Fiber	3 g
Protein	7 g
Calcium	137 mg
Iron	2 mg

Cheddar Beer Cornmeal Muffins

We love the flavor combination of Cheddar and beer, and we love cornmeal muffins, so how could we resist putting them all together? The results are divine!

■■■■■■■■■■■■■■■■

Tips

See the baking tips on page 132 before trying this recipe.

To make a dozen muffins, double all ingredients.

If GF beer is not available in your area, substitute an equal quantity of buttermilk.

For Cheddar cheese weight/ volume equivalents, see the Ingredient Glossary, page 302.

Nutritional value per serving	
Calories	211
Fat, total	11 g
Fat, saturated	3 g
Cholesterol	41 mg
Sodium	275 mg
Carbohydrate	21 g
Fiber	2 g
Protein	6 g
Calcium	166 mg
Iron	1 mg

■ **6-cup muffin pan, lightly greased**

1	portion Cornmeal Muffin Mix (page 146)	1
1/2 cup	shredded sharp (old) Cheddar cheese	125 mL
1/4 tsp	dry mustard	1 mL
Pinch	cayenne pepper	Pinch
1	large egg	1
1/2 cup	GF beer	125 mL
3 tbsp	vegetable oil	45 mL

1. In a bowl or plastic bag, combine muffin mix, cheese, mustard and cayenne. Mix well and set aside.

2. In a separate bowl, using an electric mixer, beat egg, beer and oil until combined. Add dry ingredients and mix just until combined.

3. Spoon batter into prepared muffin cups, dividing evenly. Let stand for 30 minutes. Meanwhile, preheat oven to 350°F (180°C).

4. Bake for 18 to 20 minutes or until firm to the touch. Remove from the pan immediately and let cool completely on a rack.

Variation

Substitute any tangy cheese, such as crumbled GF blue cheese or freshly grated Parmesan, for the Cheddar.

Carrot Cornmeal Muffins

Makes 6 muffins
Serving size: 1 muffin

Carrots lend moistness and added nutrition to these cornmeal muffins.

■■■■■■■■■■■■■■

Tips

See the baking tips on page 132 before trying this recipe.

To make a dozen muffins, double all ingredients.

■ **6-cup muffin pan, lightly greased**

1	portion Cornmeal Muffin Mix (page 146)	1
1 tsp	dried thyme	5 mL
1	large egg	1
1 tbsp	grated orange zest	15 mL
½ cup	freshly squeezed orange juice	125 mL
3 tbsp	vegetable oil	45 mL
3 tbsp	light (fancy) molasses	45 mL
1 tbsp	liquid honey	15 mL
⅔ cup	shredded carrots	150 mL

1. In a bowl or plastic bag, combine muffin mix and thyme. Mix well and set aside.

2. In a separate bowl, using an electric mixer, beat egg, orange zest, orange juice, oil, molasses and honey until combined. Add dry ingredients and mix just until combined. Stir in carrots.

3. Spoon batter into prepared muffin cups, dividing evenly. Let stand for 30 minutes. Meanwhile, preheat oven to 350°F (180°C).

4. Bake for 18 to 20 minutes or until firm to the touch. Remove from the pan immediately and let cool completely on a rack.

Variations

Substitute dried rosemary for the thyme. Or use 1 tbsp (15 mL) snipped fresh rosemary.

Add ½ cup (125 mL) raisins with the muffin mix.

Nutritional value per serving	
Calories	219
Fat, total	8 g
Fat, saturated	1 g
Cholesterol	31 mg
Sodium	225 mg
Carbohydrate	34 g
Fiber	3 g
Protein	4 g
Calcium	130 mg
Iron	2 mg

Figgy Bran Muffins

Makes 6 muffins
Serving size: 1 muffin

For a quick breakfast, enjoy a rich, dark bran muffin with a piece of fresh fruit and a wedge of cheese.

■ ■ ■ ■ ■ ■ ■ ■ ■ ■ ■ ■ ■ ■ ■

Tips

See the baking tips on page 132 before trying this recipe.

If you only have a 12-cup muffin pan, fill the empty cups one-quarter full with water before baking.

■ **6-cup muffin pan, lightly greased**

1/2 cup	sorghum flour	125 mL
1/3 cup	whole bean flour	75 mL
2 tbsp	tapioca starch	30 mL
2 tbsp	rice bran	30 mL
2 tsp	GF baking powder	10 mL
1/2 tsp	baking soda	2 mL
1 tsp	xanthan gum	5 mL
1/4 tsp	salt	1 mL
1	large egg	1
3/4 cup	buttermilk	175 mL
2 tbsp	vegetable oil	30 mL
2 tbsp	liquid honey	30 mL
2 tbsp	light (fancy) molasses	30 mL
1/2 cup	chopped dried figs	125 mL

1. In a bowl or plastic bag, combine sorghum flour, whole bean flour, tapioca starch, rice bran, baking powder, baking soda, xanthan gum and salt. Mix well and set aside.

2. In a separate bowl, using an electric mixer, beat egg, buttermilk, oil, honey and molasses until combined. Add dry ingredients and mix just until combined. Stir in figs.

3. Spoon batter into prepared muffin cups, dividing evenly. Let stand for 30 minutes. Meanwhile, preheat oven to 350°F (180°C).

4. Bake for 19 to 22 minutes or until firm to the touch. Remove from the pan immediately and let cool completely on a rack.

Variations

If you can tolerate oats, substitute GF oat bran for the rice bran.

Substitute chopped dates for the figs.

Nutritional value per serving	
Calories	213
Fat, total	7 g
Fat, saturated	1 g
Cholesterol	32 mg
Sodium	251 mg
Carbohydrate	38 g
Fiber	4 g
Protein	5 g
Calcium	159 mg
Iron	2 mg

Honey Applesauce Muffins

These muffins are gluten-free, fat-free, nut-free, soy-free and white sugar–free — but not flavor-free!

■■■■■■■■■■■■■■■

Tips

See the baking tips on page 132 before trying this recipe.

If you only have sweetened applesauce, reduce the honey to 3 tbsp (45 mL).

■ **6-cup muffin pan, lightly greased**

$^{2}/_{3}$ cup	sorghum flour	150 mL
$^{1}/_{3}$ cup	whole bean flour	75 mL
2 tbsp	tapioca starch	30 mL
2 tsp	GF baking powder	10 mL
$^{1}/_{2}$ tsp	baking soda	2 mL
1 tsp	xanthan gum	5 mL
$^{1}/_{4}$ tsp	salt	1 mL
1 tbsp	grated orange zest	15 mL
$1^{1}/_{2}$ tsp	ground ginger	7 mL
2	large egg whites	2
$^{3}/_{4}$ cup	unsweetened applesauce	175 mL
$^{1}/_{4}$ cup	liquid honey	60 mL
2 tbsp	freshly squeezed orange juice	30 mL

1. In a bowl or plastic bag, combine sorghum flour, whole bean flour, tapioca starch, baking powder, baking soda, xanthan gum, salt, orange zest and ginger. Mix well and set aside.

2. In a separate bowl, using an electric mixer, beat egg whites, applesauce, honey and orange juice until combined. Add dry ingredients and mix just until combined.

3. Spoon batter into prepared muffin cups, dividing evenly. Let stand for 30 minutes. Meanwhile, preheat oven to 350°F (180°C).

4. Bake for 18 to 20 minutes or until firm to the touch. Remove from the pan immediately and let cool completely on a rack.

Variation

Substitute ground allspice for the ginger.

Nutritional value per serving	
Calories	142
Fat, total	1 g
Fat, saturated	0 g
Cholesterol	0 mg
Sodium	224 mg
Carbohydrate	33 g
Fiber	2 g
Protein	4 g
Calcium	86 mg
Iron	1 mg

Orange Raisin Muffins

Makes 6 muffins
Serving size: 1 muffin

The sunny goodness of orange combined with the sweetness of raisins makes these muffins memorable.

■■■■■■■■■■■■■■■

Tip

See the baking tips on page 132 before trying this recipe.

■ **6-cup muffin pan, lightly greased**

2/3 cup	amaranth flour	150 mL
1/3 cup	teff flour	75 mL
2 tbsp	tapioca starch	30 mL
2 tsp	GF baking powder	10 mL
1/2 tsp	baking soda	2 mL
1 tsp	xanthan gum	5 mL
1/4 tsp	salt	1 mL
1 tbsp	grated orange zest	15 mL
1	large egg	1
2/3 cup	freshly squeezed orange juice	150 mL
2 tbsp	vegetable oil	30 mL
1/4 cup	liquid honey	60 mL
1/2 cup	raisins	125 mL

1. In a bowl or plastic bag, combine amaranth flour, teff flour, tapioca starch, baking powder, baking soda, xanthan gum, salt and orange zest. Mix well and set aside.

2. In a separate bowl, using an electric mixer, beat egg, orange juice, oil and honey until combined. Add dry ingredients and mix just until combined. Stir in raisins.

3. Spoon batter into prepared muffin cups, dividing evenly. Let stand for 30 minutes. Meanwhile, preheat oven to 350°F (180°C).

4. Bake for 18 to 20 minutes or until firm to the touch. Remove from the pan immediately and let cool completely on a rack.

Variation

Substitute an equal quantity of chopped walnuts or dried currants for the raisins.

Nutritional value per serving	
Calories	235
Fat, total	6 g
Fat, saturated	1 g
Cholesterol	31 mg
Sodium	217 mg
Carbohydrate	42 g
Fiber	3 g
Protein	4 g
Calcium	120 mg
Iron	4 mg

Orange Millet Muffins

Makes 6 muffins
Serving size: 1 muffin

These rich, golden muffins are studded with white dots of crunchy millet seeds. Add the refreshing flavor of orange, and you've got a real taste treat.

■■■■■■■■■■■■■■□

Tips

See the baking tips on page 132 before trying this recipe.

If millet flour is not available, increase the sorghum flour to ¾ cup (175 mL).

■ **6-cup muffin pan, lightly greased**

⅔ cup	sorghum flour	150 mL
⅓ cup	amaranth flour	75 mL
2 tbsp	millet flour	30 mL
2 tbsp	tapioca starch	30 mL
¼ cup	granulated sugar	60 mL
2 tsp	GF baking powder	10 mL
½ tsp	baking soda	2 mL
1 tsp	xanthan gum	5 mL
¼ tsp	salt	1 mL
⅓ cup	millet seeds	75 mL
1 tbsp	grated orange zest	15 mL
1	large egg	1
⅔ cup	freshly squeezed orange juice	150 mL
2 tbsp	vegetable oil	30 mL

1. In a bowl or plastic bag, combine sorghum flour, amaranth flour, millet flour, tapioca starch, sugar, baking powder, baking soda, xanthan gum, salt, millet seeds and orange zest. Mix well and set aside.

2. In a separate bowl, using an electric mixer, beat egg, orange juice and oil until combined. Add dry ingredients and mix just until combined.

3. Spoon batter into prepared muffin cups, dividing evenly. Let stand for 30 minutes. Meanwhile, preheat oven to 350°F (180°C).

4. Bake for 19 to 22 minutes or until firm to the touch. Remove from the pan immediately and let cool completely on a rack.

Variation

Substitute an equal amount of amaranth seeds for the millet seeds.

Nutritional value per serving

Calories	238
Fat, total	7 g
Fat, saturated	1 g
Cholesterol	31 mg
Sodium	215 mg
Carbohydrate	41 g
Fiber	3 g
Protein	5 g
Calcium	95 mg
Iron	3 mg

Rhubarb Pecan Muffins

A celiac we met at a conference asked us for a rhubarb muffin recipe to help her use up the extra rhubarb her garden always produces.

■■■■■■■■■■■■■■■■

Tips

Don't increase the amount of rhubarb in this recipe — the muffins will turn out soggy.

The rhubarb must be finely chopped; otherwise, the finished muffins will be crumbly.

If you use frozen rhubarb instead of fresh, it is easier to chop while still partially frozen. But let it thaw completely, then blot off excess moisture with a paper towel, before adding it to the batter.

Nutritional value per serving	
Calories	265
Fat, total	14 g
Fat, saturated	1 g
Cholesterol	32 mg
Sodium	245 mg
Carbohydrate	33 g
Fiber	3 g
Protein	6 g
Calcium	158 mg
Iron	2 mg

■ **6-cup muffin pan, lightly greased**

¾ cup	finely chopped rhubarb	175 mL
3 tbsp	liquid honey	45 mL
¾ cup	sorghum flour	175 mL
⅓ cup	quinoa flour	75 mL
2 tbsp	tapioca starch	30 mL
2 tsp	GF baking powder	10 mL
½ tsp	baking soda	2 mL
1 tsp	xanthan gum	5 mL
¼ tsp	salt	1 mL
1 tsp	ground ginger	5 mL
1	large egg	1
⅔ cup	buttermilk	150 mL
2 tbsp	vegetable oil	30 mL
½ cup	toasted chopped pecans	125 mL

1. In a small bowl, combine rhubarb and honey. Mix well and let stand for 10 minutes.

2. In a bowl or plastic bag, combine sorghum flour, quinoa flour, tapioca starch, baking powder, baking soda, xanthan gum, salt and ginger. Mix well and set aside.

3. In a separate bowl, using an electric mixer, beat egg, buttermilk and oil until combined. Stir in rhubarb mixture. Add dry ingredients and pecans; mix just until combined.

4. Spoon batter into prepared muffin cups, dividing evenly. Let stand for 30 minutes. Meanwhile, preheat oven to 350°F (180°C).

5. Bake for 19 to 22 minutes or until firm to the touch. Remove from the pan immediately and let cool completely on a rack.

Variation

Substitute ground nutmeg or allspice for the ginger.

Cranberry Pistachio Muffins

These muffins with a rich golden color feature the tartness of cranberries and the nutty flavor of pistachios.

■■■■■■■■■■■■■■

Tip

See the baking tips on page 132 before trying this recipe.

■ 6-cup muffin pan, lightly greased

¾ cup	sorghum flour	175 mL
¼ cup	quinoa flour	60 mL
2 tbsp	tapioca starch	30 mL
¼ cup	granulated sugar	60 mL
2 tsp	GF baking powder	10 mL
½ tsp	baking soda	2 mL
1 tsp	xanthan gum	5 mL
¼ tsp	salt	1 mL
1½ tsp	ground cardamom	7 mL
1	large egg	1
⅔ cup	milk	150 mL
2 tbsp	vegetable oil	30 mL
1 tsp	cider vinegar	5 mL
½ cup	dried cranberries	125 mL
½ cup	shelled unsalted pistachios	125 mL

1. In a bowl or plastic bag, combine sorghum flour, quinoa flour, tapioca starch, sugar, baking powder, baking soda, xanthan gum, salt and cardamom. Mix well and set aside.

2. In a separate bowl, using an electric mixer, beat egg, milk, oil and vinegar until combined. Add dry ingredients and mix just until combined. Stir in cranberries and pistachios.

3. Spoon batter into prepared muffin cups, dividing evenly. Let stand for 30 minutes. Meanwhile, preheat oven to 350°F (180°C).

4. Bake for 18 to 20 minutes or until firm to the touch. Remove from the pan immediately and let cool completely on a rack.

Variations

Coarsely chopped macadamia nuts are the ultimate replacement for the pistachios.

To make this recipe nut-free, you can either double the amount of cranberries or substitute raisins for the pistachios.

Nutritional value per serving	
Calories	281
Fat, total	12 g
Fat, saturated	1 g
Cholesterol	32 mg
Sodium	230 mg
Carbohydrate	40 g
Fiber	4 g
Protein	7 g
Calcium	134 mg
Iron	2 mg

Carrot Raisin Muffins

Our good friend Orma McDougall, the leader of the Brockville Celiac Chapter, requested this flavor she used to enjoy from a local bakery. These muffins bring back fond memories for her.

■■■■■■■■■■■■■■■

Tips

See the baking tips on page 132 before trying this recipe.

If you only have sweetened applesauce, reduce the sugar to ¼ cup (60 mL).

Nutritional value per serving	
Calories	192
Fat, total	6 g
Fat, saturated	1 g
Cholesterol	31 mg
Sodium	221 mg
Carbohydrate	33 g
Fiber	2 g
Protein	3 g
Calcium	91 mg
Iron	1 mg

■ **6-cup muffin pan, lightly greased**

⅓ cup	sorghum flour	75 mL
¼ cup	quinoa flour	60 mL
2 tbsp	tapioca starch	30 mL
⅓ cup	granulated sugar	75 mL
1 tsp	xanthan gum	5 mL
2 tsp	GF baking powder	10 mL
½ tsp	baking soda	2 mL
¼ tsp	salt	1 mL
1 tsp	ground nutmeg	5 mL
1	large egg	1
¼ cup	unsweetened applesauce	60 mL
2 tbsp	vegetable oil	30 mL
½ tsp	vanilla extract	2 mL
¾ cup	shredded carrots	175 mL
⅓ cup	raisins	75 mL

1. In a bowl or plastic bag, combine sorghum flour, quinoa flour, tapioca starch, sugar, xanthan gum, baking powder, baking soda, salt and nutmeg. Mix well and set aside.

2. In a separate bowl, using an electric mixer, beat egg, applesauce, oil and vanilla until combined. Add dry ingredients, carrots and raisins; mix until just combined.

3. Spoon batter into prepared muffin cups, dividing evenly. Let stand for 30 minutes. Meanwhile, preheat oven to 350°F (180°C).

4. Bake for 18 to 20 minutes or until firm to the touch. Remove from the pan immediately and let cool completely on a rack.

Variation

Substitute shredded zucchini for half the carrots. Before measuring it, make sure to squeeze out excess moisture.

Coffee Raisin Muffins

These muffins are for those who prefer a heartier flavor than most muffins offer.

■■■■■■■■■■■■■■

Tips

See the baking tips on page 132 before trying this recipe.

Be sure the coffee has cooled to room temperature. We like to use double-strength coffee.

■ **6-cup muffin pan, lightly greased**

⅔ cup	sorghum flour	150 mL
⅓ cup	teff flour	75 mL
¼ cup	tapioca starch	60 mL
2 tbsp	packed brown sugar	30 mL
2 tsp	GF baking powder	10 mL
½ tsp	baking soda	2 mL
1 tsp	xanthan gum	5 mL
¼ tsp	salt	1 mL
1	large egg	1
⅔ cup	freshly brewed strong coffee, at room temperature	150 mL
2 tbsp	vegetable oil	30 mL
2 tbsp	light (fancy) molasses	30 mL
1 tsp	cider vinegar	5 mL
½ cup	raisins	125 mL

1. In a bowl or plastic bag, combine sorghum flour, teff flour, tapioca starch, brown sugar, baking powder, baking soda, xanthan gum and salt. Mix well and set aside.

2. In a separate bowl, using an electric mixer, beat egg, coffee, oil, molasses and vinegar until combined. Add dry ingredients and mix just until combined. Stir in raisins.

3. Spoon batter into prepared muffin cups, dividing evenly. Let stand for 30 minutes. Meanwhile, preheat oven to 350°F (180°C).

4. Bake for 18 to 20 minutes or until firm to the touch. Remove from the pan immediately and let cool completely on a rack.

Variation

Add 2 tsp (10 mL) fennel, caraway or anise seeds, or a combination, with the dry ingredients.

Nutritional value per serving	
Calories	229
Fat, total	6 g
Fat, saturated	1 g
Cholesterol	31 mg
Sodium	222 mg
Carbohydrate	42 g
Fiber	3 g
Protein	4 g
Calcium	120 mg
Iron	2 mg

Chocolate Chip Muffins

You don't have to hunt for the chocolate chips in these muffins — they are full of them.

■■■■■■■■■■■■■■□

Tip

See the baking tips on page 132 before trying this recipe.

■ **6-cup muffin pan, lightly greased**

2/3 cup	amaranth flour	150 mL
1/3 cup	sorghum flour	75 mL
1/4 cup	tapioca starch	60 mL
1/4 cup	granulated sugar	60 mL
2 tsp	GF baking powder	10 mL
1/2 tsp	baking soda	2 mL
1 tsp	xanthan gum	5 mL
1/4 tsp	salt	1 mL
1	large egg	1
2/3 cup	milk	150 mL
2 tbsp	vegetable oil	30 mL
1 tsp	cider vinegar	5 mL
1/2 cup	semisweet chocolate chips	125 mL

1. In a bowl or plastic bag, combine amaranth flour, sorghum flour, tapioca starch, sugar, baking powder, baking soda, xanthan gum and salt. Mix well and set aside.

2. In a separate bowl, using an electric mixer, beat egg, milk, oil and vinegar until combined. Add dry ingredients and mix just until combined. Stir in chocolate chips.

3. Spoon batter into prepared muffin cups, dividing evenly. Let stand for 30 minutes. Meanwhile, preheat oven to 350°F (180°C).

4. Bake for 20 to 23 minutes or until firm to the touch. Remove from the pan immediately and let cool completely on a rack.

Variation

Add 1/4 tsp (1 mL) peppermint extract with the liquids.

Nutritional value per serving	
Calories	259
Fat, total	11 g
Fat, saturated	3 g
Cholesterol	32 mg
Sodium	229 mg
Carbohydrate	38 g
Fiber	3 g
Protein	5 g
Calcium	135 mg
Iron	4 mg

Special Muffins for Kids

Who can resist the combination of peanut butter, banana and chocolate? Kids of all ages will wolf these down and ask for more!

■■■■■■■■■■■■■■■

Tips

See the baking tips on page 132 before trying this recipe.

You'll need about 2 very ripe medium bananas for ¾ cup (175 mL) mashed. Do not add extra.

You can substitute GF smooth peanut butter for the crunchy.

■ **6-cup muffin pan, lightly greased**

½ cup	sorghum flour	125 mL
¼ cup	quinoa flour	60 mL
2 tbsp	tapioca starch	30 mL
¼ cup	packed brown sugar	60 mL
2 tsp	GF baking powder	10 mL
½ tsp	baking soda	2 mL
1 tsp	xanthan gum	5 mL
¼ tsp	salt	1 mL
1	large egg	1
¾ cup	mashed bananas	175 mL
¼ cup	GF crunchy peanut butter, at room temperature	60 mL
2 tbsp	vegetable oil	30 mL
1 tsp	cider vinegar	5 mL
½ cup	semisweet chocolate chips	125 mL

1. In a bowl or plastic bag, combine sorghum flour, quinoa flour, tapioca starch, brown sugar, baking powder, baking soda, xanthan gum and salt. Mix well and set aside.

2. In a separate bowl, using an electric mixer, beat egg, bananas, peanut butter, oil and vinegar until combined. Add dry ingredients and mix just until combined. Stir in chocolate chips.

3. Spoon batter into prepared muffin cups, dividing evenly. Let stand for 30 minutes. Meanwhile, preheat oven to 350°F (180°C).

4. Bake for 18 to 20 minutes or until firm to the touch. Remove from the pan immediately and let cool completely on a rack.

Variation

Substitute ¼ cup (60 mL) unsalted peanuts for half the chocolate chips.

Nutritional value per serving	
Calories	314
Fat, total	16 g
Fat, saturated	4 g
Cholesterol	31 mg
Sodium	272 mg
Carbohydrate	42 g
Fiber	4 g
Protein	6 g
Calcium	101 mg
Iron	2 mg

Cookies and Bars

██

Baking Tips for Cookies and Bars

- Granulated sugar generally results in crisper cookies than either brown sugar or honey. In the recipes in this chapter, equal amounts may be substituted one for the other, or a combination of sugars may be used. Experiment to see what you prefer.

- Using butter in a cookie usually causes the dough to spread more, creating a flatter, crisper cookie than those made with shortening. You can substitute one for the other or use part of each in a recipe to get the texture you want.

- Bake a test cookie to check the accuracy of your oven's temperature setting. You may need to increase or reduce the temperature slightly or adjust the baking time. This is a good time to check the consistency of the dough. Add 1 to 2 tbsp (15 to 30 mL) sweet rice flour if the dough is too soft, causing the cookie to spread out more than you might like.

- When creaming the butter, beat just until smooth but not airy.

- If the dough becomes too soft and sticky, refrigerate it for at least 15 minutes.

- When making cut-out cookies, roll out the dough between two layers of waxed paper or parchment paper. This allows you to reform the scraps without excessive handling of the dough.

- Roll out the dough to a uniform thickness for more even baking. Cut out shapes as close together as possible. Use as little flour as possible when rerolling dough. Sweet rice flour works well here.

- When making sugar cookies or others that are rolled out, if the dough is a bit stickier than normal, flour the board and/or your fingertips with sweet rice flour. You can use brown rice flour if it's of normal consistency.

- Shiny baking sheets produce soft-bottomed cookies, while darker pans result in crisper cookies.

- When cooking two baking sheets at once, place them in the upper and lower thirds of the oven. Switch their positions halfway through the suggested baking time.

- During baking, keep your eyes on the oven, not the clock — 1 to 2 minutes can mean the difference between undercooked and burnt cookies.

- Let the baked cookies cool on the baking sheet on a rack for 2 minutes, then remove from the baking sheet and place, without overlapping, on the rack to cool completely.

- Store moist, soft cookies and crisp, hard cookies separately. Soft cookies should be stored layered between sheets of waxed paper in an airtight container so they stay soft and moist. Crisp cookies should be lightly wrapped in a covered, but not airtight container.

- Freeze cookies and bars in an airtight container between sheets of waxed paper for up to 2 months.

- Store the dough for drop cookies wrapped airtight in the refrigerator for up to 5 days or in the freezer for up to 2 months. Thaw in the refrigerator overnight. Bring to room temperature before using.

- When making slice-and-bake cookies, make dough for about 4 to 6 dozen. Bake 1 or 2 dozen and form the remaining dough into logs. Each log should have enough dough to make 1 or 2 dozen cookies. Wrap the logs airtight and freeze. There is no need to thaw the dough completely. Let a log thaw just enough to be able to slice it into $\frac{1}{2}$-inch (2 cm) circles. This ensures you have fresh cookies without the work of making the dough each time.

Chocolate Cookie Dough

Makes enough dough for about 80 cookies
Serving size: 1 cookie

Want to make an assortment of cookies without making dozens of each kind? Start with this basic shortbread-style recipe, divide the dough into portions and make several varieties, choosing from among the recipes on pages 167 to 171.

■■■■■■■■■■■■■■■

Tips

One pound (500 g) of butter yields 2 cups (500 mL).

Set butter out on the kitchen counter to soften the night before you plan to make this cookie dough.

1 cup	sorghum flour	250 mL
1 cup	whole bean flour	250 mL
1⅓ cups	cornstarch	325 mL
1 cup	GF confectioner's (icing) sugar, sifted	250 mL
½ cup	sifted unsweetened cocoa powder	125 mL
4 tsp	xanthan gum	20 mL
1¼ tsp	salt	6 mL
1½ cups	packed brown sugar	375 mL
2	large eggs	2
2 cups	butter, at room temperature	500 mL

1. In a large bowl or plastic bag, combine sorghum flour, whole bean flour, cornstarch, confectioner's sugar, cocoa, xanthan gum and salt. Set aside.

2. In another large bowl, using a heavy-duty electric mixer, beat brown sugar, eggs and butter until light and fluffy. Gradually beat in the dry ingredients just until combined, periodically stopping to scrape the bottom and sides of the bowl with a rubber spatula.

3. Divide dough into 4 equal portions. Use right away to make cookies or wrap each portion airtight and store in the refrigerator for up to 5 days or in the freezer for up to 2 months. Thaw in the refrigerator overnight. Bring to room temperature before making cookies.

Variations

For crisper cookies, substitute granulated sugar for the brown sugar.

Substitute an equal amount of yellow pea flour for the whole bean flour.

Nutritional value per serving	
Calories	83
Fat, total	5 g
Fat, saturated	3 g
Cholesterol	18 mg
Sodium	88 mg
Carbohydrate	10 g
Fiber	0 g
Protein	1 g
Calcium	8 mg
Iron	0 mg

Chocolate Drop Cookies

Makes 20 cookies
Serving size: 1 cookie

These are the plain cookies, made without any additions to the dough.

■■■■■■■■■■■■■■■

Tip
The thinner you press the cookies, the crunchier they are when baked.

■ **Preheat oven to 350°F (180°C)**
■ **Baking sheets, lightly greased**

| 1 | portion Chocolate Cookie Dough (page 166) | 1 |
| 2 tsp | sweet rice flour | 10 mL |

1. Roll dough into 1-inch (2.5 cm) balls. Place 1½ inches (4 cm) apart on prepared baking sheets. Flatten slightly with a fork dipped in sweet rice flour.

2. Bake in preheated oven for 12 to 15 minutes or until firm. Let cool on pans on racks for 2 minutes. Transfer cookies to racks and let cool completely. Store in an airtight container at room temperature for up to 2 weeks or in the freezer for up to 2 months.

Variation
Roll the 1-inch (2.5 cm) balls in finely chopped nuts of your choice. You'll need about ½ cup (125 mL) for this size batch.

Nutritional value per serving	
Calories	84
Fat, total	5 g
Fat, saturated	3 g
Cholesterol	18 mg
Sodium	88 mg
Carbohydrate	10 g
Fiber	0 g
Protein	1 g
Calcium	8 mg
Iron	0 mg

Chocolate Orange Cookies

These chewy chocolate cookies have a hint of orange flavor.

■■■■■■■■■■■■■■■

- ■ **Preheat oven to 350°F (180°C)**
- ■ **Baking sheets, lightly greased**

1	portion Chocolate Cookie Dough (page 166)	1
$\frac{1}{2}$ cup	GF confectioner's (icing) sugar, sifted	125 mL
1 tbsp	grated orange zest	15 mL
2 tbsp	frozen orange juice concentrate, thawed	30 mL

1. In a medium bowl, combine dough, confectioner's sugar, orange zest and orange juice concentrate. Mix well.

2. Drop dough by spoonfuls $1\frac{1}{2}$ inches (4 cm) apart on prepared baking sheets.

3. Bake in preheated oven for 12 to 15 minutes or until firm. Let cool on pans on racks for 2 minutes. Transfer cookies to racks and let cool completely. Store in an airtight container at room temperature for up to 2 weeks or in the freezer for up to 2 months.

Variation

For a stronger orange flavor, add $\frac{1}{4}$ to $\frac{1}{2}$ tsp (1 to 2 mL) orange extract.

Nutritional value per serving	
Calories	98
Fat, total	5 g
Fat, saturated	3 g
Cholesterol	18 mg
Sodium	88 mg
Carbohydrate	13 g
Fiber	1 g
Protein	1 g
Calcium	9 mg
Iron	0 mg

Cherry Chocolate Cookies

Dried cherries provide the chewiness in these rich, not too sweet cookies.

Tip

You might prefer to chop the cherries, leaving them in fairly large pieces.

■ **Preheat oven to 350°F (180°C)**
■ **Baking sheets, lightly greased**

1	portion Chocolate Cookie Dough (page 166)	1
½ cup	dried sour cherries	125 mL

1. In a medium bowl, combine dough and dried cherries. Mix well.

2. Drop dough by heaping spoonfuls 1½ inches (4 cm) apart on prepared baking sheets.

3. Bake in preheated oven for 12 to 15 minutes or until firm. Let cool on pans on racks for 2 minutes. Transfer cookies to racks and let cool completely. Store in an airtight container at room temperature for up to 2 weeks or in the freezer for up to 2 months.

Variation

Substitute dried cranberries of any flavor for the cherries.

Nutritional value per serving	
Calories	103
Fat, total	5 g
Fat, saturated	3 g
Cholesterol	18 mg
Sodium	89 mg
Carbohydrate	15 g
Fiber	1 g
Protein	1 g
Calcium	12 mg
Iron	1 mg

Crunchy Mocha Cookies

You'll enjoy the strong coffee flavor of these crisp chocolate cookies.

■■■■■■■■■■■■■■■

Tips

The thinner you press the cookies, the crunchier they are when baked.

Form the dough into rough-looking 2-inch (5 cm) balls. The resulting cookies will be larger than the other recipes made with this dough.

■ **Preheat oven to 350°F (180°C)**
■ **Baking sheets, lightly greased**

1	portion Chocolate Cookie Dough (page 166)	1
2 tsp	instant coffee granules	10 mL
1 to 2 tsp	sweet rice flour	10 to 15 mL

1. In a medium bowl, combine dough and coffee granules. Mix well.

2. Form dough into 2-inch (5 cm) balls. Place 1½ inches (4 cm) apart on prepared baking sheets. Flatten slightly with a fork dipped in sweet rice flour.

3. Bake in preheated oven for 12 to 15 minutes or until firm. Let cool on pans on racks for 2 minutes. Transfer cookies to racks and let cool completely. Store in an airtight container at room temperature for up to 2 weeks or in the freezer for up to 2 months.

Nutritional value per serving	
Calories	141
Fat, total	8 g
Fat, saturated	5 g
Cholesterol	29 mg
Sodium	151 mg
Carbohydrate	16 g
Fiber	1 g
Protein	1 g
Calcium	13 mg
Iron	1 mg

Hazelnut Chocolate Chip Cookies

Here's a flavor combination everyone with a sweet tooth will love: chocolate and hazelnuts!

■■■■■■■■■■■■■■■■

Tip

Take your time when chopping the hazelnuts. If you try to chop too many at once, they travel.

■ **Preheat oven to 350°F (180°C)**
■ **Baking sheets, lightly greased**

1	portion Chocolate Cookie Dough (page 166)	1
¾ cup	semisweet chocolate chips	175 mL
½ cup	chopped hazelnuts	125 mL
1 tsp	almond extract	5 mL

1. In a medium bowl, combine dough, chocolate chips, hazelnuts and almond extract. Mix well.

2. Drop dough by spoonfuls 1½ inches (4 cm) apart on prepared baking sheets.

3. Bake in preheated oven for 12 to 15 minutes or until firm. Let cool on pans on racks for 2 minutes. Transfer cookies to racks and let cool completely. Store in an airtight container at room temperature for up to 2 weeks or in the freezer for up to 2 months.

Variation

Substitute white chocolate chips or GF toffee bits for the chocolate chips and macadamia nuts for the hazelnuts.

Nutritional value per serving	
Calories	132
Fat, total	9 g
Fat, saturated	4 g
Cholesterol	18 mg
Sodium	89 mg
Carbohydrate	14 g
Fiber	1 g
Protein	1 g
Calcium	13 mg
Iron	1 mg

Heavenly Chip Cookies

Makes 12 cookies
Serving size: 1 cookie

These classic cookies are often called Tollhouse cookies. Google the history of Tollhouse cookies!

■■■■■■■■■■■■■■■

Tip

To store the dough, form it into logs 1 inch (2.5 cm) wide and 6 inches (15 cm) long, wrap airtight and refrigerate for up to 5 days or freeze for up to 2 months. To bake, thaw slightly and cut into ½-inch (1 cm) slices. Place 2 inches (5 cm) apart on a lightly greased baking sheet. Bake as directed in step 4.

- Preheat oven to 350°F (180°C)
- Baking sheet, lightly greased

⅓ cup	sorghum flour	75 mL
¼ cup	whole bean flour	60 mL
2 tbsp	tapioca starch	30 mL
¼ tsp	xanthan gum	1 mL
½ tsp	baking soda	2 mL
⅓ cup	packed brown sugar	75 mL
1	large egg	1
⅓ cup	butter, softened	75 mL
¼ tsp	vanilla extract	1 mL
⅔ cup	semisweet chocolate chips	150 mL
⅓ cup	chopped walnuts	75 mL

1. In a bowl or plastic bag, combine sorghum flour, whole bean flour, tapioca starch, xanthan gum and baking soda. Mix well and set aside.

2. In a separate bowl, using a handheld electric mixer on low speed, cream brown sugar, egg, butter and vanilla until well blended. Gradually beat in the dry ingredients just until combined. Stir in chocolate chips and walnuts.

3. Drop dough by rounded spoonfuls 2 inches (5 cm) apart on prepared baking sheet.

4. Bake in preheated oven for 10 to 12 minutes or until set. Let cool on pan on a rack for 2 minutes. Transfer cookies to rack and let cool completely. Store in an airtight container at room temperature for up to 2 weeks or in the freezer for up to 2 months.

Variations

For a moister, softer cookie, substitute an equal amount of shortening for the butter.

To make these nut-free, omit the walnuts. If desired, increase the chocolate chips to 1 cup (250 mL).

Substitute white chocolate chips for the chocolate chips and macadamia nuts for the walnuts.

Nutritional value per serving	
Calories	159
Fat, total	10 g
Fat, saturated	5 g
Cholesterol	28 mg
Sodium	109 mg
Carbohydrate	17 g
Fiber	1 g
Protein	2 g
Calcium	18 mg
Iron	1 mg

Crunchy Peanut Butter Cookies

These classic cookies are simultaneously moist and crunchy, with peanuts in every bite.

■■■■■■■■■■■■■■■■

Tips

If you prefer, substitute smooth peanut butter for the chunky and add $1/4$ cup (60 mL) peanuts.

If the dough sticks to the fork while you're flattening the cookies, dip the fork into sweet rice flour.

To make a traditional crisscross pattern, press the fork at 90 degrees to the first imprint.

Nutritional value per serving	
Calories	232
Fat, total	14 g
Fat, saturated	3 g
Cholesterol	27 mg
Sodium	38 mg
Carbohydrate	22 g
Fiber	2 g
Protein	8 g
Calcium	35 mg
Iron	4 mg

■ **Preheat oven to 350°F (180°C)**
■ **Baking sheet, lightly greased**

$2/3$ cup	amaranth flour	150 mL
4 tsp	tapioca starch	20 mL
$1/4$ tsp	xanthan gum	1 mL
$1/8$ tsp	baking soda	0.5 mL
$1/4$ cup	packed brown sugar	60 mL
1	large egg	1
$2/3$ cup	chunky peanut butter	150 mL
$1/4$ tsp	vanilla extract	1 mL

1. In a bowl or plastic bag, combine amaranth flour, tapioca starch, xanthan gum and baking soda. Mix well and set aside.

2. In a separate bowl, using a handheld electric mixer on low speed, cream brown sugar, egg, peanut butter and vanilla until well blended. Gradually beat in the dry ingredients just until combined.

3. Roll dough into $1\frac{1}{2}$-inch (4 cm) balls. Place 2 inches (5 cm) apart on prepared baking sheet. Flatten slightly with a fork.

4. Bake in preheated oven for 8 to 10 minutes or until set. Let cool on pan on a rack for 2 minutes. Transfer cookies to rack and let cool completely. Store in an airtight container at room temperature for up to 2 weeks or in the freezer for up to 2 months.

Variation

Form the dough into a $1\frac{1}{2}$-inch (4 cm) wide log, wrap airtight and refrigerate for up to 5 days or freeze for up to 2 months. If frozen, let stand at room temperature for 1 hour so it is easier to slice. Cut into $1/4$-inch (0.5 cm) thick slices and bake for an extra 1 to 2 minutes.

Soy-Free Peanut Butter Cookies

Makes 18 cookies
Serving size: 1 cookie

Everybody's absolute favorite cookie! We've made it soy-free, as you requested.

■■■■■■■■■■■■■■■■

Tips

If you prefer, substitute smooth peanut butter for the chunky and add $\frac{1}{4}$ cup (60 mL) peanuts.

If the dough sticks to the fork while you're flattening the cookies, dip the fork into sweet rice flour.

You'll need 8 of these cookies to make 1 cup (250 mL) crumbs for the Peanut Butter Cheesecake base (page 196).

Nutritional value per serving	
Calories	86
Fat, total	4 g
Fat, saturated	2 g
Cholesterol	6 mg
Sodium	77 mg
Carbohydrate	11 g
Fiber	1 g
Protein	2 g
Calcium	14 mg
Iron	1 mg

■ **Preheat oven to 350°F (180°C)**

$\frac{2}{3}$ cup	teff flour	150 mL
3 tbsp	cornstarch	45 mL
$\frac{1}{2}$ tsp	xanthan gum	2 mL
$\frac{1}{4}$ tsp	baking soda	1 mL
$\frac{1}{4}$ tsp	salt	1 mL
$\frac{1}{4}$ cup	packed brown sugar	60 mL
$\frac{1}{4}$ cup	granulated sugar	60 mL
$\frac{1}{4}$ cup	butter, softened	60 mL
$\frac{1}{4}$ cup	chunky peanut butter	60 mL
1	large egg yolk	1
$\frac{1}{4}$ tsp	vanilla extract	1 mL
	Sweet rice flour (optional)	

1. In a bowl or plastic bag, combine teff flour, cornstarch, xanthan gum, baking soda and salt. Mix well and set aside.

2. In a separate bowl, using a handheld electric mixer on low speed, cream brown sugar, granulated sugar, butter and peanut butter. Beat in egg yolk and vanilla until light and fluffy. Gradually beat in the dry ingredients just until combined. With a rubber spatula, scrape the bottom and sides of bowl.

3. Gather the dough into a large ball, kneading in any remaining dry ingredients. Roll into 1-inch (2.5 cm) balls. Place $1\frac{1}{2}$ inches (4 cm) apart on ungreased baking sheets. Flatten slightly with a fork.

4. Bake in preheated oven for 10 to 12 minutes or until set. Let cool on pans on racks for 2 minutes. Transfer cookies to racks and let cool completely. Store in an airtight container at room temperature for up to 2 weeks or in the freezer for up to 2 months.

Variation

Form the dough into $1\frac{1}{2}$-inch (4 cm) wide logs (you decide the length, based on the number of cookies you want to bake at once). Wrap airtight and refrigerate for up to 5 days or freeze for up to 2 months. To bake, thaw slightly and cut into $\frac{1}{2}$-inch (1 cm) slices. Place $1\frac{1}{2}$ inches (4 cm) apart on ungreased baking sheets. Bake as directed in step 4.

Oatmeal Raisin Cookies

Classic oatmeal raisin cookies are always a hit. Beth Armor, of Cream Hill Estates, bakes hundreds of dozens of these, using our recipe, for sampling at celiac conferences.

■■■■■■■■■■■■■■■

Tip

Underbake for a chewy cookie. Bake longer for a crisp one. Watch carefully, as cookies can burn within an extra 1 to 2 minutes.

- Preheat oven to 350°F (180°C)
- Baking sheet, lightly greased

¼ cup	GF oat flour	60 mL
1 tbsp	tapioca starch	15 mL
¼ tsp	xanthan gum	1 mL
¼ tsp	baking soda	1 mL
¼ cup	packed brown sugar	60 mL
2 tbsp	granulated sugar	30 mL
1	large egg, lightly beaten	1
¼ cup	butter, softened	60 mL
½ tsp	vanilla extract	2 mL
⅔ cup	GF large-flake (old-fashioned) rolled oats	150 mL
½ cup	raisins	125 mL

1. In a bowl or plastic bag, combine oat flour, tapioca starch, xanthan gum and baking soda. Mix well and set aside.

2. In a separate bowl, using a handheld electric mixer on low speed, cream brown sugar, sugar, egg, butter and vanilla until well blended. Gradually beat in the dry ingredients just until combined. Stir in oats and raisins.

3. Drop dough by rounded spoonfuls 2 inches (5 cm) apart on prepared baking sheet.

4. Bake in preheated oven for 9 to 12 minutes or until set. Let cool on pan on a rack for 2 minutes. Transfer cookies to rack and let cool completely. Store in an airtight container at room temperature for up to 2 weeks or in the freezer for up to 2 months.

Variation

Oatmeal Raisin Bars: Bake dough in a lightly greased 5¾- by 3¼-inch (14 by 8 cm) loaf pan for 20 to 25 minutes or until set. Let cool in pan on a rack for 15 minutes, then cut into bars and let cool completely.

Nutritional value per serving	
Calories	119
Fat, total	5 g
Fat, saturated	2 g
Cholesterol	25 mg
Sodium	70 mg
Carbohydrate	18 g
Fiber	1 g
Protein	2 g
Calcium	15 mg
Iron	1 mg

Quinoa Flax Cookies

You'll enjoy the crunch
of these delightful
cookies. Try to eat
just one!

■■■■■■■■■■■■■■

Tips

We tried this cookie with
sprouted flax powder, flax
meal and flax flour in place
of the ground flaxseed. All
were delicious, so you can
substitute one for another.

Whole flaxseed can be
stored at room temperature
for up to 1 year. Ground
flaxseed can be stored in
the refrigerator for up to
90 days, but for optimum
freshness it is best to grind
it as you need it.

Double the recipe for your
next cookie exchange!

Nutritional value per serving

Calories	91
Fat, total	5 g
Fat, saturated	2 g
Cholesterol	19 mg
Sodium	117 mg
Carbohydrate	11 g
Fiber	2 g
Protein	2 g
Calcium	21 mg
Iron	1 mg

■ **Preheat oven to 350°F (180°C)**
■ **Baking sheets, lightly greased**

¼ cup	sorghum flour	60 mL
¼ cup	quinoa flour	60 mL
2 tbsp	ground flaxseed	30 mL
⅓ cup	cracked flaxseed	75 mL
1 tsp	baking soda	5 mL
1 tsp	xanthan gum	5 mL
⅛ tsp	salt	0.5 mL
¼ cup	packed brown sugar	60 mL
2 tbsp	granulated sugar	30 mL
¼ cup	butter or shortening, softened	60 mL
1	large egg yolk	1
½ tsp	vanilla extract	2 mL
⅓ cup	quinoa flakes	75 mL

1. In a medium bowl or plastic bag, combine sorghum flour, quinoa flour, ground flaxseed, cracked flaxseed, baking soda, xanthan gum and salt. Mix well and set aside.

2. In a large bowl, using a handheld electric mixer on low speed, cream brown sugar, granulated sugar and butter until combined. Beat in egg yolk and vanilla until light and fluffy. Gradually beat in the dry ingredients just until combined. Stir in quinoa flakes.

3. Roll dough into 1-inch (2.5 cm) balls. Place 2 inches (5 cm) apart on prepared baking sheets and flatten with the bottom of a moistened drinking glass. (The thinner they are pressed, the crisper the cookie.)

4. Bake in preheated oven for 10 to 15 minutes or until set. Let cool on pans on racks for 2 minutes. Transfer cookies to racks and let cool completely. Store in an airtight container at room temperature for up to 2 weeks or in the freezer for up to 2 months.

Variations

Substitute GF large-flake (old-fashioned) rolled oats, buckwheat flakes or amaranth flakes for the quinoa flakes.

Substitute raw hemp powder for the ground flaxseed and Hemp Hearts for half the cracked flaxseed.

Cranberry Orange Nut Cookies

Makes 12 cookies
Serving size: 1 cookie

Crisp, moist and chewy, these cookies travel well.

■■■■■■■■■■■■■■■

Tips

Zest the orange cold from the refrigerator, then warm the orange in the microwave on High for 30 seconds before juicing.

The dough can wrapped airtight and refrigerated for up to 5 days.

■ **Preheat oven to 350°F (180°C)**
■ **Baking sheet, lightly greased**

1/2 cup	amaranth flour	125 mL
1/2 cup	brown rice flour	125 mL
1/4 cup	tapioca starch	60 mL
1/4 tsp	xanthan gum	1 mL
1/2 tsp	GF baking powder	2 mL
1/8 tsp	baking soda	0.5 mL
1/2 tsp	salt	2 mL
1/2 cup	packed brown sugar	125 mL
1 tbsp	grated orange zest	15 mL
1/4 cup	unsweetened applesauce	60 mL
2 tbsp	vegetable oil	30 mL
2 tbsp	freshly squeezed orange juice	30 mL
1/2 cup	dried cranberries	125 mL
1/4 cup	coarsely chopped walnuts	60 mL

1. In a bowl or plastic bag, combine amaranth flour, brown rice flour, tapioca starch, xanthan gum, baking powder, baking soda and salt. Mix well and set aside.

2. In a separate bowl, using a handheld electric mixer on low speed, beat brown sugar, orange zest, applesauce, oil and orange juice until well blended. Gradually beat in the dry ingredients just until combined. Stir in cranberries and walnuts.

3. Drop dough by rounded spoonfuls 2 inches (5 cm) apart on prepared baking sheet.

4. Bake in preheated oven for 13 to 15 minutes or until just barely golden brown. Let cool on pan on a rack for 2 minutes. Transfer cookies to rack and let cool completely. Store in an airtight container at room temperature for up to 2 weeks or in the freezer for up to 2 months.

Variations

Substitute chopped pistachios or pecans for the walnuts.

To make this cookie nut-free, omit the walnuts and increase the cranberries to 3/4 cup (175 mL). Or substitute dried blueberries for the nuts.

Nutritional value per serving	
Calories	142
Fat, total	4 g
Fat, saturated	0 g
Cholesterol	0 mg
Sodium	115 mg
Carbohydrate	24 g
Fiber	1 g
Protein	2 g
Calcium	29 mg
Iron	2 mg

Sunshine Cookies

The orange flavor in each crisp cookie contrasts with the sweet icing. Un-iced, these make the perfect base for Orange Mini Cheesecakes (page 283).

■■■■■■■■■■■■■■

Tip

Twelve of these cookies (un-iced) yields 2 cups (500 mL) crumbs. Store crumbs in 1-cup (250 mL) amounts in airtight containers in the freezer for up to 1 month. Use as a base for cheesecake prepared in a 4½-inch (11 cm) springform pan.

Nutritional value per serving	
Calories	130
Fat, total	5 g
Fat, saturated	3 g
Cholesterol	12 mg
Sodium	46 mg
Carbohydrate	21 g
Fiber	1 g
Protein	1 g
Calcium	13 mg
Iron	2 mg

- Preheat oven to 300°F (150°C)
- Baking sheet, lined with parchment paper

Cookies

¾ cup	amaranth flour	175 mL
¼ cup	tapioca starch	60 mL
½ tsp	xanthan gum	2 mL
1 tbsp	grated orange zest	15 mL
⅓ cup	granulated sugar	75 mL
¼ cup	butter, softened	60 mL

Orange Icing

¾ cup	GF confectioner's (icing) sugar, sifted	175 mL
½ tsp	grated orange zest	2 mL
1 tbsp	butter, softened	15 mL
1 tbsp	frozen orange juice concentrate, thawed	15 mL

1. *Cookies:* In a bowl or plastic bag, combine amaranth flour, tapioca starch, xanthan gum and orange zest. Set aside.

2. In a separate bowl, using a handheld electric mixer on low speed, cream sugar and butter until fluffy. Gradually beat in the dry ingredients just until combined.

3. Shape dough by tablespoonfuls (15 mL) into balls. Place 1 inch (2.5 cm) apart on prepared baking sheet.

4. Bake in preheated oven for 15 to 18 minutes or until light brown. Let cool on pan on a rack for 5 minutes. Transfer cookies to rack and let cool completely.

5. *Icing:* In a bowl, beat confectioner's sugar, orange zest, butter and orange juice concentrate until smooth. Spread over tops of cookies. Let stand for 1 hour or until firm.

6. Store in an airtight container at room temperature for up to 1 week or in the freezer for up to 1 month.

Variation

Substitute lemon zest for the orange zest.

Snowball Surprise

These white snowballs melt in your mouth until you discover the crunchy surprise.

■■■■■■■■■■■■■■■

Tip

Be sure all chocolate chips are covered by dough.

■ **Preheat oven to 350°F (180°C)**
■ **Baking sheet, lightly greased**

⅓ cup	brown rice flour	75 mL
⅓ cup	almond flour	75 mL
2 tbsp	tapioca starch	30 mL
¼ tsp	xanthan gum	1 mL
2 tbsp	GF confectioner's (icing) sugar, sifted	30 mL
¼ cup	butter, softened	60 mL
1 tsp	almond extract	5 mL
¼ cup	semisweet chocolate chips	60 mL
	GF confectioner's (icing) sugar	

1. In a bowl or plastic bag, combine brown rice flour, almond flour, tapioca starch and xanthan gum. Mix well and set aside.

2. In a separate bowl, using a handheld electric mixer on low speed, cream 2 tbsp (30 mL) confectioner's sugar, butter and almond extract until well blended. Gradually beat in the dry ingredients just until combined.

3. Drop dough by tablespoonfuls (15 mL) at least 1 inch (2.5 cm) apart on prepared baking sheet and flatten slightly. Press chocolate chips into the center. Roll dough around chocolate, forming 1-inch (2.5 cm) balls.

4. Bake in preheated oven for 8 to 10 minutes or until puffed and golden on the bottom. Immediately transfer cookies to a rack and let cool for 5 minutes. Roll warm cookies in confectioner's sugar. Store in an airtight container at room temperature for up to 2 weeks or in the freezer for up to 2 months.

Variations

Substitute any variety of chocolate chips.

Try hazelnuts or whole blanched almonds in the center instead of chocolate chips.

Nutritional value per serving	
Calories	111
Fat, total	7 g
Fat, saturated	4 g
Cholesterol	11 mg
Sodium	45 mg
Carbohydrate	11 g
Fiber	1 g
Protein	1 g
Calcium	13 mg
Iron	0 mg

Coconut Mango Icebox Cookies

These chewy, crunchy cookies will have you believing you're in the tropics. It's a handy recipe to make ahead, so you can quickly slice off a few cookies when company drops in.

■■■■■■■■■■■■■■■

1 cup	amaranth flour	250 mL
3/4 cup	low-fat soy flour	175 mL
1/4 cup	tapioca starch	60 mL
1 tsp	xanthan gum	5 mL
2 tsp	GF baking powder	10 mL
1/2 tsp	salt	2 mL
1 cup	granulated sugar	250 mL
2	large eggs	2
3/4 cup	butter, softened	175 mL
2 cups	unsweetened desiccated coconut	500 mL
1 1/4 cups	coarsely chopped dried mango	300 mL
3/4 cup	chopped macadamia nuts	175 mL

1. In a large bowl or plastic bag, combine amaranth flour, soy flour, tapioca starch, xanthan gum, baking powder and salt. Mix well and set aside.

2. In a separate bowl, using a heavy-duty mixer, cream sugar, eggs and butter until well blended. Gradually beat in the dry ingredients just until combined. Knead in coconut, mango and nuts by hand.

3. Divide dough into 4 equal portions. Form each into a 1 1/2-inch (4 cm) wide log.

Bake Right Away

4. Preheat oven to 350°F (180°C). Cut log(s) into 1/3-inch (0.8 cm) thick rounds. Place 2 inches (5 cm) apart on lightly greased baking sheets.

5. Bake for 8 to 10 minutes or until edges are lightly browned. Let cool on pans on racks for 2 minutes. Transfer cookies to racks and let cool completely.

Nutritional value per serving	
Calories	127
Fat, total	7 g
Fat, saturated	4 g
Cholesterol	18 mg
Sodium	83 mg
Carbohydrate	15 g
Fiber	1 g
Protein	2 g
Calcium	24 mg
Iron	1 mg

Tips

We prefer to use low-fat soy flour in our baked goods, but you can substitute full-fat soy flour if you prefer.

Dried mango can be stored in an airtight container at room temperature for up to 1 year.

Refrigerate, Then Bake

4. Wrap logs airtight and refrigerate for up to 5 days. Preheat oven to 350°F (180°C). Remove log(s) from refrigerator and cut into $\frac{1}{3}$-inch (0.8 cm) thick rounds. Place 2 inches (5 cm) apart on lightly greased baking sheets.

5. Bake for 10 to 12 minutes or until edges are lightly browned. Let cool on pans on racks for 2 minutes. Transfer cookies to racks and let cool completely.

Freeze, Then Bake

4. Wrap logs airtight and freeze for up to 2 months. Remove log(s) from freezer and let stand at room temperature for 1 hour so they are easier to slice. Meanwhile, preheat oven to 350°F (180°C). Cut log(s) into $\frac{1}{3}$-inch (0.8 cm) thick rounds. Place 2 inches (5 cm) apart on lightly greased baking sheets.

5. Bake for 10 to 12 minutes or until edges are lightly browned. Let cool on pans on racks for 2 minutes. Transfer cookies to racks and let cool completely.

Variation

Substitute dried apricots for the mango and hazelnuts or walnuts for the macadamia nuts.

Amaretti

Amaretti are airy Italian macaroons traditionally made with bitter almond or apricot kernel paste. These melt in your mouth.

■■■■■■■■■■■■■■■

Tips

See the Techniques Glossary, page 308, for information on warming eggs.

We like to use the whisk attachment that comes with our handheld mixer to beat the egg whites, as it makes quick work of the task.

Add sugar gradually or the beaten egg whites will become gritty, smooth and shiny.

You'll need 8 of these cookies to make ¾ cup (175 mL) crumbs for the Amaretto Cheesecake base (page 197).

Nutritional value per serving	
Calories	161
Fat, total	9 g
Fat, saturated	1 g
Cholesterol	0 mg
Sodium	14 mg
Carbohydrate	17 g
Fiber	2 g
Protein	5 g
Calcium	49 mg
Iron	1 mg

■ **Preheat oven to 300°F (150°C)**
■ **Baking sheets, lined with parchment paper**

2	large egg whites, warmed to room temperature	2
¼ tsp	cream of tartar	1 mL
1 cup	granulated sugar	250 mL
½ tsp	almond extract	2 mL
2½ cups	almond flour	625 mL

1. In a bowl, using a handheld electric mixer, beat egg whites and cream of tartar until soft peaks form. While beating, add sugar 1 to 2 tbsp (15 to 30 mL) at a time until egg whites form stiff, glossy but not dry peaks. Beat in almond extract. Gently fold in half the almond flour at a time, making sure each addition is well blended before adding the next.

2. Drop dough by tablespoonfuls (15 mL) 2 inches (5 cm) apart on prepared baking sheet.

3. Bake in preheated oven for 40 minutes or until crisp and dry to the touch. Let cool on pan on a rack for 2 minutes. Transfer cookies to rack and let cool completely. Store between layers of waxed paper in an airtight container at room temperature for 3 days.

Variation

Substitute pecan flour for the almond flour and vanilla extract for the almond extract.

Almond Macaroons

These nutty delights will be the first to disappear from your plate of cookies.

■■■■■■■■■■■■■■■■

Tips

To avoid soft, sticky macaroons, make them on a sunny day with low humidity.

We like to use the whisk attachment that comes with our handheld mixer to beat the egg whites, as it makes quick work of the task.

■ **Preheat oven to 325°F (160°C)**
■ **Baking sheet, lined with parchment paper**

½ cup	GF confectioner's (icing) sugar, sifted	125 mL
¼ cup	almond flour	60 mL
1	large egg white	1
⅛ tsp	cream of tartar	0.5 mL
1 tbsp	granulated sugar	15 mL

1. In a small bowl, combine confectioner's sugar and almond flour. Set aside.

2. In a bowl, using a handheld electric mixer, beat egg white until foamy. Beat in cream of tartar. Continue beating until egg white forms stiff peaks. Gradually beat in granulated sugar. Continue beating until mixture is very stiff and glossy but not dry. Fold in the dry ingredients until well blended.

3. Drop dough by spoonfuls 2 inches (5 cm) apart on prepared baking sheet.

4. Bake in preheated oven for 16 to 18 minutes or until puffed, smooth and cracked around bottom edges. Let cool on pan on a rack for 2 minutes. Transfer cookies to rack and let cool completely. Store between layers of waxed paper in an airtight container at room temperature for 3 days.

Variation

Chocolate Almond Macaroons: Add 1 tbsp (15 mL) sifted unsweetened cocoa powder with the confectioner's sugar.

Nutritional value per serving	
Calories	38
Fat, total	1 g
Fat, saturated	0 g
Cholesterol	0 mg
Sodium	5 mg
Carbohydrate	7 g
Fiber	0 g
Protein	1 g
Calcium	6 mg
Iron	0 mg

Hazelnut Sticks

Cookies come in many shapes — why not sticks? These melt in your mouth. We dare you to eat just one.

■■■■■■■■■■■■■■■■

Tip
See the Techniques Glossary, page 308, for information on toasting hazelnuts.

■ **Preheat oven to 325°F (160°C)**
■ **Baking sheet, lined with parchment paper**

½ cup	teff flour	125 mL
2 tbsp	tapioca starch	30 mL
¼ tsp	xanthan gum	1 mL
¾ cup	toasted coarsely chopped hazelnuts	175 mL
⅓ cup	GF confectioner's (icing) sugar, sifted	75 mL
⅓ cup	butter, softened	75 mL
½ tsp	vanilla extract	2 mL
½ cup	hazelnut flour or toasted finely chopped hazelnuts	125 mL

1. In a bowl or plastic bag, combine teff flour, tapioca starch, xanthan gum and hazelnuts. Set aside.

2. In a separate bowl, using a handheld electric mixer on low speed, cream confectioner's sugar, butter and vanilla until fluffy. Gradually beat in the dry ingredients until just combined.

3. Shape dough by tablespoons (15 mL) into 2-inch (5 cm) long sticks. Roll sticks in hazelnut flour to coat. Place 1 inch (2.5 cm) apart on prepared baking sheet.

4. Bake for 18 to 20 minutes or until light brown. Let cool on pan on a rack for 2 minutes. Transfer cookies to rack and let cool completely. Store in an airtight container at room temperature for up to 2 weeks or in the freezer for up to 2 months.

Variations

Dust slightly warm sticks with ¼ cup (60 mL) GF confectioner's (icing) sugar.

Substitute walnuts or pecans for the hazelnuts.

Nutritional value per serving	
Calories	116
Fat, total	9 g
Fat, saturated	3 g
Cholesterol	10 mg
Sodium	37 mg
Carbohydrate	8 g
Fiber	1 g
Protein	2 g
Calcium	19 mg
Iron	1 mg

Cranberry Seed Biscotti

Biscotti, traditional Italian cookies, have become part of our Canadian cuisine.

■■■■■■■■■■■■■■

Tips

For information on toasting seeds, see the Techniques Glossary, page 310.

Biscotti will be medium-firm and crunchy. For softer, chewier biscotti, bake for only 10 minutes in step 5; for very firm biscotti, bake for 20 minutes.

Recipe can be doubled. Use a 13- by 9-inch (33 by 23 cm) baking pan and increase the baking time in step 4 by about 5 minutes, or use two 8-inch (20 cm) pans.

Nutritional value per serving

Calories	54
Fat, total	1 g
Fat, saturated	0 g
Cholesterol	16 mg
Sodium	17 mg
Carbohydrate	10 g
Fiber	1 g
Protein	1 g
Calcium	12 mg
Iron	1 mg

■ **Preheat oven to 325°F (160°C)**
■ **8-inch (20 cm) square baking pan, lightly greased**

¾ cup	amaranth flour	175 mL
¼ cup	brown rice flour	60 mL
3 tbsp	tapioca starch	45 mL
2 tbsp	cornstarch	30 mL
¾ tsp	xanthan gum	3 mL
½ tsp	GF baking powder	2 mL
Pinch	salt	Pinch
⅓ cup	granulated sugar	75 mL
2	large eggs	2
½ tsp	vanilla extract	2 mL
½ cup	dried cranberries	125 mL
⅓ cup	green pumpkin seeds, toasted	75 mL
⅓ cup	unsalted raw sunflower seeds, toasted	75 mL

1. In a bowl or plastic bag, combine amaranth flour, brown rice flour, tapioca starch, cornstarch, xanthan gum, baking powder and salt. Mix well and set aside.

2. In a separate bowl, using a handheld electric mixer on low speed, beat sugar, eggs and vanilla until combined. Gradually beat in the dry ingredients just until combined. Stir in cranberries, pumpkin seeds and sunflower seeds.

3. Spoon batter into prepared pan. Using a moistened rubber spatula, spread to edges and smooth top.

4. Bake in preheated oven for 30 to 35 minutes or until firm and top is just turning golden. Remove from oven, leaving oven on, and let cool in pan on a rack for 5 minutes. Remove from pan and let cool on a cutting board for 5 minutes. Cut into quarters, then cut each quarter into 6 slices.

5. Arrange slices upright (both cut sides exposed) at least ½ inch (1 cm) apart on an ungreased baking sheet. Bake for 15 minutes or until dry and crisp. Transfer to a rack and let cool completely. Store in an airtight container at room temperature for up to 2 weeks or in the freezer for up to 2 months.

Variation

If you like sweeter biscotti, increase the granulated sugar to ½ cup (125 mL).

Mock Graham Wafers

Here's a sweet, not savory, cracker to nibble on. Take these along on your next travel adventure.

■■■■■■■■■■■■■■■■

Tips

Don't worry that the brown sugar mixture looks curdled: it becomes smooth with the addition of the dry ingredients.

Crush these wafers into crumbs and freeze them for up to 2 months, to use when a recipe calls for graham cracker crumbs. Eight crackers yields about 1 cup (250 mL) crumbs.

- Preheat oven to 300°F (150°C)
- 15- by 10-inch (40 by 25 cm) jelly roll pan, lightly greased

³⁄₄ cup	brown rice flour	175 mL
³⁄₄ cup	whole bean flour	175 mL
¹⁄₄ cup	tapioca starch	60 mL
1¹⁄₂ tsp	GF baking powder	7 mL
1 tsp	xanthan gum	5 mL
¹⁄₂ tsp	salt	2 mL
¹⁄₂ tsp	ground cinnamon	2 mL
¹⁄₄ cup	packed brown sugar	60 mL
¹⁄₃ cup	butter, softened	75 mL
¹⁄₄ cup	fancy (light) molasses	60 mL
¹⁄₄ cup	water	60 mL
¹⁄₂ tsp	vanilla extract	2 mL

1. In a bowl or plastic bag, combine brown rice flour, whole bean flour, tapioca starch, baking powder, xanthan gum, salt and cinnamon. Mix well and set aside.

2. In a separate bowl, using a handheld electric mixer on low speed, beat brown sugar, butter, molasses, water and vanilla. Gradually beat in the dry ingredients just until combined.

3. Dollop dough by spoonfuls over entire jelly roll pan. Cover with a sheet of parchment paper. Roll out dough evenly to fill the pan completely. Press with your fingers to an even thickness on the edges and into the corners. Remove parchment paper and prick dough all over with a fork. Using a pizza wheel, cut dough into 3- by 2-inch (7.5 by 5 cm) rectangles. Using a knife, finish cutting rectangles right to the edges of the pan.

4. Bake in preheated oven for 30 minutes, watching carefully to make sure they don't become too brown or burnt. For a crisper cracker, turn off oven and let stand in oven for 1 hour. Remove from baking sheet to a rack, break into crackers and let cool completely. Store in an airtight container at room temperature for up to 2 weeks or in the freezer for up to 2 months.

Nutritional value per serving	
Calories	63
Fat, total	2 g
Fat, saturated	1 g
Cholesterol	6 mg
Sodium	72 mg
Carbohydrate	10 g
Fiber	0 g
Protein	1 g
Calcium	26 mg
Iron	0 mg

Oatmeal Chocolate Chip Bars

Makes 12 bars
Serving size: 1 bar

Bars can be made more quickly than individual cookies, which may be of the utmost importance if children are helping you bake!

■■■■■■■■■■■■■■■■

■ **Preheat oven to 350°F (180°C)**
■ **9- by 5-inch (23 by 12.5 cm) loaf pan, lightly greased and bottom lined with parchment paper**

¼ cup	sorghum flour	60 mL
¼ tsp	xanthan gum	1 mL
¼ tsp	baking soda	1 mL
¼ cup	packed brown sugar	60 mL
2 tbsp	granulated sugar	30 mL
1	large egg yolk	1
¼ cup	butter, softened	60 mL
½ tsp	vanilla extract	2 mL
⅔ cup	GF large-flake (old-fashioned) rolled oats	150 mL
½ cup	semisweet chocolate chips or chunks	125 mL

1. In a bowl or plastic bag, combine sorghum flour, xanthan gum and baking soda. Mix well and set aside.

2. In a separate bowl, using a handheld electric mixer on low speed, cream brown sugar, granulated sugar, egg yolk, butter and vanilla until well blended. Gradually beat in the dry ingredients just until combined. Stir in oats and chocolate chips.

3. Spoon batter into prepared pan. Using a moistened rubber spatula, spread to edges and smooth top.

4. Bake in preheated oven for 20 to 22 minutes or until a tester inserted in the center comes out with a few moist crumbs clinging to it. Let cool in pan on a rack for 15 minutes. Remove to rack and let cool completely, then cut into bars. Store in an airtight container at room temperature for up to 2 weeks or in the freezer for up to 2 months.

Variation

Substitute quinoa flakes for the GF oats.

Nutritional value per serving	
Calories	129
Fat, total	7 g
Fat, saturated	4 g
Cholesterol	27 mg
Sodium	65 mg
Carbohydrate	17 g
Fiber	1 g
Protein	2 g
Calcium	13 mg
Iron	1 mg

Brownies

Doubly delicious, these moist brownies appeal to the eye as well as the taste buds of any chocoholic.

■■■■■■■■■■■■■■■

Tips

Letting the batter stand for 30 minutes yields a better texture. However, if you're short on time, you can bake right away.

Pack individually wrapped bars from the freezer in your lunch bag for a mid-morning or mid-afternoon pick-me-up.

One square of baking chocolate is 1 oz (30 g).

The chocolate and butter can also be melted in a saucepan set over hot water until partially melted. Stir until melted. Be sure water doesn't touch the chocolate.

Nutritional value per serving	
Calories	137
Fat, total	11 g
Fat, saturated	5 g
Cholesterol	39 mg
Sodium	89 mg
Carbohydrate	10 g
Fiber	1 g
Protein	2 g
Calcium	25 mg
Iron	1 mg

■ **8-inch (20 cm) square baking pan, lightly greased and bottom lined with parchment paper**

1/3 cup	whole bean flour	75 mL
2 tbsp	tapioca starch	30 mL
1/2 cup	packed brown sugar	125 mL
1/2 tsp	xanthan gum	2 mL
1/2 tsp	GF baking powder	2 mL
1/8 tsp	salt	0.5 mL
2 oz	unsweetened chocolate	60 g
1/2 cup	butter or shortening, softened	125 mL
2	large eggs	2
1/2 tsp	vanilla extract	2 mL
1/2 cup	coarsely chopped walnuts	125 mL

1. In a small bowl or plastic bag, combine whole bean flour, tapioca starch, brown sugar, xanthan gum, baking powder and salt. Mix well and set aside.

2. In a microwave-safe bowl, microwave chocolate and butter, uncovered, on Medium (50%) for 3 minutes or until partially melted. Stir until melted. Whisk in eggs, one at a time. Stir in vanilla. Gradually stir in the dry ingredients just until combined. Stir in walnuts.

3. Spoon batter into prepared pan. Using a moistened rubber spatula, spread to edges and smooth top. Let stand for 30 minutes. Meanwhile, preheat oven to 350°F (180°C).

4. Bake for 20 to 25 minutes or until a tester inserted in the center comes out with a few moist crumbs clinging to it. Let cool in pan on a rack for 15 minutes. Remove to rack and let cool completely, then cut into bars. Store in an airtight container at room temperature for up to 2 weeks or in the freezer for up to 2 months.

Hazelnut Chocolate Blondies

Makes 16 blondies
Serving size: 1 blondie

Packed with hazelnuts and chocolate, these blondies are to die for.

■■■■■■■■■■■■■■

Tips

Use a ruler to mark off even bars or squares. Start by cutting in half through the center of the pan, both across and down. Then work toward the outside to keep your cuts straight.

For information on toasting hazelnuts and making your own hazelnut flour, see the Techniques Glossary, page 308.

■ **8-inch (20 cm) square baking pan, lightly greased and bottom and sides lined with parchment paper**

1 cup	low-fat soy flour	250 mL
1/4 cup	hazelnut flour	60 mL
2 tbsp	tapioca starch	30 mL
1 1/2 tsp	xanthan gum	7 mL
1/4 tsp	salt	1 mL
1 cup	packed brown sugar	250 mL
2	large eggs	2
1/2 cup	butter, softened	125 mL
2 tsp	vanilla extract	10 mL
4 oz	bittersweet (dark) chocolate, coarsely chopped, divided	125 g
2/3 cup	toasted coarsely chopped hazelnuts, divided	150 mL

1. In a bowl or plastic bag, combine soy flour, hazelnut flour, tapioca starch, xanthan gum and salt.

2. In a large bowl, using a handheld electric mixer on low speed, cream brown sugar, eggs, butter and vanilla until well blended. Stir in the dry ingredients just until combined. Stir in half each of the chocolate and hazelnuts.

3. Spoon batter into prepared pan. Using a moistened rubber spatula, spread to edges, leaving top rough. Sprinkle with the remaining chocolate and hazelnuts, pressing them into the batter. Let stand for 30 minutes. Meanwhile, preheat oven to 325°F (160°C).

4. Bake for 32 to 35 minutes or until golden. Let cool completely in pan on a rack, then cut into bars. Store in an airtight container at room temperature for up to 2 weeks or in the freezer for up to 2 months.

Variation

Substitute 1/3 cup (75 mL) bittersweet (dark) chocolate chips for the squares.

Nutritional value per serving	
Calories	220
Fat, total	13 g
Fat, saturated	6 g
Cholesterol	40 mg
Sodium	111 mg
Carbohydrate	18 g
Fiber	1 g
Protein	5 g
Calcium	39 mg
Iron	1 mg

Citus Bars

Lemon, lime and orange provide a tasty tang in these chewy coconut squares.

■■■■■■■■■■■■■■■■

Tips

Lightly greasing the pan before lining the bottom and sides prevents the parchment paper from slipping when you press it into the base.

To get more juice out of your citrus fruit, bring it to room temperature first, then roll it on the counter or between your hands before juicing.

Double the recipe and bake in an 8-inch (20 cm) square baking pan. You may need to increase the baking time by 5 to 10 minutes.

Nutritional value per serving	
Calories	103
Fat, total	4 g
Fat, saturated	2 g
Cholesterol	25 mg
Sodium	36 mg
Carbohydrate	17 g
Fiber	1 g
Protein	1 g
Calcium	9 mg
Iron	1 mg

■ **Preheat oven to 350°F (180°C)**
■ **9- by 5-inch (23 by 12.5 cm) loaf pan, lightly greased and bottom and sides lined with parchment paper**

Base

1/4 cup	amaranth flour	60 mL
1/4 cup	sweetened shredded coconut	60 mL
2 tbsp	GF confectioner's (icing) sugar, sifted	30 mL
1 tbsp	grated lime zest	15 mL
1 tsp	xanthan gum	5 mL
2 tbsp	butter, melted	30 mL

Topping

1/2 cup	granulated sugar	125 mL
2 tbsp	cornstarch	30 mL
2 tsp	grated lime zest	10 mL
1	large egg	1
2 tbsp	freshly squeezed lime juice	30 mL
1 tbsp	freshly squeezed lemon juice	15 mL
1 tbsp	freshly squeezed orange juice	15 mL

1. *Base:* In a bowl, combine amaranth flour, coconut, confectioner's sugar, lime zest and xanthan gum. Stir in butter.

2. Press evenly into bottom of prepared pan. Using a moistened rubber spatula, spread to edges and smooth top.

3. Bake in preheated oven for 10 to 15 minutes or until set. Reduce oven temperature to 325°F (160°C).

4. *Topping:* Meanwhile, in a bowl, using a handheld electric mixer, beat sugar, cornstarch, lime zest, egg, lime juice, lemon juice and orange juice until blended. Pour over hot base.

5. Bake for 20 to 25 minutes or until topping is set and firm to the touch. Let cool completely in pan on a rack. Refrigerate for at least for 1 hour before cutting into bars. Store in an airtight container at room temperature for up to 2 weeks or in the freezer for up to 2 months.

Coconut Bars

These scrumptious bars are for the true coconut lover — it's in both the base and the topping!

■■■■■■■■■■■■■■■

Tip
Butter melts quickly in a glass measuring cup in the microwave.

- Preheat oven to 350°F (180°C)
- 9- by 5-inch (23 by 12.5 cm) loaf pan, lightly greased and bottom and sides lined with parchment paper

Base

1/2 cup	amaranth flour	125 mL
1/2 cup	unsweetened shredded coconut	125 mL
1/4 cup	granulated sugar	60 mL
1 tsp	GF baking powder	5 mL
1/4 tsp	ground nutmeg	1 mL
1/8 tsp	salt	0.5 mL
1/4 cup	butter, melted	60 mL

Coconut Topping

3/4 cup	unsweetened shredded coconut	175 mL
1/4 cup	packed brown sugar	60 mL
1	large egg, lightly beaten	1
1/2 tsp	vanilla extract	2 mL

1. *Base:* In a bowl, combine amaranth flour, coconut, sugar, baking powder, nutmeg and salt. Stir in butter.

2. Press evenly into bottom of prepared pan. Using a moistened rubber spatula, spread to edges and smooth top.

3. Bake in preheated oven for 13 to 15 minutes or until golden brown. Remove from oven, leaving oven on, and let cool in pan on a rack for 5 minutes.

4. *Topping:* In a bowl, combine coconut, brown sugar, egg and vanilla. Spread over base.

5. Bake for 13 to 15 minutes or until golden brown. Let cool in pan on a rack for 5 minutes. Remove to rack and let cool completely, then cut into bars. Store in an airtight container at room temperature for up to 2 weeks or in the freezer for up to 2 months.

Variation
Add 1/2 cup (125 mL) chopped dried fruit to the base, either with or in place of the coconut. Try cranberries, apricots, cherries or maraschino cherries.

Nutritional value per serving	
Calories	209
Fat, total	11 g
Fat, saturated	9 g
Cholesterol	38 mg
Sodium	144 mg
Carbohydrate	26 g
Fiber	2 g
Protein	2 g
Calcium	48 mg
Iron	2 mg

Coconut Thins

These bars make a
delightful addition
to a dessert tray!

■ ■ ■ ■ ■ ■ ■ ■ ■ ■ ■ ■ ■ ■

Tips

Use a ruler to mark off even
bars or squares. Start by
cutting in half through the
center of the pan, both
across and down. Then
work toward the outside to
keep your cuts straight.

Crumble cooled coconut
thins to use in a crumb crust
for cheesecake. Sixteen
bars yields about 1½ cups
(375 mL) crumbs.

■ Preheat oven to 350°F (180°C)
■ 8-inch (20 cm) square baking pan, lightly greased and
bottom and sides lined with parchment paper

½ cup	amaranth flour	125 mL
½ cup	unsweetened shredded coconut	125 mL
¼ cup	granulated sugar	60 mL
1 tsp	GF baking powder	5 mL
1 tbsp	grated lemon zest	15 mL
¼ tsp	ground ginger	1 mL
⅛ tsp	salt	0.5 mL
¼ cup	butter, melted	60 mL

1. In a bowl, combine amaranth flour, coconut, sugar,
baking powder, lemon zest, ginger and salt. Stir
in butter.

2. Press evenly into bottom of prepared pan. Using
a moistened rubber spatula, spread to edges and
smooth top.

3. Bake in preheated oven for 12 to 15 minutes or
until golden brown. Let cool in pan on a rack for
5 minutes. Remove to rack and let cool completely,
then cut into bars. Store in an airtight container at
room temperature for up to 2 weeks or in the freezer
for up to 2 months.

Variation

Substitute orange zest for the lemon zest and ground
mace for the ginger.

Nutritional value per serving	
Calories	65
Fat, total	4 g
Fat, saturated	3 g
Cholesterol	7 mg
Sodium	54 mg
Carbohydrate	7 g
Fiber	1 g
Protein	1 g
Calcium	20 mg
Iron	1 mg

Hazelnut Chocolate Blondies (page 189)

Lemon Poppy Cake (page 203)

Carrot Cake
(variation, page 209)

Rhubarb Tarts (page 247) and
Pecan Butter Tarts (page 251)

Apple Cranberry Crisp
(page 256)

Peach Sponge Pudding (page 269)

Chocolate Sugar Cookies (page 280)
and Scottish Shortbread (page 281)

Individual Pavlovas (page 286)

Cakes and Cupcakes

■■■

Cheesecake Baking Tips

- Ultra-low-fat cream cheese or fat-free cream cheese should not be substituted for regular cream cheese in baked cheesecake recipes. However, light cream cheese can be used.

- If using a dark-colored springform pan, decrease the oven temperature by 25°F (10°C).

- Leaving the cheesecake in the oven after turning the oven off helps prevent large cracks.

- Be sure to loosen the cake from the edges of the springform pan before opening the clip on the side.

- Cheesecake can be made up to 1 month in advance. Let cool completely, then wrap the whole cheesecake or individual wedges tightly and freeze until ready to serve. Thaw in the refrigerator and garnish just before serving.

Cake and Cupcake Baking Tips

- We recommend sifting gluten-free flours and starches after measuring them and/or mixing them well when combining them, because cake batter is mixed very little. If the gluten-free flours and starches lump or are not mixed well, the cake or cupcakes may bake with pockets of these ingredients.

- In cake recipes, the butter or shortening is often creamed with the sugar before the eggs are added. Your cake or cupcakes will have a better texture if you cream the butter first, then gradually beat in the sugar. Then add the eggs, one at a time, beating after each, for the lightest possible cake.

- To lighten baked foods containing eggs, we like to separate the eggs and beat the whites until stiff but not dry, then fold them into the batter as the last step before spooning the batter into the baking pan.

- Letting the batter stand for 30 minutes at room temperature before baking results in lighter textured, more tender cakes and cupcakes. But if you're short on time, you can bake immediately.

- There are four ways to tell when a cake is done:
  1. The internal temperature is 200°F (100°C).
  2. The top springs back when pressed lightly.
  3. A tester inserted in the center comes out clean.
  4. The cake has just begun to pull away from the pan.

- Unless the recipe specifies otherwise, let cakes cool in the pan for 10 minutes and let cupcakes cool in the pan for 5 minutes. Then run a metal spatula or knife between the pan and cake(s) and turn the cake or cupcakes out onto a cooling rack. Let cool completely before frosting.

New York–Style Cheesecake

Makes 4 servings

This smaller version of the classic cheesecake is perfect when you only want 4 servings of dessert. Serve with fresh fruit.

■■■■■■■■■■■■■■■

Tip

Before you get started, see page 194 for tips on baking cheesecakes.

- **Preheat oven to 300°F (150°C)**
- **Roasting pan**

1	package (8 oz/250 g) brick cream cheese, softened	1
1/3 cup	granulated sugar	75 mL
1/2 tsp	grated lemon zest	2 mL
1 tsp	freshly squeezed lemon juice	5 mL
1	large egg	1
1 tbsp	amaranth flour	15 mL
1/4 cup	GF sour cream	60 mL
	Mock Graham Wafer Crumb Crust in a 4 1/2-inch (11 cm) springform pan (variation, page 235)	

1. In a large bowl, using a handheld electric mixer, beat cream cheese until smooth. Gradually beat in sugar, lemon zest and lemon juice until light and fluffy. Beat in egg. Stir in amaranth flour and sour cream. Pour into crust.

2. Place springform pan in roasting pan and place in preheated oven. Pour enough hot water into the roasting pan to fill it to a depth of at least 1 inch (2.5 cm). Bake for 45 to 50 minutes or until center is just set and the blade of a knife comes out clean. Turn oven off and let cheesecake cool in oven for 30 minutes. Carefully remove springform pan from roasting pan. Using a knife, trace around the outside edge of the cake to loosen it. Let cool in springform pan on a rack for 30 minutes. Refrigerate until chilled, about 3 hours.

Variations

Prepare this cheesecake in a 9- by 5-inch (23 by 12.5 cm) loaf pan. Decrease the baking time by about 5 minutes.

Double the recipe and bake in a 9-inch (23 cm) springform pan. Increase the baking time by 5 to 10 minutes.

Substitute 1 cup (250 mL) crumbled Sunshine Cookies (see recipe, page 178), patted into the bottom of a 4 1/2-inch (11 cm) springform pan, for the Mock Graham Wafer Crumb Crust.

Nutritional value per serving	
Calories	381
Fat, total	15 g
Fat, saturated	8 g
Cholesterol	90 mg
Sodium	308 mg
Carbohydrate	53 g
Fiber	1 g
Protein	10 g
Calcium	88 mg
Iron	3 mg

Peanut Butter Cheesecake

Makes 4 servings

Who doesn't love peanut butter cake, cookies and now cheesecake?

■■■■■■■■■■■■■■■

Tip

Before you get started, see page 194 for tips on baking cheesecakes.

- ■ Preheat oven to 300°F (150°C)
- ■ 4¹/₂-inch (11 cm) springform pan
- ■ Roasting pan

³/₄ cup	crumbled Soy-Free Peanut Butter Cookies (page 174)	175 mL
1 tbsp	butter, melted	15 mL
1	package (8 oz/250 g) brick cream cheese, softened	1
¹/₄ cup	crunchy peanut butter	60 mL
¹/₄ cup	packed brown sugar	60 mL
1	large egg	1

1. In a small bowl, combine cookie crumbs and butter; mix well. Press into bottom of pan. Refrigerate until chilled, about 15 minutes.

2. In a large bowl, using a handheld electric mixer, beat cream cheese and peanut butter until smooth. Gradually beat in brown sugar until light and fluffy. Beat in egg. Pour over base.

3. Place springform pan in roasting pan and place in preheated oven. Pour enough hot water into the roasting pan to fill it to a depth of at least 1 inch (2.5 cm). Bake for 45 to 55 minutes or until center is just set and the blade of a knife comes out clean. Turn oven off and let cheesecake cool in oven for 30 minutes. Carefully remove springform pan from roasting pan. Using a knife, trace around the outside edge of the cake to loosen it. Let cool in springform pan on a rack for 30 minutes. Refrigerate until chilled, about 3 hours.

Nutritional value per serving	
Calories	717
Fat, total	44 g
Fat, saturated	14 g
Cholesterol	128 mg
Sodium	383 mg
Carbohydrate	58 g
Fiber	5 g
Protein	25 g
Calcium	157 mg
Iron	7 mg

Variations

Prepare this cheesecake in a 9- by 5-inch (23 by 12.5 cm) loaf pan. Decrease the baking time by about 5 minutes.

Double the recipe and bake in a 9-inch (23 cm) springform pan. Increase the baking time by 5 to 10 minutes.

To make mini cheesecakes, do not crumble the cookies. Place 1 cookie in the bottom of each of 6 paper-lined muffin cups. Fill evenly with batter. Bake at 350°F (180°C) for 20 minutes or until centers are almost set.

Amaretto Cheesecake

This sky-high cheesecake is soft, smooth, cool and utterly addictive!

■■■■■■■■■■■■■■■

Tips

Before you get started, see page 194 for tips on baking cheesecakes.

If you prefer, you can substitute $1/2$ tsp (2 mL) almond extract for the liqueur.

You'll need about 8 Amaretti cookies to make $3/4$ cup (175 mL) crumbs.

- Preheat oven to 300°F (150°C)
- 4$1/2$-inch (11 cm) springform pan
- Roasting pan

$3/4$ cup	crumbled Amaretti (page 182)	175 mL
3 tbsp	butter, melted	45 mL
1	package (8 oz/250 g) brick cream cheese, softened	1
$1/3$ cup	granulated sugar	75 mL
1 tbsp	almond liqueur (such as amaretto)	15 mL
2	large eggs	2
2 tbsp	almond flour	30 mL
$1/4$ cup	plain yogurt	60 mL

1. In a small bowl, combine cookie crumbs and butter; mix well. Press into bottom of pan. Refrigerate until chilled, about 15 minutes.

2. In a large bowl, using a handheld electric mixer, beat cream cheese until smooth. Gradually beat in sugar and liqueur until light and fluffy. Beat in eggs, one at a time, beating well after each. Stir in almond flour and yogurt. Pour over base.

3. Place springform pan in roasting pan and place in preheated oven. Pour enough hot water into the roasting pan to fill it to a depth of at least 1 inch (2.5 cm). Bake for 45 to 50 minutes or until center is just set and the blade of a knife comes out clean. Turn oven off and let cheesecake cool in oven for 30 minutes. Carefully remove springform pan from roasting pan. Using a knife, trace around the outside edge of the cake to loosen it. Let cool in springform pan on a rack for 30 minutes. Refrigerate until chilled, about 3 hours.

Variations

Substitute Bailey's Irish Cream, Tia Maria or frozen orange juice concentrate, thawed, for the almond liqueur.

Prepare this cheesecake in a 9- by 5-inch (23 by 12.5 cm) loaf pan. Decrease the baking time by about 5 minutes.

Double the recipe and bake in a 9-inch (23 cm) springform pan. Increase the baking time by 5 to 10 minutes.

Nutritional value per serving	
Calories	405
Fat, total	18 g
Fat, saturated	9 g
Cholesterol	137 mg
Sodium	352 mg
Carbohydrate	48 g
Fiber	0 g
Protein	11 g
Calcium	91 mg
Iron	1 mg

Golden Cake

Makes 8 servings

This small cake is the perfect size for when you're celebrating a special occasion with just your nearest and dearest.

■■■■■■■■■■■■■■■■

Tips

Freeze cake, wrapped airtight, for up to 6 weeks. Thaw in the refrigerator.

When you're stirring in the dry ingredients alternately with the milk mixture, you can either use the handheld mixer on low speed or switch to using a rubber spatula. Mix just until blended after each addition. This technique results in a more even-textured cake.

■ **8-inch (20 cm) square baking pan, lightly greased and bottom lined with parchment paper**

⅔ cup	milk	150 mL
1 tsp	cider vinegar	5 mL
1 tsp	almond extract	5 mL
⅔ cup	brown rice flour	150 mL
½ cup	low-fat soy flour	125 mL
2 tbsp	tapioca starch	30 mL
2 tsp	GF baking powder	10 mL
1 tsp	baking soda	5 mL
1½ tsp	xanthan gum	7 mL
½ tsp	salt	2 mL
¼ cup	butter, softened, or shortening	60 mL
¾ cup	granulated sugar	175 mL
2	large eggs	2
2	large egg whites	2

1. In a small bowl, combine milk, vinegar and almond extract; mix well. Let stand for 5 minutes.

2. In a bowl or plastic bag, combine brown rice flour, soy flour, tapioca starch, baking powder, baking soda, xanthan gum and salt. Mix well and set aside.

3. In a separate bowl, using a handheld electric mixer, cream butter until fluffy. Gradually beat in sugar. Continue beating until light and fluffy. Add eggs and egg whites, one at a time, beating well after each. Stir in dry ingredients alternately with milk mixture, making three additions of dry and two of milk.

Nutritional value per serving	
Calories	226
Fat, total	8 g
Fat, saturated	4 g
Cholesterol	63 mg
Sodium	403 mg
Carbohydrate	34 g
Fiber	1 g
Protein	7 g
Calcium	104 mg
Iron	1 mg

Tips

For a lighter cake, beat the egg whites (at room temperature) until stiff but not dry, then fold into the batter just before spooning it into the pan. Bake immediately.

Letting the batter stand for 30 minutes before baking results in a lighter textured, more tender cake. But if you're short on time, you can bake the cake immediately.

4. Spoon batter into prepared pan. Using a moistened rubber spatula, spread to edges and smooth top. Let stand for 30 minutes. Meanwhile, preheat oven to 350°F (180°C).

5. Bake for 18 minutes. Check to see if cake is getting too dark and tent with foil if necessary. Bake for 8 to 12 minutes or until a tester inserted in the center comes out clean. Let cool in pan on a rack for 5 minutes. Remove from pan and let cool completely on rack.

Variations

To make a layer cake, use a long serrated knife to cut the cooled cake in half vertically. If the layers are not level, trim them until they are. Spread frosting between the layers and frost the top.

Turn this cake into a cottage pudding by serving it warm, smothered with brown sugar sauce. To make brown sugar sauce, combine ¾ cup (175 mL) packed brown sugar, 3 tbsp (45 mL) cornstarch and ¼ tsp (1 mL) salt in a large saucepan. Gradually add 2 cups (500 mL) water, stirring constantly. Bring to a boil over medium-high heat, stirring constantly. Boil for 3 minutes. Remove from heat and stir in ¼ cup (60 mL) butter and 1 tsp (5 mL) vanilla extract.

Sponge Cake

We both grew up eating versions of this classic cake. Serve with fresh strawberries on top.

■■■■■■■■■■■■■■■■

Tips

It is easier to separate eggs when they are cold, right from the refrigerator, because the yolk is less apt to break.

See the Techniques Glossary, page 308, for information on warming egg whites and yolks.

We like to use the whisk attachment that comes with our handheld mixer to beat the egg whites and yolks, as it makes quick work of the task.

Store the cakes at room temperature for up to 3 days or freeze, wrapped airtight, for up to 6 weeks.

Nutritional value per serving	
Calories	96
Fat, total	3 g
Fat, saturated	1 g
Cholesterol	106 mg
Sodium	105 mg
Carbohydrate	13 g
Fiber	1 g
Protein	4 g
Calcium	23 mg
Iron	2 mg

■ **Preheat oven to 350°F (180°C)**
■ **Two 4-inch (10 cm) mini Bundt or kugelhopf pans, lightly greased and dusted with sweet rice flour**

¼ cup	amaranth flour	60 mL
1 tbsp	tapioca starch	15 mL
1 tsp	xanthan gum	5 mL
2	large egg whites, at room temperature	2
¼ tsp	cream of tartar	1 mL
Pinch	salt	Pinch
½ tsp	freshly squeezed lemon juice	2 mL
2 tsp	granulated sugar	10 mL
2	large egg yolks, at room temperature	2
1 tbsp	granulated sugar	15 mL

1. In a small bowl or plastic bag, combine amaranth flour, tapioca starch and xanthan gum. Mix well and set aside.

2. In a separate bowl, using a handheld electric mixer, beat egg whites until foamy. Beat in cream of tartar, salt and lemon juice. Continue beating until egg whites form stiff peaks. Gradually beat in 2 tsp (10 mL) sugar. Continue beating until mixture is very stiff and glossy but not dry.

3. In a bowl, using a handheld electric mixer, beat egg yolks and 1 tbsp (15 mL) sugar for 3 to 5 minutes or until thick and lemon-colored. Fold in dry ingredients until well blended. Fold in egg whites. Spoon into prepared pans, dividing evenly.

4. Bake in preheated oven for 13 to 15 minutes or until cakes are golden and spring back when lightly touched. Invert cakes onto a rack, leaving pans on top, and let cool completely. Using a spatula, loosen edges of pans and remove.

Angel Food Cake

Makes 4 servings

White as snow and light as a feather, this fat-free cake is delicious with fresh fruit or dressed up for any special occasion.

■■■■■■■■■■■■■■■

Tips

See the Techniques Glossary, page 308, for information on warming egg whites.

This is the ideal time to use ¼ cup (60 mL) liquid egg whites, available in cartons.

We like to use the whisk attachment that comes with our handheld mixer to beat the egg whites, as it makes quick work of the task.

Make sure the mixing bowl, beaters or wire whisk and baking pans are completely free of grease.

Store the cakes at room temperature for up to 3 days or freeze, wrapped airtight, for up to 6 weeks.

Nutritional value per serving	
Calories	72
Fat, total	0 g
Fat, saturated	0 g
Cholesterol	0 mg
Sodium	101 mg
Carbohydrate	16 g
Fiber	0 g
Protein	2 g
Calcium	8 mg
Iron	0 mg

■ **Preheat oven to 350°F (180°C)**
■ **Two 4-inch (10 cm) mini Bundt or kugelhopf pans, completely free of grease**

2 tbsp	brown rice flour	30 mL
1 tbsp	tapioca starch	15 mL
2 tbsp	sifted GF confectioner's (icing) sugar	30 mL
½ tsp	xanthan gum	2 mL
2	large egg whites, at room temperature	2
¼ tsp	cream of tartar	1 mL
Pinch	salt	Pinch
2 tbsp	granulated sugar	30 mL
¼ tsp	vanilla extract	1 mL

1. In a small bowl or plastic bag, combine brown rice flour, tapioca starch, confectioner's sugar and xanthan gum. Mix well and set aside.

2. In a separate bowl, using a handheld electric mixer, beat egg whites until foamy. Beat in cream of tartar and salt. Continue beating until egg whites form stiff peaks. Gradually beat in granulated sugar. Continue beating until mixture is very stiff and glossy but not dry. Sift in half the dry ingredients at a time, gently folding in each addition until well blended. Fold in vanilla. Spoon into pans, dividing evenly.

3. Bake in preheated oven for 15 to 20 minutes or until cakes are golden and spring back when lightly touched. Invert cakes onto a rack, leaving pans on top, and let cool completely. Using a spatula, loosen edges of pans and remove.

Mocha Angel Food Cake

Makes 4 servings

This delectable cake is not quite as light and airy as the classic Angel Food Cake (page 201), but it has great flavor!

■■■■■■■■■■■■■■■

Tips

This is the ideal time to use 6 tbsp (90 mL) liquid egg whites, available in cartons.

We like to use the whisk attachment that comes with our handheld mixer to beat the egg whites, as it makes quick work of the task.

Make sure the mixing bowl, beaters or wire whisk and baking pans are completely free of grease. We wash them thoroughly just before preparing this recipe.

Store the cakes at room temperature for up to 3 days or freeze, wrapped airtight, for up to 6 weeks.

Nutritional value per serving	
Calories	91
Fat, total	2 g
Fat, saturated	0 g
Cholesterol	0 mg
Sodium	123 mg
Carbohydrate	15 g
Fiber	1 g
Protein	4 g
Calcium	14 mg
Iron	1 mg

■ **Preheat oven to 350°F (180°C)**
■ **Two 4-inch (10 cm) mini Bundt or kugelhopf pans, lightly greased**

2 tbsp	almond flour	30 mL
1 tbsp	tapioca starch	15 mL
2 tbsp	sifted GF confectioner's (icing) sugar	30 mL
1/2 tsp	xanthan gum	2 mL
2 tbsp	sifted unsweetened cocoa powder	30 mL
1 tsp	instant coffee granules	5 mL
3	large egg whites, at room temperature	3
1/4 tsp	cream of tartar	1 mL
Pinch	salt	Pinch
2 tbsp	granulated sugar	30 mL
1/4 tsp	almond extract	1 mL

1. In a small bowl or plastic bag, combine almond flour, tapioca starch, confectioner's sugar, xanthan gum, cocoa powder and coffee granules. Mix well and set aside.

2. In a separate bowl, using a handheld electric mixer, beat egg whites until foamy. Beat in cream of tartar and salt. Continue beating until egg whites form stiff peaks. Gradually beat in granulated sugar. Continue beating until mixture is very stiff and glossy but not dry. Sift in half the dry ingredients at a time, gently folding in each addition until well blended. Fold in almond extract. Spoon into prepared pans, dividing evenly.

3. Bake in preheated oven for 15 to 20 minutes or until cakes spring back when lightly touched. Invert cakes onto a rack, leaving pans on top, and let cool completely. Using a spatula, loosen edges of pans and remove.

Variation

Omit the coffee granules for a Chocolate Angel Food Cake.

Lemon Poppy Cake

Serve this cake with fresh strawberries for a pleasant treat in early summer!

■■■■■■■■■■■■■■■

Tips

We like to use the whisk attachment that comes with our handheld mixer to beat the egg white, as it makes quick work of the task.

Let cakes cool completely, then wrap tightly and freeze for up to 6 weeks.

This recipe can be doubled — just use 4 pans and bake them all at the same time.

Nutritional value per serving

Calories	248
Fat, total	8 g
Fat, saturated	1 g
Cholesterol	58 mg
Sodium	171 mg
Carbohydrate	43 g
Fiber	2 g
Protein	4 g
Calcium	154 mg
Iron	1 mg

■ Preheat oven to 325°F (160°C)
■ Two 4-inch (10 cm) mini Bundt or kugelhopf pans, lightly greased

¼ cup	sorghum flour	60 mL
2 tbsp	whole bean flour	30 mL
2 tbsp	tapioca starch	30 mL
½ tsp	xanthan gum	2 mL
1 tsp	GF baking powder	5 mL
¼ tsp	baking soda	1 mL
⅛ tsp	salt	0.5 mL
2 tbsp	poppy seeds	30 mL
1	large egg white, at room temperature	1
¼ cup	granulated sugar	60 mL
1 tsp	grated lemon zest	5 mL
1	large egg yolk	1
¼ cup	GF sour cream or plain yogurt	60 mL
1 tbsp	vegetable oil	15 mL
1 tbsp	freshly squeezed lemon juice	15 mL
¼ cup	Citrus Drizzle (page 231)	60 mL

1. In a bowl or plastic bag, combine sorghum flour, whole bean flour, tapioca starch, xanthan gum, baking powder, baking soda, salt and poppy seeds. Mix well and set aside.

2. In a small bowl, using a handheld electric mixer, beat egg white until stiff peaks form.

3. In a medium bowl, using a handheld electric mixer, beat sugar, lemon zest, egg yolk, sour cream, oil and lemon juice. Add dry ingredients and mix just until combined. Fold in beaten egg white.

4. Spoon batter into prepared pans, dividing evenly. Using a moistened rubber spatula, spread to edges and smooth tops.

5. Bake in preheated oven for 20 to 23 minutes or until a tester inserted in the center of a cake comes out clean. Let cool in pans on a rack for 5 minutes. Remove from pans and let cool completely on rack. Drizzle with Citrus Drizzle.

Applesauce Raisin Breakfast Cake

Here's a truly "everything-free" breakfast cake — gluten-free, fat-free, nut-free, soy-free, dairy-free and yeast-free — free of everything except flavor, that is!

■■■■■■■■■■■■■■■

Tips

If you only have sweetened applesauce, decrease the brown sugar to 3 tbsp (45 mL).

Letting the batter stand for 30 minutes before baking results in a lighter textured, more tender cake. But if you're short on time, you can bake the cake immediately.

Nutritional value per serving	
Calories	193
Fat, total	1 g
Fat, saturated	0 g
Cholesterol	0 mg
Sodium	120 mg
Carbohydrate	47 g
Fiber	3 g
Protein	4 g
Calcium	81 mg
Iron	2 mg

■ **Two 5³⁄₄- by 3¹⁄₄-inch (14 by 8 cm) mini loaf pans, lightly greased**

²⁄₃ cup	sorghum flour	150 mL
3 tbsp	whole bean flour	45 mL
3 tbsp	cornstarch	45 mL
¹⁄₄ cup	packed brown sugar	60 mL
1¹⁄₂ tsp	GF baking powder	7 mL
¹⁄₄ tsp	baking soda	1 mL
2 tsp	xanthan gum	10 mL
¹⁄₈ tsp	salt	0.5 mL
¹⁄₄ tsp	ground cardamom	1 mL
³⁄₄ cup	raisins	175 mL
1	large egg white	1
³⁄₄ cup	unsweetened applesauce	175 mL
¹⁄₂ tsp	cider vinegar	2 mL

1. In a large bowl or plastic bag, combine sorghum flour, whole bean flour, cornstarch, brown sugar, baking powder, baking soda, xanthan gum, salt, cardamom and raisins. Mix well and set aside.

2. In a separate bowl, using a handheld electric mixer or a whisk, beat egg white, applesauce and vinegar until combined. Add dry ingredients and stir just until combined. Spoon into prepared pans, dividing evenly. Let stand for 30 minutes. Meanwhile, preheat oven to 350°F (180°C).

3. Bake for 25 to 30 minutes or until firm to the touch. Let cool in pans on a rack for 5 minutes. Remove from pans and let cool completely on rack.

Variations

Substitute prune purée for the applesauce.

Substitute dried cranberries for the raisins.

Banana Flax Cake

Makes 6 servings

These small cakes yield
the perfect size slices
for a dessert tray!

▪▪▪▪▪▪▪▪▪▪▪▪▪▪

Tip

Use a clean coffee or
spice grinder to crack the
flaxseed.

■ **Two 5³⁄₄- by 3¹⁄₄-inch (14 by 8 cm) mini loaf pans,**
lightly greased and bottom lined with parchment paper

¹⁄₂ cup	sorghum flour	125 mL
¹⁄₄ cup	whole bean flour	60 mL
2 tbsp	cracked flaxseed	30 mL
2 tbsp	tapioca starch	30 mL
1¹⁄₂ tsp	xanthan gum	7 mL
2 tsp	GF baking powder	10 mL
1 tsp	baking soda	5 mL
¹⁄₄ tsp	salt	1 mL
¹⁄₂ tsp	ground cinnamon	2 mL
¹⁄₈ tsp	ground nutmeg	0.5 mL
Pinch	ground allspice	Pinch
¹⁄₄ cup	granulated sugar	60 mL
1	large egg	1
1	large egg white	1
³⁄₄ cup	mashed bananas	175 mL
2 tbsp	vegetable oil	30 mL
1 tsp	vanilla extract	5 mL

1. In a bowl or plastic bag, combine sorghum flour, whole bean flour, flaxseed, tapioca starch, xanthan gum, baking powder, baking soda, salt, cinnamon, nutmeg and allspice. Mix well and set aside.

2. In a separate bowl, using a handheld electric mixer, beat sugar, egg, egg white, bananas, oil and vanilla until combined. Add dry ingredients and mix just until combined.

3. Spoon batter into prepared pans, dividing evenly. Using a moistened rubber spatula, spread to edges and smooth tops. Let stand for 30 minutes. Meanwhile, preheat oven to 350°F (180°C).

4. Bake for 20 minutes. Tent with foil and bake for 5 to 8 minutes or until a tester inserted in the center of a cake comes out clean. Let cool in pans on a rack for 5 minutes. Remove from pans and let cool completely on rack.

Variation

For 6 cupcakes, bake in a 6-cup muffin pan lined with paper liners for 18 to 20 minutes.

Nutritional value per serving

Calories	190
Fat, total	7 g
Fat, saturated	1 g
Cholesterol	31 mg
Sodium	330 mg
Carbohydrate	30 g
Fiber	3 g
Protein	4 g
Calcium	96 mg
Iron	1 mg

Pineapple Upside-Down Cake

Treat yourself and enjoy this small version of a classic.

■■■■■■■■■■■■■■■

Tips

In our mini Bundt pans, we had to cut the pineapple ring so it would lie in the bottom.

Let cakes cool completely, then wrap tightly and freeze for up to 6 weeks. Thaw in the refrigerator.

- ■ **Preheat oven to 350°F (180°C)**
- ■ **Two 4-inch (10 cm) mini Bundt or kugelhopf pans, lightly greased and dusted with sweet rice flour**

2	canned pineapple rings, well drained	2
4 tsp	packed brown sugar	20 mL
3/4 cup	amaranth flour	175 mL
1/4 cup	tapioca starch	60 mL
1 tsp	GF baking powder	5 mL
1/2 tsp	baking soda	2 mL
1 tsp	xanthan gum	5 mL
1/4 tsp	salt	1 mL
1/3 cup	granulated sugar	75 mL
1	large egg	1
1/4 cup	milk	60 mL
2 tbsp	vegetable oil	30 mL
1/2 tsp	vanilla extract	2 mL

1. Place a pineapple ring in each prepared pan. Sprinkle with brown sugar. Set aside.

2. In a bowl or plastic bag, combine amaranth flour, tapioca starch, baking powder, baking soda, xanthan gum and salt. Mix well and set aside.

3. In a separate bowl, using a handheld electric mixer, beat sugar, egg, milk, oil and vanilla until combined. Add dry ingredients and mix just until combined.

4. Spoon batter over pineapple rings, dividing evenly. Using a moistened rubber spatula, spread to edges and smooth tops.

5. Bake in preheated oven for 25 minutes or until a tester inserted in the center of a cake comes out clean. Invert over small serving plates and let stand for 2 minutes. Carefully remove pans and serve warm.

Variations

Bake in two 5 1/4- by 2 1/2-inch (13 by 6 cm) mini loaf pans. Cut the pineapple rings in half and place them in an "S" shape on the bottom of the pans. Bake for 28 to 30 minutes.

For 6 cupcakes, bake in a 6-cup muffin pan lined with paper liners. Cut each pineapple ring into three sections and place one section in each muffin pan. Bake for 20 to 23 minutes.

Nutritional value per serving	
Calories	575
Fat, total	19 g
Fat, saturated	2 g
Cholesterol	95 mg
Sodium	659 mg
Carbohydrate	92 g
Fiber	5 g
Protein	10 g
Calcium	235 mg
Iron	12 mg

Hazelnut Cake

Enjoy this delightful
soft, nutty dessert cake
with a cup of green tea.

■■■■■■■■■■■■■■

Tips

Letting the batter stand for
30 minutes before baking
results in lighter textured,
more tender cakes. But
if you're short on time,
you can bake the cakes
immediately.

Let cakes cool completely,
then wrap tightly and freeze
for up to 6 weeks. Thaw in
the refrigerator.

■ **Two 4-inch (10 cm) mini Bundt or kugelhopf pans,
lightly greased**

1/3 cup	milk	75 mL
2 tsp	cider vinegar	10 mL
1/2 cup	sorghum flour	125 mL
1/4 cup	hazelnut flour	60 mL
1/4 cup	tapioca starch	60 mL
1 tsp	GF baking powder	5 mL
1/2 tsp	baking soda	2 mL
1 tsp	xanthan gum	5 mL
1/4 tsp	salt	1 mL
1/4 tsp	ground nutmeg	1 mL
1/4 cup	chopped hazelnuts	60 mL
1	large egg	1
2 tbsp	vegetable oil	30 mL
1/3 cup	liquid honey	75 mL
1/2 tsp	vanilla extract	2 mL

1. In a measuring cup, combine milk and vinegar.
   Let stand for 3 minutes.

2. In a bowl or plastic bag, combine sorghum flour,
   hazelnut flour, tapioca starch, baking powder, baking
   soda, xanthan gum, salt, nutmeg and hazelnuts. Mix
   well and set aside.

3. In a separate bowl, using a handheld electric mixer, beat
   milk mixture, egg, oil, honey and vanilla until combined.
   Add dry ingredients and mix just until combined.

4. Spoon batter into prepared pans, dividing evenly. Let
   stand for 30 minutes. Meanwhile, preheat oven to
   350°F (180°C).

5. Bake for 24 to 26 minutes or until a tester inserted in
   the center of a cake comes out clean. Let cool in pans
   on a rack for 5 minutes. Remove from pans and let
   cool completely on rack.

Variations

For extra decadence, drizzle Hazelnut Drizzle (page 230)
over the cooled cakes.

Bake in two 5 1/4- by 2 1/2-inch (13 by 6 cm) mini loaf
pans for 25 to 28 minutes.

For 6 cupcakes, bake in a 6-cup muffin pan lined with
paper liners for 20 to 23 minutes.

Nutritional value per serving

Calories	355
Fat, total	17 g
Fat, saturated	2 g
Cholesterol	48 mg
Sodium	331 mg
Carbohydrate	48 g
Fiber	3 g
Protein	6 g
Calcium	109 mg
Iron	2 mg

Maple Walnut Cake

These tasty little morsels make perfect treats for special occasions when a large cake is just too much. They're also great packed into your lunch for days when you deserve a treat.

■■■■■■■■■■■■■■■

Tips

Let cakes cool completely, then wrap tightly and freeze for up to 6 weeks. Thaw in the refrigerator.

For an extra hit of maple and walnuts, frost with Maple Buttercream Frosting (page 231), then sprinkle with toasted chopped walnuts.

Nutritional value per serving	
Calories	373
Fat, total	18 g
Fat, saturated	2 g
Cholesterol	48 mg
Sodium	344 mg
Carbohydrate	47 g
Fiber	3 g
Protein	9 g
Calcium	127 mg
Iron	4 mg

■ **Two 4-inch (10 cm) mini Bundt or kugelhopf pans, lightly greased**

1/2 cup	sorghum flour	125 mL
1/4 cup	amaranth flour	60 mL
1/4 cup	tapioca starch	60 mL
1 tsp	GF baking powder	5 mL
1/2 tsp	baking soda	2 mL
1 tsp	xanthan gum	5 mL
1/4 tsp	salt	1 mL
1/4 tsp	ground ginger	1 mL
1/2 cup	toasted coarsely chopped walnuts	125 mL
1	large egg	1
1/3 cup	buttermilk	75 mL
2 tbsp	vegetable oil	30 mL
1/3 cup	pure maple syrup	75 mL
1 1/2 tsp	maple extract	7 mL

1. In a bowl or plastic bag, combine sorghum flour, amaranth flour, tapioca starch, baking powder, baking soda, xanthan gum, salt, ginger and walnuts. Mix well and set aside.

2. In a separate bowl, using a handheld electric mixer, beat egg, buttermilk, oil, maple syrup and maple extract until combined. Add dry ingredients and mix until just combined.

3. Spoon batter into prepared pans, dividing evenly. Let stand for 30 minutes. Meanwhile, preheat oven to 350°F (180°C).

4. Bake for 26 to 28 minutes or until a tester inserted in the center of a cake comes out clean. Let cool in pans on a rack for 5 minutes. Remove from pans and let cool completely on rack.

Variations

Substitute GF sour cream or a flavored yogurt for the buttermilk.

Bake in two 5 1/4- by 2 1/2-inch (13 by 6 cm) mini loaf pans for 25 to 28 minutes.

For 6 cupcakes, bake in a 6-cup muffin pan lined with paper liners for 20 to 23 minutes.

Carrot Cake

Makes 4 servings

Love carrot cake? You don't need to wait for company — enjoy this one alone or share with a neighbor.

■■■■■■■■■■■■■■■

Tips

Let cakes cool completely, then wrap tightly and freeze for up to 6 weeks. Thaw in the refrigerator.

One medium carrot will yield about ¾ cup (175 mL) shredded.

Variations

Bake in two 5¼- by 2½-inch (13 by 6 cm) mini loaf pans for 35 to 37 minutes.

For 6 cupcakes, bake in a 6-cup muffin pan lined with paper liners for 20 to 23 minutes.

Nutritional value per serving	
Calories	622
Fat, total	27 g
Fat, saturated	7 g
Cholesterol	70 mg
Sodium	471 mg
Carbohydrate	91 g
Fiber	4 g
Protein	9 g
Calcium	191 mg
Iron	2 mg

■ **Two 4-inch (10 cm) mini Bundt or kugelhopf pans, lightly greased**

¾ cup	sorghum flour	175 mL
¼ cup	tapioca starch	60 mL
2 tsp	GF baking powder	10 mL
½ tsp	baking soda	2 mL
1 tsp	xanthan gum	5 mL
¼ tsp	salt	1 mL
½ tsp	ground cinnamon	2 mL
⅛ tsp	ground cloves	0.5 mL
⅛ tsp	ground nutmeg	0.5 mL
⅓ cup	granulated sugar	75 mL
1	large egg	1
¼ cup	milk	60 mL
3 tbsp	vegetable oil	45 mL
½ tsp	vanilla extract	2 mL
¾ cup	shredded carrots	175 mL
⅓ cup	toasted chopped walnuts	75 mL
⅓ cup	raisins	75 mL
¾ cup	Cream Cheese Frosting (page 232)	175 mL

1. In a bowl or plastic bag, combine sorghum flour, tapioca starch, baking powder, baking soda, xanthan gum, salt, cinnamon, cloves and nutmeg. Mix well and set aside.

2. In a separate bowl, using a handheld electric mixer, beat sugar, egg, milk, oil and vanilla until combined. Add dry ingredients and carrots; mix until just combined. Stir in walnuts and raisins.

3. Spoon batter into prepared pans, dividing evenly. Using a moistened rubber spatula, spread to edges and smooth tops. Let stand for 30 minutes. Meanwhile, preheat oven to 350°F (180°C).

4. Bake for 30 to 35 minutes or until a tester inserted in the center of a cake comes out clean. Let cool in pans on a rack for 5 minutes. Remove from pans and let cool completely on rack. Frost with Cream Cheese Frosting.

Carrot Snacking Cake

Here's an all-purpose cake that is wholesome as well as delicious! No one will guess that it is lower in fat than most carrot cakes, thanks to the secret ingredient: applesauce.

■■■■■■■■■■■■■■■■

Tip

Let cake cool completely, then wrap tightly, unfrosted, and freeze for up to 6 weeks. Thaw in the refrigerator.

■ **8-inch (20 cm) square baking pan, lightly greased and bottom lined with parchment paper**

¾ cup	sorghum flour	175 mL
⅓ cup	quinoa flour	75 mL
¼ cup	tapioca starch	60 mL
1½ tsp	xanthan gum	7 mL
1 tbsp	GF baking powder	15 mL
1 tsp	baking soda	5 mL
¼ tsp	salt	1 mL
1 tsp	ground cinnamon	5 mL
¾ cup	granulated sugar	175 mL
2	large eggs	2
⅓ cup	unsweetened applesauce	75 mL
¼ cup	vegetable oil	60 mL
1 tsp	vanilla extract	5 mL
1½ cups	shredded carrots	375 mL
½ cup	raisins	125 mL
¾ cup	Cream Cheese Frosting (page 232)	175 mL

1. In a bowl or plastic bag, combine sorghum flour, quinoa flour, tapioca starch, xanthan gum, baking powder, baking soda, salt and cinnamon. Mix well and set aside.

2. In a separate bowl, using a handheld electric mixer, beat sugar, eggs, applesauce, oil and vanilla until combined. Add dry ingredients and mix until just combined. Stir in carrots and raisins.

3. Spoon batter into prepared pan. Using a moistened rubber spatula, spread to edges and smooth top. Let stand for 30 minutes. Meanwhile, preheat oven to 350°F (180°C).

4. Bake for 35 to 40 minutes or until a tester inserted in the center comes out clean. Let cool in pan on a rack for 10 minutes. Remove from pan and let cool completely on rack. Frost with Cream Cheese Frosting.

Variation

For 12 cupcakes, bake in a 12-cup muffin pan lined with paper liners for 20 to 25 minutes.

Nutritional value per serving	
Calories	253
Fat, total	9 g
Fat, saturated	2 g
Cholesterol	39 mg
Sodium	216 mg
Carbohydrate	43 g
Fiber	2 g
Protein	3 g
Calcium	80 mg
Iron	1 mg

Strawberry Shortcakes

At your next summertime family reunion, serve everyone's favorite dessert: strawberry shortcake.

■■■■■■■■■■■■■■■

Tip

It's up to you how many berries to fill and top each shortcake with. We usually allow ½ to ¾ cup (125 to 175 mL) per person.

Variation

Top with yogurt or whipped cream. If using whipped cream, purchase 1 quart (1 L) heavy or whipping (35%) cream and add ½ cup (125 mL) granulated sugar when whipping. See the Techniques Glossary, page 310, for information about whipping cream.

Nutritional value per serving	
Calories	217
Fat, total	13 g
Fat, saturated	7 g
Cholesterol	32 mg
Sodium	320 mg
Carbohydrate	26 g
Fiber	2 g
Protein	3 g
Calcium	181 mg
Iron	1 mg

■ **Preheat oven to 400°F (200°C)**
■ **Baking sheets, lightly greased**

2 cups	brown rice flour	500 mL
1½ cups	sorghum flour	375 mL
⅔ cup	tapioca starch	150 mL
½ cup	granulated sugar	125 mL
2 tbsp	xanthan gum	30 mL
⅓ cup	GF baking powder	75 mL
1 tbsp	baking soda	15 mL
1½ tsp	salt	7 mL
1 tbsp	grated lemon zest	15 mL
1½ cups	cold butter or shortening, cut into 1-inch (2.5 cm) cubes	375 mL
1½ cups	plain yogurt	375 mL
3 to 4 quarts	strawberries (see tip, at left), sliced	3 to 4 L

Food Processor Method

1. In a food processor fitted with a metal blade, combine brown rice flour, sorghum flour, tapioca starch, sugar, xanthan gum, baking powder, baking soda, salt and lemon zest; pulse 3 or 4 times to combine. Add butter and pulse for 3 to 5 seconds or until mixture resembles coarse crumbs about the size of small peas. Add yogurt and pulse until the mixture holds together.

Traditional Method

1. In a large bowl, combine brown rice flour, sorghum flour, tapioca starch, sugar, xanthan gum, baking powder, baking soda, salt and lemon zest. Using a pastry blender or two knives, cut in butter until mixture resembles coarse crumbs about the size of small peas. Add yogurt all at once, stirring with a fork to make a soft, slightly sticky dough.

For Both Methods

2. Drop dough by heaping spoonfuls 2 inches (5 cm) apart on prepared baking sheets.

3. Bake in preheated oven for 13 to 15 minutes or until tops are golden. Remove from pans immediately and let cool completely on a rack.

4. Using a serrated knife, cut each shortcake in half horizontally. Arrange strawberries between the layers. Top with more strawberries.

Make Your Own Cupcake Mix

Makes about 4½ cups (1.125 L), enough for 18 cupcakes
Serving size: ¼ cup (60 mL)

This easy mix is the basis for many different cupcakes (see recipes, pages 213–219).

■■■■■■■■■■■■■■■■

Tips

Stir the mix before spooning very lightly into the dry measures. Do not pack.

Be sure to divide the mix into 3 equal portions. Depending on how much air you incorporate into the mix and the texture of the individual gluten-free flours, the total volume of the mix can vary slightly.

1¼ cups	sorghum flour	300 mL
⅔ cup	amaranth flour	150 mL
⅔ cup	brown rice flour	150 mL
¼ cup	quinoa flour	60 mL
2 tbsp	potato starch	30 mL
2 tbsp	tapioca starch	30 mL
1⅓ cups	granulated sugar	325 mL
1 tbsp	GF baking powder	15 mL
1½ tsp	baking soda	7 mL
¾ tsp	xanthan gum	3 mL
¾ tsp	salt	3 mL

1. In a large bowl, combine sorghum flour, amaranth flour, brown rice flour, quinoa flour, potato starch, tapioca starch, sugar, baking powder, baking soda, xanthan gum and salt. Mix well.

2. Immediately divide into 3 equal portions of about 1½ cups (375 mL) each. Seal tightly in plastic bags, removing as much air as possible. Store at room temperature for up to 3 days or in the freezer for up to 3 months. Let warm to room temperature and mix well before using.

Nutritional value per serving	
Calories	141
Fat, total	1 g
Fat, saturated	0 g
Cholesterol	0 mg
Sodium	204 mg
Carbohydrate	32 g
Fiber	1 g
Protein	2 g
Calcium	47 mg
Iron	2 mg

Plain Jane Cupcakes

These are for those of you who enjoy a plain cupcake with nothing added. Just frost with chocolate for a birthday party!

■■■■■■■■■■■■■■■■

Tips

To make a dozen cupcakes, double all ingredients.

Letting the batter stand for 30 minutes before baking results in lighter textured, more tender cupcakes. But if you're short on time, you can bake the cupcakes immediately.

■ **6-cup muffin pan, lined with paper liners**

1	large egg	1
$2/3$ cup	plain yogurt	150 mL
2 tbsp	vegetable oil	30 mL
1 tbsp	freshly squeezed lemon juice	15 mL
1	portion Make Your Own Cupcake Mix (page 212)	1

1. In a bowl, using a handheld electric mixer, beat egg, yogurt, oil and lemon juice until combined. Add cupcake mix and mix just until combined.

2. Spoon batter into prepared muffin cups, dividing evenly. Let stand for 30 minutes. Meanwhile, preheat oven to 350°F (180°C).

3. Bake for 20 to 23 minutes or until a tester inserted in the center of a cupcake comes out clean. Let cool in pan on a rack for 5 minutes. Remove from pan and let cool completely on rack.

Variation

For a mild spice flavor, add $1/4$ tsp (1 mL) freshly ground nutmeg.

Nutritional value per serving	
Calories	210
Fat, total	7 g
Fat, saturated	1 g
Cholesterol	33 mg
Sodium	233 mg
Carbohydrate	34 g
Fiber	1 g
Protein	5 g
Calcium	101 mg
Iron	2 mg

Apricot Prune Cupcakes

Looking for a delicious way to add fiber to your diet? Here's the answer!

■■■■■■■■■■■■■■

Tips

Instead of chopping with a knife, snip dried apricots and prunes with kitchen shears. Dip the blades in hot water when they become sticky.

To make a dozen cupcakes, double all ingredients.

Store cupcakes at room temperature for up to 3 days. Freeze individually, wrapped airtight, for up to 6 weeks.

■ **6-cup muffin pan, lined with paper liners**

1	large egg	1
1 tsp	grated orange zest	5 mL
2/3 cup	freshly squeezed orange juice	150 mL
2 tbsp	vegetable oil	30 mL
1	portion Make Your Own Cupcake Mix (page 212)	1
1/4 tsp	ground allspice	1 mL
1/2 cup	snipped dried apricots	125 mL
1/2 cup	snipped pitted prunes	125 mL

1. In a bowl, using a handheld electric mixer, beat egg, orange zest, orange juice and oil until combined. Add cupcake mix and allspice; mix just until combined. Stir in apricots and prunes.

2. Spoon batter into prepared muffin cups, dividing evenly. Let stand for 30 minutes. Meanwhile, preheat oven to 350°F (180°C).

3. Bake for 18 to 20 minutes or until a tester inserted in the center of a cupcake comes out clean. Let cool in pan on a rack for 5 minutes. Remove from pan and let cool completely on rack.

Variations

Replace the prunes with chopped dates.
Substitute ground ginger for the allspice.

Nutritional value per serving	
Calories	275
Fat, total	6 g
Fat, saturated	1 g
Cholesterol	31 mg
Sodium	215 mg
Carbohydrate	53 g
Fiber	3 g
Protein	4 g
Calcium	70 mg
Iron	3 mg

Blueberry Banana Oat Cupcakes

These blueberry-studded cupcakes are sure to please even the most discriminating palates. They are a bit larger than some of the other cupcakes made with our mix.

Tips

To partially thaw small frozen blueberries, spread them in a single layer on a microwave-safe plate and microwave on High for 45 seconds. For large berries, double the microwave time.

To make a dozen cupcakes, double all ingredients.

For a more pronounced banana flavor, serve these warm from the oven.

Nutritional value per serving	
Calories	280
Fat, total	7 g
Fat, saturated	1 g
Cholesterol	31 mg
Sodium	214 mg
Carbohydrate	53 g
Fiber	4 g
Protein	5 g
Calcium	59 mg
Iron	3 mg

■ **6-cup muffin pan, lined with paper liners**

1	large egg	1
1 cup	mashed bananas	250 mL
2 tbsp	vegetable oil	30 mL
1 tbsp	freshly squeezed lemon juice	15 mL
1	portion Make Your Own Cupcake Mix (page 212)	1
1/3 cup	GF large-flake (old-fashioned) rolled oats	75 mL
2 tbsp	GF oat bran	30 mL
3/4 cup	fresh or partially thawed frozen blueberries	175 mL

1. In a bowl, using a handheld electric mixer, beat egg, bananas, oil and lemon juice until combined. Add cupcake mix, oats and oat bran; mix just until combined. Stir in blueberries.

2. Spoon batter into prepared muffin cups, dividing evenly. Let stand for 30 minutes. Meanwhile, preheat oven to 350°F (180°C).

3. Bake for 20 to 23 minutes or until a tester inserted in the center of a cupcake comes out clean. Let cool in pan on a rack for 5 minutes. Remove from pan and let cool completely on rack.

Variations

Substitute rice bran for the GF oat bran.

Substitute chopped plums for the blueberries.

Blueberry Peach Cupcakes

As pleasing to the eye as they are to the palate, these tempting cupcakes are especially wonderful at the height of peach and blueberry season.

■ ■ ■ ■ ■ ■ ■ ■ ■ ■ ■ ■ ■ ■

Tips

To partially thaw small frozen blueberries, spread them in a single layer on a microwave-safe plate and microwave on High for 45 seconds. For large berries, double the microwave time.

To make a dozen cupcakes, double all ingredients.

Letting the batter stand for 30 minutes before baking results in lighter textured, more tender cupcakes. But if you're short on time, you can bake the cupcakes immediately.

Nutritional value per serving	
Calories	220
Fat, total	7 g
Fat, saturated	1 g
Cholesterol	33 mg
Sodium	233 mg
Carbohydrate	37 g
Fiber	2 g
Protein	5 g
Calcium	103 mg
Iron	2 mg

■ **6-cup muffin pan, lined with paper liners**

1	large egg	1
2/3 cup	plain yogurt	150 mL
2 tbsp	vegetable oil	30 mL
1 tsp	grated lemon zest	5 mL
1 tbsp	freshly squeezed lemon juice	15 mL
1	portion Make Your Own Cupcake Mix (page 212)	1
1 tsp	ground cardamom	5 mL
1/2 cup	chopped peaches	125 mL
1/4 cup	fresh or partially thawed frozen blueberries	60 mL

1. In a bowl, using a handheld electric mixer, beat egg, yogurt, oil, lemon zest and lemon juice until combined. Add cupcake mix and cardamom; mix just until combined. Stir in peaches and blueberries.

2. Spoon batter into prepared muffin cups, dividing evenly. Let stand for 30 minutes. Meanwhile, preheat oven to 350°F (180°C).

3. Bake for 20 to 23 minutes or until a tester inserted in the center of a cupcake comes out clean. Let cool in pan on a rack for 5 minutes. Remove from pan and let cool completely on rack.

Variations

For a milder spice flavor, use ground mace or nutmeg in place of the cardamom.

Substitute chopped plums for the blueberries.

Red Plum Cupcakes

With moist, tender plums popping to the surface, these cupcakes would have Little Jack Horner warming up his thumb.

■■■■■■■■■■■■■■■

Tips

For an attractive contrast in color and flavor, use both yellow and dark plums.

Two large plums will yield about 1 cup (250 mL) chopped. There's no need to peel the plums.

To make a dozen muffins, double all ingredients.

■ **6-cup muffin pan, lined with paper liners**

1	large egg	1
⅔ cup	plain yogurt	150 mL
2 tbsp	vegetable oil	30 mL
1	portion Make Your Own Cupcake Mix (page 212)	1
1 tbsp	grated orange zest	15 mL
1 tsp	ground nutmeg	5 mL
1 cup	diced plums	250 mL

1. In a bowl, using a handheld electric mixer, beat egg, yogurt and oil until combined. Add cupcake mix, orange zest and nutmeg; mix just until combined. Stir in plums.

2. Spoon batter into prepared muffin cups, dividing evenly. Let stand for 30 minutes. Meanwhile, preheat oven to 350°F (180°C).

3. Bake for 20 to 23 minutes or until a tester inserted in the center of a cupcake comes out clean. Let cool in pan on a rack for 5 minutes. Remove from pan and let cool completely on rack.

Variation

Try apricot- or peach-flavored yogurt (regular, low-fat or fat-free) instead of plain.

Nutritional value per serving	
Calories	227
Fat, total	7 g
Fat, saturated	1 g
Cholesterol	33 mg
Sodium	233 mg
Carbohydrate	38 g
Fiber	2 g
Protein	5 g
Calcium	104 mg
Iron	2 mg

Cranberry Hazelnut Cupcakes

The colors in these cupcakes are perfect for the holidays, but you may want to serve them all year round.

■■■■■■■■■■■■■■■■

Tips

Use your favorite type of marmalade — we like these with lemon, orange or three-fruit marmalade.

Purchase cranberries when they're in season, then freeze them in their original package for later use.

To partially thaw frozen cranberries, spread them in a single layer on a microwave-safe plate and microwave on High for 1 minute.

To make a dozen cupcakes, double all ingredients.

■ **6-cup muffin pan, lined with paper liners**

1	large egg	1
1/3 cup	milk	75 mL
1/4 cup	marmalade (see tip, at left)	60 mL
2 tbsp	vegetable oil	30 mL
1	portion Make Your Own Cupcake Mix (page 212)	1
1/2 tsp	ground ginger	2 mL
3/4 cup	fresh or partially thawed frozen cranberries	175 mL
1/3 cup	chopped hazelnuts	75 mL

1. In a bowl, using a handheld electric mixer, beat egg, milk, marmalade and oil until combined. Add cupcake mix and ginger; mix just until combined. Stir in cranberries and hazelnuts.

2. Spoon batter into prepared muffin cups, dividing evenly. Let stand for 30 minutes. Meanwhile, preheat oven to 350°F (180°C).

3. Bake for 20 to 23 minutes or until a tester inserted in the center of a cupcake comes out clean. Let cool in pan on a rack for 5 minutes. Remove from pan and let cool completely on rack.

Variation

For extra decadence, drizzle Hazelnut Drizzle (page 230) over the cooled cupcakes.

Nutritional value per serving	
Calories	277
Fat, total	10 g
Fat, saturated	1 g
Cholesterol	32 mg
Sodium	228 mg
Carbohydrate	44 g
Fiber	3 g
Protein	5 g
Calcium	81 mg
Iron	2 mg

Chocolate Chip Macadamia Nut Cupcakes

Make these for your kids or keep them for yourself. Either way, they will disappear quickly.

■■■■■■■■■■■■■■■■

Tips

To make a dozen cupcakes, double all ingredients.

Letting the batter stand for 30 minutes before baking results in lighter textured, more tender cupcakes. But if you're short on time, you can bake the cupcakes immediately.

■ **6-cup muffin pan, lined with paper liners**

1	large egg	1
⅔ cup	plain yogurt	150 mL
2 tbsp	vegetable oil	30 mL
1 tbsp	freshly squeezed lemon juice	15 mL
1	portion Make Your Own Cupcake Mix (page 212)	1
½ cup	white chocolate chips	125 mL
¼ cup	chopped macadamia nuts	60 mL

1. In a bowl, using a handheld electric mixer, beat egg, yogurt, oil and lemon juice until combined. Add cupcake mix and mix just until combined. Stir in white chocolate chips and macadamia nuts.

2. Spoon batter into prepared muffin cups, dividing evenly. Let stand for 30 minutes. Meanwhile, preheat oven to 350°F (180°C).

3. Bake for 20 to 23 minutes or until a tester inserted in the center of a cupcake comes out clean. Let cool in pan on a rack for 5 minutes. Remove from pan and let cool completely on rack.

Variation

Substitute raspberry-flavored chocolate chunks for the white chocolate chips and toasted chopped pecans for the macadamia nuts.

Nutritional value per serving	
Calories	319
Fat, total	15 g
Fat, saturated	4 g
Cholesterol	36 mg
Sodium	246 mg
Carbohydrate	43 g
Fiber	2 g
Protein	6 g
Calcium	131 mg
Iron	2 mg

Banana Cranberry Cupcakes for 6

Makes 6 cupcakes
Serving size: 1 cupcake

These easy-to-carry cupcakes with a delicious banana flavor can be put in a lunch bag still frozen, helping to keep your sandwich cold until lunchtime.

■■■■■■■■■■■■■■■■

Tips

Mash and freeze ripe bananas so they are ready when you need them. Thaw and bring to room temperature before using.

Store cupcakes at room temperature for up to 3 days. Freeze individually, wrapped airtight, for up to 6 weeks.

Nutritional value per serving	
Calories	237
Fat, total	6 g
Fat, saturated	1 g
Cholesterol	32 mg
Sodium	228 mg
Carbohydrate	44 g
Fiber	3 g
Protein	3 g
Calcium	79 mg
Iron	1 mg

■ **6-cup muffin pan, lined with paper liners**

½ cup	sorghum flour	125 mL
¼ cup	low-fat soy flour	60 mL
¼ cup	tapioca starch	60 mL
1 tsp	GF baking powder	5 mL
½ tsp	baking soda	2 mL
1½ tsp	xanthan gum	7 mL
¼ tsp	salt	1 mL
1	large egg	1
2 tbsp	vegetable oil	30 mL
½ cup	packed brown sugar	125 mL
½ cup	mashed banana	125 mL
¼ cup	plain yogurt	60 mL
½ tsp	vanilla extract	2 mL
½ cup	dried cranberries	125 mL

1. In a bowl or plastic bag, combine sorghum flour, soy flour, tapioca starch, baking powder, baking soda, xanthan gum and salt. Mix well and set aside.

2. In a separate bowl, using a handheld electric mixer, beat egg and oil until combined. While beating, add brown sugar, banana, yogurt and vanilla. Beat until well blended. Gradually beat in dry ingredients. Continue beating just until smooth, about 2 minutes. Stir in cranberries.

3. Spoon batter into prepared muffin cups, dividing evenly. Let stand for 30 minutes. Meanwhile, preheat oven to 350°F (180°C).

4. Bake for 20 to 25 minutes or until a tester inserted in the center of a cupcake comes out clean. Let cool in pan on a rack for 5 minutes. Remove from pan and let cool completely on rack.

Variation

Substitute fresh or dried blueberries, dried cherries or golden raisins for the cranberries.

Banana Cranberry Cupcakes for 30

When you need to take a dessert to a support group meeting, these cupcakes are a great choice.

■■■■■■■■■■■■■■■

Tips

Fill muffin cups almost level with the top. Fill empty cups one-quarter full with water.

Letting the batter stand for 30 minutes before baking results in lighter textured, more tender cupcakes. But if you're short on time, you can bake the cupcakes immediately.

If baking all three pans at once, rotate their positions in the oven after 10 minutes for even baking. We find that one pan of batter can sit on the counter while the first two pans are baking.

Nutritional value per serving	
Calories	196
Fat, total	5 g
Fat, saturated	1 g
Cholesterol	25 mg
Sodium	162 mg
Carbohydrate	35 g
Fiber	2 g
Protein	5g
Calcium	60 mg
Iron	1 mg

■ **Three 12-cup muffin pans, 30 cups lined with paper liners**

1½ cups	sorghum flour	375 mL
1½ cups	low-fat soy flour	375 mL
½ cup	potato starch	125 mL
½ cup	tapioca starch	125 mL
2 tsp	GF baking powder	10 mL
1½ tsp	baking soda	7 mL
1 tbsp	xanthan gum	15 mL
1 tsp	salt	5 mL
4	large eggs	4
½ cup	vegetable oil	125 mL
2 cups	packed brown sugar	500 mL
2 cups	mashed bananas	500 mL
1 cup	plain yogurt	250 mL
2 tsp	vanilla extract	10 mL
2 cups	dried cranberries	500 mL

1. In a large bowl or plastic bag, combine sorghum flour, soy flour, potato starch, tapioca starch, baking powder, baking soda, xanthan gum and salt. Mix well and set aside.

2. In a separate large bowl, using a handheld electric mixer, beat eggs and oil until combined. While beating, add brown sugar, bananas, yogurt and vanilla. Beat until well blended. Gradually beat in dry ingredients. Continue beating just until smooth, about 2 minutes. Stir in cranberries.

3. Spoon batter into prepared muffin cups, dividing evenly. Let stand for 30 minutes. Meanwhile, preheat oven to 350°F (180°C).

4. Bake for 20 to 25 minutes or until a tester inserted in the center of a cupcake comes out clean. Let cool in pans on a rack for 5 minutes. Remove from pans and let cool completely on rack.

Variation

Substitute fresh or dried blueberries, dried cherries or golden raisins for the cranberries.

Fudgy Cupcakes for 24

Makes 24 cupcakes
Serving size: 1 cupcake

This recipe is our answer to a special request for chocolate cupcakes for a teenager's birthday party. No one will suspect these are gluten-free.

■■■■■■■■■■■■■■■

Tips

When you're stirring in the dry ingredients alternately with the sour cream, you can either use the handheld mixer on low speed or switch to using a rubber spatula. Mix just until blended after each addition. This technique results in more even-textured cupcakes.

Store cupcakes at room temperature for up to 3 days. Freeze individually, wrapped airtight, for up to 6 weeks.

Nutritional value per serving	
Calories	177
Fat, total	8 g
Fat, saturated	5 g
Cholesterol	45 mg
Sodium	217 mg
Carbohydrate	26 g
Fiber	1 g
Protein	3 g
Calcium	55 mg
Iron	1 mg

■ **Two 12-cup muffin pans, lined with paper liners**

¾ cup	sorghum flour	175 mL
¾ cup	whole bean flour	175 mL
½ cup	potato starch	125 mL
¼ cup	tapioca starch	60 mL
½ tsp	GF baking powder	2 mL
1½ tsp	baking soda	7 mL
1 tsp	xanthan gum	5 mL
½ tsp	salt	2 mL
¾ cup	sifted unsweetened cocoa powder	175 mL
¾ cup	butter, softened, or shortening	175 mL
1½ cups	packed brown sugar	375 mL
3	large eggs	3
2 tsp	vanilla extract	10 mL
2 cups	GF sour cream	500 mL

1. In a large bowl or plastic bag, combine sorghum flour, whole bean flour, potato starch, tapioca starch, baking powder, baking soda, xanthan gum, salt and cocoa powder. Mix well and set aside.

2. In a separate bowl, using a handheld electric mixer, cream butter until fluffy. Gradually beat in brown sugar. Continue beating until light and fluffy. Add eggs, one at a time, beating well after each. Stir in vanilla. Stir in dry ingredients alternately with sour cream, making three additions of dry and two of sour cream.

3. Spoon batter into prepared muffin cups, dividing evenly. Let stand for 30 minutes. Meanwhile, preheat oven to 350°F (180°C).

4. Bake for 20 to 23 minutes or until a tester inserted in the center of a cupcake comes out clean. Let cool in pans on a rack for 5 minutes. Remove from pans and let cool completely on rack.

Variation

For milk chocolate–flavored cupcakes, decrease the cocoa powder to ½ cup (125 mL) and substitute granulated sugar for the brown sugar.

Harvest Cupcakes for 24

These moist cupcakes are perfect for a Halloween party, but serve them all year round. They make an excellent snack to carry in your lunch bag for a mid-morning break.

■■■■■■■■■■■■■■■

Tips

Be sure to buy pumpkin purée, not pumpkin pie filling, which is too sweet and contains too much moisture for these cupcakes. We often make Pumpkin Tarts (page 252) with the leftover pumpkin purée.

Letting the batter stand for 30 minutes before baking results in lighter textured, more tender cupcakes. But if you're short on time, you can bake the cupcakes immediately.

Nutritional value per serving	
Calories	120
Fat, total	5 g
Fat, saturated	3 g
Cholesterol	26 mg
Sodium	138 mg
Carbohydrate	19 g
Fiber	1 g
Protein	2 g
Calcium	34 mg
Iron	1 mg

■ Two 12-cup muffin pans, lined with paper liners

1 cup	sorghum flour	250 mL
¾ cup	whole bean flour	175 mL
¼ cup	potato starch	60 mL
¼ cup	tapioca starch	60 mL
1½ tsp	GF baking powder	7 mL
¾ tsp	baking soda	3 mL
2 tsp	xanthan gum	10 mL
½ tsp	salt	2 mL
1 tsp	ground cinnamon	5 mL
½ tsp	ground allspice	2 mL
½ tsp	ground ginger	2 mL
½ tsp	ground nutmeg	2 mL
½ cup	butter, softened, or shortening	125 mL
1 cup	packed brown sugar	250 mL
2	large eggs	2
1 cup	canned pumpkin purée (not pie filling)	250 mL
¼ cup	frozen orange juice concentrate, thawed	60 mL
1 tsp	vanilla extract	5 mL

1. In a large bowl or plastic bag, combine sorghum flour, whole bean flour, potato starch, tapioca starch, baking powder, baking soda, xanthan gum, salt, cinnamon, allspice, ginger and nutmeg. Mix well and set aside.

2. In a separate bowl, using a handheld electric mixer, cream butter until fluffy. Gradually beat in brown sugar. Continue beating until light and fluffy. Add eggs, one at a time, beating well after each. Stir in pumpkin purée, orange juice and vanilla until light and fluffy. Gradually beat in dry ingredients. Continue beating just until smooth, about 2 minutes.

3. Spoon batter into prepared muffin cups, dividing evenly. Let stand for 30 minutes. Meanwhile, preheat oven to 350°F (180°C).

4. Bake for 20 to 23 minutes or until a tester inserted in the center of a cupcake comes out clean. Let cool in pans on a rack for 5 minutes. Remove from pans and let cool completely on rack.

Sour Cream Fudge Cupcakes

With a double dose of chocolate, these cupcakes will thrill every chocoholic.

■■■■■■■■■■■■■■■

Tips

Fill muffin cups almost level with the top. Fill the empty cups one-quarter full with water.

To make 16 cupcakes, double all ingredients.

We used a dark chocolate containing 70% cacao.

Nutritional value per serving	
Calories	233
Fat, total	12 g
Fat, saturated	7 g
Cholesterol	66 mg
Sodium	241 mg
Carbohydrate	30 g
Fiber	1 g
Protein	4 g
Calcium	88 mg
Iron	1 mg

■ **12-cup muffin pan, 8 cups lined with paper liners**

2 oz	bittersweet (dark) chocolate, cut in half	60 g
¼ cup	butter	60 mL
⅓ cup	sorghum flour	75 mL
¼ cup	whole bean flour	60 mL
¼ cup	tapioca starch	60 mL
1 tsp	xanthan gum	5 mL
2 tsp	GF baking powder	10 mL
½ tsp	baking soda	2 mL
¼ tsp	salt	1 mL
½ cup	granulated sugar	125 mL
2	large eggs	2
½ cup	GF sour cream or plain yogurt	125 mL
1	recipe Dark Chocolate Drizzle (page 230)	1

1. In a microwave-safe bowl, microwave chocolate and butter on Medium (50%) for 3 minutes or until partially melted. Stir until completely melted. Set aside to cool slightly.

2. In a bowl or plastic bag, combine sorghum flour, whole bean flour, tapioca starch, xanthan gum, baking powder, baking soda and salt. Mix well and set aside.

3. In a separate bowl, using a handheld electric mixer, beat melted chocolate, sugar, eggs and sour cream until combined. Add dry ingredients and mix just until combined.

4. Spoon batter into prepared muffin cups, dividing evenly. Let stand for 30 minutes. Meanwhile, preheat oven to 350°F (180°C).

5. Bake for 20 to 23 minutes or until a tester inserted in the center of a cupcake comes out clean. Let cool in pan on a rack for 5 minutes. Remove from pan and let cool completely on rack. Drizzle with Dark Chocolate Drizzle.

Variation

For German chocolate cupcakes, substitute sweet chocolate (such as Baker's German's or Baker's) for the dark chocolate.

Heavenly Chocolate Cupcakes

Makes 6 cupcakes
Serving size: 1 cupcake

Heavenly is the only way to describe these — need we say more?

■■■■■■■■■■■■■■■■

Tips

Letting the batter stand for 30 minutes before baking results in lighter textured, more tender cupcakes. But if you're short on time, you can bake the cupcakes immediately.

Store cupcakes at room temperature for up to 3 days. Freeze individually, wrapped airtight, for up to 6 weeks.

To make a dozen cupcakes, double all ingredients.

Nutritional value per serving

Calories	282
Fat, total	13 g
Fat, saturated	4 g
Cholesterol	41 mg
Sodium	251 mg
Carbohydrate	40 g
Fiber	3 g
Protein	5 g
Calcium	103 mg
Iron	2 mg

■ **6-cup muffin pan, lined with paper liners**

½ cup	sorghum flour	125 mL
¼ cup	quinoa flour	60 mL
¼ cup	tapioca starch	60 mL
1 tsp	GF baking powder	5 mL
½ tsp	baking soda	2 mL
1 tsp	xanthan gum	5 mL
¼ tsp	salt	1 mL
2 tbsp	sifted unsweetened cocoa powder	30 mL
⅓ cup	packed brown sugar	75 mL
1	large egg	1
¾ cup	GF sour cream	175 mL
3 tbsp	vegetable oil	45 mL
⅓ cup	semisweet chocolate chips	75 mL

1. In a bowl or plastic bag, combine sorghum flour, quinoa flour, tapioca starch, baking powder, baking soda, xanthan gum, salt and cocoa powder. Mix well and set aside.

2. In a separate bowl, using a handheld electric mixer, beat brown sugar, egg, sour cream and oil until combined. Add dry ingredients and mix until just combined. Stir in chocolate chips.

3. Spoon batter into prepared muffin cups, dividing evenly. Let stand for 30 minutes. Meanwhile, preheat oven to 350°F (180°C).

4. Bake for 18 to 20 minutes or until a tester inserted in the center of a cupcake comes out clean. Let cool in pan on a rack for 5 minutes. Remove from pan and let cool completely on rack.

Variation

Substitute buttermilk for the GF sour cream.

Almond Cupcakes

In these cupcakes, we used almond flour, toasted almonds and almond extract for a true almond flavor.

■■■■■■■■■■■■■■■

Tips

For information on toasting nuts, see the Techniques Glossary, page 309. Don't skip this step.

Fill muffin cups almost level with the top.

To make a dozen cupcakes, double all ingredients.

■ **6-cup muffin pan, lined with paper liners**

1/3 cup	amaranth flour	75 mL
1/3 cup	brown rice flour	75 mL
1/4 cup	almond flour	60 mL
3 tbsp	tapioca starch	45 mL
1 tbsp	GF baking powder	15 mL
1/2 tsp	baking soda	2 mL
1 tsp	xanthan gum	5 mL
1/4 tsp	salt	1 mL
1/2 cup	toasted slivered almonds	125 mL
1/3 cup	granulated sugar	75 mL
1	large egg	1
1/2 cup	GF sour cream	125 mL
3 tbsp	vegetable oil	45 mL
2 tsp	almond extract	10 mL

1. In a bowl or plastic bag, combine amaranth flour, brown rice flour, almond flour, tapioca starch, baking powder, baking soda, xanthan gum, salt and almonds. Mix well and set aside.

2. In a separate bowl, using a handheld electric mixer, beat sugar, egg, sour cream, oil and almond extract until combined. Add dry ingredients and mix just until combined.

3. Spoon batter into prepared muffin cups, dividing evenly. Let stand for 30 minutes. Meanwhile, preheat oven to 350°F (180°C).

4. Bake for 20 to 23 minutes or until a tester inserted in the center of a cupcake comes out clean. Let cool in pan on a rack for 5 minutes. Remove from pan and let cool completely on rack.

Variation

For a refreshing twist, drizzle Citrus Drizzle (page 231) over the cooled cupcakes.

Nutritional value per serving

Calories	310
Fat, total	18 g
Fat, saturated	2 g
Cholesterol	38 mg
Sodium	237 mg
Carbohydrate	32 g
Fiber	3 g
Protein	6 g
Calcium	190 mg
Iron	3 mg

Banana Cupcakes

Lighter than banana bread, these cupcakes are a great way to use up overripe bananas.

■■■■■■■■■■■■■■■■

Tips

Letting the batter stand for 30 minutes before baking results in lighter textured, more tender cupcakes. But if you're short on time, you can bake the cupcakes immediately.

Fill muffin cups almost level with the top.

Store un-iced cupcakes at room temperature for up to 3 days. Freeze individually, wrapped airtight, for up to 6 weeks.

To make a dozen cupcakes, double all ingredients.

■ 6-cup muffin pan, lined with paper liners

½ cup	teff flour	125 mL
¼ cup	tapioca starch	60 mL
1 tsp	GF baking powder	5 mL
½ tsp	baking soda	2 mL
1 tsp	xanthan gum	5 mL
¼ tsp	salt	1 mL
½ cup	mashed banana	125 mL
⅓ cup	packed brown sugar	75 mL
1	large egg	1
¼ cup	vegetable oil	60 mL
¼ cup	GF sour cream or plain yogurt	60 mL
¾ cup	Cream Cheese Frosting (page 232)	175 mL

1. In a bowl or plastic bag, combine teff flour, tapioca starch, baking powder, baking soda, xanthan gum and salt. Mix well and set aside.

2. In a separate bowl, using a handheld electric mixer, beat banana, brown sugar, egg, oil and sour cream until combined. Add dry ingredients and mix just until combined.

3. Spoon batter into prepared muffin cups, dividing evenly. Let stand for 30 minutes. Meanwhile, preheat oven to 350°F (180°C).

4. Bake for 18 to 22 minutes or until a tester inserted in the center of a cupcake comes out clean. Let cool in pan on a rack for 5 minutes. Remove from pan and let cool completely on rack. Frost with Cream Cheese Frosting.

Variations

Frost with Maple Buttercream Frosting (page 231), then sprinkle with toasted chopped walnuts.

Drizzle cupcakes with Dark Chocolate Drizzle (page 230) instead of using frosting.

Nutritional value per serving	
Calories	360
Fat, total	16 g
Fat, saturated	5 g
Cholesterol	50 mg
Sodium	319 mg
Carbohydrate	51 g
Fiber	2 g
Protein	4 g
Calcium	100 mg
Iron	1 mg

Lemon-Lime Cupcakes

Everyone will enjoy the refreshing flavor of citrus in these springtime cupcakes.

■■■■■■■■■■■■■■

Tips

Fill muffin cups almost level with the top.

Store cupcakes, without drizzle, at room temperature for up to 3 days. Freeze individually, wrapped airtight, for up to 6 weeks.

To make a dozen cupcakes, double all ingredients.

Nutritional value per serving

Calories	236
Fat, total	7 g
Fat, saturated	1 g
Cholesterol	36 mg
Sodium	230 mg
Carbohydrate	42 g
Fiber	1 g
Protein	6 g
Calcium	154 mg
Iron	1 mg

■ **6-cup muffin pan, lined with paper liners**

½ cup	low-fat soy flour	125 mL
¼ cup	brown rice flour	60 mL
2 tbsp	tapioca starch	30 mL
1 tbsp	GF baking powder	15 mL
½ tsp	baking soda	2 mL
1 tsp	xanthan gum	5 mL
¼ tsp	salt	1 mL
½ cup	granulated sugar	125 mL
2 tsp	grated lemon zest	10 mL
2 tsp	grated lime zest	10 mL
1	large egg	1
⅓ cup	GF sour cream	75 mL
2 tbsp	freshly squeezed lemon juice	30 mL
2 tbsp	freshly squeezed lime juice	30 mL
2 tbsp	vegetable oil	30 mL
¼ cup	Citrus Drizzle (page 231)	60 mL

1. In a bowl or plastic bag, combine soy flour, brown rice flour, tapioca starch, baking powder, baking soda, xanthan gum and salt. Mix well and set aside.

2. In a separate bowl, using a handheld electric mixer, beat sugar, lemon zest, lime zest, egg, sour cream, lemon juice, lime juice and oil until combined. Add dry ingredients and mix just until combined.

3. Spoon batter into prepared muffin cups, dividing evenly. Let stand for 30 minutes. Meanwhile, preheat oven to 350°F (180°C).

4. Bake for 18 to 22 minutes or until a tester inserted in the center of a cupcake comes out clean. Let cool in pan on a rack for 5 minutes. Remove from pan and let cool completely on rack. Drizzle with Citrus Drizzle.

Pumpkin Raisin Cupcakes

These tempting cupcakes offer dark, rich color and a moist, tender crumb.

▪▪▪▪▪▪▪▪▪▪▪▪▪

Tips

Letting the batter stand for 30 minutes before baking results in lighter textured, more tender cupcakes. But if you're short on time, you can bake the cupcakes immediately.

Store cupcakes at room temperature for up to 3 days. Freeze individually, wrapped airtight, for up to 6 weeks.

To make a dozen cupcakes, double all ingredients.

Nutritional value per serving

Calories	282
Fat, total	10 g
Fat, saturated	1 g
Cholesterol	31 mg
Sodium	285 mg
Carbohydrate	47 g
Fiber	3 g
Protein	4 g
Calcium	114 mg
Iron	2 mg

■ **6-cup muffin pan, lined with paper liners**

1/2 cup	teff flour	125 mL
2 tbsp	tapioca starch	30 mL
2 tsp	GF baking powder	10 mL
1 tsp	baking soda	5 mL
1 tsp	xanthan gum	5 mL
1/8 tsp	salt	0.5 mL
1/2 tsp	ground cinnamon	2 mL
1/4 tsp	ground cloves	1 mL
1/4 tsp	ground nutmeg	1 mL
2/3 cup	granulated sugar	150 mL
1	large egg	1
1	large egg white	1
2/3 cup	pumpkin purée (not pie filling)	150 mL
1/4 cup	vegetable oil	60 mL
1/2 cup	raisins	125 mL

1. In a bowl or plastic bag, combine teff flour, tapioca starch, baking powder, baking soda, xanthan gum, salt, cinnamon, cloves and nutmeg. Mix well and set aside.

2. In a separate bowl, using a handheld electric mixer, beat sugar, egg, egg white, pumpkin purée and oil until combined. Add dry ingredients and mix just until combined. Stir in raisins.

3. Spoon batter into prepared muffin cups, dividing evenly. Let stand for 30 minutes. Meanwhile, preheat oven to 350°F (180°C).

4. Bake for 20 to 22 minutes or until a tester inserted in the center of a cupcake comes out clean. Let cool in pan on a rack for 5 minutes. Remove from pan and let cool completely on rack.

Dark Chocolate Drizzle

We like to drizzle this over Banana Cupcakes (page 227) and Brownies (page 188).

■■■■■■■■■■■■■■■

Tip
To decorate cupcakes, brownies and cookies with melted chocolate, you can either dip the tines of a fork in chocolate and drizzle or use a pastry bag fitted with a fine writing tip.

| ½ oz | good-quality bittersweet (dark) chocolate | 15 g |
| 1 tbsp | shortening | 15 mL |

1. In a microwave-safe bowl, microwave chocolate and shortening on Medium (50%) for 90 seconds or until partially melted. Stir until completely melted.

Nutritional value per serving			
Calories	31	Carbohydrate	1 g
Fat, total	3 g	Fiber	0 g
Fat, saturated	1 g	Protein	0 g
Cholesterol	0 mg	Calcium	1 mg
Sodium	5 mg	Iron	0 mg

Hazelnut Drizzle

We like to drizzle this over Hazelnut Cake (page 207) and Cranberry Hazelnut Cupcakes (page 218).

■■■■■■■■■■■■■■■

Variation
For an alcohol-free Orange Drizzle, use freshly squeezed orange juice in place of the liqueur.

½ cup	GF confectioner's (icing) sugar, sifted	125 mL
1 tbsp	butter, softened	15 mL
1 tbsp	hazelnut-flavored liqueur (such as Frangelico)	15 mL

1. In a small bowl, combine confectioner's sugar and butter. Add liqueur and stir until smooth.

Nutritional value per serving			
Calories	65	Carbohydrate	11 g
Fat, total	2 g	Fiber	0 g
Fat, saturated	1 g	Protein	0 g
Cholesterol	5 mg	Calcium	1 mg
Sodium	20 mg	Iron	0 mg

Citrus Drizzle

We like to drizzle this over **Lemon Poppy Cake (page 203)**, **Almond Cupcakes (page 226)** and **Lemon-Lime Cupcakes (page 228)**.

■■■■■■■■■■■■■■■

Tip
You can choose lemon, lime or orange for the citrus juice.

½ cup	GF confectioner's (icing) sugar, sifted	125 mL
1 tbsp	freshly squeezed citrus juice	15 mL

1. In a small bowl, combine confectioner's sugar and citrus juice. Stir until smooth.

Nutritional value per serving			
Calories	40	Carbohydrate	10 g
Fat, total	0 g	Fiber	0 g
Fat, saturated	0 g	Protein	0 g
Cholesterol	0 mg	Calcium	0 mg
Sodium	0 mg	Iron	0 mg

Maple Buttercream Frosting

This frosting is a natural complement to **Maple Walnut Cake (page 208)**, but is also delightful on **Banana Cupcakes (page 227)**.

■■■■■■■■■■■■■■■

Tip
Check to make sure your confectioner's (icing) sugar is gluten-free. It can contain up to 5% starch, which could be from wheat.

¼ cup	butter, softened	60 mL
1 cup	sifted GF confectioner's (icing) sugar	250 mL
2 tbsp	pure maple syrup	30 mL
½ tsp	maple extract	2 mL

1. In a bowl, using a handheld electric mixer, beat butter, confectioner's sugar, maple syrup and maple extract until smooth and creamy.

Variation
For a lighter frosting, fold in 1 cup (250 mL) whipped cream.

Nutritional value per serving			
Calories	163	Carbohydrate	24 g
Fat, total	8 g	Fiber	0 g
Fat, saturated	5 g	Protein	0 g
Cholesterol	20 mg	Calcium	7 mg
Sodium	78 mg	Iron	0 mg

Cream Cheese Frosting

**The traditional, all-time
favorite way to complete
a carrot cake!**

■■■■■■■■■■■■■■■

Tip

This recipe makes enough
frosting to frost a cake made
in either a 10-inch (25 cm)
Bundt pan or a 13- by 9-inch
(33 by 23 cm) baking pan.

1	package (8 oz/250 g) brick cream cheese, at room temperature	1
¼ cup	butter, softened	60 mL
2 cups	sifted GF confectioner's (icing) sugar	500 mL
1 tsp	vanilla extract	5 mL

1. In a bowl, using a handheld electric mixer, beat cream cheese and butter until light and fluffy. Beat in confectioner's sugar and vanilla until blended.

Nutritional value per serving			
Calories	102	Carbohydrate	14 g
Fat, total	5 g	Fiber	0 g
Fat, saturated	3 g	Protein	1 g
Cholesterol	13 mg	Calcium	17 mg
Sodium	85 mg	Iron	0 mg

Mini Batch Cream Cheese Frosting

**The only acceptable
topping for Carrot Cake
(page 209)!**

■■■■■■■■■■■■■■■

Tips

You can use light or regular
cream cheese in this recipe.
"Spreadable" or "whipped"
cream cheese softens too
quickly to use here.

To avoid lumps, sift the
confectioner's (icing) sugar
before measuring.

¼ cup	brick cream cheese, softened	60 mL
2 tbsp	butter, softened	30 mL
1 cup	sifted GF confectioner's (icing) sugar	250 mL
½ tsp	vanilla extract	2 mL

1. In a bowl, using a handheld electric mixer, beat cream cheese and butter until light and fluffy. Beat in confectioner's sugar and vanilla until blended.

Variation

For a thicker frosting, use an extra 2 tbsp (30 mL) GF confectioner's (icing) sugar.

Nutritional value per serving			
Calories	136	Carbohydrate	21 g
Fat, total	6 g	Fiber	0 g
Fat, saturated	4 g	Protein	1 g
Cholesterol	15 mg	Calcium	15 mg
Sodium	89 mg	Iron	0 mg

Pastry and Tarts

■ ■

Making Pastry

- In some recipes, we provide directions for both the food processor method and the traditional method of making pastry. Since this chapter contains recipes for tarts, only a small food processor (about 4 cups/1 L) can handle the small amounts of dough. The food processor method makes it easy to mix without over-handling. Process the ingredients by pulsing until the dough begins to stick together. With your fingertips, gather the dough into a light ball and gently press it together.

- In the traditional method, when using a pastry blender or two knives to cut in the shortening or butter, cut only until the pieces are the size of small peas. This results in a tender, flaky pastry. If the fat is too finely cut in or mashed, the pastry tends to be tough and heavy.

- To prepare the ice water, we add ice cubes to a small dish of water, then measure out the recipe amount once it is ice cold. Pastry is more tender when you use ice water rather than tap water.

- Form the dough into round, flattened discs before chilling. This shape is easier to roll out into a circle.

- Refrigerate the dough, tightly wrapped, for at least 1 hour before rolling out. It can be stored in the refrigerator for up to 3 days or in the freezer for up to 3 months. Thaw frozen pastry overnight in the refrigerator before rolling out.

- Roll out the dough between two sheets of parchment paper — it is easier to handle that way.

- Roll out the dough using light, long strokes from the center to the edges. Roll out to each side, then back to the center. Repeat until the dough is the desired size or thickness.

- Ease the pastry into the tart pan. Do not worry if it breaks where it touches the rim; just patch the shell with pastry scraps.

Mock Graham Wafer Crumb Crust

Missing crumb crusts?
No longer do you have
to do without. Use this
recipe to make crusts for
any of the tart recipes
in this chapter or any of
the cheesecake recipes in
the previous chapter.

■■■■■■■■■■■■■■■■■

Tip
Store the crumb mixture in
an airtight freezer bag at
room temperature for up to
2 weeks or in the freezer for
up to 3 months.

- Food processor
- Two 4¼-inch (11 cm) fluted tart pans, lightly greased

8	Mock Graham Wafers (page 186)	8
2 tbsp	butter, melted	30 mL

1. Break wafers into pieces. In a food processor, working with a few pieces at a time, pulse wafer pieces into crumbs.

2. In a bowl, combine cracker crumbs and butter, mixing well. Press into bottom and sides of prepared pans. Refrigerate for about 15 minutes, or until chilled, before carefully adding filling.

Variations

Pan size	Amount of wafers (for bottom of pan only)	Amount of butter
4½-inch (11 cm) springform pan	6	1½ tbsp (22 mL)
5¾- by 3½-inch (14 cm x 8 cm) mini loaf pan	4	1 tbsp (15 mL)
5¼- by 2½-inch (13 by 6 cm) mini loaf pan	3	2 tsp (10 mL)

Nutritional value per serving	
Calories	352
Fat, total	21 g
Fat, saturated	13 g
Cholesterol	56 mg
Sodium	291 mg
Carbohydrate	40 g
Fiber	1 g
Protein	3 g
Calcium	105 mg
Iron	1 mg

Basic Pastry

Easy as pie — truer words were never spoken, and making pastry becomes easier each time you do it. We'd like to say that this is truly a no-fail pastry.

■■■■■■■■■■■■■■

Tip

To ensure success, see page 234 for tips on making pastry.

Nutritional value per serving	
Calories	400
Fat, total	28 g
Fat, saturated	6 g
Cholesterol	53 mg
Sodium	151 mg
Carbohydrate	36 g
Fiber	2 g
Protein	2 g
Calcium	9 mg
Iron	0 mg

■ **Four 4¹/₄-inch (11 cm) fluted tart pans**

1	large egg yolk	1
3 tbsp	ice water	45 mL
1 tsp	cider vinegar	5 mL
¹/₂ cup	brown rice flour	125 mL
¹/₂ cup	cornstarch	125 mL
¹/₄ cup	tapioca starch	60 mL
2 tsp	xanthan gum	10 mL
¹/₄ tsp	salt	1 mL
¹/₂ cup	shortening	125 mL

Traditional Method

1. In a small bowl, whisk together egg yolk, ice water and vinegar. Set aside.

2. In a large bowl, sift brown rice flour, cornstarch, tapioca starch, xanthan gum and salt. Resift.

3. Using a pastry blender or two knives, cut in shortening until mixture resembles small peas. Sprinkle egg yolk mixture, a little at a time, over the flour mixture, stirring with a fork until a soft dough forms.

Food Processor Method

1. In a small bowl, whisk together egg yolk, ice water and vinegar. Set aside.

2. In a small food processor fitted with a metal blade, pulse brown rice flour, cornstarch, tapioca starch, xanthan gum and salt until combined.

3. Add shortening and pulse for 5 to 10 seconds or until mixture resembles small peas. With the motor running, add egg yolk mixture in a slow, steady stream; process until dough just holds together. Do not let it form a ball.

For Both Methods

4. Divide dough into 4 equal portions. Gently gather each portion into a ball and flatten into a disc. Wrap each disc in plastic wrap and place in a plastic bag. Refrigerate for at least 1 hour, until chilled, or overnight.

Tips

Choose a trans fat–free shortening if it is available or substitute butter for half the shortening.

Pastry can be stored in the refrigerator for up to 3 days or in the freezer for up to 3 months. Thaw frozen pastry overnight in the refrigerator before rolling out.

5. Remove 1 disc from the refrigerator. Unwrap the disc and place it on a sheet of parchment paper. Cover with another sheet of parchment paper. Roll out dough into a circle about 1 inch (2.5 cm) larger than the diameter of an inverted tart pan. Carefully remove the top sheet of parchment paper and invert the pastry over the tart pan, easing it in. Carefully peel off the remaining sheet of parchment paper. Repeat with the remaining discs.

6. Trim excess pastry to edge of tart pans and patch any cracks with trimmings. Using a sharp knife, trim the edges evenly.

To Bake Unfilled Pastry Shells

7. To prevent pastry from shrinking or puffing up, prick bottom and sides with a fork. Bake at 425°F (220°C) for 13 to 18 minutes or until golden. Let cool completely before filling.

To Bake Filled Pastry Shells

7. Do not prick the pastry. Spoon filling into unbaked pastry shells and bake according to individual recipe directions.

To Make 24 Mini Tart Shells

Remove 1 disc from the refrigerator. Unwrap the disc and place it on a sheet of parchment paper. Cover with another sheet of parchment paper. Roll out dough into an oval about $\frac{1}{8}$ inch (3 mm) thick. Using a 3-inch (7.5 cm) cookie cutter, cut out as many circles as possible. If dough sticks to parchment, loosen gently with the blade of a table knife. Ease into $1\frac{7}{8}$-inch (4.75 cm) mini tart pans. Reroll scraps. Repeat with the remaining discs. Return dough to the refrigerator if it becomes too sticky to roll.

To Make 8 Muffin Pan–Size Tart Shells

Divide dough into 8 equal discs before chilling. Remove 1 disc at a time from refrigerator and roll out 8 muffin pan–size tart shells. Follow the method above for filled or unfilled pastry shells.

Sour Cream Teff Pastry

This doesn't look like the typical white pastry, but is tasty and more nutritious. We developed it especially to bake individual tarts.

■■■■■■■■■■■■■■■■

Tip

To ensure success, see page 234 for tips on making pastry.

■ **Four 4¼-inch (11 cm) fluted tart pans**

¾ cup	teff flour	175 mL
½ cup	cornstarch	125 mL
2 tsp	xanthan gum	10 mL
¼ tsp	salt	1 mL
½ cup	cold butter, cut into ½-inch (1 cm) cubes	125 mL
2 tbsp	ice water	30 mL
¼ cup	GF sour cream	60 mL

1. In a bowl, combine teff flour, cornstarch, xanthan gum and salt. Using a pastry blender, cut in butter until mixture resembles small peas.

2. In a small bowl, combine ice water and sour cream. Sprinkle over flour mixture, stirring with a fork until a soft dough forms.

3. Divide dough into 4 equal portions. Gently gather each portion into a ball and flatten into a disc. Wrap each disc in plastic wrap and place in a plastic bag. Refrigerate for at least 1 hour, until chilled, or overnight.

4. Remove 1 disc from the refrigerator. Unwrap the disc and place it on a sheet of parchment paper. Cover with another sheet of parchment paper. Roll out dough into a circle about 1 inch (2.5 cm) larger than the diameter of an inverted tart pan. Carefully remove the top sheet of parchment paper and invert the pastry over the tart pan, easing it in. Carefully peel off the remaining sheet of parchment paper. Repeat with the remaining discs.

5. Trim excess pastry to edge of tart pans and patch any cracks with trimmings. Using a sharp knife, trim the edges evenly.

Nutritional value per serving	
Calories	378
Fat, total	26 g
Fat, saturated	16 g
Cholesterol	69 mg
Sodium	409 mg
Carbohydrate	34 g
Fiber	4 g
Protein	4 g
Calcium	73 mg
Iron	2 mg

Tips

If you prefer, you can press the dough into the tart pan rather than rolling it out.

Pastry can be stored in the refrigerator for up to 3 days or in the freezer for up to 3 months. Thaw frozen pastry overnight in the refrigerator before rolling out.

To Bake Unfilled Pastry Shells

6. To prevent pastry from shrinking or puffing up, prick bottom and sides with a fork. Bake at 425°F (220°C) for 13 to 18 minutes or until golden. Let cool completely before filling.

To Bake Filled Pastry Shells

6. Do not prick the pastry. Spoon filling into unbaked pastry shells and bake according to individual recipe directions.

To Make 24 Mini Tart Shells

Remove 1 disc from the refrigerator. Unwrap the disc and place it on a sheet of parchment paper. Cover with another sheet of parchment paper. Roll out dough into an oval about $\frac{1}{8}$ inch (3 mm) thick. Using a 3-inch (7.5 cm) cookie cutter, cut out as many circles as possible. If dough sticks to parchment, loosen gently with the blade of a table knife. Ease into $1\frac{7}{8}$-inch (4.75 cm) mini tart pans. Reroll scraps. Repeat with the remaining discs. Return dough to the refrigerator if it becomes too sticky to roll.

To Make 8 Muffin Pan–Size Tart Shells

Divide dough into 8 equal discs before chilling. Remove 1 disc at a time from refrigerator and roll out 8 muffin pan–size tart shells. Follow the method above for filled or unfilled pastry shells.

Shortbread Pastry

Makes 4 tart shells
Serving size: 1 tart shell

This pastry is richer than either our Basic Pastry (page 236) or our Sour Cream Teff Pastry (page 238).

■■■■■■■■■■■■■■■■

Tips

To ensure success, see page 234 for tips on making pastry.

To prepare the ice water, we add ice cubes to a small dish of water, then measure out the recipe amount once it is ice cold. Pastry is more tender when you use ice water rather than tap water.

■ Four 4¼-inch (11 cm) fluted tart pans

1	large egg yolk	1
¼ cup	ice water	60 mL
1 tsp	cider vinegar	5 mL
½ cup	amaranth flour	125 mL
½ cup	tapioca starch	125 mL
¼ cup	potato starch	60 mL
1 tsp	xanthan gum	5 mL
⅛ tsp	salt	0.5 mL
⅓ cup	cold butter, cut into ½-inch (1 cm) cubes	75 mL
	Sweet rice flour	

Traditional Method

1. In a small bowl, whisk together egg yolk, ice water and vinegar. Set aside.

2. In a large bowl, sift amaranth flour, tapioca starch, potato starch, xanthan gum and salt.

3. Using a pastry blender or two knives, cut in butter until mixture resembles small peas. Sprinkle egg yolk mixture, a little at a time, over the flour mixture, stirring with a fork until a soft dough forms.

Food Processor Method

1. In a small bowl, whisk together egg yolk, ice water and vinegar. Set aside.

2. In a small food processor fitted with a metal blade, pulse amaranth flour, tapioca starch, potato starch, xanthan gum and salt until combined.

3. Add butter and pulse for 5 to 10 seconds or until mixture resembles small peas. With the motor running, add egg yolk mixture in a slow, steady stream; process until dough just holds together. Do not let it form a ball.

For Both Methods

4. Divide dough into 4 equal portions. Gently gather each portion into a ball and flatten into a disc. Wrap each disc in plastic wrap and place in a plastic bag. Refrigerate for at least 1 hour, until chilled, or overnight.

Nutritional value per serving	
Calories	364
Fat, total	26 g
Fat, saturated	15 g
Cholesterol	117 mg
Sodium	318 mg
Carbohydrate	30 g
Fiber	2 g
Protein	3 g
Calcium	36 mg
Iron	4 mg

Tips

Roll out the dough using light, long strokes from the center to the edges. Roll out to each side, then back to the center. Repeat until the dough is the desired size or thickness.

Pastry can be stored in the refrigerator for up to 3 days or in the freezer for up to 3 months. Thaw frozen pastry overnight in the refrigerator before rolling out.

5. Remove 1 disc from the refrigerator. Unwrap the disc and place it between two sheets of waxed paper sprinkled with sweet rice flour. Roll out dough into a circle about $1/2$ inch (1 cm) larger than the diameter of an inverted tart pan. Carefully remove the top sheet of waxed paper and invert the pastry over the tart pan, easing it in. Carefully peel off the remaining sheet of waxed paper. Repeat with the remaining discs.

6. Trim excess pastry to edge of tart pans and patch any cracks with trimmings. Using a sharp knife, trim the edges evenly.

To Bake Unfilled Pastry Shells

7. To prevent pastry from shrinking or puffing up, prick bottom and sides with a fork. Bake at 375°F (190°C) for 22 to 25 minutes or until lightly browned. Let cool completely before filling.

To Bake Filled Pastry Shells

7. Do not prick the pastry. Spoon filling into unbaked pastry shells and bake according to individual recipe directions.

To Make 24 Mini Tart Shells

Remove 1 disc from the refrigerator. Unwrap the disc and place it on a sheet of parchment paper. Cover with another sheet of parchment paper. Roll out dough into an oval about $1/8$ inch (3 mm) thick. Using a 3-inch (7.5 cm) cookie cutter, cut out as many circles as possible. If dough sticks to parchment, loosen gently with the blade of a table knife. Ease into $1^7/8$-inch (4.75 cm) mini tart pans. Reroll scraps. Repeat with the remaining discs. Return dough to the refrigerator if it becomes too sticky to roll.

To Make 8 Muffin Pan–Size Tart Shells

Divide dough into 8 equal discs before chilling. Remove 1 disc at a time from refrigerator and roll out 8 muffin pan–size tart shells. Follow the method above for filled or unfilled pastry shells.

Pecan Pastry

This pastry is quick, easy and shortbread-tender, so there's no need to wait for holidays or special occasions to enjoy the pecan flavor. We use Pecan Pastry for fruit, pumpkin and cream tarts.

■■■■■■■■■■■■■■■■

Tips

To ensure success, see page 234 for tips on making pastry.

Work quickly to keep the pastry cold and prevent the butter from softening.

If pecan flour is not readily available, make your own (see the Techniques Glossary, page 309). Or substitute hazelnut flour or almond flour.

Nutritional value per serving	
Calories	448
Fat, total	30 g
Fat, saturated	15 g
Cholesterol	117 mg
Sodium	392 mg
Carbohydrate	40 g
Fiber	3 g
Protein	7 g
Calcium	31 mg
Iron	2 mg

■ **Four 4¼-inch (11 cm) fluted tart pans**

1	large egg yolk	1
3 tbsp	ice water	45 mL
1 tsp	cider vinegar	5 mL
½ cup	sorghum flour	125 mL
¼ cup	cornstarch	60 mL
¼ cup	tapioca starch	60 mL
¼ cup	sweet rice flour	60 mL
¼ cup	pecan flour	60 mL
1 tsp	xanthan gum	5 mL
¼ tsp	salt	1 mL
½ cup	cold butter, cut into ½-inch (1 cm) cubes	125 mL

Traditional Method

1. In a small bowl, whisk together egg yolk, ice water and vinegar. Set aside.

2. In a large bowl, sift sorghum flour, cornstarch, tapioca starch, sweet rice flour, pecan flour, xanthan gum and salt.

3. Using a pastry blender or two knives, cut in butter until mixture resembles small peas. Sprinkle egg yolk mixture, a little at a time, over the flour mixture, stirring with a fork until a soft dough forms.

Food Processor Method

1. In a small bowl, whisk together egg yolk, ice water and vinegar. Set aside.

2. In a small food processor fitted with a metal blade, pulse sorghum flour, cornstarch, tapioca starch, sweet rice flour, pecan flour, xanthan gum and salt until combined.

3. Add butter and pulse for 5 to 10 seconds or until mixture resembles small peas. With the motor running, add egg yolk mixture in a slow, steady stream; process until dough just holds together. Do not let it form a ball.

For Both Methods

4. Divide dough into 4 equal portions. Gently gather each portion into a ball and flatten into a disc. Wrap each disc in plastic wrap and place in a plastic bag. Refrigerate for at least 1 hour, until chilled, or overnight.

5. Remove 1 disc from the refrigerator. Unwrap the disc and place it on a sheet of parchment paper. Cover with another sheet of parchment paper. Roll out dough into a circle about 1 inch (2.5 cm) larger than the diameter of an inverted tart pan. Carefully remove the top sheet of parchment paper and invert the pastry over the tart pan, easing it in. Carefully peel off the remaining sheet of parchment paper. Repeat with the remaining discs.

6. Trim excess pastry to edge of tart pans and patch any cracks with trimmings. Using a sharp knife, trim the edges evenly.

To Bake Unfilled Pastry Shells

7. To prevent pastry from shrinking or puffing up, prick bottom and sides with a fork. Bake at 375°F (190°C) for 13 to 18 minutes or until firm to the touch. Let cool completely before filling.

To Bake Filled Pastry Shells

7. Do not prick the pastry. Spoon filling into unbaked pastry shells and bake according to individual recipe directions.

To Make 24 Mini Tart Shells

Remove 1 disc from the refrigerator. Unwrap the disc and place it on a sheet of parchment paper. Cover with another sheet of parchment paper. Roll out dough into an oval about $1/8$ inch (3 mm) thick. Using a 3-inch (7.5 cm) cookie cutter, cut out as many circles as possible. If dough sticks to parchment, loosen gently with the blade of a table knife. Ease into $1\frac{7}{8}$-inch (4.75 cm) mini tart pans. Reroll scraps. Repeat with the remaining discs. Return dough to the refrigerator if it becomes too sticky to roll.

To Make 8 Muffin Pan–Size Tart Shells

Divide dough into 8 equal discs before chilling. Remove 1 disc at a time from refrigerator and roll out 8 muffin pan–size tart shells. Follow the method above for filled or unfilled pastry shells.

Apple Pecan Crumble Tarts

Serve this perennial favorite with aged Cheddar cheese — the older, the better.

■■■■■■■■■■■■■■■

Tips

Choose a cooking apple variety, such as Northern Spy, Spartan or Golden Delicious.

The apple slices will shrink significantly during baking, so don't worry if they seem to be piled too high when you place them in the tart shell.

■ **Preheat oven to 375°F (190°C)**

½ cup	finely chopped pecans	125 mL
2 tbsp	packed brown sugar	30 mL
4 tsp	amaranth flour	20 mL
4 tsp	butter, softened	20 mL
2	apples, sliced	2
2	unbaked Shortbread Pastry tart shells (page 240)	2

1. In a bowl, combine pecans, brown sugar, amaranth flour and butter. Mix until crumbly.

2. Pile apple slices in tart shells, dividing evenly. Sprinkle pecan mixture over apples.

3. Bake in preheated oven for 35 to 38 minutes or until apples are tender and topping is browned. Let cool completely on a rack before removing from pans.

Variation

Add 2 tbsp (30 mL) fresh or frozen cranberries to each tart shell with the apple slices.

Nutritional value per serving	
Calories	789
Fat, total	56 g
Fat, saturated	22 g
Cholesterol	138 mg
Sodium	324 mg
Carbohydrate	72 g
Fiber	7 g
Protein	7 g
Calcium	87 mg
Iron	7 mg

Peach Blueberry Crumble Tarts

As pleasing to the eye as it is to the palate, this attractive tart makes a sweet treat at the height of summer.

■■■■■■■■■■■■■■■■

Tip

We added the filling to hot tart shells and baked immediately, and the crust did not turn out soggy. But you can also use room-temperature tart shells.

■ **Preheat oven to 375°F (190°C)**

Topping

2 tbsp	amaranth flour	30 mL
2 tbsp	packed brown sugar	30 mL
Pinch	ground cinnamon	Pinch
4 tsp	cold butter	20 mL

Filling

1¼ cups	coarsely chopped peaches	300 mL
¼ cup	blueberries	60 mL
1 tbsp	granulated sugar	15 mL
1 tbsp	amaranth flour	15 mL
¼ tsp	grated lemon zest	1 mL
Pinch	ground cinnamon	Pinch
¾ tsp	freshly squeezed lemon juice	3 mL
2	baked Sour Cream Teff Pastry tart shells (page 238)	2

1. *Topping:* In a small bowl, combine amaranth flour, brown sugar and cinnamon. Using a pastry blender or two knives, cut in butter until crumbly. Set aside.

2. *Filling:* In a large bowl, combine peaches, blueberries, sugar, amaranth flour, lemon zest, cinnamon and lemon juice.

3. Spoon filling into tart shells, dividing evenly. Sprinkle topping over top.

4. Bake in preheated oven for 30 to 35 minutes or until fruit is tender and topping is browned. Let cool completely on a rack before removing from pans.

Variation

Use any variety of chopped plums in place of the blueberries.

Nutritional value per serving	
Calories	620
Fat, total	34 g
Fat, saturated	20 g
Cholesterol	90 mg
Sodium	494 mg
Carbohydrate	76 g
Fiber	8 g
Protein	6 g
Calcium	112 mg
Iron	5 mg

Blueberry Tarts

Individual tarts are just the right size for you and your best friend. They are so easy to serve and look so elegant!

■■■■■■■■■■■■■■■■

Tip

One 6-oz (170 g) container of blueberries holds a generous cup (250 mL) of fruit.

1½ cups	blueberries	375 mL
3 tbsp	granulated sugar	45 mL
1 tbsp	cornstarch	15 mL
2 tbsp	water	30 mL
2 tsp	freshly squeezed lemon juice	10 mL
1 tsp	butter	5 mL
2	baked Pecan Pastry tart shells (page 242)	2

1. In a saucepan, combine blueberries, sugar, cornstarch and water. Bring to a boil over medium heat, stirring constantly. Reduce heat to low and simmer for about 5 minutes or until thick and shiny. Stir in lemon juice and butter.

2. Pour blueberry mixture into tart shells, dividing evenly. Refrigerate for 1 hour or until set.

Variation

Substitute blackberries or raspberries for the blueberries.

Make 4 muffin pan–size tarts.

Nutritional value per serving	
Calories	546
Fat, total	28 g
Fat, saturated	17 g
Cholesterol	75 mg
Sodium	437 mg
Carbohydrate	73 g
Fiber	7 g
Protein	5 g
Calcium	81 mg
Iron	2 mg

Rhubarb Tarts

Makes 2 tarts
Serving size: 1 tart

Freeze lots of rhubarb in the spring so you can use it to make this recipe all year round.

■■■■■■■■■■■■■■■■

Tip

If you buy frozen chopped rhubarb and the pieces are larger than 1 inch (2.5 cm), it's best to chop them into smaller pieces. We find it is much easier to chop rhubarb while it is still frozen.

■ **Preheat oven to 375°F (190°C)**

2 cups	frozen chopped rhubarb, thawed and drained	500 mL
2/3 cup	granulated sugar	150 mL
2 tbsp	amaranth flour	30 mL
2 tsp	grated orange zest	10 mL
2	unbaked Shortbread Pastry tart shells (page 240)	2
2 tsp	butter, softened	10 mL

1. In a bowl, combine rhubarb, sugar, amaranth flour and orange zest. Mix thoroughly.

2. Spoon rhubarb mixture into tart shells, dividing evenly. Dot with butter.

3. Bake in preheated oven for 35 to 38 minutes or until rhubarb is tender, filling bubbles and crust is light golden. Let cool completely on a rack before removing from pans.

Variations

Add the topping from the Apple Pecan Crumble Tarts (page 244) before baking.

Use 3/4 cup (175 mL) rhubarb and 1/4 cup (60 mL) sliced fresh strawberries.

Nutritional value per serving	
Calories	714
Fat, total	30 g
Fat, saturated	18 g
Cholesterol	128 mg
Sodium	322 mg
Carbohydrate	109 g
Fiber	5 g
Protein	5 g
Calcium	316 mg
Iron	6 mg

Lemon Meringue Tarts

Not too tangy, not too sweet — just perfect! Any excuse is a good excuse to make this recipe frequently.

■■■■■■■■■■■■■■■

Tips

It is worth the time and effort to squeeze a fresh lemon rather than use bottled juice.

For the tart shells, choose any of the pastry recipes on pages 236–242.

We like to use the whisk attachment that comes with our handheld mixer to beat the egg whites and yolks, as it makes quick work of the task.

If you don't seal the meringue to the tart shells, it will shrink and the heat from the oven will cause the filling to become thin and watery.

Nutritional value per serving

Calories	638
Fat, total	37 g
Fat, saturated	21 g
Cholesterol	247 mg
Sodium	351 mg
Carbohydrate	72 g
Fiber	2 g
Protein	7 g
Calcium	55 mg
Iron	5 mg

■ **Preheat oven to 400°F (200°C)**

1/4 cup	granulated sugar	60 mL
2 tbsp	cornstarch	30 mL
2/3 cup	water	150 mL
1 tsp	grated lemon zest	5 mL
1/4 cup	freshly squeezed lemon juice	60 mL
1 1/2 tbsp	butter	22 mL
1	large egg yolk	1
2	baked tart shells (see tip, at left)	2

Meringue

1	large egg white, at room temperature	1
1/8 tsp	cream of tartar	0.5 mL
1 tbsp	granulated sugar	15 mL

Microwave Method

1. In a microwave-safe bowl, combine sugar and cornstarch. Stir in water, lemon zest, lemon juice and butter. Microwave on High for 4 to 5 minutes, stopping several times to stir, until mixture boils and thickens.

2. Gradually whisk in egg yolk. Microwave on High for 30 seconds. Let cool for 5 minutes, then pour into tart shells, dividing evenly.

Stovetop Method

1. In a saucepan, combine sugar and cornstarch. Stir in water, lemon zest, lemon juice and butter. Heat over medium heat, stirring constantly, for 5 to 8 minutes or until mixture boils and thickens.

2. In a small bowl, beat egg yolk. Gradually whisk in half the sugar mixture until well blended. Pour egg mixture into the saucepan and stir until combined. Remove from heat and let cool for 5 minutes, then pour into tart shells.

For Both Methods

3. *Meringue:* In a separate bowl, using a handheld electric mixer, beat egg white and cream of tartar until egg white forms soft peaks. Gradually beat in sugar. Top tarts with meringue, sealing at the edges.

4. Bake in preheated oven for 5 to 6 minutes or until meringue is golden. Let cool completely on a rack. Serve immediately or cover and refrigerate for up to 1 day.

Banana Cream Tarts

Makes 2 tarts
Serving size: 1 tart

Choose a different pastry recipe each time you make these tarts so you can experience different flavor combinations.

■■■■■■■■■■■■■■■

Tip

For the tart shells, choose any of the pastry recipes on pages 236–242.

Cream Filling

3 tbsp	granulated sugar	45 mL
3 tbsp	amaranth flour	45 mL
Pinch	salt	Pinch
1	large egg yolk	1
½ cup	milk	125 mL
½ tsp	vanilla extract	2 mL
1	6-inch (15 cm) banana, thinly sliced	1
2	baked tart shells (see tip, at left)	2

1. *Filling:* In a microwave-safe bowl, whisk together sugar, amaranth flour and salt. Set aside.

2. In a small bowl or liquid measuring cup, whisk together egg yolk, milk and vanilla. Gradually whisk into dry ingredients until smooth. Microwave on High for 1 minute. Stir and microwave on High for 45 seconds. Stir and microwave on High for 15 seconds or until thick and bubbly. Let cool for 5 minutes.

3. Arrange banana slices in tart shells. Top with filling, dividing evenly. Refrigerate for 1 hour, until set, or for up to 1 day.

Variations

Omit the sliced banana to make cream tarts.

Make 4 muffin pan–size tarts.

Nutritional value per serving

Calories	603
Fat, total	30 g
Fat, saturated	17 g
Cholesterol	178 mg
Sodium	589 mg
Carbohydrate	77 g
Fiber	6 g
Protein	9 g
Calcium	178 mg
Iron	5 mg

Coconut Cream Tarts

It's fun to use a different type of pastry in this recipe each time you make it.

■■■■■■■■■■■■■■■■

Tip

For the tart shells, choose any of the pastry recipes on pages 236–242.

Coconut Cream Filling

2 tbsp	granulated sugar	30 mL
3 tbsp	amaranth flour	45 mL
Pinch	salt	Pinch
1	large egg yolk	1
1/2 cup	coconut milk or milk	125 mL
1/4 tsp	almond extract	1 mL
1/4 cup	sweetened flaked coconut	60 mL
2	baked tart shells (see tip, at left)	2

1. *Filling:* In a microwave-safe bowl, whisk together sugar, amaranth flour and salt. Set aside.

2. In a small bowl or liquid measuring cup, whisk together egg yolk, coconut milk and almond extract. Gradually whisk into dry ingredients until smooth. Microwave on High for 1 minute. Stir and microwave on High for 45 seconds. Stir and microwave on High for 15 seconds or until thick and bubbly. Let cool for 5 minutes.

3. Sprinkle coconut in bottom of tart shells. Top with filling, dividing evenly. Refrigerate for 1 hour, until set, or for up to 1 day.

Variations

Substitute coconut extract for the almond extract.

Make 4 muffin pan–size tarts.

Nutritional value per serving	
Calories	570
Fat, total	32 g
Fat, saturated	19 g
Cholesterol	178 mg
Sodium	612 mg
Carbohydrate	61 g
Fiber	6 g
Protein	9 g
Calcium	176 mg
Iron	5 mg

Pecan Butter Tarts

There is nothing more delicious than butter tarts. We know you'll love ours, which have pecan flour added to the pastry.

■■■■■■■■■■■■■■■■

Tip

To prevent the butter tarts from bubbling over as they bake, stir the filling as little as possible before spooning it into the shells.

■ **Preheat oven to 350°F (180°C)**

1/2 cup	coarsely chopped pecans	125 mL
1/3 cup	packed brown sugar	75 mL
1/4 cup	corn syrup	60 mL
2 tbsp	butter, melted	30 mL
2 tbsp	vegetable oil	30 mL
1/4 tsp	vanilla extract	1 mL
1	large egg, lightly beaten	1
2	baked Pecan Pastry tart shells (page 242)	2

1. In a small bowl, combine pecans, brown sugar, corn syrup, butter, oil and vanilla. Mix thoroughly. Add egg and mix just until blended.

2. Spoon pecan mixture into tart shells, filling them two-thirds full.

3. Bake in preheated oven for 15 to 18 minutes or until filling is puffed and set. Let cool completely on a rack before removing from pans.

Variations

Substitute raisins for the pecans, or omit the pecans for a creamier filling.

If you can't tolerate nuts, omit the pecans from the filling and bake in Basic Pastry (page 236) or Sour Cream Teff Pastry (page 238) tart shells.

Make 4 muffin pan–size tarts.

Nutritional value per serving	
Calories	1092
Fat, total	74 g
Fat, saturated	26 g
Cholesterol	193 mg
Sodium	616 mg
Carbohydrate	106 g
Fiber	7 g
Protein	10 g
Calcium	140 mg
Iron	4 mg

Pumpkin Tarts

This is not your traditional pumpkin filling: the sour cream adds a unique, delicious tang.

■■■■■■■■■■■■■■■

Tip

Freeze the remaining pumpkin purée in small quantities so you can thaw only the amount you need for a recipe.

■ **Preheat oven to 375°F (190°C)**

¼ cup	packed brown sugar	60 mL
½ tsp	ground cinnamon	2 mL
⅛ tsp	ground nutmeg	0.5 mL
Pinch	ground allspice	Pinch
Pinch	ground cloves	Pinch
1	large egg yolk	1
½ cup	pumpkin purée (not pie filling)	125 mL
¼ cup	GF sour cream	60 mL
2	unbaked Sour Cream Teff Pastry tart shells (page 238)	2

1. In a bowl, using a handheld electric mixer, combine brown sugar, cinnamon, nutmeg, allspice, cloves, egg yolk, pumpkin purée and sour cream.

2. Pour pumpkin mixture into tart shells, dividing evenly.

3. Bake in preheated oven for 25 to 30 minutes or until a knife inserted in the center comes out clean. Let cool completely on a rack before removing from pans.

Variation

For a more traditional pumpkin filling, substitute an equal amount of evaporated milk or half-and-half (10%) cream for the sour cream.

Nutritional value per serving	
Calories	571
Fat, total	30 g
Fat, saturated	18 g
Cholesterol	185 mg
Sodium	457 mg
Carbohydrate	71 g
Fiber	6 g
Protein	7 g
Calcium	174 mg
Iron	4 mg

Cobblers, Crisps, Puddings and Dessert Sauces

Tips for Cobbler Toppings

- Cobbler toppings are drop biscuits. Check out the information in Better Biscuits (page 120).

- The fruit base must be boiling and piping hot before the topping is spooned on. The bottom of the biscuit cooks from the heat of the bubbling fruit. If the fruit is cold, the center and bottom of the biscuit may be gummy and undercooked when the top is browned and baked.

- Drop the biscuit dough from a large spoon, pushing it off in one quick motion with the back of another spoon or a rubber spatula. Make sure all the dollops are the same size. Avoid adding undersized dollops, as they can cook too quickly and burn before the larger ones are baked.

- Leave a bit of room between biscuits to allow the liquid to bubble up. This prevents the biscuits from forming a seal that may burst and cause a sudden bubbling over into the oven.

- Serve the baked cobbler with the biscuit placed on top of the fruit in a fruit nappy. It looks more attractive than serving it from the baking dish.

Peach Cobbler

Enjoy this tasty cobbler at the height of peach season.

■■■■■■■■■■■■■

Tips

Be sure the cobbler topping is ready to put on the hot peaches when they come out of the oven. If by chance the base cools, reheat it until steaming. The bottom of the cobbler cooks from the heat of the peaches.

You'll need about 5 medium peaches for 3 cups (750 mL) sliced.

Nutritional value per serving	
Calories	374
Fat, total	12 g
Fat, saturated	1 g
Cholesterol	64 mg
Sodium	238 mg
Carbohydrate	65 g
Fiber	6 g
Protein	6 g
Calcium	157 mg
Iron	2 mg

■ **Preheat oven to 350°F (180°C)**
■ **3-cup (750 mL) round casserole dish, lightly greased**

Base

3 cups	sliced peaches	750 mL
2 tbsp	liquid honey	30 mL

Topping

1/4 cup	sorghum flour	60 mL
2 tbsp	quinoa flour	30 mL
1 tbsp	tapioca starch	15 mL
1/4 cup	packed brown sugar	60 mL
1 tsp	GF baking powder	5 mL
1/2 tsp	xanthan gum	2 mL
1/4 tsp	salt	1 mL
1 tsp	ground cinnamon	5 mL
1	large egg	1
1/4 cup	plain yogurt	60 mL
2 tbsp	vegetable oil	30 mL
1 tsp	almond extract	5 mL

1. *Base:* In prepared casserole dish, toss together peaches and honey. Bake in preheated oven for 15 to 20 minutes or until steaming. Remove from oven, leaving oven on.

2. *Topping:* Meanwhile, in a bowl or plastic bag, combine sorghum flour, quinoa flour, tapioca starch, brown sugar, baking powder, xanthan gum, salt and cinnamon. Mix well and set aside.

3. In a separate bowl, using a handheld electric mixer, beat egg, yogurt, oil and almond extract until combined. Add dry ingredients and mix just until combined.

4. Drop topping by 3 heaping spoonfuls over hot peaches, leaving it rough and rounded, with space between each spoonful.

5. Bake for 25 to 35 minutes or until a tester inserted in the center of the topping comes out clean. Serve warm.

Variation

Substitute blueberries for 1 cup (250 mL) of the peaches.

Apple Cranberry Crisp

Makes 3 servings

This tasty crisp brings back warm, homey memories of days gone by for those of us who live in apple country. In fact, the first Macintosh apple was grown just down the road from us.

■■■■■■■■■■■■■■■

Tips

Two medium apples yield about 1 1/2 cups (375 mL) chopped.

If you cannot tolerate cornstarch, substitute an equal amount of arrowroot starch.

If you have your oven turned on to any temperature between 325°F (160°C) and 375°F (190°C) to bake something else, you can add this crisp to it. The baking time could vary by 5 minutes.

Nutritional value per serving	
Calories	297
Fat, total	14 g
Fat, saturated	8 g
Cholesterol	31 mg
Sodium	118 mg
Carbohydrate	41 g
Fiber	5 g
Protein	4 g
Calcium	28 mg
Iron	2 mg

■ **Preheat oven to 375°F (190°C)**
■ **3-cup (750 mL) round or oval casserole dish**

Base

1 1/2 cups	coarsely chopped apples	375 mL
1 cup	fresh or thawed frozen cranberries	250 mL
1 tbsp	cornstarch	15 mL
1 tbsp	granulated sugar	15 mL

Crisp Topping

2/3 cup	GF large-flake (old-fashioned) rolled oats	150 mL
2 tbsp	GF oat flour	30 mL
1 tbsp	packed brown sugar	15 mL
1/2 tsp	ground nutmeg	2 mL
3 tbsp	butter, melted	45 mL

1. *Base:* In casserole dish, combine apples, cranberries, cornstarch and sugar. Set aside.

2. *Topping:* In a medium bowl, combine oats, oat flour, brown sugar and nutmeg. Drizzle with butter and mix until crumbly. Sprinkle topping over fruit. Do not pack.

3. Cover and bake for 15 minutes. Uncover and bake for 10 to 15 minutes or until fruit is bubbly around the edges, apples are fork-tender and topping is browned. Serve warm.

Variations

Substitute the Pear Maple Crumble topping (page 258) for the topping in this recipe.

Replace the oats with buckwheat flakes and the oat flour with amaranth flour.

Ground cinnamon or ginger can be used in place of the nutmeg.

Instead of baking, microwave the crisp, uncovered, on High for 7 minutes or until apples are fork-tender. Let stand for 5 minutes. To brown the topping, place under a preheated broiler for 1 to 2 minutes or until golden brown.

Strawberry Rhubarb Crisp

We always look forward to serving this springtime favorite.

■■■■■■■■■■■■■■

Tips

If only large strawberries are available, cut them into smaller pieces.

If you cannot tolerate cornstarch, substitute an equal amount of arrowroot starch.

If you have your oven turned on to any temperature between 325°F (160°C) and 375°F (190°C) to bake something else, you can add this crisp to it. The baking time could vary by 5 minutes.

Nutritional value per serving	
Calories	403
Fat, total	8 g
Fat, saturated	4 g
Cholesterol	15 mg
Sodium	71 mg
Carbohydrate	80 g
Fiber	6 g
Protein	7 g
Calcium	80 mg
Iron	3 mg

- Preheat oven to 350°F (180°C)
- Two 10-oz (300 mL) ovenproof bowls or ramekins, lightly greased
- Small baking sheet

Base

1 cup	strawberries, cut in half	250 mL
½ cup	chopped rhubarb (½-inch/1 cm pieces)	125 mL
2 tbsp	packed brown sugar	30 mL
1 tbsp	cornstarch	15 mL

Topping

½ cup	GF large-flake (old-fashioned) rolled oats	125 mL
¼ cup	pecan flour	60 mL
1 tbsp	packed brown sugar	15 mL
2 tsp	grated orange zest	10 mL
1 tbsp	butter, melted	15 mL

1. *Base:* In a bowl, combine strawberries, rhubarb, brown sugar and cornstarch. Spoon into prepared ovenproof bowls, dividing evenly.

2. *Topping:* In a separate bowl, combine oats, pecan flour, brown sugar and orange zest. Drizzle with butter and mix until crumbly. Sprinkle topping over fruit. Do not pack.

3. Cover and bake for 15 minutes. Uncover and bake for 10 to 15 minutes or until fruit is bubbly around the edges, juices are thickened and clear, a tester inserted in the center is hot to the touch and topping is browned. Serve warm.

Variations

If you can't tolerate nuts, substitute oat flour or brown rice flour for the pecan flour.

Instead of baking, microwave the crisp, uncovered, on High for 5 minutes or until fruit is steaming. Let stand for 5 minutes. To brown the topping, place under a preheated broiler for 1 to 2 minutes or until golden brown.

Pear Maple Crumble

Call it a crisp or call it a crumble, this is a downright delicious way to eat a serving of fruit — and one that is high in fiber to boot!

■■■■■■■■■■■■■■■■

Tips

For information on purchasing and ripening pears, see tip, page 270.

Cardamom has a strong, warmly spiced flavor and is often used in Scandinavian and Indian cuisines. Ground cinnamon, ginger or nutmeg can be used as a substitute.

If you have your oven turned on to any temperature between 325°F (160°C) and 375°F (190°C) to bake something else, you can add this crisp to it. The baking time could vary by 5 minutes.

Nutritional value per serving	
Calories	413
Fat, total	15 g
Fat, saturated	7 g
Cholesterol	15 mg
Sodium	95 mg
Carbohydrate	72 g
Fiber	8 g
Protein	5 g
Calcium	67 mg
Iron	2 mg

■ Preheat oven to 350°F (180°C)
■ 3-cup (750 mL) round or oval casserole dish, lightly greased

Base

1½ tsp	cornstarch	7 mL
2 tbsp	pure maple syrup	30 mL
2	pears, cut into 1-inch (2.5 cm) pieces	2

Crumble Topping

⅓ cup	sorghum flour	75 mL
2 tbsp	almond flour	30 mL
¼ cup	unsweetened desiccated coconut	60 mL
1 tbsp	packed brown sugar	15 mL
½ tsp	ground cardamom	2 mL
2 tbsp	butter, melted	30 mL

1. *Base:* In prepared casserole dish, combine cornstarch and maple syrup. Add pears and toss to coat. Set aside.

2. *Topping:* In a bowl, combine sorghum flour, almond flour, coconut, brown sugar and cardamom. Drizzle with butter and mix until crumbly. Sprinkle topping over fruit. Do not pack.

3. Cover and bake for 15 minutes. Uncover and bake for 10 to 15 minutes or until fruit is bubbly around the edges, pears are fork-tender and topping is browned. Serve warm.

Variations

Substitute 2 cups (500 mL) blueberries or chopped peaches, plums or plumcots for the pears.

Try the Apple Cranberry Crisp topping (page 256) in place of the topping in this recipe.

Instead of baking, microwave the crisp, uncovered, on High for 7 to 8 minutes or until pears are fork-tender. Let stand for 5 minutes. To brown the topping, place under a preheated broiler for 1 to 2 minutes or until golden brown.

Apple Meringue Dessert

Grandma often made this dessert for Heather's sons, and they asked for it every time they visited.

■■■■■■■■■■■■■■■■

Tips

Lining the bottom and sides of the pan makes it easier to remove this dessert to a plate to serve it.

See the Techniques Glossary, page 308, for information on warming egg whites to room temperature.

We like to use the whisk attachment that comes with our handheld mixer to beat the egg whites, as it makes quick work of the task.

We used Ginger Gold apples, but you can use any baking apple that holds its shape. Try Northern Spy, Spartan or Golden Delicious apples.

Nutritional value per serving	
Calories	256
Fat, total	12 g
Fat, saturated	4 g
Cholesterol	62 mg
Sodium	177 mg
Carbohydrate	31 g
Fiber	1 g
Protein	9 g
Calcium	56 mg
Iron	1 mg

■ Preheat oven to 350°F (180°C)
■ 9- by 5-inch (23 by 12.5 cm) loaf pan, lightly greased and bottom and sides lined with parchment paper

Base

1	large egg yolk	1
2 tbsp	butter, softened	30 mL
1/4 cup	almond flour	60 mL
1/4 cup	low-fat soy flour	60 mL
2 tbsp	granulated sugar	30 mL
Pinch	salt	Pinch

Topping

2	large egg whites, at room temperature	2
1/4 tsp	cream of tartar	1 mL
3 tbsp	granulated sugar	45 mL
2 tbsp	sliced almonds	30 mL

Filling

2 cups	thinly sliced apples	500 mL
1/2 tsp	ground cinnamon	2 mL

1. *Base:* In a bowl, using a handheld electric mixer on low speed, cream egg yolk and butter. Beat in almond flour, soy flour, sugar and salt until well blended.

2. Press batter into prepared pan. Using a moistened rubber spatula, spread to edges and smooth top.

3. Bake in preheated oven for 8 to 10 minutes or until golden brown.

4. *Topping:* Meanwhile, in a clean bowl, using electric mixer with clean beaters or wire whisk attachment, beat egg whites until foamy. Beat in cream of tartar. Continue beating until egg whites form stiff peaks. Gradually beat in sugar. Continue beating until mixture is very stiff and glossy but not dry. Set aside.

5. *Filling:* Spread apples evenly over hot base. Sprinkle with cinnamon. Spoon egg whites evenly over apples, sealing to the edges all the way around. Sprinkle with almonds.

6. Bake for 20 minutes or until apples are tender and meringue is golden. Let cool completely in pan on a rack.

Lemon Meringue Slices

Makes 4 servings

Heather's sons still love this dessert, which their grandmother frequently made for them when they went for a visit.

■ ■ ■ ■ ■ ■ ■ ■ ■ ■ ■ ■ ■ ■ ■

Tips

Lining the bottom and sides of the pan makes it easier to remove this dessert to a plate to serve it.

See the Techniques Glossary, page 308, for information on warming egg whites to room temperature.

Nutritional value per serving

Calories	333
Fat, total	16 g
Fat, saturated	7 g
Cholesterol	183 mg
Sodium	268 mg
Carbohydrate	41 g
Fiber	1 g
Protein	8 g
Calcium	56 mg
Iron	1 mg

■ **Preheat oven to 350°F (180°C)**
■ **9- by 5-inch (23 by 12.5 cm) loaf pan, lightly greased and bottom and sides lined with parchment paper**

Base

1	large egg yolk	1
2 tbsp	butter, softened	30 mL
1/4 cup	almond flour	60 mL
1/4 cup	low-fat soy flour	60 mL
2 tbsp	granulated sugar	30 mL
Pinch	salt	Pinch

Filling

1/3 cup	granulated sugar	75 mL
2 tbsp	cornstarch	30 mL
Pinch	salt	Pinch
2/3 cup	water	150 mL
2	large egg yolks	2
1 tsp	grated lemon zest	5 mL
3 tbsp	freshly squeezed lemon juice	45 mL
1 tbsp	butter	15 mL

Topping

2	large egg whites, at room temperature	2
1/4 tsp	cream of tartar	1 mL
3 tbsp	granulated sugar	45 mL

1. *Base:* In a bowl, using a handheld electric mixer on low speed, cream egg yolk and butter. Beat in almond flour, soy flour, sugar and salt until well blended.

2. Press batter into prepared pan. Using a moistened rubber spatula, spread to edges and smooth top.

3. Bake in preheated oven for 8 to 10 minutes or until golden brown. Let cool on a rack. Increase oven temperature to 400°F (200°C).

4. *Filling:* In a microwave-safe bowl, combine sugar, cornstarch and salt. Stir in water. Microwave on High for 2 to 3 minutes, stopping frequently to stir, until mixture boils.

Tips

We like to use the whisk attachment that comes with our handheld mixer to beat the egg whites, as it makes quick work of the task.

You can also cook the lemon filling in a small saucepan over medium heat, stirring constantly until it boils and thickens.

Use a commercial GF lemon pie filling and prepare according to the package directions.

5. In a small bowl, beat egg yolks. Gradually add ¼ cup (60 mL) of the hot syrup, whisking until blended. Whisk back into the microwave-safe bowl. Microwave on High for 30 to 60 seconds, stopping frequently to stir, until filling is thick and shiny. Stir in lemon zest, lemon juice and butter. Spoon over cooled base.

6. *Topping:* In a clean bowl, using electric mixer with clean beaters or wire whisk attachment, beat egg whites until foamy. Beat in cream of tartar. Continue beating until egg whites form stiff peaks. Gradually beat in sugar. Continue beating until mixture is very stiff and glossy but not dry. Spoon evenly over hot filling, sealing to the edges all the way around.

7. Bake for 6 to 8 minutes or until meringue is golden. Let cool completely on a rack.

Orange Sponge

This light, soufflé-like pudding is the perfect way to end a heavy meal!

■■■■■■■■■■■■■■

Tips

See the Techniques Glossary, page 308, for information on beating egg whites.

We like to use the whisk attachment that comes with our handheld mixer to beat the egg whites, as it makes quick work of the task.

Variation

Turn this into a Lemon Sponge by substituting lemon zest and juice for the orange.

Nutritional value per serving	
Calories	224
Fat, total	9 g
Fat, saturated	5 g
Cholesterol	124 mg
Sodium	185 mg
Carbohydrate	30 g
Fiber	1 g
Protein	6 g
Calcium	84 mg
Iron	2 mg

■ **Preheat oven to 300°F (150°C)**
■ **6-cup (1.5 L) round casserole dish**
■ **9-inch (23 cm) square baking pan**

³⁄₄ cup	milk	175 mL
3 tbsp	amaranth flour	45 mL
¹⁄₂ tsp	xanthan gum	2 mL
Pinch	salt	Pinch
6 tbsp	granulated sugar, divided	90 mL
2	large egg yolks	2
2 tsp	grated orange zest	10 mL
3 tbsp	frozen orange juice concentrate, thawed	45 mL
2 tbsp	butter, melted	30 mL
2	large egg whites, at room temperature	2
¹⁄₈ tsp	cream of tartar	0.5 mL
	Boiling water	

1. In a small microwave-safe bowl, microwave milk on High for 2 to 3 minutes or until small bubbles form around the edge. Set aside.

2. In a bowl or plastic bag, combine amaranth flour, xanthan gum and salt. Mix well and set aside.

3. In a separate bowl, using an electric mixer, beat 4 tbsp (60 mL) of the sugar and egg yolks until light and fluffy. Beat in milk, orange zest, orange juice concentrate and butter until blended. Beat in dry ingredients until blended. Set aside.

4. In a clean bowl, using electric mixer with clean beaters or wire whisk attachment, beat egg whites until foamy. Beat in cream of tartar. Continue beating until egg whites form stiff peaks. Gradually beat in the remaining sugar. Continue beating until mixture is very stiff and glossy but not dry. Fold in egg yolk mixture. Spoon lightly into casserole dish.

5. Place casserole dish in baking pan and place in center of preheated oven. Pour enough boiling water into baking pan to reach halfway up the sides of the casserole dish. Bake for 40 to 45 minutes or until top is set. Carefully remove casserole dish from water and let cool on a rack for 30 minutes. Serve warm.

Crème Caramel

This is our favorite restaurant dessert, and we're so glad we developed this small-quantity recipe and make it frequently. No need to wait for company!

■■■■■■■■■■■■■■■■

Tips

Individual microwaves vary; watch each of the mixtures in this recipe carefully until you figure out the exact length of time needed for each step. Make notes.

If you cook the sugar and water too long, the caramel will taste burnt.

You can also cook the custard on the stovetop over medium heat, stirring constantly.

Nutritional value per serving	
Calories	264
Fat, total	6 g
Fat, saturated	2 g
Cholesterol	192 mg
Sodium	117 mg
Carbohydrate	44 g
Fiber	0 g
Protein	10 g
Calcium	172 mg
Iron	1 mg

■ **Preheat oven to 325°F (160°C)**
■ **Two microwave-safe ³/₄-cup (175 mL) ramekins**
■ **9-inch (23 cm) square baking pan**

Caramel
¼ cup	granulated sugar	60 mL
¼ cup	water	60 mL

Custard
2 tbsp	granulated sugar	30 mL
2	large eggs	2
1 cup	milk	250 mL
¼ tsp	vanilla extract	1 mL
	Boiling water	

1. *Caramel:* In each ramekin, combine half the sugar and half the water. Microwave, uncovered, on High for 4 to 5 minutes or until sugar just begins to caramelize to a very light brown (the color of pale maple syrup; it will darken as it cools). Let stand for 15 minutes to cool and harden.

2. *Custard:* In a microwave-safe 2-cup (500 mL) measuring cup or bowl with a spout, whisk together sugar, eggs, milk and vanilla. Microwave on High for 1 to 3 minutes, stopping to stir every 30 seconds, until hot but not boiling. (Watch carefully, as you do not want to cook the eggs.) Pour over cooled caramel.

3. Place ramekins in baking pan and place in center of preheated oven. Pour enough boiling water into baking pan to reach halfway up the sides of the ramekins. Bake for 30 minutes or until a tester inserted in the center comes out clean. Carefully remove ramekins from water and let cool on a rack for 30 minutes. Cover and refrigerate for 24 hours.

4. To serve, run a knife around edge of custards and invert individual rimmed serving plates over ramekins. Quickly flip plates and ramekins over, shaking gently to unmold Crème Caramel.

Baked Quinoa Custard

You might not think of making a quinoa custard, but you will enjoy this one. An added bonus: it's very nutritious.

∎∎∎∎∎∎∎∎∎∎∎∎∎∎∎

Tips

If you are cooking quinoa for dinner, cook extra for this recipe.

For information on cooking quinoa, see the Techniques Glossary, page 310. You'll need ¼ cup (60 mL) quinoa and ¾ cup (175 mL) water to make 1 cup (250 mL) cooked quinoa.

To safely remove ramekins from the boiling water, slide a spatula under each. Lift gently and, once clear of the water, support the ramekin with an oven-mitt-covered hand while transferring it to the rack.

▪ **Preheat oven to 350°F (180°C)**
▪ **Two ¾-cup (175 mL) ramekins, lightly greased**
▪ **9-inch (23 cm) square baking pan**

1	large egg	1
1 cup	milk	250 mL
1 cup	cooked quinoa	250 mL
¼ cup	packed brown sugar	60 mL
¼ tsp	salt	1 mL
½ tsp	ground nutmeg	2 mL
	Boiling water	

1. In a bowl, whisk together egg and milk. Stir in quinoa, brown sugar, salt and nutmeg until blended. Pour into prepared ramekins.

2. Place ramekins in baking pan and place in center of preheated oven. Pour enough boiling water into baking pan to reach halfway up the sides of the ramekins. Bake for 30 minutes or until a tester inserted in the center comes out clean. Carefully remove ramekins from water and let cool on a rack for 30 minutes. Serve warm or cover and refrigerate for up to 3 days, then serve cold.

Variation

Add ¼ cup (60 mL) raisins with the quinoa and substitute ground cinnamon for the nutmeg.

Nutritional value per serving	
Calories	302
Fat, total	6 g
Fat, saturated	2 g
Cholesterol	18 mg
Sodium	397 mg
Carbohydrate	53 g
Fiber	3 g
Protein	11 g
Calcium	201 mg
Iron	2 mg

Baked Rum 'n' Raisin Rice Pudding

Makes 2 servings

When you have the oven on to bake bread or muffins, there's lots of room left to make some rice pudding too.

■■■■■■■■■■■■■■

Tips

For information on cooking rice, see the Techniques Glossary, page 310. You'll need ¼ cup (60 mL) rice for ½ cup (125 mL) cooked.

To safely remove ramekins from the boiling water, slide a spatula under each. Lift gently and, once clear of the water, support the ramekin with an oven-mitt-covered hand while transferring it to the rack.

These puddings can be covered and refrigerated for up to 3 days, then served cold.

Nutritional value per serving	
Calories	326
Fat, total	4 g
Fat, saturated	2 g
Cholesterol	98 mg
Sodium	393 mg
Carbohydrate	63 g
Fiber	1 g
Protein	9 g
Calcium	195 mg
Iron	2 mg

- **Preheat oven to 350°F (180°C)**
- **Two ¾-cup (175 mL) ramekins, lightly greased**
- **9-inch (23 cm) square baking pan**

1	large egg	1
1 cup	milk	250 mL
½ cup	cooked short-grain white rice (such as Arborio)	125 mL
¼ cup	raisins	60 mL
¼ cup	packed brown sugar	60 mL
¼ tsp	salt	1 mL
1 tbsp	dark rum	15 mL
	Boiling water	

1. In a bowl, whisk together egg and milk. Stir in rice, raisins, brown sugar, salt and rum until blended. Pour into prepared ramekins.

2. Place ramekins in baking pan and place in center of preheated oven. Pour enough boiling water into baking pan to reach halfway up the sides of the ramekins. Bake for 30 minutes or until a tester inserted in the center comes out clean. Carefully remove ramekins from water and let cool on a rack for 30 minutes. Serve warm.

Variations

Replace the rum with 1 tsp (15 mL) vanilla extract.

Substitute cooked brown or wild rice for the white rice.

Maple Walnut Tapioca Pudding

We've updated this childhood favorite to appeal to adult tastes.

████████████████

Tips

Do not omit the maple extract, as it provides a strong maple flavor.

You can also cook the tapioca mixture in a saucepan over medium heat, stirring constantly until it comes to a boil.

■ **Two ³⁄₄-cup (175 mL) ramekins**

1 tbsp	quick-cooking tapioca	15 mL
¹⁄₈ tsp	salt	0.5 mL
2	large egg yolks	2
³⁄₄ cup	milk	175 mL
¹⁄₄ cup	toasted chopped walnuts	60 mL
¹⁄₄ cup	pure maple syrup	60 mL
¹⁄₂ tsp	maple extract	2 mL

1. In a microwave-safe bowl, combine tapioca, salt, egg yolks and milk. Let stand for 5 minutes. Microwave on Medium-High (70%) for 2 to 4 minutes, stopping to stir every 30 seconds, until mixture comes to a boil.

2. Stir in walnuts, maple syrup and maple extract. Spoon into ramekins, dividing equally. Cover and refrigerate for at least 1 hour, until chilled, or for up to 3 days.

Variation

Substitute 1 cup (250 mL) strong brewed coffee for the milk, 2 tbsp (30 mL) liquid honey for the maple syrup and an equal amount of vanilla extract for the maple extract.

Nutritional value per serving	
Calories	330
Fat, total	16 g
Fat, saturated	3 g
Cholesterol	216 mg
Sodium	236 mg
Carbohydrate	40 g
Fiber	1 g
Protein	8 g
Calcium	178 mg
Iron	2 mg

Lemon Buttermilk Pudding

One day we needed to clean out the refrigerator and found extra buttermilk to use up. So we developed this light, tangy dessert we know you'll enjoy.

■■■■■■■■■■■■■■■■

Tips

It is easier to separate eggs when they are cold, right from the refrigerator, because the yolk is less apt to break.

We like to use the whisk attachment that comes with our handheld mixer to beat the egg whites, as it makes quick work of the task.

Make sure the bowl and beaters or whisk attachment are completely free of grease before beating egg whites. We wash them thoroughly just before we use them.

Nutritional value per serving	
Calories	186
Fat, total	5 g
Fat, saturated	2 g
Cholesterol	113 mg
Sodium	187 mg
Carbohydrate	30 g
Fiber	0 g
Protein	6 g
Calcium	92 mg
Iron	1 mg

■ **Preheat oven to 350°F (180°C)**
■ **6-cup (1.5 L) round casserole dish, lightly greased**
■ **9-inch (23 cm) square baking pan**

1/3 cup	granulated sugar	75 mL
2	large egg yolks	2
2 tbsp	amaranth flour	30 mL
Pinch	salt	Pinch
2 tsp	grated lemon zest	10 mL
1 cup	buttermilk	250 mL
1/4 cup	freshly squeezed lemon juice	60 mL
2 tsp	butter, melted and cooled	10 mL
2	large egg whites, at room temperature	2
1/4 tsp	cream of tartar	1 mL
2 tbsp	granulated sugar	30 mL
	Boiling water	

1. In a bowl, using an electric mixer, beat 1/3 cup (75 mL) sugar and egg yolks for 5 minutes or until thick and lemon-colored. Beat in amaranth flour and salt. Beat in lemon zest, buttermilk, lemon juice and butter until blended. Set aside.

2. In a clean bowl, using electric mixer with clean beaters or wire whisk attachment, beat egg whites until foamy. Beat in cream of tartar. Continue beating until egg whites form stiff peaks. Gradually beat in 2 tbsp (30 mL) sugar. Continue beating until mixture is very stiff and glossy but not dry. Fold in egg yolk mixture. Pour into casserole dish.

3. Place casserole dish in baking pan and place in center of preheated oven. Pour enough boiling water into baking pan to reach halfway up the sides of the casserole dish. Bake for 40 to 45 minutes or until top is set and golden. Carefully remove casserole dish from water and let cool on a rack for 30 minutes. Serve warm.

Variation

If you like a tangier pudding, decrease the 1/3 cup (75 mL) sugar to 1/4 cup (60 mL).

Lemon Snow

We both grew up eating this old-fashioned recipe, but we've updated the method just for you.

■■■■■■■■■■■■■■

Tips

Lemon zest is the bright yellow portion of a lemon's peel. It can easily be shredded with a zester.

It is worth the time and effort to squeeze a fresh lemon rather than use bottled juice.

This recipe contains raw egg whites. If the food safety of raw eggs is a concern for you, substitute 1/4 cup (60 mL) pasteurized liquid egg whites (or separate 2 pasteurized whole eggs, if available).

We like to use the whisk attachment that comes with our handheld mixer to beat the egg whites, as it makes quick work of the task.

Nutritional value per serving	
Calories	271
Fat, total	11 g
Fat, saturated	6 g
Cholesterol	129 mg
Sodium	119 mg
Carbohydrate	41 g
Fiber	0 g
Protein	3 g
Calcium	18 mg
Iron	0 mg

■ **Four 3/4-cup (175 mL) ramekins**

1/2 cup	granulated sugar	125 mL
1/4 cup	cornstarch	60 mL
2 tsp	grated lemon zest	10 mL
1 1/3 cups	water	325 mL
1/3 cup	freshly squeezed lemon juice	75 mL
3 tbsp	butter	45 mL
2	large egg yolks	2
2	large egg whites, at room temperature	2
1/8 tsp	cream of tartar	0.5 mL
2 tbsp	granulated sugar	30 mL

Microwave Method

1. In a microwave-safe bowl, combine 1/2 cup (125 mL) sugar and cornstarch. Stir in lemon zest, water, lemon juice and butter. Microwave on High for 4 to 5 minutes, stopping to stir every minute, until mixture boils and thickens.

2. In a small bowl, beat egg yolks. Gradually add 1/4 cup (60 mL) of the lemon mixture, whisking until blended. Whisk back into the lemon mixture. Microwave on High for 30 seconds. Set aside.

Stovetop Method

1. In a saucepan, combine 1/2 cup (125 mL) sugar and cornstarch. Stir in lemon zest, water, lemon juice and butter. Heat over medium heat, stirring constantly, for 5 to 8 minutes or until mixture boils and thickens.

2. In a small bowl, beat egg yolks. Gradually add 1/4 cup (60 mL) of the lemon mixture, whisking until blended. Whisk back into the lemon mixture. Simmer, whisking, for 1 minute. Remove from heat and set aside.

For Both Methods

3. In a clean bowl, using a handheld electric mixer with clean beaters or wire whisk attachment, beat egg whites until foamy. Beat in cream of tartar. Continue beating until egg whites form stiff peaks. Gradually beat in 2 tbsp (30 mL) sugar. Continue beating until mixture is very stiff and glossy but not dry. Fold in warm lemon mixture. Pour into ramekins, dividing evenly. Refrigerate for 1 hour or until set.

Peach Sponge Pudding

This self-saucing, soufflé-like pudding is just enough for three!

■■■■■■■■■■■■■■■■

Tips

See the Techniques Glossary, page 308, for information on warming egg whites to room temperature.

We like to use the whisk attachment that comes with our handheld mixer to beat the egg white, as it makes quick work of the task.

To safely remove ramekins from the boiling water, slide a spatula under each. Lift gently and, once clear of the water, support the ramekin with an oven-mitt-covered hand while transferring it to the rack.

You can double or triple this recipe if you're making it for company.

Nutritional value per serving	
Calories	141
Fat, total	4 g
Fat, saturated	1 g
Cholesterol	72 mg
Sodium	133 mg
Carbohydrate	23 g
Fiber	1 g
Protein	4 g
Calcium	54 mg
Iron	0 mg

■ **Preheat oven to 350°F (180°C)**
■ **Three ³/₄-cup (175 mL) ramekins**
■ **9-inch (23 cm) square baking pan**

¼ cup	granulated sugar	60 mL
2 tbsp	almond flour	30 mL
Pinch	salt	Pinch
1	large egg yolk	1
⅓ cup	milk	75 mL
⅓ cup	Peach Purée (page 277)	75 mL
1	large egg white, at room temperature	1
	Boiling water	

1. In a bowl, whisk together sugar, almond flour and salt. Whisk in egg yolk, milk and Peach Purée. Set aside.

2. In a clean bowl, using a handheld electric mixer, beat egg white until stiff peaks form. Gently fold in peach mixture. Pour into ramekins, dividing evenly.

3. Place ramekins in baking pan and place in center of preheated oven. Pour enough boiling water into baking pan to reach halfway up the sides of the ramekins. Bake for about 20 minutes or until tops are lightly browned and set. Carefully remove ramekins from water and let cool on a rack for 30 minutes. Serve warm or let cool completely.

Variations

If you can't tolerate nuts, use brown rice flour instead of almond flour.

Dollop 1 tbsp (15 mL) extra Peach Purée in the center of each pudding just before baking.

Baked Pear Pudding for 2

The custard puffs up around the pears as it bakes, creating a true comfort food for those who want a dessert that's not too sweet. Eat one tonight and save the other for tomorrow — or share with a friend!

■ ■ ■ ■ ■ ■ ■ ■ ■ ■ ■ ■ ■ ■ ■ ■

Tips

When purchasing pears, choose firm pears that hold up well in cooking, such as Bosc or Bartlett. Place pears in a paper bag at room temperature to ripen. To test pears for ripeness, press lightly at the stem end — it should give slightly.

Pears are very high in fiber, so enjoy them often.

If only large pears are available, bake in three ramekins or simply snack on the leftover pear cubes.

Nutritional value per serving

Calories	330
Fat, total	7 g
Fat, saturated	3 g
Cholesterol	106 mg
Sodium	243 mg
Carbohydrate	61 g
Fiber	6 g
Protein	7 g
Calcium	124 mg
Iron	3 mg

■ Preheat oven to 350°F (180°C)
■ Two 10-oz (300 mL) ovenproof bowls or ramekins, lightly greased

2	ripe small firm pears, cut into 1-inch (2.5 cm) cubes	2
2 tbsp	amaranth flour	30 mL
1 tbsp	brown rice flour	15 mL
1 tbsp	tapioca starch	15 mL
2 tbsp	granulated sugar	30 mL
½ tsp	xanthan gum	2 mL
Pinch	salt	Pinch
1	large egg	1
½ cup	milk	125 mL
1 tbsp	pure maple syrup	15 mL
½ tsp	maple extract	2 mL
2 tsp	butter, cut into small pieces	10 mL

1. Place pears in prepared ovenproof bowls.

2. In a bowl or plastic bag, combine amaranth flour, brown rice flour, tapioca starch, sugar, xanthan gum and salt. Mix well and set aside.

3. In a separate bowl, whisk together egg, milk, maple syrup and maple extract. Stir in dry ingredients. Pour over pears, dividing evenly, and dot with butter.

4. Place ovenproof bowls on a baking sheet and place in preheated oven. Bake for 25 to 29 minutes or until pears are tender and custard is set and golden. Let cool in pan on a rack for 10 minutes. Serve warm.

Variation

Add ¼ cup (60 mL) fresh or dried cranberries with the pears.

Baked Pear Pudding for 4

Here's a larger version of our pear pudding, perfect for company.

■■■■■■■■■■■■■■■

Tips

When purchasing pears, choose firm pears that hold up well in cooking, such as Bosc or Bartlett. Place pears in a paper bag at room temperature to ripen. To test pears for ripeness, press lightly at the stem end — it should give slightly.

Pears are very high in fiber, so enjoy them often.

Nutritional value per serving

Calories	299
Fat, total	7 g
Fat, saturated	3 g
Cholesterol	103 mg
Sodium	154 mg
Carbohydrate	56 g
Fiber	6 g
Protein	6 g
Calcium	102 mg
Iron	2 mg

■ **Preheat oven to 350°F (180°C)**
■ **6-cup (1.5 L) round casserole dish, lightly greased**

4	ripe firm pears, cut into 1-inch (2.5 cm) cubes	4
3 tbsp	amaranth flour	45 mL
2 tbsp	brown rice flour	30 mL
1 tbsp	tapioca starch	15 mL
1/4 cup	granulated sugar	60 mL
1/2 tsp	xanthan gum	2 mL
Pinch	salt	Pinch
2	large eggs	2
3/4 cup	milk	175 mL
2 tbsp	pure maple syrup	30 mL
1/2 tsp	maple extract	2 mL
1 tbsp	butter, cut into small pieces	15 mL

1. Place pears in prepared casserole dish.

2. In a bowl or plastic bag, combine amaranth flour, brown rice flour, tapioca starch, sugar, xanthan gum and salt. Mix well and set aside.

3. In a large bowl, whisk together eggs, milk, maple syrup and maple extract. Stir in dry ingredients. Pour over pears and dot with butter.

4. Bake in preheated oven for 40 to 45 minutes or until pears are tender and custard is set and golden. Let cool in pan on a rack for 10 minutes. Serve warm.

Variation

Add 1/2 cup (125 mL) fresh or dried cranberries with the pears.

Pumpkin Pudding

Cakelike in texture, this warm comfort food was developed with our friend Anne in mind.

■■■■■■■■■■■■■■

Tips

Serve with Hot Lemon Sauce (page 276), warm Butter Rum Sauce (page 275) or Toffee Sauce (page 275).

This pudding can also be baked in a 4-cup (1 L) casserole dish for 25 to 30 minutes.

- ■ Preheat oven to 350°F (180°C)
- ■ 3-cup (750 mL) round casserole dish, lightly greased and bottom lined with parchment paper

¼ cup	sorghum flour	60 mL
¼ cup	whole bean flour	60 mL
1 tbsp	tapioca starch	15 mL
2 tsp	GF baking powder	2 mL
¼ tsp	baking soda	1 mL
½ tsp	xanthan gum	2 mL
Pinch	salt	Pinch
⅛ tsp	ground ginger	0.5 mL
⅛ tsp	ground nutmeg	0.5 mL
Pinch	ground cloves	Pinch
¼ cup	packed brown sugar	60 mL
1	large egg	1
⅔ cup	pumpkin purée (not pie filling)	150 mL
2 tbsp	vegetable oil	30 mL
½ tsp	vanilla extract	2 mL

1. In a bowl or plastic bag, combine sorghum flour, whole bean flour, tapioca starch, baking powder, baking soda, xanthan gum, salt, ginger, nutmeg and cloves. Mix well and set aside.

2. In a separate bowl, using an electric mixer, combine brown sugar, egg, pumpkin purée, oil and vanilla. Gradually add dry ingredients and mix just until combined. Spoon into prepared casserole dish.

3. Bake in preheated oven for 28 to 32 minutes or until internal temperature of pudding registers 200°F (100°C) on an instant-read thermometer. Carefully remove casserole dish to a rack and let cool for 10 minutes. Serve warm.

Nutritional value per serving	
Calories	196
Fat, total	8 g
Fat, saturated	1 g
Cholesterol	47 mg
Sodium	176 mg
Carbohydrate	28 g
Fiber	4 g
Protein	4 g
Calcium	144 mg
Iron	2 mg

Chocolate Pudding Cake

Makes 2 servings

A comforting finale on the coldest winter day, this old-fashioned, self-saucing dessert was all the rage in the '50s. We've updated it.

■ ■ ■ ■ ■ ■ ■ ■ ■ ■ ■ ■ ■ ■

Tips

When boiling the water, heat extra and measure it after it has come to a boil. It may continue to bubble when removed from the stovetop or microwave, so be careful not to burn yourself.

When pouring hot liquid over pudding cake batter, hold a large spoon, bowl side down, over the center of the batter. Let the liquid flow over the back of the spoon to distribute evenly.

Nutritional value per serving	
Calories	290
Fat, total	2 g
Fat, saturated	1 g
Cholesterol	2 mg
Sodium	194 mg
Carbohydrate	70 g
Fiber	3 g
Protein	5 g
Calcium	331 mg
Iron	3 mg

■ Preheat oven to 350°F (180°C)
■ Two 10-oz (300 mL) ovenproof bowls or ramekins, lightly greased

Cake

2 tbsp	sorghum flour	30 mL
2 tbsp	whole bean flour	30 mL
1 tbsp	tapioca starch	15 mL
1/4 cup	granulated sugar	60 mL
2 tsp	GF baking powder	10 mL
1/2 tsp	xanthan gum	2 mL
1/8 tsp	salt	0.5 mL
2 tbsp	sifted unsweetened cocoa powder	30 mL
1/2 cup	milk	125 mL
1/4 tsp	vanilla extract	1 mL

Chocolate Sauce

1/4 cup	packed brown sugar	60 mL
1 tbsp	sifted unsweetened cocoa powder	15 mL
1/2 cup	boiling water	125 mL

1. *Cake:* In a bowl or plastic bag, combine sorghum flour, whole bean flour, tapioca starch, sugar, baking powder, xanthan gum, salt and cocoa. Mix well and set aside.

2. In a separate bowl, using a handheld electric mixer, combine milk and vanilla. Gradually add dry ingredients and mix just until combined. Spoon into prepared ovenproof bowls, dividing evenly. Place bowls on a small baking sheet.

3. *Sauce:* In a small bowl, combine brown sugar and cocoa. Sprinkle evenly over batter. Slowly pour boiling water evenly over batter. Do not stir.

4. Bake in preheated oven for 30 to 35 minutes or until cake is firm when gently touched. Serve warm.

Variations

Substitute hot brewed coffee for the boiling water in the sauce.

In place of the chocolate sauce, make a caramel sauce: In a small bowl, combine 1/3 cup (75 mL) brown sugar, 1/2 cup (125 mL) boiling water and 2 tsp (10 mL) butter. Pour evenly over batter. Do not stir. Bake as directed and serve warm. The sauce will thicken as it cools.

Apple Ginger Pudding Cake

This comforting autumnal dessert has a sweet fruit bottom and a cake top!

■■■■■■■■■■■■■■■

Tips

Choose apples that hold their shape when cooked, such as Northern Spy, Spartan or Golden Delicious.

Make sure to place the bowls on a baking sheet, as they are quite full and may boil over in the oven.

- Preheat oven to 350°F (180°C)
- Three 10-oz (300 mL) ovenproof bowls or ramekins, lightly greased

Base

2	small apples, sliced	2
1 tbsp	packed brown sugar	15 mL
2 tsp	freshly squeezed lemon juice	10 mL

Cake

1/3 cup	teff flour	75 mL
2 tbsp	amaranth flour	30 mL
1 tbsp	tapioca starch	15 mL
1/4 cup	packed brown sugar	60 mL
1 tbsp	GF baking powder	15 mL
1 tsp	baking soda	5 mL
1/2 tsp	xanthan gum	2 mL
1/8 tsp	salt	0.5 mL
1/2 tsp	ground ginger	2 mL
1/4 tsp	ground cinnamon	1 mL
1	large egg	1
1/2 cup	unsweetened apple cider or apple juice	125 mL

1. *Base:* In a small bowl, combine apples, brown sugar and lemon juice, tossing to coat apples. Evenly distribute among prepared ovenproof bowls.

2. *Cake:* In a bowl or plastic bag, combine teff flour, amaranth flour, tapioca starch, brown sugar, baking powder, baking soda, xanthan gum, salt, ginger and cinnamon. Mix well and set aside.

3. In a separate bowl, using a handheld electric mixer, combine egg and apple cider. Gradually add dry ingredients and mix just until combined. Spoon over apple mixture, dividing evenly. Place bowls on a small baking sheet.

4. Bake in preheated oven for 20 to 25 minutes or until cake is firm when gently touched. Serve warm.

Variations

Add 2 tbsp (30 mL) fresh or thawed frozen cranberries or blueberries with the apples.

Serve with Hot Lemon Sauce (page 276).

Nutritional value per serving	
Calories	251
Fat, total	3 g
Fat, saturated	1 g
Cholesterol	62 mg
Sodium	561 mg
Carbohydrate	55 g
Fiber	4 g
Protein	5 g
Calcium	290 mg
Iron	4 mg

Toffee Sauce

Drench warm Pumpkin Pudding (page 272) or Sticky Date Pudding (page 287) with this sauce.

■■■■■■■■■■■■■■■■

Tips

Substitute evaporated milk for the cream.

This sauce can be stored in an airtight container in the refrigerator for up to 1 week or in the freezer for up to 2 months.

⅓ cup	packed brown sugar	75 mL
⅓ cup	butter, cut into 1-inch (2.5 cm) cubes	75 mL
3 tbsp	liquid honey	45 mL
3 tbsp	light (5%) cream or 2% milk	45 mL

1. In a deep microwave-safe bowl, combine brown sugar, butter and honey. Microwave on Medium (50%) for 3 minutes, stopping to stir once, until sugar is dissolved. Microwave on Medium-High (70%) for 3 to 4 minutes or until sauce bubbles. Stir in cream. Serve warm.

Nutritional value per serving			
Calories	331	Carbohydrate	42 g
Fat, total	19 g	Fiber	0 g
Fat, saturated	12 g	Protein	1 g
Cholesterol	52 mg	Calcium	46 mg
Sodium	211 mg	Iron	1 mg

Butter Rum Sauce

Here's another yummy sauce that goes wonderfully well with warm Pumpkin Pudding (page 272) or Sticky Date Pudding (page 287).

■■■■■■■■■■■■■■■■

Tips

Substitute evaporated milk for the cream.

The butter separates with sitting. Whisk the sauce just before serving.

⅔ cup	packed brown sugar	150 mL
⅓ cup	butter, cut into 1-inch (2.5 cm) cubes	75 mL
⅓ cup	light (5%) cream or 2% milk	75 mL
2 tbsp	dark rum	30 mL

1. In a deep microwave-safe bowl, combine brown sugar, butter and cream. Microwave on Medium (50%) for 3 minutes, stopping to stir once, until sugar is dissolved. Microwave on Medium-High (70%) for 3 to 4 minutes or until sauce bubbles. Stir in rum. Serve warm.

Nutritional value per serving			
Calories	384	Carbohydrate	49 g
Fat, total	19 g	Fiber	0 g
Fat, saturated	12 g	Protein	1 g
Cholesterol	53 mg	Calcium	75 mg
Sodium	224 mg	Iron	1 mg

Hot Lemon Sauce

**Makes about
¾ cup (175 mL)**
Serving size: ¼ cup
(60 mL)

This warm, comforting
sauce is particularly
wonderful drizzled over
warm Pumpkin Pudding
(page 272), but you're
sure to discover many
other uses for it.

■■■■■■■■■■■■■■■

Tip

Store in an airtight container
in the refrigerator for up to
1 week.

3 tbsp	granulated sugar	45 mL
1 tbsp	cornstarch	15 mL
1 tsp	grated lemon zest	5 mL
⅔ cup	water	150 mL
2 tbsp	freshly squeezed lemon juice	30 mL
1 tbsp	butter	15 mL

1. In a microwave-safe bowl, combine sugar and cornstarch. Stir in lemon zest, water, lemon juice and butter. Microwave on High for 90 seconds. Stir and microwave on High for 1 to 2 minutes or until sauce boils and thickens. Serve warm.

Nutritional value per serving			
Calories	95	Carbohydrate	16 g
Fat, total	4 g	Fiber	0 g
Fat, saturated	2 g	Protein	0 g
Cholesterol	10 mg	Calcium	3 mg
Sodium	39 mg	Iron	0 mg

Three-Fruit Sauce

**Makes about 1 cup
(250 mL)**
Serving size: ¼ cup
(60 mL)

Serve this attractive
sauce in a small clear
glass pitcher to drizzle
over yogurt or ice cream.

■■■■■■■■■■■■■■■

Tips

Store in an airtight container
in the refrigerator for up to
1 week.

Decrease the sugar to
2 tbsp (30 mL) and serve
with turkey, chicken or pork.

½ cup	fresh or frozen cranberries	125 mL
¼ cup	granulated sugar	60 mL
1 tbsp	grated orange zest	15 mL
½ cup	freshly squeezed orange juice	125 mL
2	clementine oranges, chopped	2
1	pear or apple, peeled and diced	1

1. In a saucepan, combine cranberries, sugar, orange zest and orange juice. Bring to a boil over medium heat, stirring until sugar is dissolved. Reduce heat and simmer, stirring once halfway through, for 5 minutes or until cranberries open. Remove from heat and let cool to room temperature. Stir in clementines and pear. Serve warm or chilled.

Nutritional value per serving			
Calories	120	Carbohydrate	31 g
Fat, total	1 g	Fiber	3 g
Fat, saturated	0 g	Protein	1 g
Cholesterol	0 mg	Calcium	32 mg
Sodium	1 mg	Iron	0 mg

Peach Purée

The rich flavor and color of peaches take a dessert from simple to exotic. Drizzle this purée over GF ice cream or use it to make Peach Sponge Pudding (page 269).

■■■■■■■■■■■■■■■■

Tips

See the Techniques Glossary, page 309, for information on peeling peaches.

Purchase freestone peaches, as it is easier to remove the pits.

■ **Blender or food processor**

4	very ripe large peaches, peeled and cubed	4
1 cup	water	250 mL
2 tbsp	liquid honey	30 mL
2 tsp	freshly squeezed lemon juice	10 mL

1. In a large saucepan, combine peaches, water, honey and lemon juice. Bring to a boil over medium-high heat, stirring frequently. Reduce heat and simmer, stirring frequently, for 10 to 15 minutes or until peaches are soft.

2. Transfer to blender and purée until smooth. Store in an airtight container in the refrigerator for up to 2 days.

Variations

Substitute 2 large mangos for the peaches.

Add 2 tbsp (30 mL) white rum to the purée just before serving.

Nutritional value per serving	
Calories	42
Fat, total	0 g
Fat, saturated	0 g
Cholesterol	0 mg
Sodium	0 mg
Carbohydrate	11 g
Fiber	1 g
Protein	0 g
Calcium	3 mg
Iron	0 mg

Peach Blueberry Compote

3 cups	sliced peaches	750 mL
1 $\frac{1}{2}$ tsp	grated orange zest	7 mL
$\frac{1}{4}$ cup	freshly squeezed orange juice	60 mL
$\frac{1}{3}$ cup	liquid honey	75 mL
1 cup	blueberries	250 mL

**You can either eat this
on its own or serve it
over ice cream or gelato.**

■■■■■■■■■■■■■■■■

Tips

We don't peel the peaches
in this recipe, but if you
want to, see the Techniques
Glossary, page 309, to
learn how.

Store in an airtight container
in the refrigerator for up to
1 week.

1. In a microwave-safe bowl, combine peaches, orange
   zest, orange juice and honey. Microwave on High for
   6 minutes, stopping to stir once or twice. Let cool to
   room temperature. Gently stir in blueberries.

Variations

Vary the fruits — try sliced plums, rhubarb, apricots
or plumcots in place of the peaches, and raspberries
or chopped strawberries in place of the blueberries.
Adjust the amount of honey to suit your taste and
the sweetness of the fruit.

Substitute pure maple syrup for the honey.

Nutritional value per serving	
Calories	113
Fat, total	0 g
Fat, saturated	0 g
Cholesterol	0 mg
Sodium	2 mg
Carbohydrate	30 g
Fiber	3 g
Protein	1 g
Calcium	9 mg
Iron	0 mg

Holiday Baking

Chocolate Sugar Cookies

Just like a sugar cookie, only it's chocolate! Why not make trees for Christmas, hearts for Valentine's Day and bunnies for Easter?

■■■■■■■■■■■■■■■■

Tips

Diet margarine cannot be substituted for the butter, as it has too high a water content.

If the dough sticks to the cookie cutter, dip the cutter in a saucer of sweet rice flour or return the dough to the refrigerator until thoroughly chilled.

To bake two baking sheets at once, bake in the top and bottom thirds of the oven, rotating and switching baking sheets halfway through.

Nutritional value per serving	
Calories	109
Fat, total	5 g
Fat, saturated	3 g
Cholesterol	18 mg
Sodium	89 mg
Carbohydrate	16 g
Fiber	1 g
Protein	1 g
Calcium	12 mg
Iron	1 mg

■ 2-inch (5 cm) cookie cutter
■ Baking sheets, lightly greased and lined with parchment paper

1 cup	teff flour	250 mL
1/4 cup	quinoa flour	60 mL
1/2 cup	GF confectioner's (icing) sugar, sifted	125 mL
3/4 cup	cornstarch	175 mL
2 tsp	xanthan gum	10 mL
1/2 tsp	baking soda	2 mL
1/4 tsp	salt	1 mL
1/4 cup	sifted unsweetened cocoa powder	60 mL
1 cup	granulated sugar	250 mL
3/4 cup	butter, softened	175 mL
1	large egg	1
1 tsp	vanilla extract	5 mL

1. In a bowl or plastic bag, combine teff flour, quinoa flour, confectioner's sugar, cornstarch, xanthan gum, baking soda, salt and cocoa. Mix well and set aside.

2. In a separate bowl, using a heavy-duty electric mixer on low speed, cream granulated sugar and butter until combined. Beat in egg and vanilla until light and fluffy. Gradually beat in the dry ingredients just until combined.

3. Divide dough into 3 equal portions and place each between two sheets of plastic wrap. Roll out to 1/4 inch (0.5 cm) thick. Overwrap each portion in plastic wrap and refrigerate for at least 1 hour or overnight.

4. Preheat oven to 375°F (190°C). Place dough on a lightly floured surface and cut out shapes with the cookie cutter, rerolling scraps. Place 1 inch (2.5 cm) apart on prepared baking sheets.

5. Bake for 10 to 12 minutes or until firm. Let cool on pans on racks for 2 minutes. Transfer cookies to racks and let cool completely. Store in an airtight container at room temperature for up to 2 weeks or in the freezer for up to 2 months.

Variation

For a crisper cookie, roll out the dough to 1/8 inch (3 mm) thick and bake for 10 minutes.

Scottish Shortbread

These melt-in-your-mouth shortbread cookies are meant to be enjoyed at home, not carried to school.

■■■■■■■■■■■■■■■

Tips

Handle these cookies very gently, as they break easily.

Sprinkle the tops with a little superfine sugar while they're still warm from the oven.

■ **Preheat oven to 300°F (150°C)**
■ **Baking sheet, lined with parchment paper**

1/3 cup	brown rice flour	75 mL
1/4 cup	cornstarch	60 mL
3 tbsp	potato starch	45 mL
1/4 cup	sifted GF confectioner's (icing) sugar	60 mL
1/2 tsp	xanthan gum	2 mL
1/3 cup	butter, softened	75 mL
1 tsp	almond extract	5 mL
	Sweet rice flour (optional)	

1. Using a pencil, draw a 5-inch (12.5 cm) circle on the parchment paper; flip paper over.

2. In a bowl or plastic bag, combine brown rice flour, cornstarch, potato starch, confectioner's sugar and xanthan gum. Mix well and set aside.

3. In a separate bowl, using a handheld electric mixer on low speed, cream butter and almond extract. Gradually beat in the dry ingredients just until combined. With a rubber spatula, scrape the bottom and sides of bowl.

4. Gather the dough into a large ball, kneading in any remaining dry ingredients. Form into a disc and place in center of circle. Top with parchment paper and roll out to fit the circle. Using a sharp knife, cut almost through the dough into 8 wedges. Prick all over with a fork. Refrigerate for 1 hour.

5. Bake in preheated oven for 33 to 37 minutes or until set and lightly browned around the edges. Let cool completely on pan on a rack. Store in an airtight container at room temperature for up to 2 weeks or in the freezer for up to 2 months.

Variation

Roll the dough into 1-inch (2.5 cm) balls, place 2 inches (5 cm) apart on a baking sheet lined with parchment paper and flatten with a fork dipped in sweet rice flour. Bake for 15 to 20 minutes or until set and lightly browned around the edges. Let cool on pan for 2 minutes. Transfer cookies to racks and let cool completely.

Nutritional value per serving	
Calories	125
Fat, total	7 g
Fat, saturated	5 g
Cholesterol	19 mg
Sodium	73 mg
Carbohydrate	15 g
Fiber	0 g
Protein	0 g
Calcium	3 mg
Iron	0 mg

Almond Pistachio Bars

These yummy bars have a shortbread base and a chewy, nutty topping.

■■■■■■■■■■■■■■■

Tips

For information on toasting nuts, see the Techniques Glossary, page 309.

Don't make the topping too early, as it needs to be poured over the base as soon as the topping is cooked. When it cools, it hardens just like candy.

After pouring out the topping, fill the empty saucepan with water and bring it to a boil. This makes it much easier to clean.

Nutritional value per serving

Calories	184
Fat, total	12 g
Fat, saturated	5 g
Cholesterol	33 mg
Sodium	107 mg
Carbohydrate	16 g
Fiber	1 g
Protein	5 g
Calcium	41 mg
Iron	1 mg

■ **Preheat oven to 375°F (190°C)**
■ **8-inch (20 cm) square baking pan, lightly greased and bottom and sides lined with parchment paper**

Base

1/2 cup	almond flour	125 mL
1/4 cup	granulated sugar	60 mL
1	large egg	1
3 tbsp	butter, softened	45 mL
1/2 cup	low-fat soy flour	125 mL
1/8 tsp	salt	0.5 mL

Nut Topping

2 tbsp	granulated sugar	30 mL
1/4 cup	butter	60 mL
1/4 cup	corn syrup	60 mL
1/2 cup	toasted sliced almonds	125 mL
1/4 cup	toasted coarsely chopped pistachios	60 mL

1. *Base:* In a bowl, using a handheld electric mixer on low speed, beat almond flour, sugar, egg and butter until well blended. Gradually beat in soy flour and salt just until combined.

2. Spoon batter into prepared pan. Using a moistened rubber spatula, spread to edges and smooth top.

3. Bake in preheated oven for 8 to 10 minutes or until golden brown. Remove from oven, leaving oven on, and let cool in pan on a rack for 10 minutes.

4. *Topping:* Meanwhile, in a saucepan, heat sugar, butter and corn syrup over medium heat, stirring until sugar is dissolved. Stir in almonds and pistachios; bring to a boil. Boil, without stirring, for about 3 minutes or until slightly thickened. Quickly spread over base.

5. Bake for about 7 minutes or until topping is golden brown. Let cool in pan on rack for 5 minutes, then cut into bars. Store in an airtight container at room temperature for up to 4 days or individually wrapped in the freezer for up to 1 month.

Variation

Use brown rice flour in place of the low-fat soy flour.

Orange Mini Cheesecakes

It is so handy to have individual servings of cheesecake in the freezer for unexpected company. You can either eat these straight out of the freezer or let them thaw while you're eating your entrée.

■■■■■■■■■■■■■■■

Tips

Ultra-low-fat cream cheese or fat-free cream cheese should not be substituted for regular cream cheese in baked cheesecake recipes. However, light cream cheese can be used.

Cheesecake can be made up to 1 month in advance. Let cool completely, then wrap the cheesecakes tightly and freeze until ready to serve. Thaw in the refrigerator.

■ **Preheat oven to 300°F (150°C)**
■ **6-cup muffin pan, lined with paper liners**

6	Sunshine Cookies (page 178), un-iced	6
1	package (8 oz/250 g) brick cream cheese, softened	1
1/3 cup	packed brown sugar	75 mL
1/2 tsp	grated orange zest	2 mL
2 tbsp	freshly squeezed orange juice	30 mL
1	large egg yolk	1
1 tbsp	sorghum flour	15 mL
1/4 cup	GF sour cream	60 mL

1. Place 1 cookie in the bottom of each muffin cup, trimming to fit if necessary.

2. In a large bowl, using a handheld electric mixer, beat cream cheese until smooth. Gradually beat in brown sugar, orange zest and orange juice until light and fluffy. Beat in egg. Stir in sorghum flour and sour cream. Pour over cookies.

3. Bake in preheated oven for 25 to 30 minutes or until centers are just set and the blade of a knife comes out clean. Let cool in pan on a rack for 30 minutes. Refrigerate until chilled, about 1 hour.

Variation

Substitute 2 tbsp (30 mL) frozen orange juice concentrate, thawed, for the fresh zest and juice.

Nutritional value per serving	
Calories	289
Fat, total	12 g
Fat, saturated	7 g
Cholesterol	69 mg
Sodium	239 mg
Carbohydrate	38 g
Fiber	1 g
Protein	6 g
Calcium	89 mg
Iron	2 mg

Fudgy Brownies with Three Toppings

Makes 12 brownies
Serving size:
1 brownie

Variety is the spice of life, so we've developed three different toppings for these decadent brownies.

■■■■■■■■■■■■■■

Tips

Letting the batter stand for 30 minutes yields a better texture. However, if you're short on time, you can bake right away.

Pack individually wrapped bars from the freezer in your lunch bag for a mid-morning or mid-afternoon pick-me-up.

Nutritional value per serving (base only)	
Calories	159
Fat, total	10 g
Fat, saturated	1 g
Cholesterol	31 mg
Sodium	64 mg
Carbohydrate	17 g
Fiber	1 g
Protein	2 g
Calcium	33 mg
Iron	1 mg

■ **Three 5³/₄- by 3¹/₄-inch (14 by 8 cm) mini loaf pans, lightly greased and bottom lined with parchment paper**

¹/₃ cup	teff flour	75 mL
1 tbsp	tapioca starch	15 mL
¹/₂ tsp	GF baking powder	2 mL
¹/₂ tsp	xanthan gum	2 mL
¹/₄ tsp	salt	1 mL
¹/₃ cup	sifted unsweetened cocoa powder	75 mL
²/₃ cup	packed brown sugar	150 mL
2	large eggs	2
¹/₂ cup	vegetable oil	125 mL
1 tsp	vanilla extract	5 mL
	Mint Topping, Orange Topping and/or Coffee Topping (see recipes, opposite)	
	Dark Chocolate Drizzle (page 230) (optional)	

1. In a small bowl or plastic bag, combine teff flour, tapioca starch, baking powder, xanthan gum, salt and cocoa. Mix well and set aside.

2. In a separate bowl, whisk together brown sugar, eggs, oil and vanilla. Gradually stir in dry ingredients just until combined.

3. Spoon batter evenly into prepared pans. Using a moistened rubber spatula, spread to edges and smooth tops. Let stand for 30 minutes. Meanwhile, preheat oven to 350°F (180°C).

4. Bake for 15 to 18 minutes or until a tester inserted in the center comes out with a few moist crumbs clinging to it. Let cool completely in pan on a rack.

5. Spread with your choice of topping(s). If desired, drizzle with Dark Chocolate Drizzle. Let cool for 10 minutes, if necessary, before cutting into bars. Store in an airtight container at room temperature for up to 4 days or individually wrapped in the freezer for up to 2 months.

Mint Topping

½ cup	sifted GF confectioner's (icing) sugar	125 mL
1 tbsp	butter, softened	15 mL
1½ tsp	milk	7 mL
1 to 2	drops mint extract	1 to 2
1 to 2	drops green food coloring	1 to 2

1. In a small bowl, combine confectioner's sugar, butter, milk, mint extract and food coloring.

Nutritional value per serving			
Calories	84	Carbohydrate	15 g
Fat, total	3 g	Fiber	0 g
Fat, saturated	2 g	Protein	0 g
Cholesterol	8 mg	Calcium	3 mg
Sodium	30 mg	Iron	0 mg

Orange Topping

½ cup	sifted GF confectioner's (icing) sugar	125 mL
1 tbsp	butter, softened	15 mL
1½ tsp	frozen orange juice concentrate, thawed	7 mL
1 to 2	drops orange extract	1 to 2

1. In a small bowl, combine confectioner's sugar, butter, orange juice concentrate and orange extract.

Nutritional value per serving			
Calories	87	Carbohydrate	16 g
Fat, total	3 g	Fiber	0 g
Fat, saturated	2 g	Protein	0 g
Cholesterol	8 mg	Calcium	2 mg
Sodium	29 mg	Iron	0 mg

Coffee Topping

½ cup	sifted GF confectioner's (icing) sugar	125 mL
1 tbsp	butter, softened	15 mL
1½ tsp	very strong brewed coffee, at room temperature	7 mL

1. In a small bowl, combine confectioner's sugar, butter and coffee.

Nutritional value per serving			
Calories	84	Carbohydrate	15 g
Fat, total	3 g	Fiber	0 g
Fat, saturated	2 g	Protein	0 g
Cholesterol	8 mg	Calcium	1 mg
Sodium	29 mg	Iron	0 mg

Individual Pavlovas

A pavlova is a crisp baked meringue shell that is filled with fruit and garnished with whipped cream.

■ ■ ■ ■ ■ ■ ■ ■ ■ ■ ■ ■ ■ ■ ■

Tips

If superfine sugar (also known as berry, castor or fruit/instant dissolving sugar) is not available, use granulated sugar.

Use your favorite fruit to fill the pavlovas. We like strawberries with chocolate sauce for Valentine's Day and peaches in the summer. Cut any large fruit into small pieces; leave berries whole unless you have very large strawberries, in which case you can slice or quarter them.

For crisp, fluffy shells, bake on a sunny day with low humidity.

Nutritional value per serving	
Calories	226
Fat, total	7 g
Fat, saturated	4 g
Cholesterol	26 mg
Sodium	44 mg
Carbohydrate	39 g
Fiber	1 g
Protein	3 g
Calcium	17 mg
Iron	0 mg

■ **Preheat oven to 250°F (120°C)**
■ **Baking sheet, lined with parchment paper**

½ cup	superfine sugar	125 mL
1 tsp	cornstarch	5 mL
2	large egg whites, at room temperature	2
⅛ tsp	cream of tartar	0.5 mL
½ tsp	cider vinegar	2 mL
½ cup	fresh fruit (see tip, at left)	125 mL
½ cup	whipped cream	125 mL

1. Using a pencil, draw three 4-inch (10 cm) circles on the parchment paper; flip paper over.

2. In a small bowl, combine sugar and cornstarch. Set aside.

3. In a bowl, using a handheld electric mixer, beat egg whites until foamy. Beat in cream of tartar. Continue beating until egg whites form stiff peaks. Gradually beat in sugar mixture, 1 tbsp (15 mL) at a time. Continue beating until mixture is very stiff and glossy but not dry. Fold in vinegar.

4. Spoon one-third of the meringue into each circle on the parchment paper, filling the circle. Using the back of a large metal spoon, hollow out the center of each meringue to form a cup.

5. Bake in preheated oven for 50 to 60 minutes or until crisp but not brown. (If not crisp after 60 minutes, turn off the oven and let cool in the oven for 1 hour.) Carefully remove meringues to a rack and let cool completely.

6. Fill cooled meringues with fruit, dividing evenly, and garnish with whipped cream.

Sticky Date Pudding

We all know how the British love their puddings, often called "puds." Donna fell in love with this one on a holiday in the British Isles. The traditional way to serve it is warm, with warm toffee sauce. Try our Toffee Sauce or Butter Rum Sauce (both on page 275).

Tips

If you purchase chopped dates, check for wheat starch in the coating.

The cooled baked pudding can be wrapped airtight in the casserole dish and frozen for up to 2 months. Or freeze individual pieces, wrapped airtight, for up to 2 months; defrost in the microwave on Medium (50%) for 2 to 4 minutes or until warm.

Nutritional value per serving	
Calories	216
Fat, total	6 g
Fat, saturated	3 g
Cholesterol	73 mg
Sodium	269 mg
Carbohydrate	40 g
Fiber	2 g
Protein	3 g
Calcium	71 mg
Iron	1 mg

- Preheat oven to 350°F (180°C)
- 3-cup (750 mL) round casserole dish, lightly greased and bottom lined with parchment paper

⅓ cup	coarsely chopped pitted dates	75 mL
½ cup	water	125 mL
1 tbsp	butter	15 mL
¼ tsp	baking soda	1 mL
2 tbsp	sorghum flour	30 mL
2 tbsp	whole bean flour	30 mL
1 tbsp	tapioca starch	15 mL
½ tsp	GF baking powder	2 mL
½ tsp	xanthan gum	2 mL
Pinch	salt	Pinch
¼ cup	packed brown sugar	60 mL
1	large egg	1
½ tsp	vanilla extract	2 mL

1. In a microwave-safe bowl, combine dates, water and butter. Microwave on High for 2 minutes or until boiling. Add baking soda and stir until foaming stops. Let cool to room temperature.

2. In a bowl or plastic bag, combine sorghum flour, whole bean flour, tapioca starch, baking powder, xanthan gum and salt. Mix well and set aside.

3. In a separate bowl, using an electric mixer, beat brown sugar, egg and vanilla until blended. Stir in date mixture and dry ingredients until well combined. Spoon into prepared casserole dish.

4. Bake in preheated oven for 28 to 33 minutes or until internal temperature of pudding registers 200°F (100°C) on an instant-read thermometer. Carefully remove casserole dish to a rack and let cool for 10 minutes. Serve warm.

Variation

This pudding can also be baked in a 4-cup (1 L) casserole dish. You may need to decrease the baking time by 1 or 2 minutes.

Tips for Making and Storing Crêpes

The secret to making perfect crêpes is simple: practice, practice, practice! In fact, the first crêpe of every batch is just that — a practice one!

- The batter should be smooth and lump-free.

- Refrigerate the batter for at least 1 hour before making crêpes.

- Set the bowl of cold batter in a sink of warm water to bring it quickly to room temperature.

- A well-seasoned crêpe pan should only need to be greased very lightly. Wipe out any excess with a paper towel. Too much grease on the pan results in greasy crêpes.

- To test a crêpe pan or nonstick skillet for the correct temperature (375°F/190°C), sprinkle a few drops of water on the hot surface. If the water bounces and dances across the pan, it is ready to use. If the water sizzles and evaporates, it is too hot. Adjust the heat if necessary to accommodate differences among cooking utensils and appliances and between crêpes, as the pan continues to heat with subsequent batches.

- If crêpes stick to the pan, let the pan cool slightly, then re-grease. Wipe out any excess with a paper towel. Reheat the pan before making another crêpe.

- As each crêpe is cooked, stack them between sheets of parchment or waxed paper.

- Keep crêpes separated with parchment or waxed paper, wrap airtight and store in the refrigerator for up to 3 days or in the freezer for up to 1 month. To prevent tearing, thaw frozen crêpes in the refrigerator before separating them.

Classic Crêpes

For your next dinner party, prepare crêpes ahead of time, then assemble them with the filling of your choice at the last minute.

■■■■■■■■■■■■■■■■

Tips

For more information on making and storing crêpes, see page 288.

Crêpes can be made ahead and frozen for up to 1 month. Thaw before filling.

■ 6-inch (15 cm) crêpe pan or nonstick skillet, lightly greased

2 tbsp	amaranth flour	30 mL
2 tbsp	whole bean flour	30 mL
1 tbsp	potato starch	15 mL
1 tsp	granulated sugar	5 mL
1/2 tsp	xanthan gum	2 mL
1/4 tsp	salt	1 mL
1	large egg	1
1/4 cup	milk	60 mL
1/4 cup	water	60 mL
1 tbsp	melted butter, cooled slightly	15 mL

1. In a large bowl, combine amaranth flour, whole bean flour, potato starch, sugar, xanthan gum and salt. Mix well and set aside.

2. In a small bowl, whisk together egg, milk, water and butter. Pour over dry ingredients all at once and whisk until smooth. Cover and refrigerate for at least 1 hour or for up to 2 days. Bring batter back to room temperature before making crêpes.

3. Heat prepared pan over medium-high heat until a few drops of water sprinkled on the surface bounce across the pan. For each crêpe, add 3 to 4 tbsp (45 to 60 mL) batter, tilting and rotating pan to ensure batter covers bottom. Cook for 1 1/2 minutes or until edges begin to brown. Turn carefully with a non-metal spatula. Cook for 45 seconds. Transfer to a plate. Repeat with the remaining batter, stacking finished crêpes between sheets of parchment or waxed paper.

Nutritional value per serving	
Calories	79
Fat, total	4 g
Fat, saturated	2 g
Cholesterol	55 mg
Sodium	196 mg
Carbohydrate	7 g
Fiber	1 g
Protein	3 g
Calcium	33 mg
Iron	1 mg

Cranberry Apple Crêpes

This is one of our favorite fillings for dessert crêpes. You can make it ahead and reheat it in the microwave before filling the crêpes.

■■■■■■■■■■■■■■■■

Tips

For 2 cups (500 mL) sliced apples, you'll need about 12 oz (375 g) apples.

The apple filling can be stored in an airtight container in the refrigerator for up to 3 days. Reheat in the microwave on Medium (50%) for 2 to 4 minutes or until hot.

3 tbsp	butter	45 mL
2 cups	thickly sliced apples	500 mL
1 cup	fresh or frozen cranberries	250 mL
⅓ cup	packed brown sugar	75 mL
¾ tsp	ground allspice	3 mL
4	Classic Crêpes (page 289)	4
½ cup	GF vanilla-flavored yogurt	125 mL

Stovetop Method

1. In a saucepan, melt butter over medium heat. Add apples, cranberries, brown sugar and allspice. Reduce heat and simmer gently for 4 to 6 minutes or until apples are just tender.

Microwave Method

1. Place butter in a large microwave-safe bowl. Microwave on High for 1 minute or until melted. Add apples, cranberries, brown sugar and allspice; microwave on High for 2 to 4 minutes, stopping to stir once or twice, until apples are just tender.

For Both Methods

2. Spoon one-quarter of the apple mixture down the center of each crêpe. Roll up and serve seam side down, topped with yogurt.

Variations

Substitute 2 cups (500 mL) of your favorite prepared GF fruit pie filling for the apple filling.

Substitute whipped cream, GF frozen yogurt or GF ice cream for the GF yogurt.

Nutritional value per serving	
Calories	303
Fat, total	14 g
Fat, saturated	8 g
Cholesterol	80 mg
Sodium	314 mg
Carbohydrate	43 g
Fiber	2 g
Protein	5 g
Calcium	111 mg
Iron	2 mg

Chocolate Crêpes

Makes five 6-inch
(15 cm) crêpes
Serving size: 1 crêpe

**An elegant favorite
makes the ideal finish
to a dinner party.**

■■■■■■■■■■■■■■

Tip

For more information on
making and storing crêpes,
see page 288.

Cut any large fruit into small
pieces; leave berries whole
unless you have very large
strawberries, in which case
you can slice or quarter
them.

Nutritional value per serving	
Calories	179
Fat, total	4 g
Fat, saturated	2 g
Cholesterol	45 mg
Sodium	166 mg
Carbohydrate	33 g
Fiber	3 g
Protein	5 g
Calcium	53 mg
Iron	2 mg

■ **6-inch (15 cm) crêpe pan or nonstick skillet, lightly
greased**

1/4 cup	amaranth flour	60 mL
2 tbsp	whole bean flour	30 mL
2 tbsp	tapioca starch	30 mL
2 tbsp	granulated sugar	30 mL
1/4 tsp	xanthan gum	1 mL
1/4 tsp	salt	1 mL
2 tbsp	sifted unsweetened cocoa powder	30 mL
1	large egg	1
1/2 cup	milk	125 mL
1/4 cup	water	60 mL
1 tbsp	melted butter, cooled slightly	15 mL
1 1/2 cups	fresh fruit (see tip, at left)	375 mL
	Chocolate sauce	

1. In a large bowl, combine amaranth flour, whole bean flour, tapioca starch, sugar, xanthan gum, salt and cocoa. Mix well and set aside.

2. In a small bowl, whisk together egg, milk, water and butter. Pour over dry ingredients all at once and whisk until smooth. Cover and refrigerate for at least 1 hour or for up to 2 days. Bring batter back to room temperature before making crêpes.

3. Heat prepared pan over medium-high heat until a few drops of water sprinkled on the surface bounce across the pan. For each crêpe, add 3 to 4 tbsp (45 to 60 mL) batter, tilting and rotating pan to ensure batter covers bottom. Cook for 2 minutes or until top is dull and dry and bubbles break. Turn carefully with a non-metal spatula. Cook for 45 seconds. Transfer to a plate. Repeat with the remaining batter, stacking finished crêpes between sheets of parchment or waxed paper.

4. Fold crêpes in half, then into quarters, top with fresh fruit and drizzle with chocolate sauce.

Variation

Spoon sweetened whipped cream down the center
of each crêpe. Roll up and serve seam side down,
topped with fresh fruit.

Mini Puffs

Makes 16 mini puffs
Serving size: 1 puff

Many seasoned bakers
have asked us to develop
mini puffs, also called
profiteroles, as they
missed making one
of their favorites.

Tip

If puffs become soft before
you're ready to fill them,
reheat them in a 350°F
(180°C) oven for 5 minutes.

- Preheat oven to 425°F (220°C)
- Baking sheet, lightly greased and lined with parchment paper

½ cup	sorghum flour	125 mL
2 tbsp	potato starch	30 mL
½ tsp	xanthan gum	2 mL
Pinch	salt	Pinch
½ cup	water	125 mL
3 tbsp	butter	45 mL
2	large eggs, lightly beaten	2

1. In a small bowl, combine sorghum flour, potato starch, xanthan gum and salt. Mix well and set aside.

2. In a small saucepan, bring water and butter to a boil over medium-high heat. Add dry ingredients all at once and cook, stirring constantly, until mixture pulls away from the sides of the pan. Let cool slightly.

3. Add eggs, one at a time, beating vigorously with a wooden spoon after each addition. Return to low heat and beat for 2 minutes. The mixture will be very thick and rough in texture.

4. Drop batter by small spoonfuls 1 inch (2.5 cm) apart on prepared baking sheet.

5. Bake in preheated oven for 16 minutes or until deep golden brown. Remove from oven and immediately cut a 1-inch (2.5 cm) horizontal slit in the side of each puff. Return to oven and bake for 5 minutes. Remove from pan to a rack and let cool completely.

6. Slice off the top third of each puff. Using a small spoon or your fingers, remove and discard any moist, uncooked dough from the center of the puff, leaving a hollow shell.

Variation

Make 4 large puffs and bake in a 375°F (190°C) oven for 35 to 40 minutes.

Nutritional value per serving	
Calories	46
Fat, total	3 g
Fat, saturated	2 g
Cholesterol	29 mg
Sodium	47 mg
Carbohydrate	4 g
Fiber	0 g
Protein	1 g
Calcium	5 mg
Iron	0 mg

Mini Crab Puffs

Want your cocktail party to be remembered for serving the best gluten-free hors d'oeuvres? Be sure to include these.

■■■■■■■■■■■■■■■■

Tips

Make these ahead and freeze in an airtight container for up to 3 weeks. At the last minute, heat them in a 350°F (180°C) oven for 10 to 15 minutes or until warm.

If using packaged crabmeat, check to make sure it is gluten-free.

3 oz	cooked crabmeat	90 g
¼ cup	light or regular brick cream cheese, softened	60 mL
1 tsp	finely chopped fresh chives	5 mL
½ tsp	dill or fennel seeds	2 mL
¼ tsp	salt	1 mL
⅛ tsp	freshly ground black pepper	0.5 mL
16	cooled Mini Puffs (page 292)	16

1. In a bowl, combine crab, cream cheese, chives, dill seeds, salt and pepper. Mix thoroughly. Spoon into Mini Puffs.

Nutritional value per serving			
Calories	63	Carbohydrate	5 g
Fat, total	4 g	Fiber	0 g
Fat, saturated	2 g	Protein	2 g
Cholesterol	38 mg	Calcium	16 mg
Sodium	116 mg	Iron	0 mg

Mini Clam Puffs

These are just as popular as our Mini Crab Puffs (above) — you decide which you like better. We often serve both.

■■■■■■■■■■■■■■■■

Tips

There's no need to rinse the clams.

Make these ahead and freeze in an airtight container for up to 3 weeks. At the last minute, heat them in a 350°F (180°C) oven for 10 to 15 minutes or until warm.

1	can (5 oz/142 g) clams, drained	1
3 oz	chèvre cheese, softened	90 g
6	drops GF hot pepper sauce	6
⅛ tsp	salt	0.5 mL
⅛ tsp	freshly ground black pepper	0.5 mL
16	cooled Mini Puffs (page 292)	16

1. In a bowl, combine clams, chèvre, hot pepper sauce, salt and pepper. Mix thoroughly. Spoon into Mini Puffs.

Nutritional value per serving			
Calories	74	Carbohydrate	5 g
Fat, total	4 g	Fiber	0 g
Fat, saturated	2 g	Protein	5 g
Cholesterol	38 mg	Calcium	21 mg
Sodium	96 mg	Iron	3 mg

Prosciutto and Cheddar Puffs

Serve these terrific appetizers hot from the oven, or make them ahead and re-crisp.

■■■■■■■■■■■■■■■

Tip

If the puffs have become soft before you're ready to serve them, reheat them in a toaster oven at 425°F (220°C) for 5 minutes.

Make these ahead and freeze in an airtight container for up to 3 weeks. At the last minute, heat them in a 350°F (180°C) oven for 10 to 15 minutes or until warm.

■ **Preheat oven to 425°F (220°C)**
■ **Baking sheet, lightly greased and lined with parchment paper**

⅓ cup	sorghum flour	75 mL
2 tbsp	potato starch	30 mL
½ cup	water	125 mL
3 tbsp	butter	45 mL
2	large eggs	2
½ cup	shredded sharp (old) Cheddar cheese	125 mL
⅓ cup	finely diced GF prosciutto	75 mL

1. In a small bowl, combine sorghum flour and potato starch. Mix well and set aside.

2. In a saucepan, bring water and butter to a boil over medium-high heat. Add dry ingredients all at once and cook, stirring constantly, until mixture pulls away from the sides of the pan. Let cool slightly.

3. Add eggs, one at a time, beating vigorously with a wooden spoon after each addition. Return to low heat and beat for 2 minutes. The mixture will be very thick and rough in texture. Stir in cheese and prosciutto.

4. Drop batter by small spoonfuls 1 inch apart (2.5 cm) on prepared baking sheet.

5. Bake in preheated oven for 18 to 20 minutes or until deep golden brown. Remove from pan to a rack. Serve immediately.

Variations

Cheese Puffs: Omit the GF prosciutto and add 2 tbsp (30 mL) freshly grated Parmesan cheese with the Cheddar cheese.

Substitute 3 to 4 slices GF bacon, cooked crisp and crumbled, for the prosciutto.

Nutritional value per serving	
Calories	58
Fat, total	4 g
Fat, saturated	2 g
Cholesterol	29 mg
Sodium	110 mg
Carbohydrate	3 g
Fiber	0 g
Protein	3 g
Calcium	27 mg
Iron	0 mg

Broccoli Cheddar Mini Quiches

Here's an attractive vegetarian addition to an hors d'oeuvres platter.

■■■■■■■■■■■■■■■

Tip

Refrigerate in an airtight container for up to 2 days. Serve at room temperature or reheat in a 325°F (160°C) oven for 10 to 15 minutes or until warm.

■ **Preheat oven to 325°F (160°C)**

¼ cup	small broccoli florets	60 mL
¼ cup	shredded sharp (old) Cheddar cheese	60 mL
¼ tsp	ground nutmeg	1 mL
1	large egg, beaten	1
¼ cup	milk or half-and-half (10%) cream	60 mL
3 to 4	drops GF hot pepper sauce	3 to 4
12	Basic Pastry mini tart shells (variation, page 237), unbaked	12

1. In a bowl, combine broccoli, cheese, nutmeg, egg, milk and hot pepper sauce to taste. Spoon 1 tbsp (15 mL) filling into each tart shell, filling them evenly to the top. Place tart shells on a baking sheet.

2. Bake in preheated oven for 14 to 16 minutes or until filling puffs up and is slightly golden. Let cool in pans on a rack for 10 minutes, then loosen each around the edges, if necessary to remove from pans. Serve hot.

Nutritional value per serving	
Calories	85
Fat, total	6 g
Fat, saturated	2 g
Cholesterol	27 mg
Sodium	48 mg
Carbohydrate	7 g
Fiber	0 g
Protein	2 g
Calcium	28 mg
Iron	0 mg

Mini Quiches Lorraine

The hors d'oeuvres size of the classic quiche Lorraine is perfect for guests!

■■■■■■■■■■■■■■■■

Tip

Refrigerate in an airtight container for up to 2 days. Serve at room temperature or reheat in a 325°F (160°C) oven for 10 to 15 minutes or until warm.

■ **Preheat oven to 325°F (170°C)**

2	slices GF bacon, cooked crisp and crumbled	2
½	green onion (green part only), finely chopped	½
¼ cup	shredded Swiss cheese	60 mL
1	large egg, beaten	1
¼ cup	milk or half-and-half (10%) cream	60 mL
1 tsp	Dijon mustard	5 mL
12	Basic Pastry mini tart shells (variation, page 237), unbaked	12

1. In a bowl, combine bacon, green onion, cheese, egg, milk and mustard. Spoon 1 tbsp (15 mL) filling into each tart shell, filling them evenly to the top. Place tart shells on a baking sheet.

2. Bake in preheated oven for 14 to 16 minutes or until filling puffs up and is slightly golden. Let cool in pans on a rack for 10 minutes, then loosen each around the edges, if necessary to remove from pans. Serve hot.

Variation

Substitute ¼ cup (60 mL) finely diced cooked GF ham, crabmeat or shrimp for the bacon.

Nutritional value per serving	
Calories	112
Fat, total	8 g
Fat, saturated	2 g
Cholesterol	31 mg
Sodium	125 mg
Carbohydrate	7 g
Fiber	0 g
Protein	3 g
Calcium	37 mg
Iron	0 mg

Tomato Basil Bruschetta

Makes 6 slices
Serving size: 1 slice

Enjoy the late-summer crop of fresh tomatoes with fresh basil from your garden in this delicious topping.

■■■■■■■■■■■■■■■

Tips

Choose a meaty plum tomato, such as Roma or San Marzano.

To snip herbs, place them in a cup and cut with kitchen shears. Pack tightly to measure.

■ **Preheat broiler**

2	tomatoes, chopped	2
1	clove garlic, minced	1
1 tbsp	snipped fresh basil	15 mL
1 tbsp	snipped fresh parsley	15 mL
1 tbsp	extra virgin olive oil	15 mL
$\frac{1}{2}$	Crusty French Baguette (page 86), cut diagonally into six 1-inch (2.5 cm) thick slices, toasted on one side	$\frac{1}{2}$
$\frac{1}{3}$ cup	shredded mozzarella cheese	75 mL

1. In a bowl, combine tomatoes, garlic, basil, parsley and oil.

2. Place baguette slices, toasted side down, on a baking sheet. Spread tomato mixture over baguette slices, dividing evenly, and sprinkle with cheese. Toast under preheated broiler just until cheese melts.

Variation

Substitute snipped fresh oregano or thyme for the basil.

Nutritional value per serving	
Calories	108
Fat, total	4 g
Fat, saturated	1 g
Cholesterol	2 mg
Sodium	193 mg
Carbohydrate	16 g
Fiber	2 g
Protein	4 g
Calcium	51 mg
Iron	0 mg

Roasted Red Pepper and Shrimp Bruschetta

Bright red peppers, piled high on each baguette slice, will whet the appetite of the guests at a barbecue. The balsamic vinegar gives this colorful topping a rich, fruity character.

■■■■■■■■■■■■■■■

Tips

See the Techniques Glossary, page 307, for information on roasting bell peppers.

Use yellow and orange bell peppers for an interesting color combination.

2	roasted red bell peppers, chopped	2
1	clove garlic, minced	1
1/4 cup	snipped fresh parsley	60 mL
1 tbsp	balsamic vinegar	15 mL
1 tsp	extra virgin olive oil	5 mL
	Freshly ground white pepper	
1/2	Crusty French Baguette (page 86), cut diagonally into six 1-inch (2.5 cm) thick slices, toasted on one side	1/2
24	cooked salad shrimp	24

1. In a bowl, combine roasted peppers, garlic, parsley, vinegar and oil. Stir gently. Season with white pepper to taste. Heap mixture onto untoasted side of baguette slices. Top each with 4 shrimp.

Nutritional value per serving	
Calories	100
Fat, total	2 g
Fat, saturated	0 g
Cholesterol	22 mg
Sodium	176 mg
Carbohydrate	18 g
Fiber	2 g
Protein	5 g
Calcium	20 mg
Iron	1 mg

Equipment Glossary

Baguette pan. A metal baking pan divided into two sections shaped like long, thin loaves. The bottom surface may be perforated with small holes to produce a crisp crust and reduce the baking time.

Colander. A bowl-shaped utensil with many holes, used to drain liquids from solids.

Cooling rack. Parallel and perpendicular thin bars of metal at right angles, with feet attached, used to hold hot baked goods off the surface to allow cooling air to circulate.

Crêpe pan. A smooth, low, round pan with a heavy bottom and sloping sides. Crêpe pans range from 5 to 7 inches (12.5 to 18 cm) in diameter.

Grill. A heavy rack set over a heat source, used to cook food, usually on a propane, natural gas or charcoal barbecue.

English muffin rings. These rings hold batter in place as it bakes. They are available in sets of four or eight, and are 3³⁄₄ inches (9.5 cm) in diameter and 1 inch (2.5 cm) high.

Hamburger bun pan. A baking pan that makes six 4-inch (10 cm) hamburger buns.

Instant-read thermometer. See page 29.

Jelly roll pan. A rectangular baking pan that measures 15 by 10 by 1 inches (40 by 25 by 2.5 cm), used to bake thin cakes.

Loaf pan. A container used to bake loaves. Common pan sizes are 9 by 5 inches (23 by 12.5 cm) and 8 by 4 inches (20 by 10 cm). In this book, we also use mini loaf pans that measure 5³⁄₄ by 3¹⁄₄ inches (14 by 8 cm) or 5¹⁄₄ by 2¹⁄₂ inches (13 by 6 cm).

Mini Bundt or kugelhopf pans. Small, round cake pans with fluted or scalloped sides and an indent or tube in the center. Mini Bundt or kugelhopf pans are sold individually or in a set of four or six, connected like a muffin tin. They are made of silicone, or metal with a nonstick coating.

OXO angled measuring cups. Made to give an accurate measure while set on the counter. There's no need to hold the measuring cup at eye level — you can look straight down as you fill it, and the angled insert lets you know when it is full enough. These cups are dishwasher-safe, but not microwaveable. Sizes available include ¹⁄₄ cup (60 mL), 1 cup (250 mL), 2 cups (500 mL) and 4 cups (1 L). All sizes indicate metric and imperial amounts.

Parchment paper. Heat-resistant paper similar to waxed paper, usually coated with silicone on one side. Used with or as an alternative to other methods (such as applying vegetable oil or spray) to prevent baked goods from sticking to the baking pan. Sometimes labeled "baking paper."

Pastry blender. Used to cut solid fat into flour, this tool consists of five or six metal blades or wires held together by a handle.

Pastry brush. A small brush with nylon or natural bristles used to apply glazes or egg washes to dough. Wash thoroughly after each use. To store, lay flat or hang on a hook through the hole in the handle.

Pizza wheel. A sharp-edged wheel (without serrations) anchored to a handle.

Portion scoop. A utensil similar to an ice cream scoop, used to measure equal amounts of batter. Cookie scoops come in different sizes, for 2-inch (5 cm), $2\frac{1}{2}$-inch (6 cm) and $3\frac{1}{4}$-inch (8 cm) cookies. Muffin scoops have a $\frac{1}{4}$-cup (60 mL) capacity.

Ramekins. Usually sold as a set of small, deep, straight-sided ceramic soufflé dishes, also known as mini bakers. Used to bake individual servings of a pudding, cobbler or custard. Capacity ranges from 4 oz, or $\frac{1}{2}$ cup (125 mL), to 10 oz, or $1\frac{1}{4}$ cups (300 mL).

Rolling pin. A smooth cylinder of wood, marble, plastic or metal, used to roll out dough.

Skewer. A long, thin stick made of wood or metal, used in baking to test for doneness.

Spatula. A utensil with a handle and a blade that can be long or short, narrow or wide, flexible or inflexible. It is used to spread, lift, turn, mix or smooth foods. Spatulas are made of metal, rubber, plastic or silicone.

Springform pan. A circular baking pan, available in a range of sizes, with a separable bottom and side. The side is removed by releasing a clamp, making the contents easy to serve.

Tart pan. A shallow baking pan with a removable bottom. The sides are frequently fluted.

Tester. A thin, long wooden or metal stick or wire attached to a handle, used to test for doneness in baked products.

Thermometers.
- *Instant-read thermometer.* See page 29.
- *Oven thermometer.* Used to measure temperatures from 200°F to 500°F (100°C to 260°C). It either stands on or hangs from an oven rack.

Zester. A tool used to cut very thin strips of outer peel from citrus fruits. One type has a short, flat blade tipped with five small holes with sharp edges. Another popular style of zester is made of stainless steel and looks like a tool used for planing wood in a workshop.

Ingredient Glossary

Almond flour (almond meal). See page 20.

Almonds. An ivory-colored nut with a pointed oval shape and a smooth texture. Almonds have a thin, medium-brown skin that adheres to the nut. Sweet almonds have a delicate taste that is delicious in breads, cookies, cakes, fillings and candies. Blanched (skin off) and natural (skin on) almonds are interchangeable in recipes. Almonds are available whole, sliced, slivered or ground.

Amaranth. See page 11.

Apricots. A small stone fruit with a thin, pale yellow to orange skin and meaty orange flesh. Dried unpeeled apricot halves are used in baking.

Arrowroot. See page 21.

Asiago cheese. A pungent, grayish-white hard cheese from northern Italy. Cured for more than 6 months, its texture is ideal for grating. Weight/volume equivalents are:

4 oz (125 g) = 1 cup (250 mL) shredded
2 oz (60 g) = ½ cup (125 mL) shredded
1½ oz (45 g) = ⅓ cup (75 mL) shredded

Baking chips. Similar in consistency to chocolate chips, but with different flavors such as butterscotch, peanut butter, cinnamon and lemon. Check to make sure they are gluten-free and lactose-free.

Baking powder. A chemical leavener, containing an alkali (baking soda) and an acid (cream of tartar), that gives off carbon dioxide gas under certain conditions. Select gluten-free baking powder. See also page 18.

Baking soda (sodium bicarbonate). A chemical leavener that gives off carbon dioxide gas in the presence of moisture — particularly acids such as lemon juice, buttermilk and sour cream. It is also one of the components of baking powder.

Balsamic vinegar. A dark Italian vinegar made from grape juice that has been cooked until the water content is reduced by half, then aged for several years in wooden barrels. It has a pungent sweetness and can be used to make salad dressings and marinades or drizzled over roasted or grilled vegetables.

Bean flours. See Legume Flours, page 19.

Bell peppers. These sweet-flavored members of the capsicum family (which includes chiles and other hot peppers) have a hollow interior lined with white ribs and seeds attached at the stem end. They are most commonly green, red, orange or yellow, but can also be white or purple.

Blueberries. Wild low-bush berries are smaller than the cultivated variety and more time-consuming to pick, but their flavor makes every minute of picking time worthwhile. Readily available year-round in the frozen fruit section of most grocery stores.

Brown rice flour. See page 14.

Brown sugar. See page 23.

Buckwheat. See page 11.

Butter. A spread produced from dairy fat and milk solids, butter is interchangeable with shortening, oil or margarine in most recipes.

Cardamom. This popular spice is a member of the ginger family. A long green or brown pod contains the strong, spicy, lemon-flavored seed. Although native to India, cardamom is used in Middle Eastern, Indian and Scandinavian cooking — in the latter case, particularly for seasonal baked goods.

Cassava. The plant from which tapioca comes.

Cheddar cheese. Always select an aged, good-quality Cheddar for baking recipes. (The flavor of mild or medium Cheddar is not strong enough for baking.) Weight/volume equivalents are:

4 oz (125 g) = 1 cup (250 mL) shredded
2 oz (60 g) = 1/2 cup (125 mL) shredded
1 1/2 oz (45 g) = 1/3 cup (75 mL) shredded

Chickpea (garbanzo bean) flour. See page 19.

Cilantro. This herb has a flavor reminiscent of lemon, sage and caraway. To increase flavor in a recipe, substitute cilantro for parsley.

Coconut. The fruit of a tropical palm tree, with a hard, woody shell that is lined with a hard white flesh. There are three dried forms available, which can be sweetened or not: flaked, shredded and the smallest, desiccated (thoroughly dried).

Coconut milk. A white liquid made by pouring boiling water over shredded coconut; the mixture is then cooled and strained.

Confectioner's (icing) sugar. See page 23.

Corn flour. See page 12.

Cornmeal. See page 12.

Cornstarch. See page 22.

Corn syrup. See page 24.

Cranberries. Grown in bogs on low vines, these sweet-tart berries are available fresh, frozen and dried. Fresh cranberries are available only in season — typically from mid-October until January, depending on your location — but can be frozen right in the bag. Substitute dried cranberries for sour cherries, raisins or currants.

Cream of tartar. Used to give volume and stability to beaten egg whites, cream of tartar is also an acidic component of baking powder. Tartaric acid is a fine white crystalline powder that forms naturally on the inside of wine barrels during the fermentation of grape juice.

Currants. See Dried currants.

Dates. The fruit of the date palm tree, dates are long and oval in shape, with a paper-thin skin that turns from green to dark brown when ripe. Eaten fresh or dried, dates have a very sweet, light brown flesh around a long, narrow seed.

Demerara sugar. See page 23.

Dried currants. Similar in appearance to small dark raisins, dried currants are made by drying a special seedless variety of grape. Not the same as a type of berry that goes by the same name.

Egg replacer. The egg substitutes sold in most supermarkets contain egg products and should not be confused with commercial egg replacer. Egg replacer is a white powder containing a combination of baking powder and starches. It is added with the dry ingredients so that it is well mixed in before it touches the liquids. The oil or other fat in the recipe may have to be increased slightly.

Eggs. Liquid egg products, such as Naturegg Simply Whites, Break-Free and Omega Pro Liquid Eggs, are available in the United States and Canada. Powdered egg whites such as Just Whites can be used as a powder or by reconstituting them with warm water. A similar product is called meringue powder in Canada. Substitute 2 tbsp (30 mL) liquid egg product for each white of a large egg.

Fava bean flour. See page 19.

Fennel seeds. Small, oval, green-brown seeds with prominent ridges and a mild anise (licorice-like) flavor and aroma. Available whole or ground, they are used in Italian and Central European cookery, particularly in rye and pumpernickel breads.

Feta cheese. A crumbly white Greek-style cheese with a salty, tangy flavor. Store in the refrigerator, in its brine, and drain well before using. Traditionally made with sheep's or goat's milk in Greece and usually with cow's milk in the United States and Canada.

Figs. Pear-shaped fruits with a thick, soft skin, available in green and purple. Eaten fresh or dried, the tan-colored sweet flesh contains many tiny edible seeds.

Filberts. See Hazelnuts.

Flaxseed. See page 18.

Frangelico. A well-known hazelnut-flavored liqueur made in Italy.

Fruit sugar. See page 22.

Garbanzo bean flour. See page 19.

Garfava (garbanzo-fava bean) flour. See page 19.

Garlic. An edible bulb composed of several sections (cloves), each covered with a papery skin. An essential ingredient in many styles of cooking.

Ginger. Fresh gingerroot is a bumpy rhizome, ivory to greenish-yellow in color, with a tan skin. It has a peppery, slightly sweet flavor, similar to lemon and rosemary, and a pungent aroma. Ground ginger is made from dried gingerroot. It is spicier and not as sweet or as fresh. Crystallized, or candied, ginger is made from pieces of fresh gingerroot that have been cooked in sugar syrup and coated with sugar.

Gluten. A natural protein in wheat flour that becomes elastic with the addition of moisture and kneading. Gluten traps gases produced by leaveners inside the dough and causes it to rise.

Glutinous rice flour. See Sweet rice flour, page 14.

Golden raisins. See Raisins.

Granulated sugar. See page 22.

Guar gum. A white, flour-like substance made from an East Indian seed high in fiber, this vegetable substance contains no gluten. It may have a laxative effect for some people. It can be substituted for xanthan gum.

Hazelnut flour (hazelnut meal). See page 20.

Hazelnut liqueur. The best known is Frangelico, a hazelnut-flavored liqueur made in Italy.

Hazelnuts. Slightly larger than filberts, hazelnuts have a weaker flavor. Both nuts have a round, smooth shell and look like small brown marbles. They have a sweet, rich flavor and are interchangeable in recipes.

Herbs. Plants whose stems, leaves or flowers are used as a flavoring, either dried or fresh. To substitute fresh herbs for dried, a good rule of thumb is to use three times the amount of fresh as dried. Taste and adjust the amount to suit your preference.

Honey. See page 24.

Kalamata olives. See Olives, kalamata.

Kasha. See page 11.

Legume flours. See page 19.

Linseed. See Flaxseed, page 18.

Mangos. Mangos can be as small as an egg or as heavy as 5 pounds (2.3 kg), and can be oval, round or kidney-shaped. They have a large, tongue-shaped pit surrounded by flesh that ranges in color from yellow to red. Mangos are picked unripe and should be firm, with green skin and no blemishes. When ripe, they are completely colored with areas of green, yellow and red and should be quite firm to the touch, with a sweet, fruity smell. Dried mango, available in chunks and strips, is leathery in texture, burnt orange in color, sweet and non-acidic. It has four to five times as many calories as the fresh fruit. Dried mango can be stored at room temperature for up to 1 year.

Maple syrup. See page 24.

Margarine. A solid fat derived from one or more types of vegetable oil. Do not use lower-fat margarines in baking, as they contain too much added water.

Mesclun. A mixture of small, young, tender salad greens such as spinach, frisée, arugula, oak leaf and radicchio. Also known as salad mix, spring mix or baby greens and sold prepackaged or in bulk in the grocery produce section.

Millet. See page 12.

Mixed candied fruit. A mixture of orange and lemon peel, citron and glacé cherries. Mixed candied peel includes orange, lemon and citron peel. Expensive citron may be replaced by candied rutabaga.

Molasses. See page 23.

Montina. See page 12.

Muscovado sugar. See page 23.

Nonfat dry milk. See Skim milk powder.

Nut flours (nut meals). See page 20.

Oats. See page 13.

Olive oil. Produced from pressing tree-ripened olives. Extra virgin oil is taken from the first cold pressing; it is the finest and fruitiest, pale straw to pale green in color, with the least amount of acid, usually less than 1%. Virgin oil is taken from a subsequent pressing; it contains 2% acid and is pale yellow. Light oil comes from the last pressing; it has a mild flavor, light color and up to 3% acid. It also has a higher smoke point. Product sold as "pure olive oil" has been cleaned and filtered; it is very mild-flavored and has up to 3% acid.

Olives, black. A variety of olive that is black after ripening and is picked when overripe.

Olives, green. A variety of olive that is green both before and after ripening. They are usually sold packed in olive oil or vinegar.

Olives, kalamata. A large, flavorful variety of Greek olive, typically dark purple in color and pointed at one end.

Parsley. A biennial herb with dark green curly or flat leaves, used fresh as a flavoring or garnish. It is also used dried in soups and other mixes. Substitute parsley for half the amount of a strong-flavored herb, such as basil.

Pea fiber. See page 19.

Pea flours. See page 19.

Pecan flour (pecan meal). See page 20.

Pecans. This sweet, mellow nut is smooth and oval, golden brown on the outside and tan on the inside. You can purchase pecans whole, halved, chopped or in chips.

Peel (mixed, candied or glacé). This type of peel is crystallized in sugar.

Peppers. See Bell peppers.

Pinto bean flour. Interchangeable with whole bean flour in any of the recipes in this book.

Plumcots. This new hybrid, also called a pluot, is a cross between a plum and an apricot, with speckled skin. Plumcots are available in various colors and sizes.

Poppy seeds. These tiny, kidney-shaped seeds have a mild, sweet, nutty, dusty flavor. They are available whole or ground. They are most flavorful when roasted and crushed.

Potato flour. See page 21.

Potato starch (potato starch flour). See page 21.

Provolone cheese. An Italian cheese with a light ivory color, mild mellow flavor and smooth texture that cuts without crumbling. Available shapes are sausage, squat pear and piglet. Weight/volume equivalents are:

4 oz (125 g) = 1 cup (250 mL) shredded
2 oz (60 g) = ¹/₂ cup (125 mL) shredded
1¹/₂ oz (45 g) = ¹/₃ cup (75 mL) shredded

Pumpkin seeds. Available roasted or raw, salted or unsalted, and with or without hulls. Raw pumpkin seeds without hulls — often known as pepitas ("little seeds" in Spanish) — are a dull, dark olive green. Roasted pumpkin seeds have a rich, almost peanuty flavor.

Quinoa. See page 14.

Raisins. Dark raisins are sun-dried Thompson seedless grapes. Golden raisins are treated with sulfur dioxide and dried artificially, yielding a moister, plumper product.

Raw sugars. See page 23.

Rhubarb. A perennial plant with long, thin red- to pink-colored stalks resembling celery, and large green leaves. Only the tart-flavored stalks are used for cooking, as the leaves are poisonous. For 2 cups (500 mL) cooked rhubarb, you will need 3 cups (750 mL) chopped fresh, about 1 lb (500 g).

Rice bran. See page 14.

Rice flours. See page 14.

Rice polish. See page 14.

Sanding sugar. See page 22.

Sesame seeds. These flat oval seeds, which can be ivory, red, brown, pale gold or black, have a nutty, slightly sweet flavor. Black sesame seeds have a more pungent flavor and bitter taste than white or natural sesame seeds.

Shortening. A solid, white flavorless fat made from vegetable sources.

Skim milk powder. The dehydrated form of fluid skim milk. Use ¹/₄ cup (60 mL) skim milk powder for every 1 cup (250 mL) water.

Sorghum. See page 14.

Sour cream. A thick, smooth, tangy product made by adding bacterial cultures to pasteurized, homogenized cream containing varying amounts of butterfat. Check the label: some lower-fat and fat-free brands may contain gluten.

Soy flour. See page 19.

Starches. See page 21.

Sun-dried tomatoes. Available either dry or packed in oil, sun-dried tomatoes have a dark red color, a soft chewy texture and a strong tomato flavor. Use dry, not oil-packed, sun-dried tomatoes in recipes. Use scissors to snip. Oil-packed and dry are not interchangeable in recipes.

Sunflower seeds. These plump, nutlike kernels grow in teardrop shapes within gray-and-white shells. They are sold raw or roasted, and salted, seasoned or plain. Shelled sunflower seeds are sometimes labeled "sunflower kernels" or "nutmeats." When buying seeds in shell, look for clean, unbroken shells.

Superfine sugar. See page 23.

Sweet peppers. See Bell peppers.

Sweet rice flour. See page 14.

Tapioca starch. See page 22.

Tarragon. An herb with narrow, pointed, dark green leaves and a distinctive anise-like flavor with undertones of sage. Use fresh or dried.

Teff. See page 15.

Turbinado sugar. See page 23.

Vegetable oil. Common oils used are canola, corn, sunflower, safflower, olive, peanut, soy and walnut.

Walnuts. Inside a tough shell, a walnut's curly nutmeat halves offer a rich, sweet flavor, and the edible, papery skin adds a hint of bitterness to baked goods. Walnuts are available whole (shelled and unshelled), halved and chopped.

White (granulated) sugar. See page 22.

White (navy) bean flour. Interchangeable with whole bean flour in any of the recipes in this book.

Whole bean flour. See page 19.

Wild rice flour. See page 14.

Xanthan gum. See page 24.

Yeast. See page 18. To test for freshness, see page 19.

Yogurt. Made by fermenting cow's milk using a bacteria culture. Plain yogurt is gluten-free, but not all flavored yogurt is.

Zest. Strips from the outer layer of rind (colored part only) of citrus fruit. Avoid the bitter part underneath. Used for its intense flavor.

Techniques Glossary

Almond flour (almond meal). *To make:* See Nut flour. *To toast:* Spread in a 9-inch (23 cm) baking pan and bake at 350°F (180°C), stirring occasionally, for 8 minutes or until light golden.

Almonds. *To blanch:* Cover almonds with boiling water and let stand, covered, for 3 to 5 minutes. Drain. Grasp the almond at one end, pressing between your thumb and index finger, and the nut will pop out of the skin. Nuts are more easily chopped or slivered while still warm from blanching. *To toast:* see Nuts.

Baking pan. *To grease:* See page 28.

Bananas. *To mash and freeze:* Select overripe fruit, mash and package in 1-cup (250 mL) amounts in freezer containers. Freeze for up to 6 months. Defrost and warm to room temperature before using. Two to 3 medium bananas yield 1 cup (250 mL) mashed.

Beat. To stir vigorously to incorporate air, using a spoon, whisk, handheld beater or electric mixer.

Bell pepper. *To roast:* Place whole peppers on a baking sheet, piercing each near the stem with a knife. Bake at 425°F (220°C) for 18 minutes. Turn and bake for 15 minutes or until the skins blister. (Or roast on the barbecue, turning frequently, until skin is completely charred.) Place in a paper or plastic bag. Seal and let cool for 10 minutes or until skin is loose. Peel, and discard seeds.

Blanch. To completely immerse food in boiling water and then quickly in cold water, to loosen and easily remove skin, for example.

Blueberries, frozen. *To partially defrost:* Place 1 cup (250 mL) frozen blueberries in a single layer on a microwave-safe plate and microwave on High for 80 seconds.

Bread crumbs. *To make fresh:* For best results, the GF bread should be at least 1 day old. Using the pulsing operation of a food processor or blender, process until crumbs are of the desired consistency. *To make dry:* Spread bread crumbs in a single layer on a baking sheet and bake at 350°F (180°C) for 6 to 8 minutes, shaking pan frequently, until lightly browned, crisp and dry. (Or microwave, uncovered, on High for 1 to 2 minutes, stirring every 30 seconds.) *To store:* Package in airtight containers and freeze for up to 3 months.

Chocolate. *To melt:* Foods high in fat, such as chocolate, soften and then become a liquid when heated. Microwave on Medium (50%) for 1 minute per 1-oz (30 g) square or until soft. Stir until completely melted.

Combine. To stir two or more ingredients together for a consistent mixture.

Cream. To combine softened fat and sugar by beating to a soft, smooth creamy consistency while trying to incorporate as much air as possible.

Cut in. To combine solid fat and flour until the fat is the size required (for example, the size of small peas or meal). Use either two knives or a pastry blender.

Drizzle. To slowly spoon or pour a liquid (such as frosting or melted butter) in a very fine stream over the surface of food.

Dust. To coat by sprinkling GF confectioner's (icing) sugar, cocoa powder or any GF flour lightly over food or a utensil.

Eggs. *To warm to room temperature:* Place eggs in the shell from the refrigerator in a bowl of hot water and let stand for 5 minutes.

Egg whites. *To warm to room temperature:* Separate eggs while cold. Place bowl of egg whites in a larger bowl of hot water and let stand for 5 minutes. *To beat to soft peaks:* Beat to a thickness that comes up as the beaters are lifted and folds over at the tips. *To beat to stiff peaks:* Beat past soft peaks until the peaks remain upright when the beaters are lifted.

Egg yolks. *To warm to room temperature:* Separate eggs while cold. Place bowl of egg yolks in a larger bowl of hot water and let stand for 5 minutes.

Flaxseed. *To grind:* Place whole seeds in a coffee grinder or blender. Grind only the amount required. If necessary, store extra ground flaxseed in the refrigerator. *To crack:* Pulse in a coffee grinder, blender or food processor just long enough to break the seed coat but not long enough to grind completely.

Fold in. To combine two mixtures of different weights and textures (for example, gluten-free flours into stiffly beaten egg whites) in a way that doesn't deflate the batter. Place the lighter mixture on top of the heavier one. Use a large rubber spatula to gently cut down through the two mixtures on one side of the bowl, then gently move the spatula up the opposite side. Rotate the bowl a quarter-turn and repeat until the mixtures are thoroughly combined.

Garlic. *To peel:* Use the flat side of a sharp knife to flatten the clove of garlic. Skin can then be easily removed. *To roast:* Cut off top of head to expose clove tips. Drizzle with 1/4 tsp (1 mL) olive oil and microwave on High for 70 seconds or until fork-tender. Or bake in a pie plate or baking dish at 375°F (190°C) for 15 to 20 minutes or until fork-tender. Let cool slightly, then squeeze cloves from skins.

Glaze. To apply a thin, shiny coating to the outside of a baked, sweet or savory food to enhance the appearance and flavor.

Grease pan. See page 28.

Hazelnut flour (hazelnut meal). *To make:* See Nut flour. *To toast:* Spread in a 9-inch (23 cm) baking pan and bake at 350°F (180°C), stirring occasionally, for 8 minutes or until light golden. Let cool before using.

Hazelnuts. *To toast and remove skins:* Place hazelnuts in a 350°F (180°C) oven for 15 to 20 minutes. Immediately place in a clean, dry kitchen towel. With your hands, rub the nuts against the towel. Skins will be left in the towel. Be careful: hazelnuts will be very hot.

Herbs. *To store full stems:* Fresh-picked herbs can be stored for up to 1 week with stems standing in water. (Keep leaves out of water.) *To remove leaves:* Remove small leaves from stem by holding the top and running fingers down the stem in the opposite direction of growth. Larger leaves should be snipped off the stem using scissors. *To clean and store fresh leaves:* Rinse under cold running water and spin-dry in a lettuce spinner. If necessary, dry between layers of paper towels. Place a dry paper towel along with the clean herbs in a plastic bag in the refrigerator. Use within 2 to 3 days. Freeze or dry for longer storage. *To measure:* Pack leaves tightly into correct measure. *To snip:* After measuring, transfer to a small glass and cut using the tips of sharp kitchen shears/scissors to avoid bruising the tender leaves. *To dry:* Tie fresh-picked herbs together in small bunches and hang upside down in a well-ventilated location with low humidity and out of sunlight until the leaves are brittle and fully dry. If they turn brown (rather than stay green), the air is too hot. Once fully dried, strip leaves off the stems for storage. Store whole herbs in an airtight container in a cool, dark place for up to 1 year and crushed herbs for up to 6 months. (Dried herbs are stored in the dark to prevent the color from fading.) Before using, check herbs and discard any that have faded, lost flavor or smell old and musty. *To dry using a microwave:* Place $1/2$ to 1 cup (125 to 250 mL) herbs between layers of paper towels. Microwave on High for 3 minutes, checking often to be sure they are not scorched. Then microwave for 10-second intervals until leaves are brittle and can be pulled from stems easily. *To freeze:* Lay whole herbs in a single layer on a flat surface in the freezer for 2 to 4 hours. Leave whole and pack in plastic bags. Herbs will keep in the freezer for 2 to 3 months. Crumble frozen leaves directly into the dish. Herb leaves are also easier to chop when frozen. Use frozen leaves only for flavoring and not for garnishing, as they lose their crispness when thawed. Some herbs, such as chives, have a very weak flavor when dried, and do not freeze well, but they do grow well inside on a windowsill.

Instant-read thermometer. *To test baked goods for doneness:* See page 29.

Leeks. *To clean:* Trim roots and wilted green ends. Peel off tough outer layer. Cut leeks in half lengthwise and rinse under cold running water, separating the leaves so the water gets between the layers. Trim individual leaves at the point where they start to become dark in color and coarse in texture — this will be higher up on the plant the closer you get to the center.

Line pan. See page 28.

Mango. *To ripen:* Place mangos in a paper bag at room temperature for 3 to 5 days. Once ripe, they can be refrigerated in a plastic bag for up to 1 week. *To pit:* Lay mango narrow side up on a cutting board. Cut flesh from each side of the pit and discard pit, then slice flesh lengthwise. You can also try using a mango splitter,

a tool similar in appearance to an apple corer. Its sharp, elliptical, centered metal blade slides down around the pit, slicing the fruit in half at the same time. Two handles, opposite each other, prevent your hands from slipping. It works best on large mangos. *To cube:* After pitting, cut a grid pattern in the flesh, down to (but not through) the skin. Gently push skin to turn inside out; cut off flesh.

Mix. To combine two or more ingredients uniformly by stirring or using an electric mixer on a low speed.

Nut flour (nut meal). *To make:* Toast nuts (see Nuts), let cool to room temperature and grind in a food processor or blender to desired consistency. *To make using ground nuts:* Bake at 350°F (180°C) for 6 to 8 minutes, let cool to room temperature and grind finer.

Nuts. *To toast:* Spread nuts in a single layer on a baking sheet and bake at 350°F (180°C) for 6 to 8 minutes, shaking the pan frequently, until fragrant and lightly browned. (Or microwave, uncovered, on High for 1 to 2 minutes, stirring every 30 seconds.) Nuts will darken upon cooling.

Oat flour. *To make:* In a food processor or blender, pulse oats until finely ground, or to desired consistency.

Olives. *To pit:* Place olives under the flat side of a large knife; push down on knife until pit pops out.

Peaches. *To peel:* Blanch peaches in a pot of boiling water for 1 to 2 minutes or until skin starts to peel away. Using a slotted spoon, transfer to a bowl of ice water until cool enough to handle; remove skins.

Pecan flour (pecan meal). *To make:* See Nut flour.

Pumpkin seeds. *To toast:* See Seeds.

Quinoa. *To cook:* For 1 cup (250 mL) cooked quinoa, bring $1/4$ cup (60 mL) quinoa and $3/4$ cup (175 mL) water to a boil over high heat. Reduce heat to low, cover and simmer for 20 minutes. Remove from heat. Let stand, covered, for 5 to 10 minutes or until water is absorbed, quinoa grains have turned from white to transparent and the tiny spiral-like germ is separated.

Rice. *To cook short-grain white rice:* In a saucepan, combine 1 cup (250 mL) rice and $1^{1}/_{2}$ cups (375 mL) water. Bring to a boil over high heat. Reduce heat, cover and simmer for 15 to 20 minutes (12 to 14 minutes for Arborio rice) or until rice is tender and liquid is absorbed. Makes 3 cups (750 mL). *To cook brown rice:* In a saucepan, combine 1 cup (250 mL) rice and 2 cups (500 mL) water. Bring to a boil over high heat. Reduce heat, cover and simmer for 45 to 50 minutes or until rice is tender and liquid is absorbed. Makes 3 cups (750 mL).

Sauté. To cook quickly at high temperature in a small amount of fat.

Seeds. *To toast:* There are three methods you could use: 1) Spread seeds in a single layer on a baking sheet and bake at 350°F (180°C) for 6 to 10 minutes, shaking the pan frequently, until aromatic and lightly browned; 2) Spread seeds in a single layer in a large skillet and toast over medium heat for 5 to 8 minutes, shaking pan frequently; or 3) Microwave seeds, uncovered, on High for 1 to 2 minutes, stirring every 30 seconds. Seeds will darken upon cooling.

Sesame seeds. *To toast:* See Seeds.

Skillet. *To test for correct temperature:* Sprinkle a few drops of water on the surface. If the water bounces and dances across the pan, it is ready to use. If the drops of water evaporate, it is too hot.

Stir in. To gently incorporate additional ingredients into an existing mixture. Can be done with an electric mixer on low speed or by hand, using a spoon or spatula.

Sunflower seeds. *To toast:* See Seeds.

Tent with foil. When you want to prevent further browning in the oven, place a sheet of foil, shiny side up, lightly over the pan, making a tent that allows hot air to circulate underneath the foil. Do not tuck the foil around the pan.

Whipped cream. *For greater volume when whipping cream:* Chill beaters and bowl in refrigerator for at least 1 hour before whipping.

Wild rice. *To cook:* Rinse 1 cup (250 mL) wild rice under cold running water. Add to a large saucepan, along with 6 cups (1.5 L) water. Bring to a boil over high heat. Reduce heat and simmer for 35 minutes. Cover and simmer for 10 minutes or until wild rice is tender and liquid is absorbed. Makes 3 cups (750 mL).

Yeast. *To test for freshness:* See page 19.

Zest. *To zest:* Use a zester, the fine side of a box grater or a small sharp knife to peel off thin strips of the colored part of the skin of citrus fruits. Be sure not to remove the bitter white pith below.

About the Nutrient Analysis

THE NUTRIENT ANALYSIS done on the recipes in this book was derived from The Food Processor Nutrition Analysis Software, version 7.71, ESHA Research (2001). Where necessary, data were supplemented using the following references:

1. Shelley Case, *Gluten-Free Diet: A Comprehensive Resource Guide*, Expanded Edition (Regina, SK: Case Nutrition Consulting, 2006).

2. Bob's Red Mill Natural Foods. Nutritional information product search. Retrieved May 12, 2011, from www.bobsredmill.com/catalog/index.php?action=search.

3. Gluten-free oats and oat flour from Cream Hill Estates (www.creamhillestates.com). Certificate of Analysis of Pure Oats (Lasalle, QC: Silliker Canada Co., 2005). Certificate of Analysis of Oat Flour (Lasalle, QC: Silliker Canada Co., 2006).

4. Flax Council of Canada. Nutritional information product search. Retrieved May 12, 2011, from www.flaxcouncil.ca.

5. USDA Agricultural Research Service. USDA National Nutrient Database for Standard Reference Release 18. Retrieved May 30, 2011, from www.nal.usda.gov/fnic/foodcomp/search/.

Recipes were evaluated as follows:

- The larger number of servings was used where there is a range.
- Where alternatives are given, the first ingredient and amount listed were used.
- Optional ingredients and ingredients that are not quantified were not included.
- Calculations were based on imperial measures and weights.
- Nutrient values were rounded to the nearest whole number.
- Defatted soy flour and brown rice flour were used, including where these ingredients are listed as soy flour and rice flour.
- Calculations involving meat and poultry used lean portions without skin.
- Canola oil was used where the type of fat was not specified.
- Recipes were analyzed prior to cooking.

It is important to note that the cooking method used to prepare the recipe may alter the nutrient content per serving, as may ingredient substitutions and differences among brand-name products.

Index

Library and Archives Canada Cataloguing in Publication

Washburn, Donna
    The gluten-free baking book : 250 small-batch recipes for everything from brownies
to cheesecake / Donna Washburn, Heather Butt.

Includes index.
ISBN 978-0-7788-0274-7

    1. Gluten-free diet — Recipes. 2. Baking. 3. Cookbooks —. I. Butt, Heather. II. Title.

RM237.86.W382 2011   641.5'638   C2011-903208-2